BRITISH STRATEGY
AND POLITICS
1914 to 1918

Oxford University Press, Amen House, London E.C.4

GLASGOW NEW YORK TORONTO MELBOURNE WELLINGTON
BOMBAY CALCUTTA MADRAS KARACHI LAHORE DACCA
CAPE TOWN SALISBURY NAIROBI IBADAN ACCRA
KUALA LUMPUR HONG KONG

BRITISH STRATEGY
AND POLITICS
1914 to 1918

BY

PAUL GUINN

OXFORD
AT THE CLARENDON PRESS
1965

TO OLWEN

ADDITIONAL NOTE

I HAVE taken account of what new data and interpretations have
appeared since the preceding was written through emendations
of the proof sheets.

21 September 1964

CONTENTS

LIST OF PLATES

PREFACE

THIS is an interpretation of British grand strategy during the 'Great War' in the light of war aims, national politics, and tactical developments. It also examines the interaction between war policy and domestic politics.

One of the purposes of this study was to demonstrate that the actual course of military operations can only be rendered meaningful through an understanding of the grand strategies of the war. Another was to show that a strategic policy is the outcome of a variety of political and military pressures, is in fact closely related to the over-all fabric of national life.

This book was written at a time of revival in First World War studies on both sides of the Atlantic. In retrospect, involvement in that struggle can be seen to mark at once the apogee and the beginnings of decline in British power. The bitterness and passion of the controversies over the course of that involvement have hardly abated over the ensuing years, and are faithfully reflected in much of the literature. This emotion is part of the experience history must seek to recapture, and in itself calls for explanation. On such subjects as the relationship between shifting attitudes toward violence and personal loss and the politics of the war, however, much—or perhaps everything —still remains to be done.

Though books on British military operations, politics, and war direction during the period 1914–18 are exceedingly numerous, this study is the only attempt by a student rather than a participant in that mighty drama to view all of these aspects of national policy as parts of one whole.

I have a number of acknowledgements to make for help afforded me. In England, officials of the Public Record Office, the National Register of Archives of the Historical Manuscripts Commission, the Library of the Trades Union Congress, the State Paper Room of the British Museum, and the Cabinet Office, and, in the United States, of the National Archives and the Division of Manuscripts of the Library of Congress, facilitated my access to a number of important materials. The late Sir Maurice Bonham-Carter and the present Lord Kitchener allowed me to examine the Asquith and Kitchener Papers respectively. Unpublished Crown-copyright material in the Public Record Office has been reproduced by permission of the Controller of H.M. Stationery Office. The late Lord Hankey and Major-General Sir E. L. Spears answered a number of questions, and the former gave me a lengthy personal interview. Captain B. H. Liddell Hart afforded me not only documentary material, personal information, and 'gossip' of interest, but also hospitality and a critical reading of the typescript.

My greatest debt, however, is to Michael Howard, Lecturer[1] in War Studies, King's College in the University of London, under whose observation I did the real mental work on this subject. I am very grateful to him for his patient helpfulness and intellectual responsiveness, as well as for encouraging me to persevere.

Finally, I am most thankful to my mother, Mrs. J. Caroline Guinn, for typing the manuscript.

I have been reproached for a certain irony of tone in writing on grave matters. This stricture may overlook the historian's obligation faithfully to record—and even heighten—whatever he sees. I do not think anything in these pages need detract from one's awe at the British, and Imperial, role in this tragic episode in European history.

P. G.

Institute for Defense Analyses
Washington, D.C.
22 March 1963

[1] Now Professor.

LIST OF MAPS

'He that commands the Sea is at great liberty, and may take as much and as little of the Warre as he will.'
FRANCIS BACON, 'Of the True Greatnesse of Men and Estates'.

'Unfortunately we have to make war as we must and not as we should like to.'
LORD KITCHENER, Dardanelles Committee, 20 August 1915.

PROLOGUE

'As we have created it, the G.S. [General Staff] is going to be our Frankenstein. I can see that clearly. . . . The German model is going to be our curse. However, we cannot now go back.'

LORD ESHER, letter to SIR GEORGE CLARKE, 18 February 1906.

BEFORE—and after—the 'Great War' of 1914–18 England's strategic policy during her participation in the principal European conflicts has been so much of a pattern as to confirm belief in a 'British way' in warfare. England is an island: therefore a potential invader must first cross the seas. The enemy's only other recourse was naval interference with British trade and communications. Against invasion the British Isles had long provided a militia—the 'Constitutional Force'. But Britain's main reliance against both threats was traditionally upon the weapon of sea-power—a pre-eminent navy. By means of superior naval strength she could also take the offensive as she chose: a commercial blockade, the seizure of the enemy's merchant ships and colonies. The colonies could serve her either as hostages against the coming peace; or, more often, as permanent possessions.

A happy state of affairs! England was certainly fortunate in being so protected by her geographical position, because she had always been unable to furnish large military forces—professional or conscript—in the European pattern. 'Standing armies' were the creation of monarchs; and in the seventeenth and eighteenth centuries Britain's sovereigns had neither the political power nor the financial resources of their fellow princes on the Continent. During the nineteenth century the financial burdens and the interference with the liberty of the subject which a large army necessarily entailed were alike intolerable to British statesmen. The Houses of Parliament, remembering both military rule (Cromwell's major-generals) and the threat of a *coup d'état* (James II's assembled army of Hounslow Heath), regarded the British Army with either suspicion or indifference. The Navy, on the other hand, had repeatedly ensured the safety and glory of England, the liberty and prosperity of her citizens. The Pax Britannica was imposed by British sea-power.

At the beginning of the present century, however, these platitudes had become increasingly unacceptable as signposts for the future; or so, at any rate, many prominent Englishmen had come to believe. England, to the imperialists of all parties, was not an isolated island; but the centre and governing head of a vast empire. Communications within the Empire had still to be maintained by sea-power, but naval strength was no longer sufficient guarantee of British security. Much of the British Empire was now composed of subject peoples who needed to be both protected and dominated by military force. There was chronic anxiety over a Russian invasion of India. The hinterland of Egypt, the Sudan, once it had been reconquered and defended against the French, had to be kept secure.

Imperial needs had called forth the means, but in a typically empirical British fashion. The Indian and, largely, the Egyptian, armies were British-trained and officered; but statesmen in London refused to consider these and the British Army as interconnected parts of one Imperial force, in spite of the growing consciousness within the officer corps of the necessity for a continental army on a scale suited to the demands of a great land empire. Major-General Haig, in 1910 Chief of Staff in India, persistently expounded 'an imperial outlook upon military affairs'; but the Radical John Morley, then Secretary of State for India, ordered—though in vain—that all plans for the employment of the Indian Army outside the frontiers of that subcontinent should be destroyed.[1]

The existence of these two concepts of England—island and empire—is a key to the understanding of British history between the Boer War and August 1914. The older liberal ideal of an England governed by parliament, inefficient though it might be, was challenged by the new 'dynamic' imperialist view of an authoritarian Empire administered with impartial efficiency by an *élite* military and civil bureaucracy composed of men of 'British race'. Between the pressures engendered by these two concepts of British society successive Conservative and Liberal governments threaded their way as governments at all times and places must. The conflict, which cut—though not

[1] Duff Cooper, *Haig* (1936), i. 118–19.

impartially—across party lines, goes far to explain home politics, foreign policy, and military and naval direction during this troubled period.

Our story really begins with the South African War. In 1899 the Conservative and 'traditional' administration of Lord Salisbury allowed itself to be pushed into a war with the Boer republics by its imperialist faction—and in particular by Sir Alfred Milner as High Commissioner for South Africa supported from home by the Colonial Secretary, 'Joe' Chamberlain. After an unexpected three years of warfare Imperial rule had been clamped upon South Africa; but British prestige and popularity, and—in the eyes of some—even her moral repute, had sharply fallen. The Royal Navy, or so it appeared, had helped to foil any plans for continental intervention; but the Army had once again demonstrated its inefficiency to the world and to the British public.

Warned and perhaps a trifle shaken by the experiences of the Boer War, the government that succeeded Lord Salisbury's in July 1902 pursued a policy of chastened rather than aggressive imperialism. The original draft treaty that followed upon the Younghusband expedition to Tibet and which was designed to make of that ancient society a British satellite was repudiated by the Balfour government; and the Viceroy of India, Lord Curzon, the sponsor of the expedition, was, unlike Milner, dis-entered. The attempt at 'splendid'—that is to say, militant—isolation was abandoned, and the Conservative government recalled upon a series of hopefully protective agreements which were to lead Great Britain further than the statesmen who concluded them foresaw. The Anglo-Japanese Alliance of 1902 was an attempt to stop further Russian encroachments in the Far East. When the terms of this agreement[1] threatened to draw

1 'II. If either Great Britain or Japan in the defence of their respective interests as above described, should become involved in war with another Power, the other High Contracting Power will maintain a strict neutrality, and use its efforts to prevent other Powers from joining in hostilities against its Ally.

III. If in the above event any other Power or Powers should become involved in hostilities against the Ally, the other High Contracting Power will come to its assistance and will conduct the war in common, and make peace in mutual agreement with it.' Anglo-Japanese Agreement, 30 January 1902, *British Documents on the Origins of the War, 1898–1914*, eds. Gooch and Temperley (1926–38), ii, no. 125.

England into the obviously impending Russo-Japanese War
Lord Lansdowne hastened to conclude the long negotiations that
in April 1904 sealed the reconciliation with France. When these
diplomatic triumphs had been achieved British public opinion
could from a distance safely applaud the victories of the Japanese
and notably the annihilation of the Russian battle fleet off the
island of Tsushima.

The destruction of the Russian Navy in May 1905 made all the
more strikingly manifest the menace posed by another new factor
in the strategic balance of power—the rise of a German navy as
a factor in 'world' politics. The construction of the German High
Seas Fleet had riveted the attention of responsible officials from
the winter of 1902–3 onwards. Germany soon became in English
eyes the principal menace to the Royal Navy, and thereby to the
security and world power of the British Empire. The Anglo-
French Entente, its effect reinforced both by the notorious
inefficiency of the French Navy and the disappearance of the
Russian Navy, made possible a radical reorganization of British
naval dispositions to meet and overcome the threat from the
North Sea.

On the need to make the Royal Navy strong enough to inflict
overwhelming defeat on the German High Seas Fleet in battle
there was no difference in opinion between Liberals and Conservatives, between imperialists and 'Little Englanders'. The
only subject for political controversy—which was very acute—
on the naval question over the forthcoming years was whether
the personnel and organizational reforms, ship construction,
and new fleet dispositions did in fact serve to achieve this
commonly shared goal.

Under the despotic driving power of Admiral Sir John Fisher,
First Sea Lord from October 1904, the Royal Navy was bullied
into preparation for what Fisher consistently called 'Arma-
geddon'. The Mediterranean Fleet, long the strongest in the
navy, was gradually reduced; a number of the overseas squadrons were abolished; and a new Home Fleet was built up for
deployment in the North Sea. The overwhelming preponderance
of British capital ships was gradually concentrated in these
waters. A series of naval scares and the introduction of the
dreadnought ensured a superiority in battleship numbers and
fire range—if not fire effectiveness—over the German Navy.

During these early years—before January 1906—of the
'German menace' it was generally assumed, in military as well
as in other circles, that a war with Germany would be of the
traditional naval character. Two examples will serve to make
this expectation clear. As Chief of the Imperial General
Staff from December 1915 to February 1918 General William R.
Robertson was to fasten a military policy of attrition upon
England and her Empire, but in March 1902 Robertson, then
a lieutenant-colonel and head of the Foreign Intelligence Section of the War Office Directorate of Military Operations and
Intelligence, stated in a paper for the government that in the
event of a violation of Belgian neutrality by either France or
Germany,[1] 'Naval aid would . . . seem to be the most important,
while military assistance would be restricted to the number of
troops adequate to afford ocular proof of our share in the war.'

In February 1903 Lieutenant-Colonel E. A. Altham, head of
the operations section, perplexedly observed in a paper subse-
quently printed for the Committee of Imperial Defence that[2]

A war between Germany and Great Britain would in some ways
resemble a struggle between an elephant and a whale, in which

[1] Treaty Obligations of the British Empire. Directorate of Military Operations
and Intelligence, War Office. March 1902. W.O. 106/44, Public Records Office
[P.R.O]. The minutes of the Prime Minister and of the Secretary of State for Foreign
Affairs on this document are of interest. Lord Salisbury commented reprovingly
(Minute 5),

'It does not seem to me that much profit will be derived from meditations of
this kind. I am sure, I can make no useful contribution. It seems to me that any
invasion of Belgium . . . must be preceded and caused by some strong sympathising
movement from the inside. We cannot foresee the extent of such a movement . . .
or its effect on English opinion here.

'Into whose hands under such circumstances the direction of English policy
will fall it is idle to speculate. Our treaty obligations will follow our national
inclinations and will not precede them. Remember the fate in 1877 of the tripartite
guarantee of Turkey signed in 1856 by Austria, France and England.'

Lord Lansdowne, however, affirmed (Minute 3),

'If we were to intervene [against a violation of Belgian neutrality] we should no
doubt do so with all our might, and the most effective mode of doing this would be
by means of at sea. It would be for our experts to tell us whether we could usefully
land a force in Belgium or elsewhere. I have always understood that our military
system provided for the immediate despatch of a small force beyond the limits of
these islands, and that we contemplated the possibility of sending out an Army
Corps as soon as we had time to mobilize.'

[2] Memorandum on the Military Policy to be adopted in a War with Germany.
Intelligence Department, War Office. Mar. 1904. C.I.D. 20A. W.O. 106/46,
P.R.O.

each, although supreme in its own element, would find difficulty in bringing its strength to bear on its antagonist. . . .

    Our power of offence against Germany is . . . limited to—

    (a) The destruction of her sea-borne trade.

    (b) The seizure of her Colonies and Heligoland.

The existence of the Entente with France made possible a less restricted, but still flexible, war policy. The two Moroccan crises of 1905–6 and 1911, provoked by the German desire to disrupt the Entente, not only drew France and Britain closer together but provided an opportunity for planning and preparations of a military nature for war against Germany. During the first—'Algeciras'—the decision was taken to create a striking force; during the second—'Agadir'—it was implicitly settled that this tiny army would be employed as an extension of the French left wing to counter a German invasion. The Liberal Secretary of State for War, Richard B. Haldane, took the first decision and imposed the second over the objections of the Admiralty. That the opportunity for military preparations presented by the Entente and the recurrent war scares prior to August 1914 was seized was due to two factors: the reorganization of the supreme command begun under Balfour and the replacement of the Conservatives in December 1905 by a government in which the 'Lib Imps' Grey and Haldane held the key posts of Foreign Affairs and War.

The creation of a supreme command structure adapted to cabinet government had been one of the after-effects of the Boer War. Army reform, though constantly a subject of discussion, had lain dormant since Cardwell[1] and the Franco-Prussian War. Now further reforms, at any rate on the relatively painless organizational level, could no longer be resisted by either privileged Conservatives or frightened Liberals. At the end of 1902 the war and naval ministers forced upon Balfour the creation of the Committee of Imperial Defence. This body, served by a small secretariat and responsible directly and only to the Prime Minister, who was also its chairman, consisted primarily of key ministers and the chief staff officers of the two services. The Committee would serve, in the tactful phraseology of its first secretary, Sir George Clarke, 'To bring about a

---

[1] Edward Cardwell, Gladstone's Secretary of State for War, 1868–74.

settlement of questions which might otherwise involve long correspondence between two Departments of State'.[1]

Among the usual attendants at the meetings of the Committee of Imperial Defence before the war were two military officers occupying newly created posts: the Chief of the Imperial General Staff (the 'Imperial' having been added in 1909) and the Director of Military Operations, his subordinate. For in 1904 the three-man War Office (Reconstitution) Committee, more usually known as the Esher Committee, had renewed earlier demands for a General Staff such as had long been a feature of continental armies. That 'damnable dictatorial domineering Trio' (Campbell-Bannerman's reputed phrase) had now prevailed. The British Army from 1904 onwards had a governing instrument, the Army Council, and was soon to be furnished with a 'brain', the General Staff. The General Staff as a body of officers was constituted by Haldane in September 1906, but since 1904 a Chief of the General Staff had sat as first and principal military member of the Army Council.[2]

The constitution of a General Staff with headquarters in the War Office in London meant that military officers could now systematically formulate strategy from a national or Imperial rather than a local 'theatre of operations' viewpoint, and that with assurance of support from within the Army; the creation of the Committee of Imperial Defence ensured that the Army's views would receive a hearing from ministers. Sir Henry Campbell-Bannerman, a Gladstonian Liberal, had in 1890 opposed the establishment of a Chief of Staff responsible for advising on military operations because he foresaw and feared precisely these results. Continental nations, he had then observed, were[3]

concerned in watching the military conditions of their neighbours, in detecting points of weakness and strength, and in planning possible operations in possible wars against them. But in this

[1] Sir George Clarke, Memorandum on the functions of the Committee of Imperial Defence, Enclosure, Letter of Clarke to Campbell-Bannerman, 24 Jan. 1907. Campbell-Bannerman Papers, *British Museum Additional Manuscripts*, v. 41, 213, f. 259.

[2] *Journals and Letters of Reginald Viscount Esher* (1934–8), ii. 50, iii. 72; Colonel John K. Dunlop, *Development of the British Army, 1899–1914* (1938), 198–218.

[3] Further Report of the Hartington Commission, 11 Feb. 1890, Cd. 5979, xxix, as cited in Field-Marshal Sir William Robertson, *Soldiers and Statesmen, 1914–1918* (1926), i. 7.

country there is in truth no room for 'general military policy' in this larger and more ambitious sense of the phrase. We have no designs against our European neighbours. Indian 'military policy' will be settled in India itself, and not in Pall Mall. In any of the smaller troubles with which we may be drawn by the interests of our dependencies, the plan of campaign must be governed by the particular circumstances, and would be left (I presume and hope) to be determined by the officer appointed to direct the operations. ... I am therefore at a loss to know where, for this larger branch of their duties, the new department could find an adequate field in the circumstances of this country. There might indeed be a temptation to create such a field for itself, and I am thus afraid that while there would be no use for the proposed office, there might be some danger to our best interests.

Campbell-Bannerman's fears were to be strikingly confirmed under his own prime ministership fifteen years later.

The Liberal government took office in early December 1905, eight months after the First Moroccan Crisis began with the theatrical landing of the Emperor William II at Tangier. Lord Lansdowne, still Foreign Secretary, had given the French his assurances of support in their plans for the conquest of Morocco, for the Germans could not be allowed to obtain a port in the western Mediterranean. The King, it was rumoured, had told the French Foreign Minister, Delcassé, that should war ensue the British Navy would seize the Kiel Canal and land an army of one hundred thousand men in Schleswig-Holstein. This daring project was long attributed to Sir John Fisher. French newspaper reports on the British 'offer' of armed support met however with icy reserve in the British press; and the Under-Secretary of State for Foreign Affairs, Sir Thomas Sanderson, went to the heart of the matter when he volunteered a denial to the German Ambassador with the observation that, 'To begin with we have not got one hundred thousand men to land anywhere'.[1] If staff talks did take place between British and French military authorities during the last months of the Balfour government, they could hardly have done much more than underline this fundamental fact.

The first concern of the Committee of Imperial Defence

---

[1] *Die grosse Politik der europäischen Kabinette, 1871–1914*, eds. Bartholdy and Thimme (Berlin: Lipsius, 1922–7), xx². 6873.

during the summer of 1905 appears to have been an attack on Belgium. In August Balfour asked the General Staff:[1]

I. In the event of a Franco-German war, would there be a strong inducement for either of the belligerents to violate the neutrality of Belgium?

II. [Could Belgium resist invasion] by holding the defences of Namur and Liége?

III. In what time from the order to mobilize could two British Army Corps be disembarked in Belgium?

The General Staff's reply, dated 29 September and circulated to the Committee, minimized the danger of the crisis. Violation of Belgian neutrality was improbable in the first stages of war, though 'quite possible' later on:

the weight of opinion among military writers of both France and Germany appears to be that the prospective military advantages to be gained by France or Germany by making an advance through Belgium either as their main effort or as a subsidiary movement, do not afford sufficient justification for such a serious step as the violation of a neighbouring state.

The rest of the memorandum was less hopeful. The Belgians could not be expected to offer any serious resistance; it would take twenty-three days after the mobilization orders for the two army corps to disembark. This last was almost certainly a gross overestimate; the new army corps existed only as largely 'paper' administrative units; the British Army was still what it had been since Cardwell, a congeries of regiments whose function it was to train and supply troops for Empire service.

In the spring of 1905 a General Staff war game postulated a British decision to go to Belgium's assistance against German invasion. A British army was thereupon landed at Antwerp; but, according to Robertson, who 'commanded' the German army, the results showed that there was little hope of stemming the German tide unless the British units arrived speedily and in substantial numbers.[2] A 'need' for an Expeditionary Force for employment in Belgium, if not in France, had been demonstrated; but no such force as yet existed. The crisis, however,

---

[1] The Violation of the Neutrality of Belgium during a Franco-German War. General Staff, War Office. 29 Sept. 1905. C.I.D. 65B. W.O. 106/46, P.R.O.

[2] Robertson, *Soldiers and Statesmen*, i. 24; G. Aston, 'The Entente Cordiale and the Military Conversations', *Quarterly Review*, Apr. 1932, p. 368.

appeared to end in late September when the French and
Germans agreed on the agenda of the international conference
on Morocco to be held in Algeciras the following January.
Balfour, whose parliamentary credit had long been exhausted,
took advantage of public disagreements among the Liberal
leaders and resigned on 4 December. The next day Campbell-
Bannerman accepted office.

The Liberal party had been no less convulsed than the Conservatives by the imperialist impulse. Campbell-Bannerman's
'methods of barbarism'[1] speech during the height of the Boer
War had gravely offended sections of the party. The Liberal
League, with Grey and Asquith as two of its three vice-presi-
dents, was founded eight months later, in February 1902, as an
organ to rally the imperialists within the party and propagate
their creed. In 1905 Grey, Asquith, and Haldane agreed in the
'Relugas Compact'[2] that when a Liberal government was formed
the three would combine to force Campbell-Bannerman into
the Lords as a mere figurehead prime minister. With Asquith
leading the party in the House and Grey and Haldane as
minister for foreign affairs and Lord Chancellor respectively,
the Liberal Imperialists would be free to impose their own policy
free of the restraining hand of a 'Little Englander' prime
minister.

The 'Lib Imps' ultimatum, delivered by Grey on 4 December,
failed. Campbell-Bannerman declined to be displaced, and
Asquith broke ranks and accepted the Chancellorship of the
Exchequer. Grey and Haldane thereupon gave way; the former,
despite the Prime Minister's opposition, secured the Foreign
Office; while Haldane had to content himself with the despised
War Office. The combination proved ideal for an imperialist
policy. These two men, intimate friends, did more than any
other statesmen to prepare England for a war against Germany
within the framework of a Continental alliance system.

The portly, rather self-satisfied Haldane entered into office
with an obsession for organization and clear thinking, but as
yet no substantive programme. What kind of a military force

---

[1] A reference to Kitchener's concentration camp policy. 'One was told that no
war was going on, that it was not war. When was a war not a war? When it was
carried on by methods of barbarism in South Africa.' Speech of 14 June 1901.
The camps were used to confine the enemy's non-combatant population.

[2] Grey's fishing lodge in Scotland.

did he wish? A 'Hegelian Army' was his quip by way of response to one of his generals. Since, however, he considered
himself still 'a young and blushing virgin' no results were to be
expected for at least nine months.[1] The Expeditionary Force
was constituted just twelve months later.

On New Year's Day 1906 Haldane foreshadowed, as his two
post-Boer War predecessors had done before him, the creation
of a 'striking force', but for traditional Imperial purposes only.
'Our wars', he explained in a memorandum for the Army Council,[2]

take place, so far as the actual fighting is concerned, mainly over-sea,
at a long distance, and we require an Army wholly different from
that of any other nation . . . what is obviously required is a highly-
organized and well-equipped striking force which can be transported,
with the least possible delay, to any part of the world where it is
required. Its possible work may vary between the defence of India,
against a Russian invasion, to some small war on a Crown Colony.

While the Secretary of State for War was thus occupied, his
colleague at the Foreign Office was confronted with a more
urgent military problem closer home. The Conference at
Algeciras was about to assemble. On the 9th Sir Edward Grey
warned the Prime Minister,[3]

Indications keep trickling in that Germany is preparing for war in
the spring; France is very apprehensive. I do not think there will be
war; I believe the steps taken imply precautions, but not intentions.
But the War Office ought, it seems to me, to be ready to answer the
question, what could they do, if we had to take part against Germany,
if for instance the neutrality of Belgium was violated? Fisher of
course is prepared to answer the question for the Admiralty at any
moment; but that only means driving the German fleet to anchor in
Kiel and staying there.

The next day the French Ambassador, Paul Cambon, asked
Grey to sanction the continuance of 'unofficial communications'

---

[1] *Richard Burdon Haldane: An Autobiography* (1929), 183–5.
[2] A preliminary memorandum of the present situation. Being a rough note for
consideration by the Members of the Army Council. R. B. H., 1 Jan. 1906, Campbell-
Bannerman Papers, v. 41, 218, f. 169.
[3] Letter of Grey to Campbell-Bannerman, 9 Jan. 1906, ibid., f. 50. Also in
Viscount Grey of Fallodon, *Twenty-Five Years, 1892–1916* (Frederick A. Stokes,
N.Y., 1925), i. 115.

between the military and naval authorities of the two countries.[1]

Amid these alarums the new Government prepared to face the electorate. On 12 January Haldane came to speak for Grey in the latter's constituency at Berwick, near the Scottish border. This chore completed, the two men went off on a carriage drive for a private talk. Haldane agreed to military 'conversations' with the French, and, impressed by Grey's anxieties, immediately returned to London, where he summoned the French military attaché and his own advisors. Thereupon[2]

I became aware at once that there was a new army problem. It was, how to mobilise and concentrate at a place of assembly to be opposite the Belgian frontier, a force calculated as adequate (with the assistance of Russian pressure in the East) to make up for the inadequacy of the French armies for their great task of defending the entire French frontier from Dunkirk down. . . .

In a Franco-German War the Russian Army, weakened by their defeat by the Japanese at Mukden the previous March, would for a time be of little active assistance. Major-General J. M. Grierson, the Director of Military Operations, now argued, in a memorandum of 4 January 1906, that since the French had made their eastern frontier so strong[3]

it is . . . not improbable that the Germans may be compelled to attempt a turning movement through Belgium, whose neutrality they would violate. This would probably throw Belgium on to the side of the allies, and its army of 120,000 troops into the field. A British force of the same strength added to this and based on the fortress of Antwerp would produce a field army of over 200,000 combatants which would be advantageously placed to operate against the communications of the Germans endeavouring to turn the line of the French eastern fortresses.

The Germans, Grierson generously estimated, could put four million men into the field, the French but three and a half. Should the Germans be so unobliging as not to enter Belgium, 'our only course will be to send what troops we can to reinforce

---

[1] Grey to Bertie, 10 Jan. 1906, *British Documents on the Origins of the War, 1898–1914*, eds. Gooch and Temperly (H.M.S.O., 1926–38), iii. 210 (a).

[2] Viscount Haldane, *Before the War* (1920), 30–31.

[3] Memorandum upon the Military Forces Required for Over-Sea Warfare. J. M. Grierson, Major-General, 4 Jan. 1906, W.O. 106/44, P.R.O.

the French Army in the field and so help to stem the tide of German invasion. . . . British aid to the French field force must come *at once*, owing to the fact that the moral effect of a first success would have an enormous influence on the course of such a war.'

Grey's warnings and the General Staff opinions furnished Haldane with the *raison d'être* he had been so anxious to find for the British Army. He could now devote his six-year tenure of the War Office to a drastic reorganization of the entire military establishment, reserve as well as regular. The term 'Striking Force' was dropped, probably so as not to alarm the Radicals, but in January 1907 an Army Order provided that in time of war the Regular Army at home should be formed into an Expeditionary Force of one cavalry and six infantry divisions. Later measures constituted an Army and Special Reserve of 80,000 men to maintain the Force in the field and a Territorial Force of fourteen divisions.[1] That same year, 1907, Sir Edward Grey brought the long estrangement with Russia to an end by an agreement with the Russian Empire on respective spheres of influence in Persia, Afghanistan, and Tibet.

Where would the (as yet non-existent) Striking Force strike? In the Anglo-Belgian conversations of January–April 1906 the Belgian Chief of General Staff, General Ducarne, was anxious that the British should, in the event of a German invasion, sail directly into the Scheldt Estuary to Antwerp. They could then join the Belgian Army at Brussels, whence the two forces could attack the enemy flank, whether the Germans reached out toward Antwerp or contented themselves with a less extended march along the Meuse on Liége and Namur. To this the British Military Attaché refused to agree, not out of any concern for violating the Dutch territorial waters of the Scheldt; but because, he explained, the Admiralty insisted on

---

[1] Great Britain. War Office, 1908. Army Orders, 1907. Army Order 28. Organization of the Regular Field Army in the United Kingdom; Lieut.-Col. C. à Court Repington, *The First World War, 1914–1918* (Boston, 1921), i. 14 ('I believe that I suggested the name of the Expeditionary Force. It was first called the Striking Force, and I thought that this would alarm the Radicals unduly'). For the transformation of the British Army under Haldane, see Col. John K. Dunlop, *Development of the British Army, 1899–1914* (1938), and Paul Kluke, *Heeresaufbau und Heerespolitik Englands vom Burenkrieg bis zum Weltkrieg* (Munich, 1932). There were some 20,000 men to a division. See also George Monger, *The End of Isolation: British Foreign Policy, 1900–1907* (1963).

keeping the waters of the North Sea clear until the German fleet
had been destroyed. Till then British troop movements could take
place only south of the Dover Straits. The troops therefore would
be disembarked between Boulogne and Dunkirk, and would then
be sent where they were most needed. Grierson was confident
that the Germans were more likely to be at Namur than at
Antwerp. Once the great naval battle had taken place the British
base could be changed to Antwerp.[1]

The Moroccan crisis finally came to an end, and the General
Staff soon began to have second thoughts. Was it not very risky
to join up with the small Belgian Army? Might not the two
together be simply rounded up and defeated by an overwhelmingly superior German force? The 'decisive point' would be that
of impact between the French and the German Armies; should
not the B.E.F. be in a position where it could affect the decision?
By January 1907 a War Office minute emphasized these considerations and came to the conclusion that 'the General Staff . . .
after careful consideration of the circumstances, are strongly of
opinion that whether Germany in a war with France violates
Belgian territory or whether she does not, our wisest course will
be not to commit ourselves to independent operations in that
country but to land in France; to support the French left rather
than the Belgian right'. A General Staff memorandum of November 1908 merely confirmed this view. Lieutenant-Colonel
Maurice Hankey, who joined the secretariat of the Committee
of Imperial Defence that year, informed the present writer in
1959, 'Within my own recollections the War Office General
Staff always wanted to line on the left of the French Army as
actually they did in 1914.' Doubtless this is not far from the truth.[2]

As yet the plans of the 'soldiers' committed only themselves.
But during the winter of 1908–9, during the Bosnian Crisis,[3]

---

[1] British Documents, iii. 169–203; J. Wullüs-Rudiger, La Belgique et l'équilibre
européen (Paris, 1935), 311–17. See also Carl Hosse, Die englisch-belgischen Auf-
marschpläne gegen Deutschland vor dem Weltkriege (Vienna, 1930).

[2] War with Germany in defence of Belgian Neutrality. Jan. 1907. W.O. 106/46,
P.R.O.; Memorandum by the General Staff. Nov. 1908. W.O. 106/47, P.R.O.;
Letter, Lord Hankey to the present writer, 23 Jan. 1959.

[3] Austria-Hungary proclaimed her annexation of the former Turkish provinces
of Bosnia and Herzegovina, occupied by Austro-Hungarian forces since 1878, in
October 1908. The resulting acute European crisis terminated with Serbia's—and
Russia's—capitulation to Germany's demand for recognition of the fait accompli
the following March.

the Committee of Imperial Defence first considered plans for British participation in a Franco-German war.

By then Campbell-Bannerman, who in 1907 had informed the French premier, Clemenceau, that the British contribution to a war with Germany must needs be exclusively naval,[1] had died, to be succeeded by Asquith. The Sub-Committee on the Military Needs of the Empire, over which Asquith himself now presided, had been[2]

informed by the Foreign Office that: 'In the event of Germany provoking hostilities with France, the question of armed intervention by Great Britain is one which would have to be decided by the Cabinet; but the decision would be more easily arrived at if German aggression had entailed a violation of the neutrality of Belgium, which Great Britain has guaranteed to maintain.'

The decision of the question of whether Great Britain should intervene on behalf of France cannot, in our opinion, be left to turn on the mere point of violation of Belgian neutrality. We are strengthened in this conclusion by the opinion expressed by the General Staff as follows: 'It is considered generally unlikely that Belgium will form part of the theatre of war during the first operations. . . .'

Whether Belgium was so afflicted or not, 'The plan to which preference is given by the General Staff is . . . one in which the British force shall be concentrated in rear of the left of the French army, primarily as a reserve.' The subcommittee in its report of 24 July 1909 confined itself to the conclusion that

in the event of an attack on France by Germany, the expediency of sending a military force abroad, or of relying on naval means only, is a matter of policy which can only be determined when the occasion arises by the Government of the day.

In view, however, of the possibility of a decision by the Cabinet to use military force, the Committee have examined the plans of the General Staff, and are of opinion that, in the initial stages of war between France and Germany, in which the Government decided

[1] *British Documents*, vi, nos. 9, 10; France: *Documents diplomatiques français (1871–1914)* [DDF] (Paris, 1929–?), second series, x, no. 472; R. B. Jones, 'Anglo-French negotiations, 1907: a memorandum by Sir Alfred Milner', *Bulletin of the Institute of Historical Research*, xxxi (1958), 224–7.

[2] C.I.D. 109B. Report of the Sub-Committee of the Committee of Imperial Defence on the Military Needs of the Empire, 24 July 1909. P.R.O. The conclusion is cited in *British Documents*, vii, no. 639.

to assist France, *the plan to which preference is given by the General Staff is a valuable one, and the General Staff should accordingly work out all the necessary details.*[1]

The War Office, in view of Admiralty and Radical opposition —the former most truculently expressed to the subcommittee by Fisher—could hardly have wished for more encouragement. The 'necessary details', all save one, were worked out with enthusiasm and devotion after Major-General Sir Henry Wilson became Director of Military Operations the following year.[2]

The lean, talkative, feverishly active figure of Henry Wilson will often reappear in these pages. His influence was largely attributed to his active cultivation of leading politicians, a source of mingled admiration and exasperation to his fellow senior officers. Here it will only be noted that Wilson personally drew up the initial memorandum for the creation of a General Staff before Haldane had taken over the War Office, and that as D.M.O. from 1910 onwards he made himself responsible for seeing that all the arrangements were in fact made for the immediate dispatch of the B.E.F. in aid of the French. Henceforth French military documents referred to the B.E.F. as 'L'armée "W" '.

In April 1911 the French resumed their advance in Morocco, and in May entered Fez, the capital of the sultanate. In order to compel 'compensation' the Germans on the 1st of July dispatched the gunboat *Panther* to Agadir. During the whole of the ensuing Second Moroccan Crisis[3] the attitude of the British Government was markedly firmer than in 1905–6. The Prime Minister referred in the House on 6 July to the need for 'the fulfilment of our treaty obligations to France'. A speech by finance minister David Lloyd George clearly threatened war. The crisis converted both Lloyd George and Churchill—by 1911 the most powerful personalities in the Cabinet—to belief in the reality of the 'German menace'.

It also precipitated fundamental decisions in both France and England on war strategy. In Paris General Michel, who favoured a defensive policy, was replaced as head of the French

---

[1] Present author's italics.

[2] Maj.-Gen. Sir C. E. Callwell, *Field-Marshal Sir Henry Wilson: His Life and Diaries* (1927), i. 86–99.

[3] Which lasted till in November the Germans received a disappointingly small compensation in the French Congo.

PLATE I

b. Richard B. Haldane
Secretary of State for War 1905–12

a. Sir Edward Grey
Secretary of State for Foreign Affairs 1905–16

PLATE 2

Major-General Sir Henry H. Wilson
Director of Military Operations 1910–14

Army by General Joffre, behind whose ample bulk and impassive countenance a dedicated staff preached the doctrine of an unthinking and ceaseless offensive. On 20 July, at a meeting in Paris with the then French Chief of General Staff, General Dubail, Henry Wilson pledged that the British Army would (always subject to government approval) devote to the operations against Germany all the forces available for overseas employment. The 150,000-man Expeditionary Force would be concentrated in north-eastern France, in the triangle Arras–Saint-Quentin–Cambrai.[1]

The B.E.F. was ready to depart, the French eager to welcome it. There was only one difficulty: the Royal Navy would not agree to transport the troops across the Channel!

For, during all the period that the War Office had painfully evolved a strategy for war against Germany in the context of an alliance with France, the Admiralty had been engrossed in its own preparations and concept of the war.

An Anglo-German war, in the eyes of Sir John Fisher and his assistants in the Admiralty, would continue to be primarily naval in character. The strategic aim of the struggle would be 'command of the sea', to be attained preferably and most decisively by the destruction in battle of the German High Seas Fleet. The difficulty lay in how to obtain this, particularly if the Germans should refrain from offering opportunity.

If the High Seas Fleet declined to steam out to its doom on the outbreak of the war, the Royal Navy would have to establish command of the sea by a blockade of the German North Sea coast. Despite the development of the mine, the torpedo, the airplane, and the submarine, the Admiralty continued against criticisms and its own increasing misgivings to rely, as in the Napoleonic Wars, on a *close* blockade of the enemy's ports and of the Kiel canal. Such a blockade, it was hoped and expected, would flush the German High Seas Fleet, forcing it to confront the stronger British battle squadrons. The blockade, moreover, would be effective in the important, but subsidiary, function of economic warfare. German overseas trade would be prevented, British and allied trade protected, and neutral trade controlled in accordance with the dictates of British war policy.

In such a concept of maritime war the General Staff plan had

[1] *British Documents*, vii, nos. 364, 640.

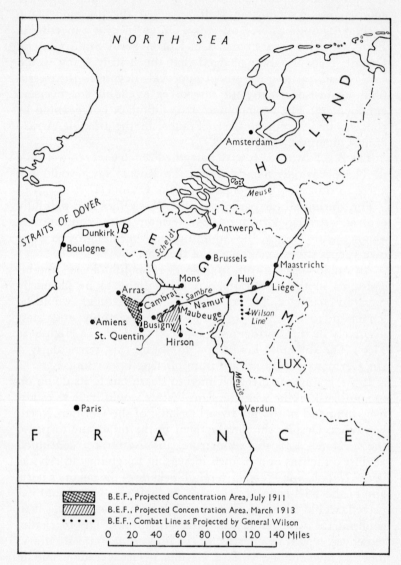

Map 1: The Defence of France and Belgium.

PROLOGUE   19

no place. The B.E.F. was first seen as a tiresome nuisance, the
mere existence of which was an affront to the Navy's exclusive
claims to the nation's attention and support. In the beginning
of a war the B.E.F. must not be allowed to interfere with the
smooth execution of naval plans. At that time the Navy would
be 'too busy' to ferry or to guard an expeditionary force;
besides, was it not a basic principle of war that no overseas
transport should be effected until command of the sea had been
unequivocally secured through destruction of the enemy fleet?
Once the B.E.F. was in existence, its functions were viewed by
authoritative naval opinion in a less blankly negative light. If
trained troops were available *within* the British Isles when war
broke out the Navy could be ensured protection against the
pressure from a fearful public opinion to divert British battle-
craft from their preassigned offensive mission to that of coastal
defence. The periodic pre-war controversies on the German
'invasion bogey' had thoroughly alerted naval and political
circles to this danger.[1]

British military units could also, however, be put to more
direct naval use. The Army, as Fisher never tired of pointing
out, 'should be regarded as a projectile to be fired by the Navy!
The Navy embarks it and lands it where it can do most mis-
chief!'[2] That location, in naval opinion, was not in northern
France in independent support of the French Army, but along
the north German coast under direction of the Royal Navy.

To air, if not to resolve the conflict between Army and Navy,
a move now finally made inescapable by the Admiralty refusal
to transport the B.E.F. across the Channel, Asquith convened
the Committee of Imperial Defence for 23 August. Sir Henry
Wilson was in his element. Tall and self-assured, he fluently
made out a plausible case for the immediate dispatch of the
Expeditionary Force to France in case of war. The Germans, he
said, had available for an invasion of France up to eighty-four

[1] The only source on pre-war British naval policy worth mentioning is Arthur
J. Marder's recent (1961) *From the Dreadnought to Scapa Flow: The Royal Navy in the
Fisher Era, 1904–1919*, vol. i, *The Road to War, 1904–1914*, an excellent account.
Ch. XII is on 'Evolution of Pre-War Strategy and Tactics'. The present writer
gained instructive insights into naval opinion through his personal interviews with
the late Lord Hankey and with Mr. Brian Tunstall.
[2] Letter to Lord Esher, 19 Nov. 1903, *Fear God and Dread Nought: The Correspondence of Admiral of the Fleet Lord Fisher of Kilverstone* (1952–9), i. 291.

divisions, the French—after detaching nine divisions to keep
an eye on the Italians—sixty-six for defence. The most probable
invasion route would be through Belgium,[1] but east of the line
formed by the rivers Meuse and Sambre, thereby avoiding
the fortress towns of Liége, Huy, and Namur, as well as,
perhaps, serious Belgian resistance. Along the ninety-mile gap
between the two fortified towns of Maubeuge (on the Sambre
just south of the Belgian border) and Verdun there were fortunately only thirteen through roads, each of which could accommodate no more than three divisions. Besides, the fighting front
of each division would take up from two to two and a half miles.
Therefore at the first shock of battle the Germans could furnish
no more than forty divisions, against which the French could
probably place from thirty-seven to thirty-nine.

The six British divisions, therefore, might prove to be the
deciding factor! And the moral effect of the British contingent
would be equal to twice their number of French troops. But for
these results to take place the Expeditionary Force must arrive on
the battleground in time for the first general action, some seventeen to twenty days after the French and Germans had mobilized.

Sir John Fisher was no longer present to defend the Navy's
prerogatives. In 1910 he had been displaced and pushed into
the House of Lords. The naval case was instead presented by
First Sea Lord Admiral Sir Arthur Wilson, who, though possess-
ing the same strength of character as his predecessor, commanded neither Fisher's loquacity nor his personal force. The
Navy's objectives were sketched out in a faltering and poorly
prepared exposition. There would be a *close* blockade of the
German North Sea coast, to be enforced by seizure of several
offshore islands—Wangeroog and Schelighlorn off the Jade Bay
—and perhaps more extensive ventures to threaten the Kiel
Canal. These combined operations would require the services
of at least one regular division. If the desired general fleet action
were thus precipitated, the Navy might then force its way into
the Baltic and blockade the Prussian coast. The capture of bases
for the fleet, such as Fehmarn Island, would be required, while
Swinemünde and Danzig might be attacked. For these, small
contingents of British troops would again be necessary. One

---

[1] Sir Henry Wilson appears to have been the first responsible General Staff
officer to commit himself to the view that the Germans would invade Belgium.

division was essential to ensure the capture of the island of Heligoland, envisaged shortly after the outbreak of hostilities. There was, as a matter of fact, no clear limit to the number of divisions that could be kept busy harassing the German littoral. In response to pressure from Haldane, however, the Admiral conceded—though remarking that he had not inquired into the matter—that the Navy could probably transport the Expeditionary Force across the Channel without serious difficulty.[1]

It was clear that the naval exposition, which had been the object of much destructive criticism on the part of the military, had made an unsatisfactory impression. Seizing his opportunity, Haldane determined to force the issue between the services to a, or rather his, solution. That same day he informed the Prime Minister orally—and later in writing—that he would resign unless the Navy were reorganized and furnished with a 'War Staff, working in the closest co-operation with the military General Staff under the general direction of the War Office', and proposed himself as successor to Reginald McKenna as First Lord of the Admiralty. Asquith, unwilling to deal so damaging a blow to Admiralty prestige, did not accept this last suggestion, but instead appointed the thirty-seven-year-old Home Secretary, Winston Churchill. Churchill took over the office in October. He twice changed the composition of the Board of Admiralty, instituted a—purely advisory—War Staff, and substituted a distant for the earlier close blockade policy. The Admiralty Transport Department after many lengthy delays agreed to transport the Army across the Channel, though still only south of the Dover Straits, and made the necessary arrangements. By March 1912 the French by agreement with the War Office had moved the B.E.F.'s concentration area further north and east along the river Sambre, to the region Maubeuge–Busigny–Hirson just south of the Belgian border— the very area to which Sir Henry Wilson prophesied that the German extreme right flank might extend, but not overreach.[2]

---

[1] Minutes, C.I.D. meeting of 23 Aug. 1911. Asquith Papers, Bodleian, Oxford; *British Documents*, viii, no. 314; Adm. Sir Edward E. Bradford, *Life of Admiral of the Fleet Sir Arthur Knyvet Wilson* (1923), 235–8; Callwell, *Henry Wilson*, i. 99–100; Winston S. Churchill, *The World Crisis, 1911–1918* (4 vols.; Odhams Press edn., n.d., but c. 1950), i. 41; Haldane, *Autobiography*, 225–7.

[2] Haldane, *Autobiography*, 228; Maj.-Gen. Sir Frederick Maurice, *Haldane: The Life of Viscount Haldane of Cloan* (1937–9), i. 283–4; Frank Owen, *Tempestuous*

By then the French were in process of adopting an offensive strategy by which the French forces south of the Belgian border would advance into Belgium to meet any incoming German troops. The B.E.F.'s new concentration area—and its initial movements therefrom in August 1914—clearly fitted into this strategy.[1]

The after-effects of the meeting of 23 August 1911 had taken place as a result of the demand of the Secretary of State for War, supported by Churchill and Lloyd George, an insistence made possible by the existence of the Committee of Imperial Defence as a forum for conflicting service views and by the impression of weakness, inconsistency, and lack of preparation made by the naval representative within this body.[2]

In this shift the Cabinet as such had taken no part. The Liberal government—a coalition of imperialists, Gladstonians, and Radicals—found it easier, and far more interesting, to focus on the struggle against the Tories and on questions of social reform than on the obscure, remote, and internally divisive issues of foreign policy and over-all strategy for a war that, hopefully, might either not take place at all or else, as in 1870, leave the British Isles unscathed. Questions that impinged on war strategy were examined by the Cabinet primarily in the light of their internal political or budgetary implications. The invasion controversy was closely connected with the conscription or national service issue. The pressure for increased naval expenditures was viewed in the light of their effect on the budget, and hence on the Liberal programme for social reform.

Besides, the Asquith cabinet was mainly a group of independent departmental heads. They were not encouraged to 'meddle' in foreign policy or national strategy, nor did they

---

Journey: Lloyd George His Life and Times (N.Y., 1955), 221; Churchill, *World Crisis*, i. 49–70, 112–35; Callwell, *Henry Wilson*, i. 119; *DDF*, third series, ii, no. 272.

[1] In Aug. (?) 1913 Wilson indicated that the line 'on which I want to fight' extended directly north from Verdun into Belgium, the British holding a twenty-five mile front from Rochefort, 15 miles east of Dinant (on the Meuse) to Andenne, on the right bank of the Meuse some 10 miles east of Namur. Wilson hoped Belgian garrisoning of the Meuse forts would 'confine the Germans south of the Meuse'. (See Basil Collier, *Brasshat: a Biography of Field-Marshal Sir Henry Wilson* [1961], pp. 119–20, 135.) Both the British and the French failed to appreciate the boldness —or the rashness—of the Schlieffen–Moltke plan.

[2] Marder, *Dreadnought to Scapa Flow*, i. 246–9; Lord Riddell, *More Pages from My Diary, 1908–1914* (1934), 25.

insist on being informed on these sensitive matters. Sir Edward Grey, as is notorious, had not informed the Cabinet of his authorization of the 'military conversations' with the French Army Staff. Neither Campbell-Bannerman nor Asquith had directed that Grey should do so; no minister—and no member of parliament—insisted that the persistent rumours of Franco-British military collaboration should be authoritatively and unambiguously confirmed or denied. 'The country did not know because it refused to know. There is an ignorance whose true name is connivance.'[1]

It is easy in retrospect to make a fetish of Cabinet responsibility. All governments have their key figures; all Cabinets their inner circles of power. Members of the Government present at the Committee of Imperial Defence meeting of 23 August 1911 were Asquith, Churchill, Grey, Haldane, Lloyd George, and McKenna; none of the Cabinet's most energetic personalities or politically powerful members was excluded.

What was striking was the important role now played by the Committee of Imperial Defence. The new organization, responsible not to the Cabinet but to the Prime Minister, had had a slow and difficult start. Regarded with hostility and treated with indifference by the Senior Service, the Committee was saved from an existence of strictly limited and obscure usefulness partly by the support of Haldane, partly by its involvement in spectacular issues that caught the public attention: the charges of Admiralty maladministration made by Admiral Lord Charles Beresford; and the allegations as to Great Britain's vulnerability to invasion made by Lieutenant-Colonel Repington, Military Correspondent of *The Times*, and Field-Marshal Earl Roberts, former Commander-in-Chief in South Africa, as part of their campaign for conscription. The August 1911 meeting brought the C.I.D. for the first and last time in the very centre of the decision-making process. One could say that if the Committee had not then existed it would have had to be invented.

Still, those jealous of the influence exerted through the C.I.D. and resentful of the adverse reception given to the Navy's proposals could find much to criticize in the procedures adopted. Parliament was in recess. Of the regular members of the Committee of Imperial Defence, Crewe, Secretary for India;

---

[1] Elie Halévy, *The Rule of Democracy, 1905–1914* (Benn, 1961), 438.

Harcourt, Colonial Secretary; Morley, Lord President of the Council; and Esher, unofficial representative of the Crown, were absent at the August meeting. According to Almeric Fitzroy, Clerk of the Privy Council, 'At that time no Cabinets met, . . . and I received and acted upon instructions conveyed by the Secretary of State for War, with the assumed concurrence of the Prime Minister.'[1]

The Agadir crisis gave Grey's and Haldane's critics some rein. In September Asquith tried to put a stop to the joint Franco-British military staff talks, but Grey, alluding to the danger of such a rebuff to political relations with the French, proved adamant. Warm debates took place within the Cabinet on British obligations to France. The existence of the 'conversations' was made formally known to the Cabinet the following spring. Haldane was moved from the War Office to become Lord Chancellor. The next major British strategic question, on which there were divided opinions, the proposed withdrawal of the bulk of the Mediterranean Fleet to the North Sea, was repeatedly examined both in the C.I.D. and in the Cabinet before a decision was reached.[2]

The strategic implications of the aftermath of the August 1911 meeting were perhaps not as clear then as they are now. Asquith seems to have regarded his replacement of McKenna by Churchill as an administrative rather than a policy decision, designed to bring efficiency and readiness to the Admiralty. Asquith himself stated, both to McKenna and to Esher, that he was opposed to the General Staff plan, which would not be carried out so long as he remained Prime Minister.[3]

These reservations notwithstanding, when the last major crisis in Anglo-German relations erupted in the summer of 1914, no resistance could avail against the long-matured General Staff preparations. In vain did the Cabinet on 2 August 1914 decide—perhaps as a means of retaining their less belligerent members—to concentrate on naval warfare and to keep the

---

[1] Almeric Fitzroy, *Memoirs* (n.d.), ii. 539. See also Lord Hankey, *The Supreme Command, 1914–1918* (1961), i. 78, and Marder, *Dreadnought to Scapa Flow*, i. 392.

[2] Grey, *Twenty-Five Years*, i. 92–95; G. M. Trevelyan, *Grey of Fallodon* (1940), 139–40; Marder, *Dreadnought to Scapa Flow*, i. 287 ff.; J. A. Spender and Cyril Asquith, *Life of Herbert Henry Asquith, Lord Oxford and Asquith* (1932), i. 349; Esher, Reginald Viscount, *Journals and Letters*, Maurice V. Brett [ed.] (1934–8), iii. 74.

[3] Marder, *Dreadnought to Scapa Flow*, i. 248–51; *Esher Journals*, iii. 61–62.

Expeditionary Force in the country. Once war was declared, in vain did Lord Kitchener, the new Secretary of State for War, express his fears that a German 'large enveloping movement' through Belgium *west* of the Meuse would swallow up the tiny British army. In vain—after Henry Wilson and others of the General Staff had persuaded the hastily improvised 'War Council' of 5 August to send four of the six divisions overseas, a decision endorsed by the Cabinet the following day—did Kitchener insist that the Force be kept at Amiens until the direction of the German offensive should be made manifest. On 12 August the French Military Attaché, Colonel Huguet; two emissaries from the French Commander-in-Chief, General Joffre; and the Commander of the British Expeditionary Force, Sir John French with his two chief staff officers (one of them Henry Wilson), combined to beard Kitchener in his lair in the War Office. Finally they prevailed upon him to allow the British troops to proceed to Maubeuge, thence to participate in Joffre's two-pronged general—not to say scattered—offensive. Eight days later the B.E.F., its command and staff intent on the forthcoming offensive through Belgium into Germany, completed their concentration. The next day they moved up to the Mons canal, and forty-eight hours later, after their encounter with the German right, were in precipitate if well-ordered retreat.[1]

So a small David went off to join a battle between two Goliaths. Of the some two million troops in the three Allied armies in the western theatre of operations, the British Expeditionary Force—even after the two divisions originally retained for home defence were dispatched—furnished but 160,000.

[1] Spender and Asquith, *Life of Asquith*, i. 82, ii. 107; *British Documents*, xi, no. 487; Russia. *Mejdounarodnia Otnochenia v epokhou imperialisma*, third series, 1914-17 (Moscow, 1930 ff.), v, no. 456; Churchill to Lloyd George, 1 Aug. ('Naval War will be cheap, not more than 25 millions a year'), Owen, *Lloyd George*, 265; Earl of Oxford and Asquith, *Memories and Reflections* (Boston, 1928), ii. 12 ('The dispatch of the Expeditionary Force to help France at this moment is out of the question and would serve no object'); Asquith to Bonar Law, 2 Aug., Robert Blake, *The Unknown Prime Minister: The Life and Times of Andrew Bonar Law, 1858-1923* (1955), 223-4; Blanche E. C. Dugdale, *Arthur James Balfour* (1936), ii. 117; P. C. Newton, *Lord Lansdowne: A Biography* (1929), 440-1; Callwell, *Henry Wilson*, i. 162-3; Sir George Arthur, *Life of Lord Kitchener* (1920), iii. 21-23; Lucy Masterman, *C. F. G. Masterman: A Biography* (1939), 269 ('The German main attack is coming *there* . . . and I can't make the French believe it').

What was now the B.E.F. had been the Regular Army on home service; and under the 'linked-battalion' system introduced by Cardwell in 1871 the strength of the home Army was set at the number required to replenish the overseas garrisons.

The reasons for the persistence of this limitation are clear. Plans for an expeditionary force more expensive or larger than the 'two complete Army Corps, with Cavalry Division and Line of Communication'[1] tentatively proposed as long before as 1891 by the then Secretary of State for War, Mr. Edward Stanhope, would not have overcome the pacific and 'economy' factions within the Cabinet and Commons. The cost of an ever-expanding fleet and of the new social services were quite sufficient burdens to the Liberal—and still in part Radical—cabinets of 1906–14. The General Staff had little difficulty in making the fixed size of the Expeditionary Force meet not only the strategic demands of the British in a Franco-German war but also the supposed needs of India in the event of a Russian invasion. Pre-war official War Office estimates of reinforcements after the first encounter battle never went beyond those required to keep the Force up to strength and the additional dispatch of, at most, one British and perhaps two or three native Indian divisions. The French had been warned to expect no further military assistance.[2]

The constitution and sending of an expeditionary force in aid of a Continental ally could therefore be viewed as a complement to, rather than a departure from, traditional British strategy.

In a Franco-German war the British Government feared above all the defeat of France and the occupation of the Belgian coast. These, the course of the war was to show, were two distinct dangers. The General Staff, with but one expeditionary unit available, had long been convinced that the B.E.F. should be sent to join the French, and not the Belgian, Army. But the chosen area of concentration—at Maubeuge—seemed to ensure not only action at 'the decisive point' and comparative security for the tiny British force but also an ideal vantage point for operations in Belgium itself. Once the Germans were stopped in the west, one might well hope that they could not long hold fast

---

[1] Stanhope Memorandum, Dunlop, *Development of British Army*, App. A, p. 307
[2] *DDF*, second series, xiii, no. 180.

against the overwhelming numbers of the more slow-moving Russian Army.[1]

When the war finally materialized, the Germans did make the wide enveloping move that Kitchener, but not the General Staff, foresaw and feared. The bulk of the French forces, at least equal in numbers to the German forces in the west, was employed in a vain offensive in Lorraine and the Ardennes. Only the French Fifth Army—and the B.E.F.—were left to meet the full force of the overwhelmingly preponderant (five armies) German right wing.

The dispatch of the Expeditionary Force to France, together with that of the First Fleet to Scapa Flow a week before the war began, set the pattern of British strategy for the duration of the war. For four years the Grand Fleet was to cruise in the North Sea; for four years British military authorities in France were to clamour, on the whole with success, for limitless reinforcements and efforts on the Western Front.

This pattern, however, was unknown in August 1914. British military critics had long pressed—as they do still—for the creation of an expeditionary force ready for instant use. When for once a Secretary of State for War succeeded in actually constituting such a force the General Staff firmly decided that it would be sent to France to help to stem, perhaps even to turn, the tide of German invasion. During the last five months of 1914 the British Expeditionary Force amply fulfilled that task. Its successors, the vast British Armies in France, were to attempt, with less success, to defeat in battle the entire German Army. But neither this self-imposed task nor the sacrifices demanded thereby from the peoples of Great Britain and her Empire were evident in August 1914, or for many months thereafter.

[1] 'If the German Emperor is Napoleon the campaign of 1814 will repeat itself. If he is not, he is done a month hence when Russia advances.' Letter of Lord Esher to M. V. B., 5 Aug. 1914, *Journals and Letters*, iii. 175.

PART ONE

THE GOVERNMENT'S WAR

'I pointed out to Lord K. that our greatest weakness is the want of co-ordination between the naval, military and political forces of the Empire.'

LORD ESHER, *Journal*, 27 December 1914.

I

THE PHASE OF MOVEMENT

'Anticipations of an early defeat by the Allies of Germany have
been falsified by events, and all indications to-day point to a long
continuance of the struggle.'

LORD ESHER, *Journal*, 7 October 1914.

THE higher direction of the war, in August 1914 as in previous conflicts, was the function of the Government. The
Cabinet assumed responsibility for decisions on strategic
policy; these decisions were in fact made by an inner group of
members, with the Prime Minister as arbiter. Of these ministers
the two service secretaries—Kitchener and Churchill—were
naturally the most important and active.

The new Secretary of State for War, Field-Marshal Horatio
Herbert Earl Kitchener of Khartoum, was by general consent
the Empire's most distinguished soldier-statesman. Over the
past thirty years he had conquered the Sudan and South Africa,
and under one title or another ruled Egypt and India. His
exploits in the marches of Empire, his enigmatic but striking
personality, and the apparent austerity of his private life combined to project an image of implacable determination, self-
sacrifice, and devotion to duty. His appointment as war
minister the day after the declaration of hostilities became a
symbol of Britain's will to persevere till victory.

The elderly man behind the image was more human, and
more fallible. Kitchener had not resided in England since his
youth. Of English or European politics, of War Office or British
Army organization, of Haldane's reforms he knew nothing and
cared less. As with all his previous enterprises, the war was to
be a 'one-man show'. He kept his own counsel as much as he
was able, slaved in solitude from morning into the night, and
corresponded freely only with his own coterie, the members of
which were still for the most part in Egypt and India.

Within the War Office he neither found nor looked for advice.

The leading lights of the General Staff had departed for France
in accordance with pre-war plans as members of General
Headquarters of the British Expeditionary Force. The Chief
of the Imperial General Staff, General Sir Charles Douglas,
had been chosen by Asquith several months earlier uniquely
for his reputation as a disciplinarian, and at the outbreak of
the war was already a sick man. He died in office in October.
Kitchener appointed to this high position a diffident clerk,
Lieutenant-General Sir James Wolfe-Murray, who hardly
dared speak in his master's presence. Kitchener did not even
bother to make him a member of the Army Council. The
Director of Military Operations, Major-General Sir Charles
Callwell, had been called back from retirement. During the
first months of the war he was sometimes consulted by the
Admiralty, but never by his chief. Kitchener, an ageing ignorant man armed only with a giant's reputation, now had to
perform by himself a gigantic task. The reputation itself,
proving insufficient, was soon lost.[1]

The youthful First Lord of the Admiralty, Winston Spencer
Churchill, was, unlike his colleague at the War Office, a professional politician. He had, however, for a brief period in his
meteoric career been an officer in the Regular Army, and had
always displayed an informed interest in military questions.
Since his appointment to his present office three years earlier
Churchill had absorbed himself in the problems of the Navy—
too much so for the good of his political career, thought some
observers. Within the Admiralty he headed—and perhaps dominated—'The War Staff Group', which met at least once a day
and in principle made all major decisions on naval policy. The
First Sea Lord and the Chief of Staff were both members. After
Admiral Prince Louis Alexander of Battenberg had been
forced to resign on 28 October because of his German parentage
Churchill forced the appointment of the aged but still torrential Baron Fisher as First Sea Lord; and Acting Vice-Admiral

---

[1] Sir George Arthur, *Life of Lord Kitchener* (1920), iii. 1–6, 12–15; Philip Magnus,
Kitchener: Portrait of an Imperialist (1958), 277–9, 281–8; Great Britain, *History of
the Great War*, based on official documents by direction of the Historical Section,
Committee of Imperial Defence. Compiled by Brig.-Gen. C. F. Aspinall-Oglander.
Military Operations Gallipoli, i (1929), 46–47, 51 n. 1; Maj.-Gen. Sir C. E. Callwell,
Experiences of a Dug-Out, 1914–1918 (1920), *passim*; Dardanelles Commission. First
Report. Cd. 8490 (1917), 12–13.

PLATE 3

Field-Marshal Earl Kitchener of Khartoum and of Broome
Secretary of State for War 1914–16

PLATE 4

Winston S. Churchill, First Lord of the Admiralty, and Admiral Sir John
Fisher (taken in 1913)

Sir Henry F. Oliver, formerly Fisher's Naval Assistant, there-upon became Chief of the Staff. Thereafter the War Staff Group also included Churchill's Naval Secretary, Commodore Charles M. De Bartolomé; the Secretary to the Board of Admiralty, Sir William Graham Greene; and as attendants two officers of great distinction but no official responsibility: Admirals Sir Arthur Wilson (recalled also from retirement) and Sir Henry Jackson. In fact naval policy was determined by Churchill and Fisher in the light of advisers chosen—and replaceable—by themselves.[1]

The Admiralty and the War Office were far from controlling all the armed forces of the Empire. The Indian Army was still under the policy direction of the India Office, administered by the patrician Marquess of Crewe. During the first days of the war Kitchener exchanged telegrams directly with the Com-mander-in-Chief of the Indian Army, General Sir Beauchamp Duff; but was persuaded by Crewe, whose views on the place of the Indian Army in the imperial structure appear to have been similar to those expressed by Morley in 1910 and Camp-bell-Bannerman in 1890, to discontinue this practice 'on constitutional grounds'. Other colonial forces were under the direction of the Secretary of State for Colonies, Lewis Harcourt.[2]

The possibilities for confusion and cross-purposes, particu-larly in the event of combined operations, were many. This eventuality might have been foreseen from the start but was conclusively demonstrated by the fiasco off Tanga, in German East Africa, at the beginning of November. The Cabinet there-after (on the 22nd) gave the War Office control over operations in East Africa;[3] and on 25 November the Committee of Imperial Defence, though formally still in existence, was replaced as

[1] Winston S. Churchill, *The World Crisis, 1911–1918* (Odhams Press edn.), i. 193–7, 357–63; Dardanelles Commission. First Report, 10–12; Lord Beaverbrook, *Politicians and the War, 1914–1916*, i (N.Y., 1928), 137–40; Earl of Oxford and Asquith, *Memories and Reflections* (Boston, 1928), ii. 56; *Mil. Opns. Gall.* i. 100; *Fear God and Dread Nought: The Correspondence of Admiral of the Fleet Lord Fisher of Kilver-stone* (1952–9), iii. 73 ('We meet daily for an hour or two to discuss the world "from China to Peru" '); Admiral Sir William James, *A Great Seaman: The Life of Admiral of the Fleet Sir Henry F. Oliver* (1956), 137–8.

[2] Great Britain, *History of the Great War*, based on official documents. *The Campaign in Mesopotamia, 1914–1918*. Compiled at the request of the Government of India, under the direction of the Committee of Imperial Defence, by Brig.-Gen. F. I. Moberly (1923–7), ii. 30 n. See also Magnus, *Kitchener*, 286–7.

[3] See below, p. 42.

a forum for those ministers concerned with the conduct of the war by a 'War Council'.[1] The members were Asquith, Kitchener, Churchill, Crewe, Grey, Lloyd George, Chancellor of the Exchequer, and Haldane, now Lord Chancellor. Mr. A. J. Balfour, who had attended the pre-war meetings of the Committee of Imperial Defence, was regularly present, as were, in an advisory capacity, Admiral Fisher and General Wolfe-Murray. The indispensable, acute, and obliging Lt.-Col. Maurice Hankey, together with his tiny staff, was taken over from the C.I.D. to act as Secretary and informal adviser.[2]

Neither the existence of the War Council, however, nor the separate control over the Indian and colonial forces need disguise the realities of power within the Liberal Government. Strategy during the first ten months of the war was formulated by Kitchener and Churchill. Of these two strong personalities, Kitchener had by far the greater prestige and power. But Churchill's was the more active and fertile mind. Kitchener dominated by his presence and reputation, Churchill by his aggressiveness and resource. Churchill initiated strategic decisions, but without the means or power to carry them out. Hence the failures of 1915.

When strategy impinged on foreign policy, as it usually did throughout that year, both Kitchener and Churchill had to accommodate themselves to the decisions or indecisions of Sir Edward Grey, who had long been used to complete freedom in his own domain. The Secretary of State for Foreign Affairs had little interest or talent in the complexities of strategy, nor did he see much relationship between them and his own responsibilities in time of war. Disagreements between the two service ministers, or with Grey, could only be resolved by Asquith, who, also in accordance with his pre-war custom, intervened but seldom and always with reluctance.[3]

---

[1] But Lloyd George in a letter of 31 Dec. 1914 referred to 'the War Committee of the C.I.D.'. See his *War Memoirs*, Odhams Press edn., 2 vols. (n.d. but c. 1939), i. 213.

[2] Dardanelles Commission. First Report, 5–9; Lord Hankey, *The Supreme Command, 1914–1918* (1961), i. 237 ff. (according to whom the War Council first included only Asquith, Churchill, Fisher, Grey, Kitchener, Lloyd George, Wolfe-Murray, and Hankey himself as secretary. Crewe joined on 1 Dec., and Haldane and Arthur Wilson on 7 Jan. On 10 Mar. 1915 McKenna and Harcourt were added.)

[3] G. M. Trevelyan, *Grey of Fallodon* (Longman Library, 1940), 117, 135, 267

Within the Government the differences between the Radicals
and the Liberal Imperialists, resolved by the German invasion
of Belgium, were bound to re-emerge. During the first months
of the war the most serious potential danger to the Kitchener–
Churchill domination of war strategy was presented by Lloyd
George, a Radical turned war enthusiast. His prestige was
shaken since his involvement in the Marconi financial scandal
the preceding year. The war now largely effaced the memory of
these past details. Eager to play a leading part in the struggle, he
needed to find scope for his talents. The shortage of high-
explosive shells was to furnish this supreme opportunist with a
suitable task and issue; and in his struggle to improve the organization of the supply of war material generally he entered into
fierce and eventually successful combat with Kitchener. The
'shells' question, however, though eventually playing its part
in the formation of the First Coalition and the decline of
Kitchener, did not—though doubtless it should have—directly
affect strategy formulation. Kitchener and Churchill could at
the outset pursue what policies they wished.

The Liberal Government could do the same without fear of
external political repercussions. The German invasion of
Belgium had presented Asquith with the priceless gift of national
approval for British intervention; while the Conservative
party through its leader Bonar Law had promised even earlier
its 'unhesitating support' for a war policy. The Prime Minister's
appointment of Kitchener—in response to appeals from both
Liberals and Conservatives—'as an emergency man until the
War comes to an end' not only met with almost universal
approval but also stifled Conservative criticism of war manage-
ment. One could not attack a demigod, and one in the 'Imperial'
pantheon at that. The Tories were left to rail at the renegade
Churchill. Though since the last general election the Conservatives had had within the Commons the same number of seats
as the Liberals, Asquith, once the invasion of Belgium had made
it possible for him to unite his Cabinet on the war issue, determined to ignore all talk of coalition and continue party government. The consequent placing of the Irish Home Rule and
Welsh Church bills on the Statute Book in September 1914

('His want of interest in the military side of things may be held a serious shortcoming
in his equipment as Foreign Minister').

—while postponing their entry into effect until peacetime—
enraged Asquith's opponents, but for the moment they were
helpless.[1]

Both the advantages and the handicaps of the organization
such as existed in the first months of the war are evident. The
concentration of responsibility and initiative in the hands of a
few ministers made national rather than service or local interests the aim of strategic policy. But it also unduly accentuated
considerations of national and political—even personal—
prestige. The presence of a small number of highly skilled but
irresponsible advisers at the very apex of the governmental
machine rather than of more conventionally trained staff
officers from the two services made for a flexible and imagi-
native strategy. But the danger that what was technically
possible would be ignored in the light of what was politically
desirable was real. So were the temptations of slovenliness and
imprecision. Finally, the lack of any effective co-ordination
between the services and between various theatres of war save
that imposed by a prime minister with little staff assistance and
with a multitude of other duties and preoccupations would
mean at best confusion and waste and at worst disaster. The
narrative of events will make the meaning of these observations
plain.

From the beginning of the war until the end of the year the
struggle between the German and French armies and the German
advance along the Belgian channel coast dominated ministers'
minds. In the series of battles between French and Germans
the B.E.F. must play—must be made to play—its part. The
'Retreat from Mons', undertaken in conformity with the withdrawal of the French Fifth Army, began in the small hours of
23/24 August. Within the week Sir John French in a series of
missives communicated his intention to leave the line of battle
altogether to rest and refit at a location well south and west of
Paris, such as his new base at Saint-Nazaire, on the south
coast of Brittany! After the midnight receipt of a particularly

---

[1] Letter, Bonar Law to Asquith, 2 Aug. 1914. Robert Blake, *The Unknown Prime
Minister: The Life and Times of Andrew Bonar Law, 1858–1923* (1955), 222; Asquith,
Memories and Reflections, ii. 30; R. C. K. Ensor, *England, 1870–1914* (Oxford, 1936),
427.

gloomy telegram Kitchener went over to the Prime Minister's residence, where a hastily convoked group of ministers (Asquith, Churchill, Lloyd George, McKenna, and Pease) authorized him to go see the British commander. Kitchener crossed the Channel that same night, and at the British Embassy in Paris the next afternoon, 1 September, instructed Sir John French to remain in the fighting line in conformity with 'the movements of the French Army'.[1]

The intervention of the Secretary of State for War contributed directly to the thwarting of Germany's strategy for victory. Sir John French consented to move his weary troops northward again across the river Marne. The B.E.F.'s unexpected appearance—together with the French Fifth Army—in the gap between the German First and Second Armies took the German High Command unawares, and was an important factor in its decision to withdraw to the Aisne. The first German bid for victory had failed, due in part to Kitchener's swift, vigorous, and authoritative action, supported by the full powers of the British Government.

There followed the attempts of the French and German armies to turn the other's flank on the west—the so-called 'Race to the Sea'. During these operations Sir John French—with Churchill's encouragement—moved the B.E.F. from the Aisne to, in Churchill's words, 'its natural station on the sea flank in contact with the Navy'. By mid-October the British forces were in their new positions south of the Belgian town of Ypres.[2]

Thereupon the B.E.F., the optimism of its command renewed, entered into what began as an encounter battle but continued as a desperate attempt to withstand annihilation. Sir John French's qualities of personal leadership here found full scope. The decision at what only later became known as 'First Ypres' would also determine the fate of the remaining Channel ports and of the Dover Straits.

The Cabinet had already made, with pitifully inadequate and untrained forces, three attempts to slow the German

---

[1] Arthur, *Kitchener*, iii. 55–56. See also ibid. 45–56; Asquith, *Memories and Reflections*, ii. 36–38; Field-Marshal Viscount French of Ypres, *1914* (1919), 92–101, 293–7; Brig.-Gen. J. E. Edmonds, *Mil. Opns. Fr. and Bel. 1914*, i (1st edn., 1922), App. 22, pp. 471–5; ibid. (3rd edn., 1933), 263–4.

[2] Churchill, *World Crisis*, i. 235–6; French, *1914*, 157, 164–74, 190–2.

advance down the Belgian coast. On 16 August Churchill
had ordered the formation of a Royal Naval Division to absorb
surplus naval reservists. 'The use of these brigades need not
be considered until the organization has advanced sufficiently
to allow of their military value to be judged.'[1] None the less, so
pressing was the need and so obdurate was Kitchener in his
refusal to employ units of the Territorial Force that the marine
brigade was within the next two months to be sent to Ostend
and to Dunkirk, and the entire division to Antwerp. Such
desperate expedients, and the loss of both the Belgian ports,
were the price of the pre-war General Staff decision to send the
B.E.F. in support of the French.

The landings at Ostend and Dunkirk were intended primarily to attract the enemy's attention. On 27 August—
at Hankey's suggestion—the Navy disembarked some three
thousand men at Ostend. Churchill announced the landings
in the House of Commons, and the rumours in England—
the product of wishful thinking—that a great Russian force
would follow were encouraged. This movement was undertaken in hopes of distracting German troops from the hard-
pressed B.E.F. and facilitating the sortie of the Belgian Army
from Antwerp on the 24th. After a few days' patrolling the
brigade was re-embarked.[2]

Two weeks after the marines' return General Joffre telegraphed Kitchener requesting that they be sent to Dunkirk to
delude the enemy into the belief that the entire coastal area was
strongly held. Churchill agreed and the marine brigade once
again departed for the Continent. For this adventure, un-
officially dubbed the 'Dunkirk Circus', were added a regiment
of Yeomanry Cavalry, some armoured cars, and ninety-seven
motor omnibuses—all under the command of a Marine officer.
This bizarre array made its presence known in the coastal area
of France and Belgium during the remainder of September.[3]

[1] W. S. C., Formation of the Royal Naval Division, 16 Aug. 1914: Churchill,
World Crisis, iv, App. E, p. 1390.

[2] Asquith, *Memories and Reflections*, ii. 35–36; Churchill, *World Crisis*, i. 263–4;
Hankey, *Supreme Command*, i. 194–7; Sir Julian S. Corbett, *Naval Operations*, i
(1920), 94–98, 121–4.

[3] Asquith, *Memories and Reflections*, ii. 41–42; Beaverbrook, *Politicians and the
War*, ii (n.d. but *c.* 1932), 26–33; Churchill, *World Crisis*, i. 271–3; Hankey,
Supreme Command, i. 197–8; Magnus, *Kitchener*, 308; *Mil. Opns. Fr. and Bel. 1914*,
ii. 28–30; *Naval Opns*. i. 169–71.

These expedients had logic while the main strength of the German Army was elsewhere engaged and while awaiting the results of the first great clash of arms.[1] On the outcome of that clash all other measures, including those which might have saved the great Belgian port of Antwerp, had to wait. A proposal by Churchill on 7 September (during the battle of the Marne), urging the dispatch of units of the Territorial Force to Antwerp through the Dutch territorial waters of the Scheldt, was rejected by Grey and Kitchener; and on the following day Asquith noted that the Cabinet 'of course' refused 'on military grounds' a Belgian request to send some twenty to thirty thousand men to join an equal number of Belgian troops to keep open the road from Antwerp south to Ostend. France continued to take precedence over the Belgian coast.[2]

The German armies disengaged at the Marne and William II ordered the capture of Antwerp. On 28 September the Germans opened fire with their new huge howitzers; the outer lines began to crumble and the defending forces to weaken. On 2 October Kitchener and Grey belatedly made appeals to Joffre, Sir John French, and the French Government to come to the relief of Belgium's chief port. 'If not', Grey commented fatalistically, 'the loss of Antwerp must be contemplated.'[3]

That same night the British Minister at Antwerp telegraphed that the Belgian Army—a force of some 150,000 men—Government, and King would evacuate the city the next day.

Grey thereupon convoked Kitchener and Churchill (the Prime Minister being in Wales) to another midnight ministerial conference, in the course of which the First Lord prevailed upon his colleagues to agree to his immediate departure for the beleaguered city in hopes of persuading the Belgians to hold out. The entire Royal Naval Division—together with the extra regular (the Seventh) that had earlier been contemplated

[1] The Ostend and Dunkirk landings more than fulfilled the hopes of their originators; the German command became seriously concerned at the 'threat' to its flank, a preoccupation which affected German indecision at the Marne and after. (See Liddell Hart, *A History of the World War, 1914–1918* (1938), 112 ff.)

[2] Churchill, *World Crisis*, i. 299–302; J. A. Spender and Cyril Asquith, *Life of Herbert Henry Asquith, Lord Oxford and Asquith* (1932), ii. 125–6; Hankey, *Supreme Command*, i. 199–201; *Naval Opns.* i. 181.

[3] Churchill, *World Crisis*, i. 303–5; Arthur, *Kitchener*, iii. 67–68; Hankey, *Supreme Command*, i. 201–3; *Mil. Opns. Fr. and Bel. 1914*, ii. 32–39.

as a reinforcement for the B.E.F., and a cavalry division—
would be sent to Antwerp to hearten the dispirited Belgian
troops.

Churchill and the Royal Naval Division departed immediately. The activities of the First Lord in Antwerp postponed
the admission of defeat perhaps four or five days, but on 10
October the city formally capitulated. The Seventh and
cavalry divisions, still on the road from Ostend, were ordered
to join the B.E.F. The promised French assistance of two
territorial divisions had not appeared.[1]

The several days' delay, however, proved an invaluable
advantage in the 'Race to the Sea'. After the fall of Antwerp,
that of the coastal towns of Ostend and Zeebrugge followed
almost automatically. But by the time the German forces had
arrived near the French coast the Belgian Army made a stand
on the Yser and the B.E.F. had completed its entrainment from
the Aisne. There ensued a month-long (c. 20 October–22
November) series of ferocious combats between the German
and Allied forces.

'First Ypres' was a 'soldiers' battle'. It was also, as has
perhaps not been sufficiently observed, the encounter battle
which had long been looked to before the war as decisive but
had been declined by the Germans at the Marne. Kitchener
fed the conflict with the two native divisions of the Indian
Corps, another regular division (the Eighth) just constituted
from battalions recalled from overseas, and, *mirabile dictu*, no
fewer than nineteen battalions (the equivalent of almost two
divisions) of the Territorial Force.[2]

While these great events took place in France and Belgium,
the 'traditional' extra-Continental elements of British strategy
were not neglected. Minor military operations were undertaken against the German colonies mainly to please the Navy
but also with the advantage in mind of obtaining hostages for
the release of Belgium at the time of peace negotiations. As

[1] Asquith, *Memories and Reflections*, ii. 48–54; Churchill, *World Crisis*, i. 305–23;
Viscount Grey of Fallodon, *Twenty-Five Years* (N.Y., 1925), ii. 80–83; Hankey,
Supreme Command, i. 203–5; *Mil. Opns. Fr. and Bel. 1914*, ii. 39–67; *Naval Opns.* i.
180–201.

[2] Arthur, *Kitchener*, iii. 91, 319–21; *Mil. Opns. Fr. and Bel. 1914*, ii; App. 4,
pp. 487–8.

early as 6 August the Cabinet approved recommendations on the subject made the preceding day by a subcommittee of the Committee of Imperial Defence under the chairmanship of Admiral Sir Henry Jackson.

The German colonies in the Pacific and South-West Africa were to be captured so that their cable and wireless telegraph stations could be destroyed, thus cutting off all communications between the German Naval High Command and its ships overseas. An expedition from India would be sent to the port of Dar es Salaam in German East Africa to forestall any German ships from using that harbour as a base.

The German islands and possessions in the Pacific were promptly seized: those north of the equator by the Japanese, those south by the Australians and New Zealanders. Togoland was captured within the month by the West African Rifles from the Gold Coast with the aid of French colonial units. Elsewhere operations went less smoothly. A Franco-British expedition to the Cameroons under an officer of the West African Rifles attacked and took the main port, Duala, but the enemy garrison escaped into the hinterland. The South African expedition to German South-West Africa precipitated a Boer rebellion, and the force had to be temporarily withdrawn. As for the expedition to German East Africa, it turned out a fiasco.[1]

This last venture had been cursed from the beginning. The Government of India, which preferred the seizure of the head of the Persian Gulf to the occupation of German East Africa, had initially succeeded in avoiding compliance with the C.I.D. subcommittee recommendations on Dar es Salaam. In September, however, the British Cabinet forced India to send the expedition. The reason for this insistence was the threat, real or apparent, to sea communications posed by Admiral von Spee's Far East Squadron. The capture of the German

---

[1] Asquith, *Memories and Reflections*, ii. 31; Churchill, *World Crisis*, i. 237–8; *Mil. Opns. Fr. and Bel. 1914*, ii. 20–25; Brig.-Gen. Sir James E. Edmonds, *A Short History of World War I* (1951), 394–402; *Naval Opns.* i. 128 ff. ('The governing principle . . . on which the Committee set out, was that all operations were to be regarded primarily as designed for the defence of our maritime communications and not for territorial conquest. The single object was to deprive the enemy of his distant coaling and telegraphic stations'); Proceedings of a Sub-Committee of the Committee of Imperial Defence, assembled on 5 Aug. 1914 to consider the question of offensive operations against German colonies. Asquith Papers, The Bodleian Library, Oxford.

possessions in the Pacific had deprived this unit of the German Navy of a base. Shortly thereafter one of von Spee's cruisers, the *Emden*, began raids in the Indian Ocean. The *Königsberg*, on permanent station off East Africa, was still at large.

On 14 September the Indian Government was therefore ordered to send a force to East Africa to forestall Admiral von Spee's expected movements. The Government of India and Indian Army, unconcerned as they were with naval pre-occupations, chose the units they could most easily spare; and on 31 October an inferior 8,000-man force arrived at the British-ruled island of Mombasa. By then the *Königsberg* had been discovered hiding in the river Rufiji and von Spee's squadron was off the South American coast, two of his vessels having been located in the Eastern Pacific over three weeks before. The expedition had lost its *raison d'être*.[1]

The actual ensuing operations reflected no credit on the good sense of any of the British local authorities. Since the British naval commander off East Africa had, without bothering to consult the Admiralty, negotiated a no hostilities agreement with the German leaders at Tanga and Dar es Salaam he felt in honour obliged to warn them of the impending attack. Not till some twelve hours after the surrender of Tanga had been demanded did two battalions disembark on the peninsula, and the main attack was not delivered till the next morning. This proved unsuccessful and after a three-day struggle the expedition, many of its troops in a state of panic, withdrew.

No news of this humiliation to British arms was allowed to appear in the public press, but the Cabinet thereafter made the India Office transfer responsibility for subsequent operations in East Africa to the War Office. Three days after this decision, on 25 November, the War Council held its first meeting.[2]

All these far-flung colonial operations, dictated as they were

[1] Lieut.-Col. Charles Hordern, *Military Operations East Africa*, i (1941), 60–79, 101–3; Churchill, *World Crisis*, i. 239–46, 254–6, 366; Col. R. Meinertzhagen, *Army Diary, 1899–1926* (1960), 81–82; Mesopotamia Commission. Report of the Commission Appointed by Act of Parliament to Enquire into the Operations of War in Mesopotamia. Cd. 8610 (1917), 11.

[2] *Mil. Opns. East Africa*, i. 79–109; Meinertzhagen, *Army Diary*, 83–109; Edmonds, *Short History*, 405; *Mil. Opns. Fr. and Bel. 1914*, ii (1925), 10 ('A War Council was formed, mainly for the purpose of curtailing the number of the members of the Cabinet who personally participated in the conduct of the war').

primarily by naval demands, did not affect the determination of the British Government to prevent the extension of the war. A Greek offer on 18 August to join the Triple Entente was rejected by Grey lest intervention precipitate hostilities by Bulgaria and Turkey. Various provocatory actions by the leaders of the Ottoman Empire were resolutely overlooked.[1]

The imminence of hostilities with Turkey, however, did give rise to one genuinely colonial expedition. The pressure of the Indian military authorities led to the seizure of the head of the Persian Gulf. The entire Persian Gulf area had long been a special British preserve, and concern over the 'loyalty' of the local sheiks in the event of a Turkish 'holy war' against an infidel power was widespread. It is therefore perhaps not surprising that as early as 26 September the Military Secretary of the India Office, General Sir E. Barrow, should urge a landing of troops from India into *Persian* territory at the head of the Gulf, 'ostensibly to protect the oil installation but in reality to notify to the Turks that we meant business and to the Arabs that we were ready to support them'.[2] The Cabinet's approval was obtained on 2 October, and by the 23rd a brigade and supporting units from India had made a rendezvous off the island of Bahrein. They then waited until the formal declaration of war. At the end of the month two ships of the Turkish Navy manned by German crews bombarded Russia's Black Sea ports. On 2 November Russia accordingly declared war, followed by England and France three days later. The following day the Indian expeditionary force landed on Abadan Island. Hostilities with Turkish troops just above the oil installations were so successful that the Cabinet sanctioned the capture of Basra, seventy-five miles north of the Persian Gulf. This town was taken without difficulty on 22 November, and by early December British troops had advanced fifty-five miles northward to the junction of the Tigris and Euphrates rivers. The entire head of the

[1] Grey, *Twenty-Five Years*, ii. 178–85; Prime Minister to the King, Report on the Cabinet of 17 Aug. 1914 (Crewe and Kitchener, in view of Moslem sensitivity in India and Egypt, desire that Turkey, and not the British, make the aggressive act). Asquith Papers. The policy of refusing proffered Balkan co-operation lest Turkey be offended was protested by Churchill, but to no effect. See his *World Crisis, 1911–1918* (Odhams Press edn.), ii. 446–7.

[2] The Role of India in a Turkish War. *Campaign in Mesopotamia*, i. 87.

Persian Gulf was now securely under British control; a proclamation informed the local population that they would never be
returned to Turkish rule. This expedition of the Indian Army,
unlike the one to German East Africa, had ended in complete
success. Its mission was terminated.[1]

During the last weeks of 1914 three series of events changed
the conditions under which the war had been fought and
closed the phase of movement. The outer seas were swept
clean of German warships; a stalemate was imposed in the
Western theatre; and the Russian 'steamroller' was unmistakably brought to a halt while still in Russian Poland. The existence of the 'new war' was evident to ministers, who thereupon
set about without delay to formulate a new strategy along
traditional lines.

The Battle of the Falklands, on 8 December, destroyed
Admiral von Spee's cruiser squadron. An earlier attempt by
Rear-Admiral Cradock, commanding the South American
Station, to engage the German force with but three armed
cruisers had ended in disaster. To retrieve the situation the
First Lord and First Sea Lord did what had before appeared
impossible. Three battle cruisers were wrested from the Grand
Fleet, two more very powerful ones were extracted from their
dockyards, and a new projected operation against von Spee
was placed under the direct command of the outgoing Chief of
Staff, Admiral Sturdee. In the next encounter between the
Royal Navy and von Spee only one of his ships, the *Dresden*,
escaped; and even this cruiser was later cornered off the Chilean
coast finally to be blown up by her own crew. The oceans of
the world were cleared of German warships; trade and transport could proceed unhampered; and the Admiralty could
make its dispositions without regard to any German war vessels
save those in or near home waters.[2]

---

[1] *Campaign in Mesopotamia*, i. 75–153; Mesopotamia Commission. Report, 12–15;
Edmonds, *Short History*, 378–9; Lieut.-Col. R. Evans, *A Brief Outline of the Campaign
in Mesopotamia, 1914–1918* (1930), 8–19; Meinertzhagen, *Army Diary*, 82 ('16. x.
1914. At sea off Bombay. "I believe we have been at war with Turkey for a week
or so, but nothing official has as yet been announced. But we are sending a force
to occupy the mouth of the Tigris and Euphrates, Mohammerah, Basra and perhaps
Baghdad. If this does not mean war with Turkey I don't know what does." ')

[2] Churchill, *World Crisis*, i. 364–94; *Fear God and Dread Nought*, iii. 67–77, 82–92;
Naval Opns. i. 341–58, 400–36.

On the Western Front the desperate struggles along the Belgian coast died away, leaving the contesting forces still dug in trenches. 'First Ypres' was the B.E.F.'s great ordeal; by the time the tide of battle ebbed over half its original strength had been expended. But the German Army, despite more than one fierce attempt to break the Allied front, had been held, thus largely justifying even the more optimistic pre-war estimates of the B.E.F.'s function. More could hardly be expected from the hard-used little army, as for the moment even Sir John French was prepared to admit. The B.E.F. contributed little more than a half-hearted demonstration to Joffre's mid-December offensive, and the troops celebrated the Christmas season by fraternizing with their German companions in bondage.[1]

If in the Western theatre the German Army had been held, in the Eastern sector the Russian Army had been similarly thwarted. The latter giant force, however, was now dangerously vulnerable. A premature invasion of East Prussia, undertaken in response to French pleas, had been smashed at Tannenberg. The pleas, however, supported by Sir Edward Grey, continued. A subsequent Russian counter-attack through Silesia fared no better, for the Germans consistently outfought and out-manoeuvered their enemies. In early December Lodz, in Russian Poland, was lost. The Russian armies were still in being; but, as a series of dispatches in December warned, had all but exhausted their ammunition. Russia, moreover, was in a peculiarly unfavourable position for remedying this now common want.[2]

Elsewhere in Europe military operations had come to no decision, but were on the whole advantageous to the Allies. Two Austrian attempts to conquer Serbia had been repulsed, and the Austrian armies forced back to the frontier. The long-drawn-out battles between the Austrian and Russian forces had destroyed much of the officer corps whose loyalties and interests had made possible the existence of a monarchical army

---

[1] Arthur, *Kitchener*, iii. 77–79; Maj.-Gen. Sir E. Callwell, *Field-Marshal Sir Henry Wilson: His Life and Diaries* (1927), i. 189–94; C. R. M. F. Cruttwell, *A History of the Great War, 1914–1918* (2nd edn., 1936), 108–9; French, *1914*, 338; *Mil. Opns. Fr. and Bel. 1915*, i. 23.

[2] Cruttwell, *History of the Great War*, 38–54, 79–93; Arthur, *Kitchener*, iii. 81; Callwell, *Henry Wilson*, i. 183, 193, 196; French, *1914*, 334–6; Churchill, *World Crisis*, ii. 471.

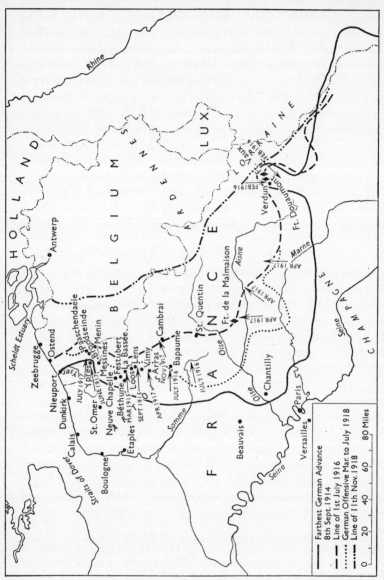

Map 2: The Western Front, 1914-18.

in the multi-national Austro-Hungarian state. At the end of 1914 south-eastern Europe offered favourable opportunities to the Entente.

As the implications of the events of December 1914 became evident, ministers reverted—by instinct as by reason—to the older traditions of British war policy. The B.E.F. had held the Germans. If victory could not be obtained in the West, why not try elsewhere? In January 1915 there were no lack of projects or of opportunities. Whether the will and the means existed was, however, less certain.

II

THE DARDANELLES EXPEDITION

'The object in forcing the Dardanelles is ultimately to . . . overawe Constantinople.'
Telegram, LORD KITCHENER to LIEUT.-GEN. SIR JOHN MAXWELL, C.I.C.,
Egypt, 24 February 1915.

ON 29 December 1914 the Prime Minister received 'two very interesting memoranda' from Hankey and Churchill on the future conduct of the war, and three days later yet another from Lloyd George. All three emphasized the existence and probable continuance of stalemate in the West. The whole country from Ypres to the German frontier, Asquith noted, was being transformed into a series of 'fortified entrenchments'. 'I am profoundly dissatisfied with the immediate prospect—an enormous waste of life and money day after day with no appreciable progress.'[1]

The War Council, which had been meeting at weekly intervals, held from 7 January onwards a series of daily conferences to consider the suggestions being made for new strategic policies. Meanwhile, on 2 January, Kitchener wrote Sir John French that[2]

The feeling here is gaining ground that, although it is essential to defend the line we hold, troops over and above what is necessary for that service could be better employed elsewhere.

I suppose we must now recognize that the French Army cannot make a sufficient break through the German lines of defence to cause a complete change of the situation and bring about the retreat of the German forces from Northern Belgium. If that is so, then the

---

[1] Earl of Oxford and Asquith, *Memories and Reflections* (Boston, 1928), ii. 61–63; Lord Hankey, *The Supreme Command, 1914–1918* (1961), i. 244–50; Winston S. Churchill, *The World Crisis, 1911–1918* (4-vol. Odhams Press edn.), ii. 484–5; *War Memoirs of David Lloyd George* (2-vol. Odhams Press edn., 1938), i. 219–26.
[2] Sir George Arthur, *Life of Lord Kitchener* (1920), iii. 85–86.

German lines in France may be looked upon as a fortress that cannot be carried by assault, and also cannot be completely invested—with the result that the lines can only be held by an investing force, while operations proceed elsewhere.

The question of *where* anything effective can be accomplished opens a large field, and requires a good deal of study. What are the views of your Staff?

That Kitchener should ask the leader of the British Forces in the Field this question was only natural, since the pre-war General Staff was now largely incorporated in the latter's command. Sir John French had himself been Chief of the Imperial General Staff for two years until his reluctant resignation from that post in April 1914. His temperament however had always been far from judicious, and his outlook was now simply that of a field commander both short of munitions and desirous of more troops. His alarm was such that he determined to make his views known to the Prime Minister, and it was to Asquith that French had his reply to Kitchener's inquiry personally delivered. The memorandum is of interest: the faith now newly placed in weight of ammunition to ensure tactical success was to serve as the principal military argument of the Westerners for the next two years. Yet Sir John, unlike his successor, did not believe that it was in France that the war could be won:[1]

Breaking through the enemy's lines is largely a question of expenditure of high explosive ammunition. If sufficient ammunition is forthcoming, a way out can be blasted through the line. If the attempt fails, it shows, provided that the work of the infantry and artillery has been properly co-ordinated, that insufficient ammunition has been expended, i.e. either more guns must be brought up, or the allowance of ammunition per gun increased.

Until the impossibility of effective action in France and Flanders is fully proved, there can be no question of employing British or French troops elsewhere. I consider that the Eastern theatre of war is one in which a success on the part of the Allies would have the most decisive results. On the other hand a great German success in the West would be fatal.

[1] Sir John French, Memorandum, 5 Jan. 1915, 6 pp. Kitchener Papers, National Register of Archives, London; Philip Magnus, *Kitchener: Portrait of an Imperialist* (1958), 311–12; Arthur, *Kitchener*, iii. 86–87; Hankey, *Supreme Command*, i. 261–2 ('Ultimate victory must be sought for in the eastern theatre of war').

This special pleading did not change ministers' views or basic decisions; Sir John French proved unconvinced by his own arguments.[1] On 8 January the War Council vetoed a proposed advance on Zeebrugge,[2] informing Sir John that he was not thereby prevented from 'co-operating—to the utmost extent compatible with *your present resources*—with any offensive move-ment contemplated by General Joffre' (author's italics).[3]

On 13 January the War Council reached the important con-clusion, 'That if the position in the Western theatre becomes in the spring one of stalemate, British troops should be despatched to another theatre and objective'.[4] A C.I.D. subcommittee was appointed to discover these last.

So quickly, so without hesitation, so unanimously did the British Government formally express their desire to free them-selves from their commitment to the Western Front. Their readiness to search without delay for 'another theatre and objec-tive' doubtless reflected both the empiricism on which British statesmen have long prided themselves and their wish to con-serve Britain's traditional military policy of limited Continental commitments. It also manifested unquestioning faith in the potentialities of British sea-power.

The mobility afforded by the Royal Navy's command of the sea could be used in one of several possible theatres. An out-flanking sea and land attack could be delivered, it was proposed, from either the north (the Baltic) or the south (the Adriatic or the Aegean). The Baltic, the Austrian, and the Turkish schemes all had their advocates within the War Council.

The 'Baltic operation' was the most strategically promising, but also the most dangerous and uncertain of the alternative campaigns proposed. Since 1905 it had in one form or another

---

[1] Hankey, *Supreme Command*, i. 264 (War Council, 13 Jan. 'Sir John admitted that in the west we were not strong enough to break down the German resistance'); *The Intimate Papers of Colonel House*: Arranged as a Narrative by Charles Seymour, i (1926), 360–1; Burton I. Hendrick, *The Life and Letters of Walter H. Page* (1924), i. 427–8.

[2] This prohibition was lifted three days later, but Sir John remained unable to convert either the French or Belgian military authorities, so Flanders coast operations were abandoned until the command of the British Armies in France conceived itself strong enough for the task—two and one-half years later.

[3] Arthur, *Kitchener*, iii. 92. On the Zeebrugge project see ibid. 86–92; Magnus, *Kitchener*, 305–8; Hankey, *Supreme Command*, i. 258–60, 263–5; Churchill, *World Crisis*, ii. 490–5, 506–7.

[4] Hankey, *Supreme Command*, i. 267.

been advocated and worked for by Admirals Fisher and Wilson. Returned to positions of power in November 1914, these naval officers could now look for military assistance from the mammoth Russian armies. The essence of the project—in so far as the few scattered available sources permit reconstruction—was that the Navy should break into the Baltic, destroy the German fleet, and land a *Russian* army on the Pomeranian coast. British troops would be employed in operations designed to prevent the German ships from escaping through the Kiel canal into the North Sea. These actions could scarcely lead to less than apocalyptic results, though to which of the contenders' benefit it is not easy to say.

The Russians, however, seem to have greeted the idea with favour. In November 1914 the Admiralty commissioned the building of a fleet of some six hundred ships for this particular mammoth operation. Among them were over two hundred motor barges ('lighters') for use as troop landing craft. They were eventually to see service elsewhere.

Churchill for his part urged the merits of the Baltic naval offensive on the Prime Minister. But the First Lord was unable to elicit from either Fisher or Wilson or from the reluctant War Staff a practicable plan of operations. The complications and difficulties seemed strange and overwhelming. The Navy could only 'break into' the Baltic through the very narrow waters of the Belts—traversing Denmark—or the Sound, between Denmark and Sweden. The reactions of these neutral nations and the effects of enemy minelaying in these waters were all the more feared for being unknown. The escape of the German fleet through the Kiel canal could only be prevented by closing the Elbe by operations from captured Frisian Islands—Borkum, Sylt, even Heligoland. The prospect of seizing these islands evoked no enthusiasm within the War Staff. Captain Richmond, Assistant Director of its Operations Division, advised against such combined operations in waters the 'command' of which would not yet have been secured. The commander of the Grand Fleet, Admiral Jellicoe, was opposed to the whole scheme. So it fell out of sight, while Churchill became engrossed in the Dardanelles. No 'northern flank' operation was to be attempted until the next war, in the spring of 1940.[1]

[1] The account of the projected 'Baltic' operation is derived from the following

The War Council as a body was more impressed by the advantages to be gained on the 'southern flank' through an attack on Austria or Turkey; the committee appointed to search for a new theatre, with Kitchener as its chairman, on 28 January recommended the Greek port of Salonika. Not only were the risks less appalling, but allies—or so it appeared—were more attainable. In the north the peaceful Netherlands and Scandinavian states were determined to guard their neutrality. But in the south the territorial ambitions of the Balkan powers— Greece, Rumania, Bulgaria—and of Italy might well be exploited at the expense of the Austrian and Turkish Empires. The willingness of Greece's Prime Minister, M. Venizelos, to make that country an ally of Britain was well known.[1]

The leading advocate of an attack directed against Austria was Lloyd George. He conceived of the operation as a strike from Salonika (or, alternatively, the Dalmatian coast) 'in conjunction with the Serbians, the Roumanians, and the Greeks'. These last two powers, it was estimated, could well furnish half a million troops. By April Great Britain could send as many as six hundred thousand. Even if the Austrian forces were undefeated, Austria would be forced to transfer so many of her troops as to leave Silesia indefensible against the Russians. Either Germany would send reinforcements making her vulnerable to attack elsewhere, or Austria would be defeated, leaving Germany isolated and forced to defend herself on still another front. And the Balkans would have entered the war on the side of the Entente.

sources: Adm. Sir R. H. Bacon, *The Life of John Rushworth, Earl Jellicoe* (1936), 188; Adm. Sir Edward E. Bradford, *Life of Admiral of the Fleet Sir Arthur Knyvet Wilson* (1923), 239–42; Maj.-Gen. Sir C. E. Callwell, *Experiences of a Dug-Out, 1914–1918* (1920), 119–22; Churchill, *World Crisis*, ii. 479–86; Churchill, 'Lord Fisher and his Biographer', *Great Contemporaries* (Fontana Books edn., 1959), 277–8; *Fear God and Dread Nought: The Correspondence of Admiral of the Fleet Lord Fisher of Kilverstone*, iii (1959), 42–47, 121–2, 259–60; Admiral of the Fleet Lord Fisher, *Memories* (1919), 55, *Records* (1919), 217–24; *Portrait of an Admiral: The Life and Papers of Sir Herbert Richmond*, (ed.) Arthur J. Marder (1952), 134–45, 138–40.

[1] Hankey, *Supreme Command*, i. 268, 272–3; *Mil. Opns. Gallipoli*, i (1929), 64; *Mil. Opns. Fr. and Bel. 1915*, i. 63 n.; Callwell, *Henry Wilson* (1927), i. 200, 205–6; Asquith, *Memories and Reflections*, i. 68 ('I have urged Grey to put the strongest possible pressure upon Rumania and Greece to come in without delay, and to promise them that if they will form a real Balkan *bloc* we will send some of our troops to join them. I am sure that this is right and that all our side-shows, Zeebrugge, Alexandretta, even Gallipoli, must be postponed for this.')

The Chancellor of the Exchequer also suggested a landing in Syria to cut off the Turkish Army then congregating for an attack on the Suez canal. These '*two independent operations* . . . would have the common purpose of bringing Germany down by the process of knocking the props under her'. So soon was formulated the characteristic argument by phraseology of the Easterners.[1]

The Secretary of the War Council had meanwhile circulated a memorandum suggesting the merits of a military offensive against Turkey with Constantinople as the prize. At this early stage of the war, we emphasize, the 'Austrian' and 'Turkish' projects were complementary rather than competitive. As far back as September 1914 Churchill had urged that in the event of war with Turkey the Gallipoli Peninsula be seized by a Greek army, thus enabling the Anglo-Greek fleet to destroy the Turkish Navy in the Sea of Marmora and thereafter 'dominate the situation' with the help of the Russian military forces. And at the first meeting of the War Council, in November, he had suggested a British attack, which would, however, require 'a large force'.[2]

Now, in a memorandum dated 28 December 1914, Lieutenant-Colonel Maurice Hankey amplified this proposal:[3]

Has not the time come to show Germany and the world that any country that chooses a German alliance against the great sea-power is doomed to disaster? Is it impossible now to weave a web round Turkey which will end her career as a European power?

. . . Left to themselves [the] Balkan States, all of whom [Greece, Roumania, Bulgaria] stand to gain from the ejection of Turkey from Europe and from the dismemberment of Austria, will be unable to realize their overwhelming opportunity, so great is their mutual distrust.

But supposing Great Britain, France and Russia . . . were themselves to participate actively in the campaign and to guarantee to each nation concerned that fair play should be rendered. . . . It is presumed that in a few months time we could, without endangering the position in France, devote three army corps, including one original first line army corps, to a campaign in Turkey, though sea transport might prove a difficulty. This force, in conjunction with

---

[1] Lloyd George, *War Memoirs*, i. 219–26; Hankey, *Supreme Command*, i. 260–2.
[2] Churchill, *World Crisis*, ii. 443–4; Dardanelles Com. First Rpt. Cd. 8490 (1917), 14; Hankey, *Supreme Command*, i. 242–3, 262.
[3] Hankey, *Supreme Command*, i. 248–9.

Greece and Bulgaria, ought to be sufficient to capture Constantinople.
If Russia, contenting herself with holding the German forces on an
entrenched line, could simultaneously combine with Serbia and
Roumania in an advance into Hungary, the complete downfall of
Austria–Hungary could simultaneously be secured.

The difficulty with both 'southern flank' projects was that on
the one hand the necessary troops were as yet unavailable, and
on the other ministers, or at any rate Churchill, could not or
would not wait until they were. It was in vain that Admiral
Fisher, attracted by 'the peculiar merit of Hankey's Turkish
plan', urged that one hundred thousand men be withdrawn
from the B.E.F. The first of Kitchener's New Armies was in
training. The Territorials the Secretary of State for War declined
to employ. The withdrawal of effectives from Sir John French's
command, now three hundred thousand strong, might or might
not affect the security of the line but would certainly evoke
apoplectic protests not only from G.H.Q. but also from General
Joffre and his obedient servants the French Council of Ministers.
Elsewhere, Lord Kitchener affirmed, 'We have no troops to land
anywhere'. From this judgement there was as yet no appeal.[1]

It was while these discussions on the future employment of the
New Armies were still being pursued that a naval strike in the
Sea of Marmora was decided upon, apparently as an interim
measure. Some of the Navy's now expendable warships would
find employment in an enterprise which by the almost magical
effect of sea-power might even attain the same goals as the more
ambitious plans for a great combined military offensive on
Austria or Turkey. In response to Churchill's promptings the
War Council as early as 13 January artlessly authorized the
preparation, and then on the 28th the dispatch, of 'a naval
expedition . . . to bombard and take the Gallipoli Peninsula,
with Constantinople as its objective'.[2] Neither the adverse pre-
war Committee of Imperial Defence reports concerning an
attack on Gallipoli nor the First Sea Lord's current objections
were at this stage made known to the Council.

---

[1] *Fear God and Dread Nought*, iii. 17–19; Churchill, *World Crisis*, ii. 529; Dardanelles Com. First Rpt. 30.
[2] Dardanelles Com. First Rpt. 21; Hankey, *Supreme Command*, i. 266–7 (Hankey
states that Asquith himself drew up this thoughtless phrase).

The immediate origin of the Dardanelles expedition was a telegram received by Lord Kitchener on 2 January from the Commander of the Russian Armies. The Grand Duke Nicholas requested a British 'demonstration' for the purpose of diverting a Turkish offensive through northern Persia to the Caucasus, where the Russian forces were threatened with envelopment. An affirmative reply was sent on Grey's advice. Kitchener was naturally of the opinion that the only area where a demonstration 'might have the desired effect was at the Dardanelles'. Churchill agreed, but, being desirous of guarding Britain's capability of making a genuine attack in that area, was opposed to giving the Turks prior warning by a mere feint. To resolve this dilemma there was needed only the belief that sea-power might topple the Turks unaided, and this hope the First Lord was quick to grasp. The very next day Churchill telegraphed Admiral Carden, commander of the British squadron in the Eastern Mediterranean,[1] 'Do you consider the forcing of the Dardanelles by ships alone a practicable proposition?' The Dardanelles 'might be forced', Carden cautiously replied, 'by extended operations with large number of ships'. This was enough for Churchill who told Carden to submit a detailed operational plan. '*Your* view' (author's italics), he telegraphed, 'is agreed with by high authorities here.'[2]

Carden's plan of operations arrived on the 11th and two days later Churchill obtained provisional approval from the War Council for a purely naval attempt to force the Dardanelles through methodical reduction of the forts. These would provide a remunerative target for the new battleship *Queen Elizabeth*, about to conduct her trials. Some fourteen older ships hitherto used for operations against German cruisers overseas or about to be dismantled so that their guns could be installed on monitors for the Baltic project would also sail for the Eastern Mediterranean. Could not the success of the German howitzers in silencing the fortresses of Liége, Namur, and Antwerp now be duplicated at the expense of Constantinople?

So the British Government, as in 1807 and 1878, ordered a fleet to sail the Dardanelles to 'overawe' Constantinople. As in

---

[1] Churchill, *World Crisis*, ii. 527–32; Arthur, *Kitchener*, iii. 100–1; Dardanelles Com. First Rpt. 15–16.

[2] Churchill, *World Crisis*, ii. 533.

these previous operations, bluff played a large part. Lord
Kitchener thought the plan was worth trying. 'We could leave
off the bombardment if it did not prove effective.' Once in the
Sea of Marmora, the fleet would, Grey and Kitchener believed,
cause panic in the capital and provoke a *coup d'état* which
would bring into power a government favourable to the Entente.
'Sir Edward Grey thought that the Turks would be paralysed
with fear when they heard that the forts were being destroyed
one by one.' In any event, Churchill trusted, Russia would in
her own interests combine her Black Sea Fleet with Admiral
Carden's forces and land troops to make sure of the great prize
of Constantinople. Success of the naval attack, Grey stated,
would 'finally settle the attitude of Bulgaria and the whole of
the Balkans'. This last was certainly a very weighty influence
in the War Council decision. 'It was difficult to imagine',
Balfour summed up, 'a more helpful operation.' All these aims
were to be achieved by a force of eighteen obsolete warships.[1]

The Council's decision was made in at any rate official ignorance of the objections of Admiral Fisher. The First Sea Lord
had not been included among the 'high authorities' who
Churchill had stated were in agreement with Admiral Carden
on the practicability of forcing the Dardanelles. Admirals Oliver
and Jackson, Churchill later explained, were the authorities in
question. Fisher, though he had favoured the Hankey project,
was opposed to a purely naval operation which might weaken
the Grand Fleet and would certainly postpone further preparations for a Baltic offensive. Nevertheless he and Sir Arthur Wilson
at the War Council of 13 January expressed no disapproval. But
on the 25th the First Sea Lord submitted to Churchill a formal
memorandum with a request that it be submitted to the War
Council. In view of the continued existence of the German High
Seas Fleet it was[2] 'imperative and indeed vital that no operation
whatever should be undertaken by the British Fleet, calculated
to impair its present superiority. . . . Even the older ships should

---

[1] Arthur, *Kitchener*, iii. 105, 114 ('the object . . . is . . . ultimately to . . . overawe
Constantinople'); Churchill, *World Crisis*, ii. 534–53; Dardanelles Com. First Rpt.
17–21, 23–27, 51, 53; Hankey, *Supreme Command*, i. 265–8, 271; *Mil. Opns. Gallipoli*,
i. 74.

[2] Churchill, *World Crisis*, ii. 583. See also ibid. 576–84; *Fear God and Dread Nought*,
iii. 141, 147–8; Dardanelles Com. First Rpt. 20–21, 25–26; Hankey, *Supreme
Command*, i. 269.

not be risked, for they cannot be lost without losing men and they form our only reserve behind the Grand Fleet.'

Churchill forwarded the memorandum to Asquith and in a covering paper had little difficulty in demonstrating the Grand Fleet's secure margin of superiority over the High Seas Fleet. Asquith summoned Fisher and Churchill to a private conference at his office the morning of the 28th and insisted upon Fisher's presence at the War Council that same day. The First Sea Lord's memorandum was never circulated. At the Council meeting that day Churchill asked for approval of the naval attack. Fisher objected to discussion of the project, and, remarking that the Prime Minister knew his views, rose to leave the room. He was, however, followed by Kitchener who after some discussion prevailed upon him to return.

After the meeting Churchill in a long talk with Fisher persuaded him to give his report. Thereafter, Fisher maintained, 'I went the whole hog, *totus porcus*'. At a later session of the Council that same day Churchill, with Fisher and Oliver at his side, announced that the Navy would force the Dardanelles. For Churchill, this was 'the point of final decision. After it, I never looked back.'[1]

Churchill's absorption in the Gallipoli adventure was not, however, shared by his colleagues. They did not know to what extent they had committed the future. The War Council, unaware of the importance of the decision it had just taken, continued to discuss at its leisure strategic alternatives which no longer existed. At this same meeting of 28 January Lloyd George continued to press his plan for a landing at Salonika. Kitchener agreed in the importance of such a move in order to influence the Balkan neutrals. Britain might ultimately send a 500,000-man army to Serbia. But when? His last man was being sent to France, and it was easier to send troops than to retrieve them.

The 'last man' was the Twenty-Ninth Division, the last of the units constituted since the outbreak of the war from regular troops recalled from overseas garrisons. Kitchener had already promised the Twenty-Ninth to the French War Minister, M. Millerand, on the latter's visit to England. Millerand, faithfully

---

[1] Churchill, *World Crisis*, ii. 591. See also ibid. 584–94; Asquith, *Memories and Reflections*, ii. 70–71; Dardanelles Com. First Rpt. 25–29; Fisher, *Memories*, 59, 80; Hankey, *Supreme Command*, i. 271–2, 275.

reflecting General Joffre's views, had then done his best to discourage any Balkan expedition. But on 28 January the Greek minister in Petrograd informed the Russian Foreign Minister that Greece would be willing to intervene if Bulgaria or Rumania did likewise. In the latter event it was suggested that the Entente provide a contingent of troops as a caution to the Bulgars. The Russians showed no enthusiasm, but Lloyd George leapt at the suggestion and in a visit to Paris persuaded the French Government to agree to an Anglo-French force of two divisions. The British would contribute the Twenty-Ninth.[1]

On Lloyd George's return to London he vainly attempted to persuade Sir Edward Grey to preside over a Foreign Ministers' conference in Greece of the Entente and Balkan States—an interesting anticipation of Lloyd George's own exercises in Summitry. The War Council approved the dispatch of the Twenty-Ninth Division to Salonika on 9 February, and Major-General Sir Hubert Gough, then leading the Second Cavalry Division in France, was offered its command. But M. Venizelos, much to British ministers' irritation, flatly refused to accept the proposed joint Anglo-French army corps until after a firm understanding with Rumania had in fact been reached. An approach to Bulgaria met with no more success. That country had, indeed, just made a loan in Berlin.[2]

A proposal by Sir Edward Grey for a joint appeal to Rumania for intervention was deprecated by Delcassé, the French Foreign Minister, who urged that further Balkan démarches be suspended until the Dardanelles operation, to which the French would contribute a squadron, had been successfully completed. The Entente's suggestions might then be more favourably received.[3]

[1] Secretary's Notes of a Meeting of a War Council held at the War Office, 28 Jan. 1915, at 4 p.m. Asquith Papers, Bodleian, Oxford; Churchill, World Crisis, ii. 600; Hankey, Supreme Command, i. 272–5.

[2] France. Ministère de la Guerre. Etat-Major de l'Armée. Service historique. Les Armées françaises dans la Grande Guerre (Paris: Imprimerie nationale, 1922–39) [hereinafter cited as AF], tome ii, Annexes nos. 662, 786; Russia. Mejdounarodnia Otnochenia v epokhou imperialisma, third series, 1914–1917 (Moscow, 1930 ff.) [hereinafter cited as Rus. Dip. Docs.],vii (1), nos. 93, 98, 170, 191, 194; Lloyd George, War Memoirs, i. 238–46; General Sir Hubert Gough, The Fifth Army (1931), 75; Hankey, Supreme Command, i. 276–9. See also Asquith, Memories and Reflections, ii. 71–75; Churchill, World Crisis, ii. 601–2; Russia. Constantinople et les détroits (Paris: Éditions Internationales, 1930–2), ii, nos. 16, 21, 38.

[3] Constantinople et les détroits, i, no. 179; Albert Pingaud, Histoire diplomatique de la France pendant la Grande Guerre (Paris: Éditions 'Alsatia', n.d.), i. 211–14.

The fate of the offer of the Twenty-Ninth Division certainly pointed to this conclusion. But at least it demonstrated that England did have troops, if not an army, to spare and that there was no law of nature decreeing that they be sent to France as soon as raised. The Admiralty, generally supported by the War Council, began to press Kitchener to send the Twenty-Ninth Division and other troops to join Admiral Carden's forces. The Navy would contribute the Royal Naval Division.[1]

The British did have, after all, outside of France other military units besides the Twenty-Ninth Division and Kitchener's New Armies, the first of which was still in training. There was still the Territorial Force. Kitchener, through ignorance, the crassest prejudice, and perhaps a touch of vainglory, had refused to employ the Territorial Force in accordance with pre-war expectations as a basis for expansion of the Regular forces. He had instead elected to conjure up the New Armies associated with his name. Four Territorial divisions had been sent out of the country in 1914 for garrison duties in the Empire. But even so this still left, at the end of 1914, ten first-line Territorial divisions, though thirty-one of their battalions—the equivalent of not quite three divisions—had been sent overseas independently.[2] Another twenty-four battalions had been promised to the French by mid-February.[3]

In addition to the Territorial Force there were now the contributions in man-power from the Empire. The Canadian Division had not only come to England but on 2 February embarked for France, henceforth to be employed as élite troops. The Indian Division, too, had been sent to the Western Front. But the Australian Imperial Force and the New Zealand Expeditionary Force, together comprising some 39,000 men, the strength of

---

[1] Asquith, *Memories and Reflections*, ii. 75; Churchill, *World Crisis*, ii. 602–3; Dardanelles Com. First Rpt. 29–30; Hankey, *Supreme Command*, i. 277–9.

[2] The Territorial Force had originally been constituted as an organization comprising fourteen divisions, fourteen cavalry brigades and corps troops. There were in all 204 infantry battalions, over fourteen to a division.

[3] *Mil. Opns. Gallipoli*, i. 45–46; *AF*, ii, Annexe no. 662; Col. John K. Dunlop, *Development of the British Army, 1899–1914* (1938), 287; General Sir Ian Hamilton, *Gallipoli Diary* (1920), i. 5 ('Did I myself, speaking as . . . Commander . . . executively responsible for the land defence of England, think the 29th Division could be spared at all? "Yes", I said, "and four more Territorial Divisions as well!" K. used two or three very bad words and added . . . that I would find myself walking about in civilian costume instead of going to Constantinople if he found me making any wild statements of that sort to the politicians').

two divisions, had disembarked not in England but in Egypt, due to reports which had reached Australian officials on the Canadian Division's ordeal caused by the inadequate facilities at the training grounds on Salisbury Plain. The Anzacs were therefore completing their training in the more salubrious Egyptian desert, conveniently far from France.[1]

If, however, only limited numbers of unequally trained troops could be released or diverted to the East, their strategic function must needs be defined in severely limited terms—how else obtain the men at all? It was in vain that from within the Admiralty Admirals Fisher and Jackson urged a military occupation of the Gallipoli Peninsula in conjunction with the naval attack. This view, which as Churchill himself states, 'neither Lord Kitchener nor the War Council would at this time have entertained', was not pressed outside Admiralty walls. Balfour called it 'altogether absurd'.[2]

Churchill argued that troops should rather be used 'to reap the fruits' of the naval successes by seizing the Gallipoli Peninsula 'when it has been evacuated, or to occupy Constantinople if a revolution takes place'. The Dardanelles operation was still conceived as basically a naval enterprise with what army troops might be available acting as auxiliaries. 'I wish to make it clear', the First Lord wrote Kitchener on 4 March, 'that the naval operations in the Dardanelles cannot be delayed for troop movements, as we must get into the Marmora as soon as possible in the normal course.'[3]

Kitchener assured Churchill that military assistance would be forthcoming in case of need. However (and on this point Balfour agreed), once the Navy had penetrated the Straits the Turkish troops in the Peninsula would be cut off, doomed to surrender or to starve. In Constantinople a *coup d'état* or a general *sauve qui peut* was probable. To be sure, if 'the Fleet would not get through the Straits unaided, the Army ought to

[1] Col. A. Fortescue Duguid, *Official History of the Canadian Forces in the Great War, 1914–1919*, i (Ottawa, 1938), 150; C. E. W. Bean (ed.), *The Official History of Australia in the War of 1914–1918*, twelve volumes (Australia: Angus & Robertson Ltd., 1921–42), i. 110–14.

[2] Dardanelles Com. First Rpt. 17–18, 21–22, 29–30; *Fear God and Dread Nought*, iii. 142, 158, 165; Churchill, *World Crisis*, ii. 602–3; Lloyd George, *War Memoirs*, i. 104; Hankey, *Supreme Command*, i. 277–9.

[3] Letter, Churchill to Kitchener, 8 Feb. 1915, Kitchener Papers; Churchill, *World Crisis*, ii. 615. See also Lloyd George, *War Memoirs*, i. 248.

see the business through'. But Kitchener was opposed to a preliminary military attack on the Gallipoli Peninsula, where as many as forty thousand Turks were estimated (erroneously) to be in occupation. How the expeditionary force would be employed could really only be decided *after* the naval attack.[1]

In retrospect it is easy to see that the contrasting views and consequent semi-deliberate misunderstandings on the function of troops at the Dardanelles were largely responsible for the manifest inadequacy of the 'Mediterranean Expeditionary Force' for the task it had actually to perform—were indeed responsible for the ultimate failure of the entire campaign.

It was only during the course of these discussions—on 19 February, when naval bombardment of the outer forts on the southern tip of the Gallipoli Peninsula had already begun—that the Prime Minister read to the War Council extracts from memoranda submitted in December 1906 by the General Staff and the Director of Naval Intelligence to the Committee of Imperial Defence on the advisability of either a purely naval or a combined operation against the Dardanelles. Copies of the memoranda were later circulated. The General Staff document opined that the risk of failure in either event was unacceptable; the naval memorandum expressed belief that a military landing on the Peninsula if supported by naval covering fire would succeed, but at the cost of 'heavy losses'.

It was late in the day for such opinions, though they might induce—and surely should have—realization of the need for direct naval support of a military landing should such be found necessary, and for a decision one way or another on the acceptance of the probable losses. It was argued, probably with justice, that developments in ordnance since 1906 now made a naval strike technically feasible. In the event the physical obstacle, in itself the least important, to the forcing of the Dardanelles was not forts but mines.[2]

[1] Dardanelles Com. First Rpt. 29, 32–33; Lloyd George, *War Memoirs*, i. 104, 259; Arthur, *Kitchener*, iii. 114–15; *AF*, viii (1) Annexe no. 1. There were actually under 20,000 Turkish troops on the Peninsula.

[2] C.I.D. 92B. The Possibility of a Joint Naval and Military Attack upon the Dardanelles. I. Memorandum by the General Staff. II. Note by the Director of Naval Intelligence. 20 Dec. 1906. Public Record Office; The Final Report of the Dardanelles Commission (Part II—Conduct of Operations, &c.). Cmd. 371 (1919), pp. 7–8; Hankey, *Supreme Command*, i. 279–80 ('The plan of a prolonged naval operation with the object of silencing the forts one by one, as

Even if no decision had yet been made on the employment of military forces at the Dardanelles, advance preparations for their dispatch were deemed desirable. M. Venizelos had already agreed to the use by the Royal Navy of the island of Lemnos as a concentration point. On 16 February Kitchener was persuaded to agree to the sending of the Twenty-Ninth Division to Lemnos, only to withdraw his permission three days later. On the 20th Kitchener wired the British Commander-in-Chief in Egypt, where a Turkish attack had just been repulsed with ease, that 'in order to assist the Navy a force is being concentrated in Lemnos Island to occupy any captured forts', and ordered him to prepare the Australian and New Zealand contingents for this service. Would these, plus the Naval Division and assorted marines, form an effective military force? Quite enough for a cruise in the Sea of Marmora, Kitchener assured the Prime Minister. He was reluctant to accept in addition the services of a proffered French division.[1]

Even so the Twenty-Ninth Division, as a part of the Regular Army, was considered the indispensable core of the proposed patchwork expeditionary force. What a contrast to the care and planning lavished on the original B.E.F.! In withdrawing his permission to employ the division at the Dardanelles Kitchener was moved by fears of the effect of a débâcle in Russia, where at the beginning of February Hindenburg and Ludendorff had undertaken with the aid of poison-gas shells an offensive from eastern Prussia: the 'Winter Battle of Masuria'. A German success might lead to renewed attempts on the Western Front, perhaps even to a renewal of the war of manœuvre. The Secretary of State for War would then need the Twenty-Ninth as a mobile reserve to be thrown in where needed. From this position, in spite of a personal appeal from Asquith, he refused to be swayed.

These anxieties were played upon by Field-Marshal French and General Joffre. For several weeks there was a tug-of-war between these two commanders in France and the War Council for the Twenty-Ninth Division, with Kitchener as the perplexed

conceived by Carden, was not mentioned, and the papers, therefore, had little bearing . . .').

[1] Dardanelles Com. First Rpt. 30, 32; Arthur, *Kitchener*, iii. 113; Churchill, *World Crisis*, ii. 602, 605; Hankey, *Supreme Command*, i. 279, 281; Minutes, War Council, 24 Feb. 1915, Asquith Papers.

arbiter. General Joffre in particular exerted the strongest pressure. He could not, he informed Kitchener on the 21st, guarantee the immunity of the Allied line in the West unless the Twenty-Ninth Division were held available. M. Millerand complained bitterly that Kitchener had given him a formal promise of the truant division. Sir John French contented himself with stating that he needed the division for an operation whose nature he refused to discuss. Confronted with so many pressures, Kitchener decided for the time being to keep the Twenty-Ninth in England, out of both Churchill's and Sir John French's reach. Perhaps he also wanted to ensure that military operations in the Dardanelles would be postponed until the results of the naval attack were clear.[1]

Kitchener's decision to retain the Twenty-Ninth Division in England had unexpected repercussions upon the Western Front. Sir John French had made arrangements to take over part of the line in order to relieve the French operations at Arras. The British would then support the offensive there by a separate attack. But when the Twenty-Ninth was formally withheld the British commander refused to carry out the relief, alleging that he could not do so in security. Joffre thereupon cancelled the French operations, but Sir John, sensitive to the French command's aspersions on the B.E.F.'s inactivity during Joffre's offensive of the preceding December, persevered in his own scheduled attack. In the resultant battle of Neuve-Chapelle (10–13 March 1915), conducted by the commander of the First Army, Sir Douglas Haig, the British through surprise pushed back the German line two thousand yards but their overly deliberate advance was then brought to a halt by some six machine-guns. The Cabinet, ignorant of Sir John's motives, expressed irritation that their allies had not supported the British attack.[2]

[1] Telegrams between French and Kitchener, 24–27 Feb. 1915. Minutes, War Council, 26 Feb. 1915, Asquith Papers; Letter, Millerand to Kitchener, 2 Mar. 1915, Kitchener Papers; Arthur, *Kitchener*, iii. 117. See also Sir George Arthur, *Not Worth Reading* (1938), 230; Asquith, *Memories and Reflections*, ii. 76; Churchill, *World Crisis*, ii. 604–10; Dardanelles Com. First Rpt. 33–34; Hankey, *Supreme Command*, i. 281–4; Magnus, *Kitchener*, 320–33; Major the Hon. Gerald French, *Life of Field-Marshal Sir John French* (1931), 278.

[2] Correspondence between Joffre and French, 18 Feb.–9 Mar. 1915, *AF*, ii, Annexes nos. 916, 917, 927, 979, 1108, 1124, 1125; Capt. G. C. Wynne, 'Pattern for Limited (Nuclear) War: the Riddle of the Schlieffen Plan—I', *Journal of the*

By then Kitchener had, on 10 March, agreed to abide by his earlier consent to send the Twenty-Ninth Division to the Dardanelles. It would form the nucleus of a 'Constantinople Expeditionary Force' under the command of General Sir Ian Hamilton. The Russian armies in the north had escaped from the German grip and formed a new line, thenceforth themselves to assume the offensive. The security of the Western Front was therefore once again assured. Meanwhile, the publicity given to the Dardanelles had been so great, and the progress of the operations themselves so slow, that the decision to send a military expedition appeared as a timely and necessary measure of reinforcement.[1]

As early as 19 February Admiral Carden's forces had begun their bombardment of the 'outer' forts on the Peninsula and Asian coast protecting the entrance to the Dardanelles. By the 25th the Turkish guns had all been either reduced or evacuated. Thereafter a mere three of Carden's ships (out of a total strength of nineteen, eleven of them battleships) entered the Straits, where they began a cautious and leisurely bombardment of the intermediate forts. These attacks met with less success, and the minesweepers, manned by civilian crews, would not face enemy fire. The pace of operations slackened, and on 9 March Admiral Carden reported that no further progress in reducing the forts could be made until his air reconnaissance service had been reinforced.[2]

Hopes and expectations in England and elsewhere were however now at their high point. The Russians had detailed an army corps to co-operate with the British fleet upon its arrival in the Sea of Marmora. Asquith and Bonar Law had each emphasized in the House of Commons the results which would be attained at the Dardanelles, while at the same time carefully drawing attention (ominous sensitivity!) to the need not to weaken either the Western Front or the Grand Fleet. Ministers urged the neutral powers on the 'southern flank' to seize opportunities such as would surely never again occur. The response

---

Royal United Service Institution (1957), 495; Report to the King on the Cabinet of 16 March 1915, Asquith Papers; Hankey, *Supreme Command*, i. 293 ('the attack had been organized without the Council having any knowledge of it'), 297–8.

[1] Dardanelles Com. First Rpt. 33; Churchill, *World Crisis*, ii. 615–16.

[2] Churchill, *World Crisis*, ii. 611–14, 623–5; Sir Julian S. Corbett, *Naval Operations*, ii (1921), App. B, pp. 414–15; Hankey, *Supreme Command*, i. 282–3.

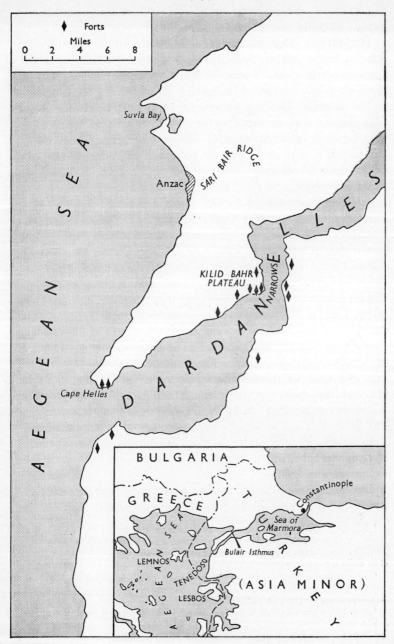

Map 3: The Gallipoli Peninsula.

was certainly heartening: both Greece and Italy now made serious offers to join the Entente.[1]

The Greek offer was no sooner made than rejected—by Russia. On 2 March Asquith reported to the King that the accommodating M. Venizelos had proffered the support of three divisions for use at Gallipoli.[2]

The Russian Minister at Athens, however, clearly indicated that Russia was determined not to tolerate the presence of Greek troops or warships at Constantinople. The Greek King, Constantine, was thereupon emboldened to refuse Venizelos's demand for Greek entry into the war and proceeded to form a new government. By the time Sir Edward Grey had overcome Russian resistance by a formal written agreement to cede to Russia the whole of Constantinople and its environs the Entente's opportunity had passed. The Greek Government now stated that it would not intervene until joined by Bulgaria. If Allied troops were to be used south of the Sea of Marmora England herself would have to furnish them.[3]

The prospect of Italian belligerency, however, now loomed large. On 10 March the Italian ambassador to London intimated that 'on certain conditions' Italy would enter the war that April. The territorial concessions demanded at the expense of Serbian aspirations were high, but then it was not British interests that would suffer. Ministers generally ascribed the greatest importance to Italian intervention. It would, Grey and Kitchener expected, finally precipitate similar action throughout the Balkans. The Italian overture proved at once the international significance of the Dardanelles operations and the need to prosecute them to success.[4]

On 12 March General Sir Ian Hamilton, long one of 'K.'s' protégés,[5] presented himself by instruction at the War Office.

---

[1] Minutes, War Council, 3 Mar. 1915, Asquith Papers; W. W. Gottlieb, *Studies in Secret Diplomacy during the First World War* (1957), 113; Great Britain. *5 Parliamentary Debates* (Commons), lxx (1 Mar. 1915), 596, 603–4; *Constantinople et les détroits*, i. 44, ii. 183.

[2] Report to the King on the Cabinet of 2 Mar. 1915, Asquith Papers.

[3] *Constantinople et les détroits*, i, nos. 56, 80, ii, nos. 105, 107, 109, 114, 117, 118; *Rus. Dip. Docs.* vii (1), nos. 340, 352.

[4] *Rus. Dip. Docs.* vii (1), no. 348, (2), nos. 419, 451; Hankey, *Supreme Command*, i. 285–90.

[5] The preceding November the War Secretary had offered to appoint Sir Ian

Kitchener informed his susceptible and courteous—but surprised—subordinate that he was to command a force of some eighty thousand men to 'support the Fleet' at the Dardanelles. After Hamilton, who had no knowledge of Turkey or its army, pressed for more information the Secretary of State for War called in the Chief of the Imperial General Staff and the Director of Military Operations. General Wolfe-Murray, Hamilton noted, 'seemed to be quite taken aback'; while General Callwell could only inform Hamilton of the supposed outlines of a Greek plan, requiring one hundred and fifty thousand men, for a landing at the Narrows.

Hamilton received in addition a 1912 handbook of the Turkish Army, an Admiralty report—also pre-war—on the Dardanelles defences, and an inaccurate map of the Peninsula; but no military appreciation of the enemy and no plan of campaign.[1]

Kitchener's written instructions, dated the following day, consisted largely of negative admonitions. His caution was understandable, for the Turkish military strength upon the Peninsula was now estimated at sixty thousand. 'The employment of military forces on any large scale for land operations' was 'only contemplated in the event of the Fleet failing to get through *after every effort has been exhausted*' (author's italics). After the Straits had been forced Hamilton might employ some of his forces on the Peninsula, but only at Bulair, at the neck of the Peninsula, 'to retain the Turkish forces . . . and prevent reinforcements arriving'. 'Under present conditions it seems undesirable to land any permanent garrison, or hold any lines on the Gallipoli

to the command of the B.E.F.—a suggestion which Generals Joffre and Foch had decided to oppose. The two French generals then informed Sir John French of the favour they had done him, thus further embroiling relations between the War Office and G.H.Q., and, for the future, between the latter and Hamilton's force. Maj.-Gen. Sir E. Callwell, *Field-Marshal Sir Henry Wilson: His Life and Diaries* (1927), i. 186–7; *Mémoires du maréchal Joffre* (Paris: Plon, 1932), i. 479. Ian Hamilton is the subject of a brilliant—and possibly unfair—sketch in Alan Moorehead, *Gallipoli* (Arrow edn., 1959), 94–96.

[1] It was just four days later that Colonel Hankey wrote: 'It must be borne in mind that up to the present time the employment of military forces has been proposed only to clear up the situation *after* the Dardanelles have been forced. Now . . . so far as the War Council is concerned, we are faced with a new and very formidable operation to be carried out by the land forces.' He therefore urged that the War Council ensure that the most careful advance preparations were being made for the new combined operations. Otherwise, he warned, 'a serious disaster may occur'. (Brig.-Gen. C. F. Aspinall-Oglander, *Military Operations, Gallipoli* [1929], i. 101 ff.)

Peninsula.' Once the fleet was in the Sea of Marmora, the military force would probably be best employed in holding the railway line in European Turkey. That way, Kitchener explained, the British troops could be withdrawn again without difficulty. The contingent did not receive the usual 10 per cent. margin of reserves to replace casualties.[1]

The Admiralty, much relieved at the decision to send troops, sped Sir Ian Hamilton on his way and revived the flagging naval operations. Only four days after leaving the War Office the new Commander-in-Chief arrived at the island of Tenedos just in time to witness the first naval attack. In a letter to Kitchener he expressed his hope that the Navy would manage to break through, for the tip of the Peninsula, contrary to 'K.'s' expectations, was fully occupied by Turkish troops.[2]

The naval attack on the Narrows on 18 March had been pressed upon Admiral Carden by the Admiralty War Group a week before. Carden agreed to resume operations and abandon in theory as well as in fact the plan of a progressive reduction of the forts along the Straits, but added that 'In my opinion military operations on a large scale should be commenced immediately' upon the Peninsula 'to ensure my communication line'. In this view he was supported by Admirals Fisher and Jackson. The Admiralty in its reply confined itself to noting that no attempt would be made 'to rush the passage without having previously cleared a channel through the mines and destroyed the primary armament of the forts'.[3] The decision on any such attempt should be referred to the Admiralty, for (significant and revealing misapprehension!) 'it might then be found that decisive military action to take the Kilid Bahr plateau[4] would be less costly than a naval rush'.

The prospect of a direct, concentrated, and undelayed naval attack upon the Narrows was in fact too great a challenge to the former Superintendent of Malta Dockyard. Admiral Carden

[1] General Sir Ian Hamilton, *Gallipoli Diary* (1920), i. 1–18; Dardanelles Com. First Rpt. 34–35, Final Rpt. 10–11; *Mil. Opns. Gallipoli*, i. 88–90, 101–2; Churchill, *World Crisis*, ii. 625–7 n.; Hankey, *Supreme Command*, i. 290–5.

[2] Letter, Hamilton to Kitchener, H.M.S. *Phaeton*, 18 Mar. 1915. Kitchener Papers; Hamilton, *Gallipoli Diary*, i. 27–28; Churchill, *World Crisis*, ii. 626–7; Final Rpt. of the Dardanelles Com., 11–12.

[3] Churchill, *World Crisis*, ii. 634–5. See also ibid. 628–34.

[4] On the Peninsula overlooking the Narrows.

broke down and was replaced by the officer appointed his second-in-command when the Dardanelles operation had first been decided upon—Vice-Admiral John M. de Robeck. The latter declared himself in agreement with the Admiralty policy of an attack upon the Narrows, which thereupon proceeded.

The naval strike proved a spectacular failure. Some of the forts were silenced, though not destroyed; but of the sixteen ships employed three were sunk and three others put out of action. A single row of mines had been responsible for most of these losses. Admiral de Robeck, appalled at this 'disaster' to the force for which he was responsible, broke off the action.[1]

To Churchill and the War Council—and even to Admirals Fisher and Wilson—the events of 18 March seemed instead a deplorable beginning. The ships lost had been expendable, and in fact steps were taken immediately to replace them. The very next day the War Council authorized de Robeck to proceed with the operations 'if he thought fit'. Yet opinions must even then have been divided on the general issue of continuing the operations, for Asquith was careful not to convene the War Council again until 14 May, when the failure of the first military attack made a meeting inescapable.[2]

To Churchill's surprise and mortification, however, de Robeck declared on 23 March his intention of suspending further naval operations until such time as the Army would land 'on its own' and occupy the entire Gallipoli Peninsula. The First Lord was understandably unwilling to accept such a decision, and proceeded to draft a telegram directing de Robeck in forthright terms to resume the interrupted naval attack upon the Narrows.[3]

But now for the first time in the Gallipoli expedition Churchill was successfully thwarted by the professional naval officers he had himself chosen as his advisers. The Admiralty War Group[4] refused to agree to the telegram being sent. If de Robeck considered that a renewed purely naval attempt was technically

---

[1] Moorehead, *Gallipoli*, 51–59, 71–72; Churchill, *World Crisis*, ii. 635–45, 661; *Naval Opns.* ii. 204–30; Admiral of the Fleet Lord Wester-Wemyss, *The Navy in the Dardanelles Campaign* (1924), 41–43; *The Naval Memoirs of Admiral of the Fleet Sir Roger Keyes, 1910–1918*, i (1934), 219–20, 248.

[2] Churchill, *World Crisis*, ii. 645–6; Dardanelles Com. First Rpt. 38; Hankey, *Supreme Command*, i. 292.

[3] Churchill, *World Crisis*, ii. 646–8, 650–1; Dardanelles Com. First Rpt. 38, Final Rpt. 13–14.

[4] With the exception of Admiral Oliver and Commodore Bartolomé.

unfeasible they had no right to overrule him. Besides, military occupation of the Peninsula was precisely what the Navy had long been urging. Why not let events take their natural course?

In spite of 'high words' Churchill was unable to change the War Group's decision. The Prime Minister, to whom Churchill appealed, agreed, as did Balfour, that a renewed naval attack was desirable, and even noted his opinion that 'the Admiral seems to be in rather a funk'. But he declined to overrule the War Group. The original conception of the Dardanelles expedition as a mainly naval strike was now—though never explicitly—abandoned. The ministerial direction of strategy had received its first check. Never again would it recover its earlier freedom of action.[1]

This drastic change in the policy of what now became the Dardanelles *campaign*—from primarily naval to exclusively military—had been decided on the spot in a matter of moments without the strain of taking thought. Four days after the failure of the naval attack upon the Narrows, the Admiral and the General, as they were henceforth generally called, met in conference with their respective staffs on the *Queen Elizabeth*. 'The moment we sat down,' Ian Hamilton recorded, 'de Robeck told us *he was now quite clear he could not get through without the help of all my troops* . . . there was no discussion. At once we turned our forces to the land scheme.' The chivalric Hamilton did not mention that his instructions had begun by emphasizing that his forces were to be used 'on any large scale' only 'after every effort has been exhausted' by the Fleet. Nor did the Secretary of State for War himself allude to the fact. Instead Kitchener approved of a full-scale military attack aimed at the occupation of the Peninsula and informed the Cabinet that the Army would assume the burdens of the expedition.[2]

If no further naval operations were to be attempted, the only other alternative to inactivity would be withdrawal of the entire task force. Such an eventuality had earlier been accepted (even

---

[1] Asquith, *Memories and Reflections*, ii. 80; Churchill, *World Crisis*, ii. 648–53, 661–4; Dardanelles Com. First Rpt. 38; *Fear God and Dread Nought*, iii. 168–9; Hankey, *Supreme Command*, i. 299 ('Jackson . . . and Fisher . . . very angry with Churchill, as they had warned him that troops were necessary to carry the Dardanelles'), 300.

[2] Hamilton, *Gallipoli Diary*, i. 41–42; Churchill, *World Crisis*, ii. 665. See also Final Rpt. Dardanelles Com. 12, and Hankey, *Supreme Command*, i. 300–1.

welcomed), but now ministers—or at any rate those whose prestige was most involved—proved unwilling to swallow the pill. Not that it was a matter of prestige and emotional commitment alone. The intervention of two of the neutrals on the 'southern flank' appeared imminent. Negotiations on Italian entry had just begun. On 25 March Rumania finally came forward. That day its minister in London informed Sir Edward Grey that Rumania would definitely join the Entente powers, and would be ready to begin hostilities in May.[1] He intimated, however, that Italian entry would make Rumanian intervention more certain still. But surely neither would declare war if Britain and the Royal Navy admitted failure at the Dardanelles.

Kitchener's decision to come to the Navy's rescue was therefore mutely accepted. A small military force thrown together to exploit a naval success was now to be the expedition's sole reliance.

This crucial decision, so casually taken, was never submitted to or discussed by the War Council, which Asquith continued to refuse to convene. Admiral Fisher's repeated written requests that the War Council meet to examine the Dardanelles operation in the light of the naval reverse 'before the final plunge is taken and the troops are landed' were ignored. A similar suggestion by Hankey met the same fate. The War Council never sanctioned a landing on the Gallipoli Peninsula.[2]

As for de Robeck, he made no more attempts on Turkish installations, and refused a request by Hamilton, supported by the War Office, to renew the naval attack. No true combined operation was in fact ever attempted. The Navy at the Dardanelles became a transport service, and its demands for equipment and reinforcements were increasingly resented by the officers of the Admiralty. The Dardanelles had become an 'army show'.[3]

Kitchener for his part made, despite the commitment he had assumed, no attempt to increase the Mediterranean[4]

---

[1] Report to the King on the Cabinet of 26 Mar. 1915, Asquith Papers. See also *Rus. Dip. Docs.* vii (2), nos. 429, 476; Asquith, *Memories and Reflections*, ii. 86; Hankey, *Supreme Command*, i. 301–2.

[2] *Fear God and Dread Nought*, iii. 172–81; *Mil. Opns. Gallipoli*, i. 101–2.

[3] Churchill, *World Crisis*, ii. 664; *AF*, viii (1), Annexe no. 50; *Fear God and Dread Nought*, iii. 183, 186, 188–95, 200.

[4] Changed from 'Constantinople' at Hamilton's plea 'to avert Fate's evil eye'.

Expeditionary Force to a size reasonably adequate for its new task. Instead at a conference at Joffre's headquarters at Chantilly on 29 March he agreed to British participation in an offensive projected in Artois that May under General Pétain and for that operation promised Sir John French two more Territorial Divisions, thus bringing the British forces in France to half a million men. The M.E.F. numbered just seventy-five thousand. French was assured that no more troops would be sent to the Dardanelles. Kitchener did finally at Hamilton's promptings authorize the transfer of one Indian *brigade* from Egypt, but even this arrived too late to take part in the military attack.[1]

Hamilton's three divisional commanders did not believe the landing could succeed. But Hamilton himself was so loyal to his old chief that he would correspond with no one else in London, and yet so fearful of crossing him that he made no further requests for reinforcements. An appeal *to the War Office* for some of the Navy 'lighters' built for Fisher's Baltic operation as landing craft went unanswered.[2]

The unfortunate Hamilton was yet further handicapped not only by his own nature, but also by Grey's bungling diplomacy. To obtain Greek intervention the Foreign Secretary had been willing enough to offer Smyrna. But in exchange for a direct offer of Greek intervention he refused to guarantee that country's northern frontier. At the beginning of May the Greek Government offered the British their full naval co-operation, reserving the army for defence against any Bulgarian incursion into Macedonia. The Cabinet, however, obsessed by the mirage of Bulgarian intervention on the side of the Entente, as they were to be for the remainder of the war, refused to make any move, no matter how otherwise advantageous, that might jeopardize their dreams. If Bulgaria wanted Greek and Serbian Macedonia, she must have it. The Cabinet decided on 6 May both to inform Bulgaria of the Greek desire to intervene and to decline the Greek offer. The Greek overture was not even acknowledged.

---

[1] Hamilton, *Gallipoli Diary*, i. 15; Report to the King on the Cabinet of 30 Mar. 1915, Asquith Papers; *AF*, iii, Annexe no. 23; *Some War Diaries, Addresses, and Correspondence of Field-Marshal the Right Honourable the Earl of Ypres*, Gerald French (ed.) (1937), 187–8; Callwell, *Henry Wilson*, i. 218–19; *Mil. Opns. Gallipoli*, i. 124, 127 n.

[2] Hamilton, *Gallipoli Diary*, i. 44–45, 54–55, 86–94, 161.

For Greece to communicate with the Entente she must first once again make M. Venizelos premier. It is difficult to recall a more disastrous example of feeble Machiavellism.[1]

Further to reduce Sir Ian's chances, Grey vigorously opposed a Russian proposal that the Bulgarian port of Burgas be seized by the Russian fleet as a basis for prosecuting operations against Turkey. The Foreign Secretary urged his 'objections' to 'a most serious political error'. Thus real gains were yet again, and not for the last time, sacrificed to the delusion of a Bulgarian alliance. Operations from Bulgaria were to win the war against Turkey in October 1918, but only after Bulgaria herself had first been vanquished. In 1915 and after the statesmen of the Entente, with England in the lead, continued to attempt to reconcile the irreconcilable.[2]

On 25 April, when the weather finally cleared, Sir Ian Hamilton's forces stormed the tip and waist of the Gallipoli Peninsula. Kitchener on 3 May assured the Prime Minister that there was 'no doubt that we shall break through'. This optimism, though it must have been widespread in London (how else explain the cavalier rejection of the Greek offer?), is difficult to understand, for British troops were inferior in numbers to the defending Turks and equally pinched for ammunition. That they were successful in landing at all is a tribute both to their courage and to Hamilton's generalship. Severe fighting continued for some weeks, but by 9 May Hamilton had to report that he could no longer offer any hope of occupying the Peninsula along the Dardanelles without further reinforcements in troops and munitions. In view of the military stalemate the Admiral now indicated his willingness to try another naval strike on the Narrows, but in terms that expressed his conviction of his own quixotism. Admiral Jackson opined that the proposed operation would end in disaster. As for Fisher, he formally warned his chief, and informed the Prime Minister, that he could not 'under any circumstances' be party to such an attempt. The whole

---

[1] Reports to the King on the Cabinets of 4 and 6 May 1915, Asquith Papers; Hankey, *Supreme Command*, i. 303.

[2] *Rus. Dip. Docs.* vii (2), nos. 569, 736. See also *Constantinople et les détroits*, ii, nos. 134, 239; Gottlieb, *Studies in Secret Diplomacy*, 115; C. Jay Smith, *The Russian Struggle for Power: A Study of Russian Foreign Policy During the First World War* (N.Y. Philosophical Library, 1956), 242.

Dardanelles venture had come to deadlock. It was time to face realities and give up false hopes.[1]

It was not just from the Eastern Mediterranean that bad news came. On all the fronts the Allied position was deteriorating. In the West the Germans on 22 April had made a gas attack at Ypres—to 'cover', their Chief of General Staff later alleged, their subsequent offensive in Russia. The surprise lost the British most of their salient north-east of the town. Thereafter they were able to stand their ground, but were left in no condition to participate effectively in the French push at Artois beginning 9 May. The British attack near Béthune that day, again under Haig's leadership, ground to a halt within the hour; the French advanced three miles at a bound but could make no further progress. On 15 May Asquith offered Sir John French his condolences.[2]

No strategic change had occurred in the West, but in the Eastern theatre the Russian armies sustained a serious reverse. In the beginning of May the Germans and Austrians began an offensive in Galicia. By 14 May, when the War Council reconvened to consider operations at Gallipoli, the Central Powers had covered eighty miles to reach the river San. This enemy success not only imperilled the entire Eastern Front but also affected Gallipoli, for the Russian army corps detailed for employment at the Dardanelles had now to be diverted to Galicia.[3]

The only silver lining to be discerned was in Italy. That nation, anxious not to miss an opportunity to share in the spoils in the Eastern Mediterranean, had signed a treaty on 25 April, the day of the landings, committing her to war against Austria. But on 13 May the Italian premier, confronted with a parliamentary revolt against this decision, was forced to resign. British efforts everywhere appeared frustrated.[4]

[1] Asquith, *Memories and Reflections*, ii. 89; Final Rpt. Dardanelles Com. 21; Churchill, *World Crisis*, ii. 741–50; *Fear God and Dread Nought*, iii. 215–21; Hankey, *Supreme Command*, i. 314. See also *Mil. Opns. Gallipoli*, i. 155, 302; Churchill, *World Crisis*, ii. 721–35; Moorehead, *Gallipoli*, 107–39.

[2] C. R. M. F. Cruttwell, *A History of the Great War, 1914–1918* (2nd edn., Oxford, 1936), 158–9; French, *Life of French*, 376; Hankey, *Supreme Command*, i. 304.

[3] Liddell Hart, *A History of the World War, 1914–1918* (1934), 198; M. Larcher, *La guerre turque dans la guerre mondiale* (Paris, 1926), 102; *AF*, viii (1), 14; Hankey, *Supreme Command*, i. 304.

[4] C. Howard, 'The Treaty of London', *History* (Mar. 1941), 350–5; Pierre

These external misfortunes and disappointments were aggravated by dissensions within the Government and political pressures from without. The morning's *Times* carried a report that the reason for the failure of the British offensive in France was lack of shells. And Kitchener, thus publicly if indirectly attacked, was infuriated by an Admiralty decision to withdraw the *Queen Elizabeth*, the finest vessel of de Robeck's command, from the Dardanelles altogether. No wonder Churchill in his memoirs describes the Council meeting as 'sulphurous'.[1]

The recall of the *Queen Elizabeth* was Fisher's doing. The First Sea Lord's wishes could no longer be denied. Since the German declaration of a submarine blockade in February there had been general and increasing anxiety over the submarine peril. The sinking of the *Lusitania* on 7 May demonstrated to all the world how effective a weapon the submarine could be. The Admiralty reported that one or more U-boats were definitely heading toward the Aegean. The sinking of the battleship *Goliath*, of de Robeck's force, with the loss of most of her crew, by a Turkish *destroyer* on the morning of 12 May decided Fisher to action. He demanded that the *Queen Elizabeth* be immediately recalled. Churchill agreed, but stipulated that two older battleships be sent at once in exchange, as well as the two new monitors originally constructed for the Baltic operation which were nearing completion.

Kitchener on a visit to the Admiralty that night learned of the decision with consternation. His expostulations were in vain; Fisher, now in a state of acute nervous tension, excitedly insisted that he would resign that very night if the *Queen Elizabeth* were not recalled.

In a letter to the Prime Minister Kitchener reiterated his complaint. The Army had agreed to come to the Navy's aid, only to be rewarded with 'desertion'. Under these circumstances, he suggested, the M.E.F. might best be returned to Alexandria, 'as there may be a Moslem rising in Egypt'.[2]

At the War Council meeting of 14 May Kitchener was less

Renouvin, *La Crise europëenne et la Premiere Guerre mondiale* (3rd edn., Paris, 1948), 299.
[1] Churchill. *World Crisis*, ii. 754.
[2] Magnus, *Kitchener*, 338-9. See also Churchill, *World Crisis*, ii. 751-3; *Fear God and Dread Nought*, iii. 221-2; Hankey, *Supreme Command*, i. 305 n., 314.

capricious but even more sombre. All attempts to break through the German lines in the West had entirely failed. The tactical position in Gallipoli was similar. He did not see how the Turks could ever be driven from their positions at the Narrows. He would like to withdraw from the Dardanelles altogether, but this too was impracticable.[1]

Fisher intervened only to remind the Council that he had been opposed to the Dardanelles from the beginning. Lloyd George was doubtful of the success of a renewed attack. But the rest of the Council believed the British Empire could not now afford to withdraw. The first of Kitchener's New Armies was now ready. That night Asquith informed the King that the Cabinet had already decided on the day before that two more divisions would be sent to the Dardanelles within the week, and Kitchener wired Hamilton that[2] 'The War Council would like to know what force you consider would be necessary to carry through the operations on which you are engaged. You should base this estimate on the supposition that I have adequate forces to place at your disposal.'

By the time Hamilton's answer was received the Dardanelles crisis had forced a drastic reconstruction of the Government.

The 'shells scandal' and Fisher's resignation—both the result of the internal pressures engendered by the Dardanelles venture—precipitated this political convulsion. On the morning of 14 May a front-page news item appeared in *The Times* on the abortive attack at Festubert. It began

NEED FOR SHELLS

BRITISH ATTACKS CHECKED

LIMITED SUPPLY THE CAUSE

A LESSON FROM FRANCE

'The need of an unlimited supply of high explosive was a fatal bar to our success.' The story was filed by Colonel Repington, *The Times* military correspondent, and a leading authority in

---

[1] Draft Statement for War Council, Kitchener Papers; War Council, 14 May 1915, Asquith Papers. The meeting is discussed in Churchill, *World Crisis*, ii. 854–6, and Hankey, *Supreme Command*, i. 303–6.

[2] Final Rpt. Dardanelles Com. 24; Report to the King on the Cabinets of Wednesday and Thursday, 14 May 1915, Asquith Papers.

his own right on military affairs.[1] 'It is certain', he concluded, 'that we can smash the German crust if we have the means. So the means we must have, and as quickly as possible.'[2]

The next morning Lord Fisher resigned in protest against further naval reinforcements to the Dardanelles. Four days later Asquith announced in the House that a new government would be formed.

Neither of these dramatic events would have had such profound effects had it not been for the political pressure from backbenchers in the House of Commons and from Lloyd George in the Cabinet. The reader will recall Asquith's earlier refusal to contemplate a coalition government. Bonar Law had accepted the situation with philosophy, but many of his followers had become increasingly restive. At the beginning of 1915 a Unionist Business Committee was established as a 'ginger group'—as much for the benefit of its own leaders as for the Government. 'There is really nothing wrong with the party except the Front Bench', commented Professor Hewins, the guiding spirit of the Committee, 'and that reduces itself to the question of Bonar Law.' The House and the Conservative party were aware of Sir John French's repeated complaints on munitions supplies and of G.H.Q.'s disapprobation of the Dardanelles venture, but Bonar Law, who still adhered to the policy of 'patriotic Opposition', had so far been able to discourage public discussion.[3]

Within the Cabinet Lloyd George, who had never favoured the military attack on Gallipoli, had been long engaged in a struggle with Lord Kitchener over the organization and scale of munitions production. In April Asquith agreed to the

---

[1] Lieut.-Col. C. à Court Repington (1852–1925), the 'Playboy of the Western Front', was a retired officer turned journalist. Despite the marital scandal that ended his army career, he enjoyed very useful connexions in the worlds, not only of the services and journalism, but also of politics and society. As a journalist he was extremely successful—or notorious—and helped to stir up some of the more stormy political-military controversies of pre-war England. He had an important, if rather obscure, role in the beginnings of the Franco-British military staff conversations in 1905. Reactions to his personal character were very mixed. A knowledgeable, uninhibited biography based on his papers would be informative, and exciting.   [2] *The Times*, 14 May 1915, 8 (3).

[3] W. A. S. Hewins, *The Apologia of an Imperialist: Forty Years of Empire Policy* (1929), ii. 15. See also Lord Beaverbrook, *Politicians and the War, 1914–1916* (1928), 10, 41–42, 46–53, 87–92; A. J. P. Taylor, *Politics in the First World War*, The Raleigh Lecture on History, British Academy, 1959, pp. 72–74; Robert Blake, *The Unknown Prime Minister: The Life and Times of Andrew Bonar Law* (1955), 231–40.

formation of a Cabinet Munitions of War Committee under the chairmanship of Lloyd George, but its work was condemned to futility by Kitchener's refusal to share his responsibility or furnish information. The committee last met on 13 May.[1]

Under these conditions of burgeoning political crisis the Repington telegram had the effect of a lighted match in a gas-filled oven. Its dispatch had been precipitated by the effects of the Dardanelles on the Western Front. Sir John French had assured Kitchener that there would be sufficient munitions for the British Army to participate in the May offensive. But the night of 9 May, after the British attack, French received an order to direct twenty-five thousand rounds of artillery ammunition—20 per cent. of his reserve supply—to a ship at Marseille for the Dardanelles. His stock would be replaced within twenty-four hours. This was in fact done.[2]

The shock of this directive was too great for French, who had just witnessed the failure of Haig's attack. He now accepted an earlier suggestion by Lord Northcliffe, proprietor of *The Times* and many other London journals, that he publicize his griefs. He dispatched two of his personal staff to London to see Bonar Law and as many members of Parliament as they could gather and ventilate the Army's needs for more high-explosive shells. Lloyd George was among those the envoys saw first. Newspaper correspondents were not yet allowed at G.H.Q., but Colonel Repington was staying as an 'old friend'. At French's directions he was furnished the material for the famous telegram.[3]

The Times was glad to print the report. Not only had it no love for the Government, but Northcliffe had been reliably informed by General Joffre that munitions for the Dardanelles was material wasted. After the beginning of the military attack on the Dardanelles *The Times* had warned its readers to keep their attention fixed on the Western Front, which was the only

---

[1] Asquith, *Memories and Reflections*, ii. 79–80, 83–85, 88, 91; Lloyd George, *War Memoirs*, i. 110–11, 248; Beaverbrook, *Politicians and the War*, 55–65.

[2] Asquith, *Memories and Reflections*, ii. 92; Arthur, *Kitchener*, iii. 235–6; French, *Life of French*, 301–4; Field-Marshal Viscount French of Ypres, *1914* (1919), 356–61; Callwell, *Experiences of a Dug-Out*, 204–5.

[3] French, *1914*, 301–4; Reginald Pound and Geoffrey Harmsworth, *Northcliffe*, (1959), 475 ('A short and very vigorous statement from you to a private correspondent . . . would . . . bring public pressure upon the Government to stop men and munitions pouring away to the Dardanelles'); Lloyd George, *War Memoirs*, i. 119–20; Magnus, *Kitchener*, 336–7.

'decisive' one. The Director of Military Operations, General Callwell, allowed the telegram to be published. He had no love for Kitchener and was opposed to the Dardanelles.[1]

The effect on the House of Commons was instantaneous. Hewins informed the Prime Minister that he would raise the munitions question in the House. Bonar Law was in a quandary. Not only was his hand being forced by the hotheads in his own party, but a public discussion of the munitions scandals might ruin all chance of Italy's joining the Entente. The delicacy of the Italian position has already been indicated. And Bonar Law in particular had the highest hopes of the effect of Italian entry, suggesting to Kitchener that it would bring the end of the war in sight. The problem which confronted both the leaders of the two great parties was how to keep the House of Commons from asserting political power.[2]

The resignation of Sir John Fisher afforded the solution. His increasing opposition to naval action in the Dardanelles and his uneasiness over the military attack there has been traced in these pages and may be studied in the edition of his correspondence. In his stand he had been supported by the junior Sea Lords, who were also concerned about the margin of superiority enjoyed by the Grand Fleet. 'If . . . you think there would be any value in the support of the Board (which still exists, at all events in name), we shall consider it our duty to give it to you.'[3]

The night of 14 May Churchill sent for Fisher's confirmation a series of minutes ordering reinforcements for the Dardanelles: four cruisers; fifteen monitors, drifters, and trawlers; and two submarines—all the miscellaneous craft, in fact, which Churchill could secure. It was Fisher's turn to explode. On reading the minutes early next morning he sent Churchill a letter of resignation and left the Admiralty, no one knew where, never to return. He also, however, took care to write Bonar Law a long letter urging that Parliament discuss his departure. '*A very great national disaster is very near us in the Dardanelles!*' This letter was received on 17 May.[4]

[1] Harmsworth, *Northcliffe*, 473; *The Times* leader, 27 Apr. 1915; Callwell, *Experiences of a Dug-Out*, 323–4.

[2] Letter, Bonar Law to Kitchener, 3 May 1915, Kitchener Papers; Hewins, *Apologia*, ii. 33.   [3] *Fear God and Dread Nought*, iii. 188–90.

[4] Ibid. 222–6, 237–8; Blake, *Unknown Prime Minister*, 244; Churchill, *World Crisis*, iv. 1419–22.

Bonar Law's—and Lloyd George's—opportunity had come. The Leader of the Conservative party went to consult with the Chancellor of the Exchequer, the bugbear of the Tories. Lloyd George records Law as saying, 'Matters . . . had come to such a pitch that it would be impossible for him to restrain his followers.' Lloyd George then 'went alone to see Mr. Asquith and put the circumstances quite plainly before him'. Adding fuel to the flames, George talked to Northcliffe and Repington that same day. Asquith, his back to the wall, agreed to Bonar Law's demand for a coalition and asked for his colleagues' resignations. 'The resignation of Lord Fisher . . . and the more than plausible case in regard to the alleged deficiency of high-explosive shells', he explained, 'would, if duly exploited (as they would have been) in the House of Commons at this moment, have had the most disastrous effect on the general political and strategic situation: in particular, such a discussion might have had the result of determining adversely to the Allies the attitude of Italy.'[1]

The effects of the change in régime on war strategy were both profound and noxious.

[1] Lloyd George, *War Memoirs*, i. 135–7; Asquith, *Memories and Reflections*, ii. 114–15. See also *Lord Riddell's War Diary, 1914–1918* (n.d. but c. 1933), 87; Blake, *Unknown Prime Minister*, 246–7, 257; Lieut.-Col. C. à Court Repington, *The First World War, 1914–1918* (Boston, 1921), 39; Beaverbrook, *Politicians and the War*, 93.

III

COLLAPSE

'We are (as you realize) in a most critical situation. . . . So long as you and I stand together, we carry the whole country with us. Otherwise, the Deluge!'

Letter, ASQUITH to KITCHENER, 17 October 1915.

'There is only one answer that can satisfy the public and that is that you have already made an end of the futile régime that tumbled along from one fatuity to another.'

Letter, LLOYD GEORGE to ASQUITH, 31 October 1915.

THE First Coalition was formed in response to acute parliamentary and public discontent with the Government's direction of the war. The Conservative leaders, who fully shared the general dissatisfaction, pressed for a purge of ministers and for a closer supervision over the leaders of the military and naval departments rather than for any basic change in reorganization. The resultant machinery for war direction, which persisted in essentials until the end of the year, marked no improvement. It had the defects but not the virtues of its predecessor.

Churchill's exclusion from the Admiralty was demanded not only by the Conservative leaders, indignant at Antwerp and the Dardanelles, but also by Liberal members of the House, who unjustly suspected him of having intrigued to bring the shell scandal into the public gaze. He was shunted, energetically protesting, into the largely honorific position of Chancellor of the Duchy of Lancaster.[1]

Admiral Fisher's departure was finally accepted by Asquith in a one-sentence letter just twenty-one words long. 'I am commanded by the King to accept your tendered resignation of the Office of First Sea Lord of the Admiralty.' Whatever

[1] Letters to Asquith from Churchill, Mrs. Churchill, and Pringle (20 May 1915), Asquith Papers; Lord Beaverbrook, *Politicians and the War 1914–1916* (N.Y., 1928), 124–35; Winston S. Churchill, *The World Crisis, 1911–1918* (4 vols., Odhams Press edn.), ii. 773–5.

chances Fisher may have had of staying in power after Churchill's dismissal—and they seem to have been substantial—
were destroyed by his own action. In an ultimatum to the
Prime Minister dated 19 May he demanded the ejection of
Churchill from the Cabinet, a veto on Balfour as First Lord,
an entirely new Board of Admiralty chosen by Fisher himself,
the dismissal of Sir Arthur Wilson, and 'complete professional charge of the war at sea, together with the absolute sole
disposition of the Fleet and the appointment of all officers of
all ranks whatsoever, and absolutely untrammeled sole command of all the sea forces whatsoever. These six conditions
must be published verbatim.' The Sea Lords, scandalized by
Fisher's absence from his post, had deputized the Director of
Naval Intelligence to press on the Government their view that
Fisher's resignation must be accepted. Asquith commented
to the King that Fisher's bid 'indicated signs of mental
aberration'. 'Fisher went mad', Churchill—unaware of this
particular document—wrote in a note to Kitchener. He had
certainly become a man possessed.[1]

The new leaders of the Navy—Balfour as First Lord and
Admiral Sir Henry Jackson as First Sea Lord—brought a long-
absent atmosphere of placidity and quiet into the Admiralty.
Perhaps that was one of the reasons for their appointments.
Visitors noted the drop in pressure.[2] 'In Winston's time one
felt the whole machine pulsating. To-day, a marked calm
pervaded the First Lord's room.' Balfour, in contrast to his
predecessor, was careful not to override or even to influence
his professional advisers, whatever his penetrating intellect
might indicate as the best direction for naval policy. Sir Henry
Jackson's career had been made as a scientific officer. In this
field he had accomplished much; he was particularly noted for
having adapted wireless telegraphy to the needs of the Navy.
But 'technical' officers lacked prestige; and Admiral Jackson's
personality struck his colleagues as colourless, his character as
wanting in force. 'J. is, well, rather like a white rabbit that has

---

[1] *Fear God and Dread Nought: The Correspondence of Admiral of the Fleet Lord Fisher
of Kilverstone* (1952–9), iii. 213 n. 2, 241–3, 247; Harold Nicolson, *King George the
Fifth: His Life and Reign* (1952), 263; Philip Magnus, *Kitchener: Portrait of an
Imperialist* (1958), 340; Lord Hankey, *The Supreme Command, 1914–1918* (1961),
i. 315–16.
[2] *Lord Riddell's War Diary, 1914–1918* (1933), 103.

come suddenly into the glare of the footlights from the depth of a conjurer's hat.'[1] The real effect of this absence of drive at the centre was to give greater control of naval policy to the commander of the Grand Fleet, Sir John Jellicoe. So it remained throughout the life of the First Coalition.

No such clean sweep could be made at the War Office. Lloyd George, by threatening further exposure of the delays and obstructions in munitions supply, was able to procure the formation of a Ministry of Munitions with himself at the head, thereby depriving the War Office of one of its most important functions. Lloyd George, Asquith, and Bonar Law were at this time angry at Kitchener over the 'shells' crisis. The latter for his part would have been glad to dismiss Sir John French and assume command of the British Armies in France. The leaders of both political parties, however, came to the reluctant decision that Kitchener's hold on the public—foreign as well as British—was too great to permit his supersession. Their estimate of his prestige was certainly correct.[2]

Both Kitchener's friends and enemies—and Kitchener himself—toyed with the notion of his becoming Commander-in-Chief of all British forces at Home and Overseas, a post which might mean everything or nothing. In France Briand was at the end of the year to hit on this same expedient for General Joffre. Kitchener then awaited a bitterer fate. But for the moment his prestige protected him from any further overt change in his functions. Instead a new Coalition Cabinet observed him with suspicion, forced him to dance attendance at their committees, and made decisions in his despite. Nor was Sir John French disturbed in his office.[3] Meanwhile G.H.Q. in

---

[1] *Portrait of an Admiral: The Life and Papers of Sir Herbert Richmond*, (ed.) Arthur J. Marder (1952), 194. See also Beaverbrook, *Politicians and the War*, 135–6; Churchill, *World Crisis*, ii. 768; Blanche E. C. Dugdale, *Arthur James Balfour* (1936), ii. 140, 144–9; Sir Almeric Fitzroy, *Memoirs* (Hutchinson, n.d.), ii. 596; Hankey, *Supreme Command*, i. 316–17, 333–5.

[2] The vendetta of the *Daily Mail*, beginning on the twenty-first with a leader headlined THE SHELLS SCANDAL. LORD KITCHENER'S TRAGIC BLUNDER—written by Northcliffe himself—only succeeded in reducing the circulation of that journal from 1,400,000 to less than 250,000 copies. *War Memoirs of David Lloyd George* (2 vols., Odhams Press, n.d. but c. 1938), i. 121–2; Sir Charles Petrie, *Life and Letters of the Right Hon. Sir Austen Chamberlain* (1939–40), ii. 21–23, 26–27; Fitzroy, *Memoirs*, ii. 594–5; *Riddell War Diary*, 90–92; Reginald Pound and Geoffrey Harmsworth, *Northcliffe* (1959), 476–9.

[3] *Journals and Letters of Reginald Viscount Esher* (1934–8), iii. 233–6, 241, 247–8;

France agitated for the re-creation of an effective General
Staff within the War Office that would give advice palatable
to 'Western' interests. In September Asquith directed Kitchener
to form such an organization to submit reports and advice to
the Cabinet.[1]

The strategic issue which demanded immediate attention
was the position at the Dardanelles, and on this operation
opinions were almost irreconcilable. Hence the name of the
successor to the War Council was the Dardanelles Committee,
and hence the members of that body, made up originally of
ministers only, numbered as many as twelve, and thirteen after the
inclusion of Sir Edward Carson in August—that is to say everybody and his brother. The roster first consisted of Asquith,
Balfour, Churchill, Crewe, Curzon, Lloyd George, Grey,
Kitchener, Lansdowne, Bonar Law, McKenna, and Selborne.[2]

The disagreements on strategic policy were none the less so
many and so tenacious that the major decisions of the Dardanelles Committee had usually to be discussed all over again in
a Cabinet composed of the leaders of three parties.[3] The party
leaders cordially distrusted and in many cases despised each
other. There were steadily widening rifts within the Liberal
leadership. Among the Conservatives, it was only the 'notables'
who had attained office. The First Coalition was not greeted
with any enthusiasm in the House, least of all by the 'ginger
group' that had forced its formation.[4]

Hankey, *Supreme Command*, i. 315; General Sir Ivor Herbert, 19 May 1915. Great
Britain. *5 Parliamentary Debates* (Commons), lxxi, 2393–402; Jere Clemens King,
*Generals and Politicians: Conflict between France's High Command, Parliament and
Government, 1914–1918* (Berkeley, 1951), 85–86; Asquith and Kitchener Papers.

[1] See below, pp. 98–99. Maj.-Gen. Sir E. Callwell, *Field-Marshal Sir Henry
Wilson: His Life and Diaries* (1927), i. 228, 230; Field-Marshal Sir William Robert-
son, *Soldiers and Statesmen 1914–1918* (1926), i. 161–2; Major the Hon Gerald French,
Life of Field-Marshal Sir John French (1931), 305.

[2] The Final Report of the Dardanelles Commission. (Part II—Conduct of
Operations, &c.) Cmd. 371 (1919), p. 24; Hankey, *Supreme Command*, i. 336–7.
Hankey does not list Reginald McKenna.

[3] The Labour Party, which now entered a government for the first time, had
one cabinet post.

[4] Churchill, *World Crisis*, ii. 785–6; J. A. Spender and Cyril Asquith, *Life of
Herbert Henry Asquith, Lord Oxford and Asquith* (1932), ii. 180–6; Robert Blake, *The
Unknown Prime Minister: The Life and Times of Andrew Bonar Law, 1858–1923* (1955),
256–7, 261–4; Sir Charles Petrie, *Walter Long and His Times* (1936), 191–2; Ian
Colvin, *The Life of Lord Carson*, iii (1936), 52; John Bowle, *Viscount Samuel: A
Biography* (1957), 125; S. Salvidge, *Salvidge of Liverpool* (1934), 162; Beaverbrook

The continued existence, to say nothing of the smooth working of the new government, was rendered even more difficult by the emergence into practical politics—for the first time in British history—of the issue of what was euphemistically called National Service. Among themselves, the party leaders were more specific. 'I am *certain*', wrote the 'die-hard' Walter Long to Bonar Law, 'we must have compulsion for Army and Labour.'[1] The campaign for both conscription and the forced direction of labour was opened by a letter from Lord Milner to *The Times* on 27 May, supported by a leading article. *The Times* editor in a private letter a few days later commented[2] '. . . we have got a good movement going in the direction of National Service, the introduction of which is really the main justification of this change of Government'.

The demand for compulsory service, be it 'national' or merely 'military', thus further tormented the Cabinet, and not along clearly marked party lines. During the summer Churchill and Lloyd George joined the ranks of the 'compulsionists'. The bulk of the Radicals, the 'economists', and the Labour Party, however, would not hear of it, and Kitchener, greatly to the compulsionists' annoyance, refused to declare conscription either necessary or desirable. His presence in the War Office thereby acted as a shield for the Radicals and an added obstacle to the compulsionists, among whom the high command in France was numbered.[3]

Churchill has rightly called the new administration 'A Defective War Instrument'. Divided in itself, it was at the mercy of field commanders, other governments, most of all of the enemy. As will be clear, it was German successes that really dictated British strategy during the remainder of 1915. The First Coalition, like the Liberal government, continued to make decisions primarily in the light of its own apprehensions and the insufficient and poorly evaluated intelligence at its disposal. Protests and revolts from within the Cabinet itself

---

Politicians and the War, 140, 154–5; A. J. P. Taylor, *Politics in the First World War*, The Raleigh Lecture on History, British Academy, 1959, pp. 74–75; W. A. S. Hewins, *Apologia of an Imperialist* (1929), ii. 34–36.   [1] Petrie, *Walter Long*, 192–3.

[2] *The History of The Times*, iv (1952), 1, pp. 275–6; *The Times*, 27 May 1915.

[3] Churchill, *World Crisis*, iii. 1098–1100; Beaverbrook, *Politicians and the War*, 223–5; Hankey, *Supreme Command*, i. 425–7 n.; A. M. Gollin, *Proconsul in Politics* (1964), 275–87.

at the lack of order were not lacking, but effective only when the opportunities for well directed action had passed. Yet the need for clear decisions at the centre had rarely been more pressing.[1]

The Dardanelles Committee first met on 7 June, three weeks after General Hamilton had wired his estimate that with two extra army corps [i.e. four divisions] he could 'finish the task'. At the end of May, in a memorandum (largely written by Hankey) for the Committee, Kitchener had recommended that the M.E.F. be allowed to persevere, but without any substantial reinforcements. He doubted, viewing Sir John French's troubles as a comparison, that 'a rapid conclusion' was in fact possible. A further telegram went out from the War Office to Hamilton asking him if he were convinced that with the required reinforcements he could in fact force the Kilid Bahr position and thus finish the Dardanelles operations. Hamilton's answering messages indicated that without reinforcements his command would be reduced to a 'state of close siege' but that with them he believed he could 'eventually . . . take the Kilid Bahr and . . . assuredly expedite the decision'. The choice between 'getting on' and 'getting out' seemed inescapable. But in June the only purpose Kitchener and the new government appeared to discern in the Gallipoli expedition was the need to 'get on' in order to be able later 'to get out' in safety and honour.[2]

Thereupon Kitchener informed the Dardanelles Committee that he would resign if the operations at Gallipoli were not continued. The Committee agreed to dispatch to Hamilton the four divisions which he had requested (one of them had already been sent) and in addition a number of monitors, submarines, and two light cruisers.[3]

Cabinet approval of this decision was not reached without difficulty, and the Cabinet and Dardanelles Committee continued to be divided over the entire Gallipoli venture. Opponents of the expedition, however, were temporarily won

[1] Churchill, *World Crisis*, ii. 785; Hankey, *Supreme Command*, i. 334.

[2] Final Rpt. Dardanelles Com. 24–26; General Sir Ian Hamilton, *Gallipoli Diary* (1920), i. 264, 266, 276; Churchill, *World Crisis*, ii. 786–93; Hankey, *Supreme Command*, i. 335–6, 339–40.

[3] Final Rpt. Dardanelles Com. 24–26; Churchill, *World Crisis*, ii. 793–4; Hankey, *Supreme Command*, i. 340.

over by arguments based on fear of loss of face, continuing hopes of neutral intervention, and the no less delusive expectations of limited operations.[1]

Of these three the prestige factor was probably the most important, and particularly attractive to the 'elder statesmen' such as Curzon and Selborne.[2] The shock of evacuation, it was argued, would be a great blow to British power throughout the East, particularly in the eyes of the Empire's Moslem subjects, and might lead to widespread insurrection and revolt.[3]

Then, too, the shimmering vistas of Balkan intervention still persisted. Rumania, despite its promises, had remained neutral; but Italy declared war against Austria-Hungary on 23 May, and Sir Edward Grey promptly took advantage of this unaccustomed piece of good fortune to try to win over Bulgaria with promises of Serb and Greek territory. This overture had met with no positive response, but the mirage still held ministers' gaze. A key Conservative minister indicated that he would not persist at all with the Dardanelles operation if he did not think there was considerable hope that Bulgaria might be brought in. He felt that Bulgaria was essential to success.[4]

Finally, doubters were encouraged to hope that the attack might now take the form of an occupation of the Bulair isthmus rather than a renewed offensive upon the Turkish troops on the Peninsula itself—a 'starving' rather than a 'storming' operation. This new tactic had been suggested to the Prime Minister by one of the expedition's two official war correspondents, Ellis Ashmead-Bartlett. Admiral de Robeck however had refused to agree, nor on this point did Hamilton press him. For enemy submarines, as Fisher had feared, had now made their appearance off Gallipoli. In May two British warships were torpedoed. The Mediterranean Fleet had now left the Peninsula entirely and until the new offensive took place would

---

[1] Churchill, *World Crisis*, ii. 794–5; Final Rpt. Dardanelles Com. 26; Hankey, *Supreme Command*, i. 340–1.

[2] Lord Selborne's support was crucial at this stage.

[3] Hankey, *Supreme Command*, i. 339–41; Beaverbrook, *Politicians and the War*, 168.

[4] Telegram, Grey to Rodd, 26 May 1915. Viscount Grey of Fallodon, *Twenty-Five Years* (N.Y., 1925), ii. 205–6; Russia. *Mejdounarodnia Otnochenia v epokhou imperialisma*, third series, 1914–17 (Moscow, 1930 ff.) [hereinafter cited as *Rus. Dip. Docs.*], viii (1), no. 2; C. Jay Smith, *The Russian Struggle for Power: A Study of Russian Foreign Policy during the First World War* (N.Y., 1956), 309–11; Hankey, *Supreme Command*, i. 343–4; Asquith Papers.

remain in shelter at Lemnos. A landing as far north as Bulair, the Admiral contended, would be an unacceptable naval risk.[1]

Kitchener's decision to award the command of these modest reinforcements for Gallipoli in blind adherence to traditional Army organization and rules of seniority destroyed the expedition's chance of success. The divisions being sent out were to be formed into an army corps. Kitchener refused Hamilton's request to be given the services of two experienced Western Front commanders—Generals Byng and Rawlinson—though the latter, for one, would have been delighted at the chance. One of the commanders of the divisions to be sent out held the exceptionally high rank of lieutenant-general. Kitchener declined to deprive that officer of his position and insisted that the new army corps must also be commanded by a lieutenant-general. Only two were deemed available. One of them was too stout for physical efforts, so Hamilton reluctantly accepted the elderly and ailing Sir Frederick Stopford. Stopford, an agreeable incompetent, had never commanded troops in war; before 1914 he had been Lieutenant of the Tower of London, a post for which he was better suited and to which he was afterwards to return. Never had Hamilton's gentlemanly qualities played him or his troops so false.[2]

The decision to continue the operations in Gallipoli made even more pressing the need to determine some definite policy in the West. The eruption of the 'shells crisis' confirmed belief that the British for want of ammunition could not as yet pursue major attacks on more than one front. As for current operations, the Franco-British offensive at Ypres and in Artois had ground on till mid-June to no effect. Since April, Churchill pointed out, on the Western Front the British and French together had lost some 320,000 men. German losses he estimated at less than a third of that number. 'The results are that the French

---

[1] Report to the King on the Cabinets of 18 and 19 June 1915. Asquith Papers; E. Ashmead-Bartlett, *The Uncensored Dardanelles* (1928), 118–32; Churchill, *World Crisis*, ii. 796–800; Hamilton, *Gallipoli Diary*, i. 289–93; Hankey, *Supreme Command*, i. 341; *Mil. Opns. Gallipoli*, ii. 68; Alan Moorehead, *Gallipoli* (Arrow edn., 1959), 175–83; *Naval Opns.* iii (2nd edn.), 69; Spender, *Asquith*, ii. 180.

[2] Final Rpt. Dardanelles Com. 29; Hamilton, *Gallipoli Diary*, i. 285, 302–3, 306–7; *Mil. Opns. Gallipoli*, ii. 74; 'Stopford, Sir Frederick William', *D.N.B. 1922–1930* (1937); Kitchener Papers.

have gained 1½ miles on a front of about 5, and the British have gained, in face of La Bassée, less than half the ground they have lost around Ypres. Out of approximately 19,500 square miles of France and Belgium in German hands we have recovered about 8.'[1]

The Cabinet decided in mid-June that the whole question of future strategy in France and Flanders should undergo fundamental review. At the same time the British military representatives at a conference on munitions at Boulogne under the chairmanship of Lloyd George concluded that sufficient munitions for a successful offensive in the West could not be furnished until the spring of 1916. Consequently it was recommended that an 'active defensive' be maintained in that theatre. Haig in a letter to Asquith expressed similar views.[2]

The Cabinet, divided on Gallipoli, continued the easy course of sending troops to the Western Front in the pathetic hope that they would not be employed in battle. On 3 July there was a cabinet meeting with Sir John French and Sir Henry Wilson in attendance. The Cabinet affirmed that 'the western theatre was the principal one for our efforts', but came to the conclusion, drawn up in a memorandum by Asquith himself, that[3]

For the moment we believe that the best service we can render may probably be to be ready to take over additional lengths of the French line, which will set free so many French troops either for offensive or defensive purposes.

In view of the still imperfect equipment of our New Army in the matter of artillery ammunition, and of the uncertainties of the strategic situation, *it should be strongly represented to the French that they should defer any offensive operations.* If they nevertheless think it necessary to undertake such an operation, Sir John French will lend such co-operation with his *existing* forces *as, in his judgment, will be useful for the purpose, and not unduly costly to his army* [present author's italics].

[1] A Further Note Upon the General Military Situation, 18 June 1915. Churchill, *World Crisis*, 807–8. The quotation is on p. 803; Hankey, *Supreme Command*, i. 342; *Mil. Opns. Fr. and Bel. 1915*, ii. 77.

[2] Report to the King on the Cabinets on 16 and 22 June 1915. Letter, Haig to Asquith, 25 June 1915, Asquith Papers; Hankey, *Supreme Command*, i. 346–7; *Mil. Opns. Fr. and Bel. 1915*, ii. 117.

[3] Spender, *Asquith*, ii. 182. See also Callwell, *Henry Wilson*, i. 236–7, and Hankey, *Supreme Command*, i. 343.

In an attempt to convert the French to this view the British Government requested a conference.[1] Asquith at first excluded Kitchener from the participants, but this was apparently found impossible. Anyway, Kitchener was as dubious about the prospects on the Western Front as anyone.[2]

The first conference of the war between the French and British Governments[3] took place at Calais on 6 July. Joffre and Sir John French attended. No minutes were taken, but Sir John French's diary—all the more accurate for its artlessness—records the confusion and deliberate misunderstandings.[4]

K. . . . spoke at some length and laid down the view of the Government as to the future conduct of the War. The necessity for *prudence* and economy of men and ammunition. He deprecated a too vigorous offensive.

Balfour then spoke in much the same sense.

Joffre replied at considerable length advocating the strongest possible offensive and giving all his reasons.

Everyone then spoke and the whole subject was discussed at length. The upshot of it all was that Joffre's views were accepted by both Governments with the proviso that we must exercise *prudence* and caution.

A private meeting between Kitchener and Joffre, arranged by Wilson, took place just before the conference itself. What they said no one knows, but the French President, Poincaré, noted the next day that as a result of the various meetings Kitchener had agreed to send to France that same month six new divisions to be followed each succeeding month by six more. He had for the moment no intention of sending further reinforcements to the Dardanelles. All six divisions of the Second New Army embarked for France that same month—to what purpose was left unclear.[5]

[1] Reports to the King on the Cabinets of 30 June and 3 July 1915, Asquith Papers; *Mil. Opns. Gallipoli*, ii. 63.

[2] Nevertheless Henry Wilson recorded that in a private interview on the 5th Kitchener stated that 'he wants to see Joffre alone and . . . come to an agreement as to what he shall say in front of the politicians whom he (Kitchener) hates and distrusts as much as, I told him, Joffre did' (Callwell, *Henry Wilson*, i. 237–8).

[3] There had been earlier journeys of individual ministers to Paris or London. The proceedings of the Calais conference, curiously enough, were all in French.

[4] French, *Life of French*, 311.

[5] Callwell, *Henry Wilson*, i. 238; Hankey, *Supreme Command*, i. 347–51, and esp. p. 349; *Mil. Opns. Fr. and Bel. 1915*, ii. 86 n. 3; Raymond Poincaré, *Au service de la France*, vi (Paris, 1930), 314–15.

The Central Powers had not been idle while these indecisive half-measures on the Dardanelles and the Western Front were being taken. The Austro-German offensive begun in Galicia in May continued with visible and disquieting success. By the end of June the Russians had retreated one hundred miles and abandoned all of Galicia and Bukovina. Then on 13 July the Germans mounted complementary attacks from northern Poland and the Baltic provinces. These too made striking progress and the Russian Commander-in-Chief, the Grand Duke Nicholas, appealed with some bitterness for Allied action to prevent the arrival of further German reinforcements from the West. Germany meanwhile made overtures to the Russian Government for a separate peace. Throughout the summer and autumn the continued Russian retreat was the dominant feature of the war. The British Government, having itself no settled military policy, could for the remainder of the year only improvise a series of reactions to the consequences of Russian defeat.[1]

The first of these repercussions of the Russian situation, too late to be of practical effect, was on the Dardanelles. For the first time the Government attempted, though in vain, to adopt in this theatre a policy devoted wholeheartedly to victory rather than one of continued drift. Victory at the Dardanelles and consequent Balkan intervention would certainly be the best help the Entente could give Russia in her time of trial. Besides, if that Power should collapse, the troops at Gallipoli must needs return to France to meet the dangers of a new gigantic German onslaught on the West. Hence the urgency, it was argued, of a quick decision at the Peninsula.[2]

By early July Churchill had already prevailed upon Kitchener and the Dardanelles Committee to sanction the dispatch of the two first-line Territorial divisions still left in England. Hamilton, now provided with a total of five divisions as reinforcements, injudiciously stated 'success would be generally assured'. But no attempt was made to fill up the cadres of the divisions employed in the first military attack, and munitions continued to

[1] *Rus. Dip. Docs.* viii (1), no. 340; Pierre Renouvin, *La Crise européenne et la première guerre mondiale* (Paris, 3rd edn., 1948), 301–3, 345–6; General Erich von Falkenhayn, *General Headquarters, 1914–1916, and its Critical Decisions* (Hutchinson, n.d.), 153–5.
[2] *Mil. Opns. Gallipoli*, ii. 64; Churchill, *World Crisis*, iii. 810.

be allotted to the M.E.F. with a miserly hand. Hamilton's request for a temporary priority over the Western Front in ammunition supply was refused with some contempt by the War Office.[1]

Under the impact of the Russian defeats the Government belatedly attempted to overcome the effect of its earlier divisions and hostilities to Hamilton's enterprise. Churchill was to go to the Dardanelles to make a personal report for the Cabinet. The opposition within the Cabinet to this proved too strong, and Hankey was sent instead. He was not at first made to feel welcome by Hamilton or his cliquish staff, resentful at the intrusion. In the last days of July Kitchener telegraphed that 'we are most anxious to give you everything you can possibly require and use', and promised preference over France in munitions delivery. Once again, as in May, but only in response to pressure from Churchill, high explosives were dispatched from Marseille. Lord Selborne by private letter informed Hamilton of the existence of the Dardanelles Committee and asked for a frank statement of his needs, only to be snubbed for his pains.[2]

These last-minute efforts did not compensate for the neglect which had been the lot of the Mediterranean Expeditionary Force since its formation. 'Although we have all along had resources available which would have placed the issue of this battle beyond doubt', Churchill commented, 'it can now only be regarded as one of the great hazards of war.'[3]

General Hamilton's second military attack on Gallipoli began on 6 August. By then the opposing forces were again equal in numbers, for the May cabinet crisis had delayed the dispatch of reinforcements for six weeks. Hamilton, unwilling to venture beyond the letter of his prerogatives, had refused to follow his own inclinations and once more urge upon the Admiral a simul-

[1] Churchill, *World Crisis*, iii. 820, 825–6; Final Rpt. Dardanelles Com. 27; Hamilton, *Gallipoli Diary*, i. 307–10, 321–2, 351, 386, ii. 10–13; Hankey, *Supreme Command*, i. 342–4; *Mil. Opns. Gallipoli*, ii. 60–63.

[2] Churchill, *World Crisis*, iii. 826–7; Hamilton, *Gallipoli Diary*, ii. 24, 37–39; Hankey, *Supreme Command*, i. 376–7, 390; *Mil. Opns. Gallipoli*, ii. 65; Letters between Asquith and Churchill, 16/19 July, 12 Aug. 1915, Asquith Papers; Correspondence, 17/18 July 1915; Letter, Hamilton to Kitchener, 26 July 1915. (The reply to Selborne avoided saying anything of the least importance. After all, the latter is not owed any responsibility!), Kitchener Papers.

[3] Memorandum, mid-July 1915, Churchill, *World Crisis*, iii. 821.

taneous naval strike upon the Narrows. He pinned all his hopes on the thrust of his own forces across the waist of the Peninsula. From their lodgement at 'Anzac' the Australian and New Zealand Army Corps would attempt to scale the ranges of the hills before them and debouch on to the Narrows. These troops would be supported by an attack just north of Anzac, at Suvla Bay, where a landing would be effected by the reinforcements from the New Armies and Territorial Force.

The 'dug-outs' who commanded the New Army divisions under General Stopford turned the prospects of victory into defeat. The landing at Suvla, aided by Fisher's monitors, was made with ease. Almost no Turkish troops were in the area, but the commanders at Suvla, obsessed by second-hand reports of the new trench warfare, devoted all their attention to the problem of holding the beaches against a non-existent enemy force. They could not be prevailed upon to advance to the hills above, and by the time Hamilton had dismissed the ineffectual Stopford and several of his equally hopeless fellow sexagenarians the enemy was present in strength. The chance of victory had disappeared. At Suvla no further progress was made. From Anzac the few isolated units which attained the heights of the Sari Bair Range above them could not maintain their position in the absence of support from Suvla. They were driven back. The second military attack had failed to effect any change in the strategic position.[1]

As the first intelligence of Hamilton's reverses came to London Kitchener changed his mind on the command question and ordered the transfer of Byng and two other Western Front generals to the Dardanelles. The Admiralty informed de Robeck that his 'old battleships' could now be used for the support of the 'land operations' in any way he saw fit. This strong hint met with no response. Hamilton once again refused to urge the Admiral on.[2]

But the reaction to Hamilton's admission of defeat in his telegram of 17 August, requesting ninety-five thousand more

---

[1] Final Rpt. Dardanelles Com. 87; Hamilton, *Gallipoli Diary*, ii. 32, 49; Hankey, *Supreme Command*, i. 391 ff.; *Mil. Opns. Gallipoli*, ii. 127–329; Moorehead, *Gallipoli*, 201 ff. and esp. p. 236 ('The Suvla plan, which was a good plan, had failed because the wrong commanders and soldiers had been employed, and at Anzac the best officers and men were employed upon a plan that would not work').

[2] Hamilton, *Gallipoli Diary*, ii. 105; *Mil. Opns. Gallipoli*, ii. 327, 365–6.

troops to give him 'the necessary superiority', boded ill for the expedition and for Hamilton himself. At the meeting of the Dardanelles Committee two days later all the speakers save Churchill blamed the failure on the commander-in-chief. Had he not received all the troops he had asked for? He had been confident, but now blamed two or three generals. Neither Liberal nor Conservative leaders favoured sending him re-inforcements without a critical examination of their probable effectiveness. A Coalition Cabinet would not be responsible for sending out more troops.[1]

In the absence of Lord Kitchener, however, no decision on Hamilton's request was made.

Kitchener was in France, where he had been invited by General Joffre and M. Millerand in order that they might constrain him to order fuller British participation in the next French 'great offensive'. The novel feature of this operation was General Joffre's intention to bite off both extremities of the great German salient—in Champagne and at Artois—simultaneously. Sir John French had earlier welcomed the renewal of the offensive in principle, but his enthusiasm withered when he was made acquainted with the area the French strategic plan had of necessity allotted him. The British were to prolong the attack some six miles northwards from Lens to the La Bassée canal, in a mining area interspersed with villages, mineheads, and slag-heaps. The British command, accustomed since the winter to what had already become their old fighting grounds, viewed this new area with disdain. Haig and French argued that the British could meet with no success. Generals Joffre and Foch insisted, however; Sir John French, while deferring to their judgement, ordered that 'The attack . . . is to be made chiefly with artillery, and a large force of infantry is not to be launched to the attack of objectives which are so strongly held as to be liable to result in the sacrifice of many lives.' The Cabinet's injunctions of 3 July were being strictly obeyed.[2]

[1] Hamilton, *Gallipoli Diary*, ii. 110–18, 126; Report to the King on the Cabinet of 18 Aug. 1915. Meeting . . . Dardanelles Committee . . . 19 Aug. 1915, Asquith Papers. A year later 'Crewe said, and the P.M. agreed, that the failure of the Dardanelles expedition was entirely the failure of one man—Ian Hamilton', *Old Men Forget: The Autobiography of Duff Cooper* (1953), 56.

[2] *Mil. Opns. Fr. and Bel. 1915*, ii. 125. See also ibid. 111–30, 144–8; France. *Les Armées françaises dans la Grande Guerre*, iii, nos. 736, 860, 889, 1026, 1040, 1102, 1143,

Thereupon the apprehensive Joffre and Millerand invited Kitchener's presence. By then Russia appeared as if it might be heading for collapse. Warsaw fell on 4 August, and thereafter 'the Russians multiplied their speed in retreat'.[1] A War Office paper warned (erroneously) that the enemy was aiming, not at the line of the Vistula river, but at the destruction of the Russian Army.[2]

From Russia reports of revolutionary unrest and rumours of a separate peace multiplied. That the Russians were resentful of the quiet on the Western Front was indisputable. The French military authorities drew the conclusion that an offensive was necessary to make the Russians feel better, and hinted to Kitchener not obscurely at the possibilities of France herself concluding peace. Sir Henry Wilson stressed that if Joffre and Millerand were not allowed to launch their offensive their consequent fall and replacement by a new team would mean an opportunity for French politicians 'wanting in reality to make peace'.[3]

Kitchener, sick at heart over the failure at Suvla, gave in to these interested—even absurd—solicitations and informed the British command that it must, to cite Haig's report of his verbal instructions, *act with all our energy, and do our utmost to help the French, even though, by so doing, we suffered very heavy losses indeed*.[4]

On his return to England Kitchener on 20 August informed the Dardanelles Committee and the Cabinet of his decision to have the British participate in Joffre's autumn offensive for the

1156, 1174 (Conferences at Chantilly on 24 June and 7 July 1915 and at Saint-Omer on 11 July, Correspondence between Joffre and French, 27 July–14 Aug.); French, *Life of French*, 313, 315; General Sir Hubert Gough, *The Fifth Army* (1931), 95–96.

[1] C. R. M. F. Cruttwell, *A History of the Great War, 1914–1918* (2nd edn., Oxford, 1936), 180.

[2] The War Office, 5 Aug. 1915, Asquith Papers.

[3] Callwell, *Henry Wilson*, i. 245–6. See also Grey, *Twenty-Five Years*, ii. 216–18; Maj.-Gen. Sir John Hanbury-Williams, *The Emperor Nicholas II as I Knew Him* (1922), 48–49; *Mil. Opns. Fr. and Bel. 1915*, ii. 127; Précis of Conversation with Officers of the Cabinet de la Guerre, Paris, 3 July 1915, Kitchener Papers (Germany may offer France Alsace-Lorraine, retaining Belgium, at close of Galician campaign. Some Frenchmen would be ready to accept, and the situation might become very delicate).

[4] *The Private Papers of Douglas Haig, 1914–1919*: Being selections from the private diary and correspondence of Field-Marshal the Earl Haig of Bemersyde, Robert Blake (ed.) (1952), 102.

sake of ensuring that France and Russia remained in the war. He offered no hopes of military success, but his decision was after much discussion none the less accepted. This was the second major effect of the Russian retreats on British military policy. There is no record of any comments by Sir Edward Grey on the absurdity (so far as France was concerned) of connecting cancellation of the campaign with a separate peace. The Government was not informed of the nature or location of the impending offensive. Hamilton was informed that he must make do without reinforcements. His reply left no doubt that henceforth the British in the Peninsula could only stand on the defensive.[1]

The British Government had hardly made the grave decision to participate in a militarily unproductive offensive on the Western Front out of fear of mortally offending their allies than the French proposed to share the burden at the Dardanelles and suggested that one of their own generals be placed in command! On 3 September Kitchener informed the amazed Dardanelles Committee that the French had requested transport facilities for four French divisions for an attack on Asia Minor. The British Government agreed with 'gratification' and expressed their hope but not their will that Joffre's 'grand offensive' might now be abandoned.[2]

In vain. The French offer was due less to an appreciation of the strategic possibilities in the Aegean, though this awareness existed, than to the desire to find a berth for the controversial General Sarrail. In an army led primarily by Catholics and suspected royalists, a general officer who was an anticlerical, a member of the Masons, and friendly with parliamentarians had gained popularity among the governors of the Third Republic. 'Whatever dispute there might be about his military achievements, his irreligious convictions were above suspicion.'[3] General Joffre had relieved him from his command in July.

---

[1] Churchill, *World Crisis*, iii. 854-6; Hamilton, *Gallipoli Diary*, ii. 135; Poincaré, *Service*, vii (1931), 48-49; Report to the King on the Cabinet of 20 Aug. 1915. Minutes. Dardanelles Committee, 20 Aug. 1915 (Lord Kitchener: On the Western Front there was no more than a reasonable chance of success. British inaction there, however, implied some chance of the Russians and the French concluding separate peace agreements in October).

[2] Spender, *Asquith*, ii. 183.

[3] Churchill, *World Crisis*, iii. 858.

PLATE 5

a. Field-Marshal Sir John French, Commander-in-Chief, British Expeditionary Force, August 1914–December 1915

b. Commodore Keyes, Vice-Admiral de Robeck, General Sir Ian Hamilton, and Major-General Braithwaite aboard the *Triad* (taken the afternoon of Hamilton's departure for England)

But Joffre himself had gained no laurels in 1915. Left-wing politicians proceeded to agitate for Sarrail's being given a new and independent command, while M. Millerand was desirous that any such command be far removed from Paris. Hence the offer of the four French divisions for a campaign on the Asiatic side of the Straits. But the Joffre–Millerand team was still strong enough to resist the transfer of any troops from France to General Sarrail's new command until after the autumn offensive, which would proceed as scheduled. Lord Kitchener was so informed on his trip to Calais on 11 September. No troops would move from France till mid-October. As for General Sarrail, he refused to move from Paris. Once again it was evident to all those who had eyes to see that the British would have to win their own battles at Gallipoli. But for this victory a definite military policy was needed in London, and that did not exist.[1]

While this lamentable comedy was being played the German successes in the East coaxed Bulgaria into the war on the side of the Central Powers, crushed Serbia, and in Britain posed harsh choices on a government incapable of taking controversial decisions. The effort to do so destroyed Cabinet control of military operations for the next two and a half years. On 21 September the Bulgarian Army began general mobilization.

During the summer of 1915 the effort to procure Bulgar intervention on the side of the Entente had been the principal concern of Allied, and particularly British, policy in the Balkans. The British minister at Sofia, who did not believe this volte-face was possible, was replaced by an official who could carry out British policy more whole-heartedly. It is conceivable that a Bulgarian alliance might have been secured through success at the Dardanelles, but the united will in London to assure this had never existed. Instead reliance was placed on pressure upon the Serbs and Greeks to return their conquests in the Balkan Wars to the dissatisfied Bulgaria. Meanwhile the stalemate at the Dardanelles and the Russian retreats continued. The fall of the fortress and railway junction of Kovno on 18

---

[1] Arthur, *Kitchener*, iii. 174–5; Callwell, *Henry Wilson*, i. 247–51; Colvin, *Carson*, iii. 84–85; Final Rpt. Dardanelles Com. 52–53; Hankey, *Supreme Command*, i. 410–12; King, *Generals and Politicians*, 67–88.

August had particularly wide repercussions in both Petrograd
and Sofia. In the former capital the British ambassador reported that the 'News . . . has created something almost like
consternation amongst the pessimists . . ., who seem convinced
that the Brest–Litovsk line will have to be abandoned, and
that road to Petrograd will be opened'; while the envoy at
Sofia noted that the news had 'made a deep impression in the
governing and military circles, giving rise to anticipations of a
coming disaster to Russian arms'. A Bulgarian attack on Serbia,
he warned Sir Edward Grey, was probable in the near future.[1]

The British reaction was to increase the pressure on Serbia
for concessions, and by the beginning of September that country
agreed 'in principle' to give up Macedonia. 'The more desperate
the situation,' Grey later recalled, 'the more frantic grew the
promises.' These were powerless now to affect the Bulgarian
decision.[2]

The reaction of the Cabinet, tenacious of its illusions, at the
news of the Bulgarian mobilization was one of indignation.
The Serbs were blamed for not having agreed to give up more
territory sooner. Serbia's 'obstinacy and cupidity', Asquith
reported to the King, 'have now brought her to the verge of
disaster'.[3] But Kitchener, again absent in France, also incurred
the condemnation of a Cabinet become most resentful of his
secrecy. Why had they not been told sooner? Asquith now
decided upon the reconstitution of the General Staff. The
phantom who held the office of C.I.G.S. was to be replaced by
his deputy, Lieutenant-General Sir Archibald Murray. Murray
after a series of pre-war high staff appointments had been Chief
of the Staff of the British Expeditionary Force until the French,
irritated at his obstructionism, had succeeded in having him
sent home at the beginning of 1915. Since then his principal
assignment as D.C.I.G.S. had been to watch over the training
of the New Armies. His personality was chill and reserved, his
outlook narrow and conventional, and as a theatre commander
he was later to show no distinction. But he had made a reputation for tactical skill during the Boer War, and may well have

    [1] Grey, *Twenty-Five Years*, ii. 211–12, 217–18. See also Lieut.-Col. H. D. Napier,
The Experiences of a Military Attaché in the Balkans (Crane, n.d.), 167.
    [2] Grey, *Twenty-Five Years*, ii. 204. See also Hankey, *Supreme Command*, i. 413–17, and
Rus. Dip. Docs. viii (1) no. 618.
    [3] Spender, *Asquith*, ii. 184–5. See also Hankey, *Supreme Command*, i. 417.

been a competent administrator. In any event a change was necessary, and Murray was in the right place. Sir John French would not accept him back at G.H.Q. On 23 September Asquith by formal letter directed Kitchener to institute new procedures:[1]

At yesterday's Cabinet—from which you were unfortunately absent—the question was raised and much discussed of the importance of having a General Staff here, to guide and advise the Cabinet and its Committees, in matters of strategy and of naval and military policy.

It was felt, and expressed, that . . . it has become essential that both you yourself, and the Government, should have the best intelligence that the Army can supply for our common purpose. . . . In these circumstances I suggest to you

1) that Sir A. Murray should be at once made Chief of the Imperial General Staff,

2) that he should have associated with him for the daily conduct of the Staff here three or four of the best staff officers who have seen service at the front,

3) that there should be drawn up, for circulation to the Cabinet, once in every week a considered appreciation by the General Staff here of the military situation, actual and prospective,

4) that there should be a systematic inter-change for Staff purposes of officers at the front and officers at home.

After over a year of hostilities the British Government had made arrangements to be regularly informed on the progress of the war.

Sir Archibald was duly appointed C.I.G.S. on the twenty-sixth; his first chore was to advise on the Balkans.[2] The prospect was perplexing. The 'great offensive' in France was due to begin, so for the moment no troops could be withdrawn from the West. Any immediate aid to the Serbs would be at the expense of the troops at Gallipoli. If only an enemy offensive in the Balkans could yet be averted! Hoping against hope, the Government pursued its 'Munich' policy of appeasing the Bulgars. 'There was nothing except dignity to be lost by trying

---

[1] Letter, French to Kitchener, 14 Sept. 1915; Asquith to Kitchener, 23 Sept. 1915, Kitchener Papers. There is a summary with excerpts in Magnus, *Kitchener*, 350–1.

[2] Hankey, *Supreme Command*, i. 428. There is an article on Murray in the *D.N.B. 1941–1950*.

at Sophia, and we all tried', Grey later commented.[1] But
honour too was compromised. Kitchener and Grey warned the
unfortunate Serbian leaders not to attack Bulgaria first while
time yet remained. The British Government refused to associate
itself with a Russian ultimatum to Bulgaria to cease mobilization. In Parliament Grey and Crewe expressed British friendship for Bulgaria, while warning that if it should join the Central
Powers 'we are prepared to give our friends in the Balkans
all the support in our power, in the manner that would be
most welcome to them, in concert with our Allies, without
reserve and without qualification'.[2] It will be seen how this
pledge was fulfilled.

To this policy of appeasement the French enforced one
exception. M. Venizelos had after new elections again become
premier of Greece. According to a treaty concluded in 1913
Greece was obligated to come to Serbia's assistance in the event
of Bulgarian attack. The treaty in truth was meant to apply
only to a purely Balkan struggle, but M. Venizelos was willing
to ignore this limitation in his desire to join the Entente. His
opponents in Greece, however, were able to point out that the
Serbs were not fulfilling the stipulated condition for Greek
entry—the concentration of one hundred and fifty thousand
troops opposite the Bulgarian frontier—for Serbia was now
forced to dispose her men so as to meet not only a Bulgar but
also an Austro-German offensive. Venizelos therefore requested
the Entente to furnish the one hundred and fifty thousand men
themselves. Grey deprecated the suggestion, but the French
insisted, and ordered one of their divisions currently assigned
to Sir Ian Hamilton withdrawn forthwith to Salonika. Now at
last General Sarrail could find really useful employment! 'It
was impossible', Asquith reported, 'for us in the circumstances
to hold back',[3] and the British thereupon agreed to furnish part
of the contingent. If Bulgaria were to be deterred some troops

[1] Grey, *Twenty-Five Years*, ii. 204.

[2] Grey, House of Commons, 28 Sept. 1915; Crewe, Lords, 29 Sept. 5 *Parliamentary Debates* (Commons), lxxiv. 731–2, (Lords) xix. 935–40. See also *AF*,
viii (1) no. 87; Maj.-Gen. C. E. Callwell, *Experiences of a Dug-Out, 1914–1918* (1920),
75–77; Hankey, *Supreme Command*, i. 418–21; Capt. Cyril Falls, *Military Operations
Macedonia* (1933–5), i. 31–32; *Rus. Dip. Docs.* viii (2) nos. 801, 819, 821, 843; G. M.
Trevelyan, *Grey of Fallodon* (Longman Library edn., 1940), 287.

[3] Spender, *Asquith*, ii. 184–5. See also Trumbull Higgins, *Winston Churchill and
the Dardanelles* (N.Y., 1964), 220.

would have to land at Salonika immediately. The Gallipoli
Peninsula was the obvious source. At the end of September the
British Tenth Division, Lieutenant-General Bryan T. Mahon
commanding, was ordered from Suvla to Salonika. This was the
third effect of the Russian defeat on British strategy. In spite of
Kitchener's express assertion to the contrary, the withdrawal
from Gallipoli had begun. For the present, Hamilton was informed, no more ammunition could be sent him; it was all
needed in France.[1]

In the first week of October the Balkan theatre became the
centre of events. The Tenth and one French division—together
constituting but thirteen thousand weak, tired, and dispirited
troops—landed at Salonika; an invading Austro-German army
from the north, supported a few days later by a Bulgarian army
from the east, crossed the Serbian frontier; and M. Venizelos
his rash interventionist policy yet again repudiated by King
Constantine, yet again resigned office. At the news of Venizelos'
fall Kitchener hastily countermanded the movement orders for
the Tenth Division, but the Dardanelles Committee overruled
this decision.[2]

The implications of the attack on Serbia for British strategy
were considered at a meeting on 11 October of the War Committee (so renamed from Dardanelles Committee on 7 October),
and for advice it now had a paper from Sir Archibald Murray
and the presence of Sir William Robertson, Chief of the General
Staff of the British Armies in France. On Salonika and the
Western Front these two authorities were agreed. No British
troops should be sent to Greece or Serbia. On the Western
Front it might be thought that there would be some difference of
opinion. The offensive begun on 25 September had—even with
the help of gas—met with no success; General Joffre had not
only ordered the cessation of French attacks but also indicated
his intention of staying on the defensive for some months.
Nevertheless Robertson advocated, and Murray agreed, that
G.H.Q. in France should be allowed to continue its operations
with a view to 'consolidation'. The Murray paper, however,
argued that if Joffre could not be prevailed upon to continue

---

[1] Hamilton, *Gallipoli Diary*, ii. 209-11, 213, 227; *AF*, viii, no. 367; Russia. *Constantinople et les détroits* (Paris, 1930-2), ii, no. 157; *Rus. Dip. Docs.* viii (2) no.
781; Hankey, *Supreme Command*, i. 417-20.   [2] *Mil. Opns. Macedonia*, i. 42-43.

the offensive and thus win the war the only way it could be won—
the destruction of the German armies—sufficient troops (calculated at eight divisions) should be sent to Gallipoli to 'complete
the capture of the peninsula'. In an appendix the First Sea
Lord indicated that once this was done a naval attack would be

Map 4: The Balkan and Italian Fronts.

pressed regardless of losses. Robertson counselled evacuation
pure and simple.

The War Committee was now so distracted and divided that
its conclusions expressed only its own impotence and desire to
satisfy all parties:[1]

[1] Lloyd George, *War Memoirs*, i. 297. See also ibid. 295–7; Arthur, *Kitchener*,
iii. 183; Churchill, *World Crisis*, iii. 866–7; Hankey, *Supreme Command*, i. 428–30;
Mil. Opns. Gallipoli, ii. 381–2; Victor Bonham-Carter, *Soldier True* (1963), 130.

Instructions to be given for the dispatch, *so soon as the present operations are over*, of an adequate substantial force from France to Egypt without prejudice to its ultimate destination. . . .

A specially selected general to proceed without delay to the Near East and to consider and report as to which particular sphere, and with what particular objective, we should direct our attention.

The abdication of the Government was complete.

The Bulgarian entry and its expected consequence, the crushing of Serbia, meant that transport between Germany and Turkey would be unrestricted. The Turks would have free access to German ammunition and artillery; thereafter, it was somewhat hastily concluded, the position of the British on the Gallipoli Peninsula would be untenable. And winter would soon be coming. The policy of half-measures at Gallipoli, always unfortunate, was now manifestly disastrous. Some attempt at a definite decision there had to be made. Sir John French was ordered to prepare eight divisions for transfer to Egypt. These would serve either to take the Peninsula or, should evacuation be decided upon, to hold Egypt against the external attack or internal revolts that Kitchener and the other guardians of Empire within the Cabinet feared would inevitably follow. As early as 7 October Asquith had insisted that a plan for evacuation be prepared; after the War Committee meeting on the 11th Kitchener wired Hamilton requesting an estimate on what losses would be incurred by evacuation.[1]

The delay recommended by the War Committee in the dispatch of troops from France meant the abandonment of Serbia. Sir Edward Carson immediately resigned from the Cabinet in protest, and Bonar Law and Lloyd George urged that a Salonika expedition be formed at the expense of Gallipoli. At Lloyd George's goading Grey consented to make one last effort, desperate but at any rate not trivial, to induce Rumanian and Greek intervention. Two hundred thousand Entente troops were promised in the Balkans by the end of the year, if need be all British. As an extra lure Greece was offered Cyprus. At last Great Britain was offering her own and not other

[1] Hamilton, *Gallipoli Diary*, ii. 249; *Mil. Opns. Fr. and Bel. 1915*, ii. 406; *Gallipoli*, ii. 378; Callwell, *Henry Wilson*, i. 255; Churchill, *World Crisis*, iii. 870–3; Hankey, *Supreme Command*, i. 429.

powers' territory. But the offer was far too late, and was
immediately rejected by both Greece and Rumania, fearful
of German revenge.[1]

Thereafter the British Government gave up hope for the
Balkan theatre and in effect wrote off Eastern Europe. Grey,
questioned in the House, would now only give the chill assurance
that decisions on Serbia would be governed by 'sound strategy'.[2]

The only question now was how to counter the repercussions
outside Europe of these successes of the Central Powers. Serbia
was being rapidly overrun. Even tactical success at Gallipoli,
increasingly harder to obtain, could not have the same strategic
consequences as before. When Hamilton reported that evacuation would mean loss of half his total force the War Committee
immediately ordered his recall. He had failed in the August
attack; the New Army generals he had sent home were com-
plaining of his leadership; and Ashmead-Bartlett and an
Australian journalist friend, Keith Murdoch, had both just
returned from the Peninsula for the express purpose of cir-
culating highly coloured memoranda—supported by personal
interviews—to members of the Cabinet and men of prominence
urging Sir Ian Hamilton's recall and the withdrawal of the
entire expedition. In the House of Lords Lord Milner publicly
called for evacuation. The opponents of Gallipoli were beginning again to exert public as well as private pressure.[3]

Into this brewing maelstrom walked the 'specially selected
general' deputized to tell the Government what its military
policy in the Balkans, the Dardanelles, and Egypt ought to be.
For this imposing assignment Kitchener had chosen a Western
Front general who was an expert on infantry-fire tactics: General
Sir Charles Carmichael Monro. On his return to London
from command of the Third Army this cool and capable officer
was informed that his main task would be to advise on the
future of the Gallipoli expedition. He was shown the Murdoch

---

[1] Blake, *Bonar Law*, 267–8; Churchill, *World Crisis*, iii. 868–9; Hankey, *Supreme Command*, i. 429–32; Lloyd George, *War Memoirs*, i. 298–306; *Rus. Dip. Docs.* viii (2), no. 909; Smith, *Russian Struggle for Power*, 337–8.

[2] Statement by Sir E. Grey, Events in Balkans, 14 Oct. 1915, 5 *Parliamentary Debates* (Commons), lxxiv, 1502.

[3] Ashmead-Bartlett, *Uncensored Dardanelles*, 240–3; Hamilton, *Gallipoli Diary*, ii. 235, 240, 245–6, 253, 259; Hankey, *Supreme Command*, i. 430; Harmsworth, *Northcliffe*, 486–9; *Mil. Opns. Gallipoli*, ii. 383–6; Moorehead, *Gallipoli*, 305–13; 5 *Parliamentary Debates* (Lords), xix, 1053–6 (14 Oct. 1915); Gollin, *Proconsul*, 303–12.

allegations (these referred primarily to the incompetence and callousness of the Army Command and Staff on the Peninsula); and left London, as probably he had arrived there, disposed to advise evacuation.[1]

While events were thus moving to compel withdrawal from the Western extremity of the Ottoman Empire the Government moved to counter the expected ill effects by an advance from the East. The Mesopotamia Expedition had been almost forgotten in the press of greater events since the bloodless conquest of Basra in December 1914. Its ambitious commander General Sir John Nixon had so far overcome the restraints of the home and Indian governments as by October 1915 to have by an almost imperceptible series of advances reached Kut-el-Amara, some one hundred miles from Baghdad. The capture of this last had not evoked any enthusiasm before in London, but now it was hoped that in the eyes of Persia, the Arabs, and the British Empire's Moslem subjects Baghdad would compensate for the loss of prestige at Gallipoli. Baghdad, one minister explained, was 'the one bright spot on the military horizon'. The General Staff, to which the question was referred, was dubious; Baghdad could probably be captured, but could it be held without further reinforcements? Kitchener was totally opposed, but the Government was no longer disposed to accept his advice. On 23 October the Government of India was informed that 'Nixon may march on Baghdad'. The Indian Corps, the two divisions of which had been included in the force due to be sent from France to Egypt, would be sent as reinforcements to Mesopotamia instead. It would arrive when transportation permitted.[2]

Meanwhile discussions on the Balkans proceeded with the French, who refused to be guided by 'sound strategy'. The French Government and General Joffre insisted that Britain was bound to provide her agreed share (ninety thousand men) of

<hr/>

[1] 'Monro, Sir Charles Carmichael, 1860–1929', *D.N.B. 1922–1930*; General Sir Edmund George Barrow, *Life of General Sir Charles Carmichael Monro* (1931), 62–73; Callwell, *Experiences of a Dug-Out*, 102–3; Hankey, *Supreme Command*, ii. 456; Harmsworth, *Northcliffe*, 486.

[2] Lieut.-Col. R. Evans, *A Brief Outline of the Campaign in Mesopotamia* (1930), 20–45; Mesopotamia Commission, Report of the Commission Appointed by Act of Parliament to Enquire into the Operations of War in Mesopotamia, Cd. 8610 (1917); *Rus. Dip. Docs.* ix, no. 70; Robertson, *Soldiers and Statesmen, 1914–1918*, ii. 42.

the one hundred and fifty thousand troops promised at Salonika, where General Sarrail had now arrived. To the British argument that the commitment had lapsed with the fall of M. Venizelos and that it was too late to save Serbia the French replied that the British promise had been to France as well and that the Serbian Army, if not Serbia itself, could still be saved to fight another day. At the end of October General Joffre travelled to London and informed the British that unless they sent their divisions from France not to Egypt but to Salonika he would resign in protest and that the alliance between France and England would be imperilled. While he was in London the French Government fell due to parliamentary indignation at the invasion of Serbia and was replaced by an administration headed by M. Briand, a leading advocate of the Salonika venture. At the same time General Monro's report arrived from Gallipoli. In one day he had visited all three battlegrounds on the Peninsula (an unprecedented feat), briefly questioned their commanders, and on military grounds promptly advised evacuation. 'He came, he saw, he capitulated.' The British force, he reported, could not withstand a determined Turkish attack employing substantial quantities of ammunition. The estimated casualties on evacuation would be about one-third of the Allied force. But Lord Kitchener would not accept his recommendation; the effect on Egypt, he was convinced, would be disastrous.[1]

As if there were not troubles enough in the Western Mediterranean, both the Western and Home Fronts at the end of October promised an explosion which might again destroy the Government. In the Western Front operations had made no progress. This failure could cause no surprise, but the British chief staff officer—Lieutenant-General Sir William Robertson—and Army commanders, headed by Sir Douglas Haig, were in open revolt against Sir John French's leadership. He had, they claimed, kept control of the reserves in his own hand too

[1] Formula agreed to between the French and British Governments on 19 Oct. (150,000 men to be sent via Egypt, their final destination to be decided later). Crewe. Report to the King on the Cabinet of 18 Oct. 1915 (the agreement was made necessary by the French Government's statements in their parliament). Letter, Kitchener to Asquith, 1 Nov. 1915, Asquith Papers; *AF*, viii, Annexes nos. 88, 108, 185, 206, 305; Churchill, *World Crisis*, iii. 867–8, 878; Hankey, *Supreme Command*, i. 432–4, ii. 456.

long. If Haig had been allowed these sooner, a breakthrough would have been assured. Sir John was accused of falsifying his dispatch on the operations. French's subordinates informed the King of these views on his visit to France, and George V agreed that the Commander-in-Chief must be recalled.[1]

Greater political dangers impended at home. The Coalition Government was breaking down due to internal divisions and the weight of its own numbers. On the conscription issue the 'compulsionists' had forced Asquith to make his last evasion. On 5 October the popular Lord Derby agreed to become Director of Recruiting and administer the scheme associated with his name. All men between eighteen and forty-one were asked to agree to serve when the Government should find it necessary. It was hoped that the expected failure of the scheme would induce Labour and old-line Liberals to agree to conscription. But their hostility showed no signs of diminishing. In mid-October Asquith had to send a personal letter of appeal —couched in most uncharacteristic emotional tones[2]—to Kitchener not to insist that conscription had now become necessary. But to the House of Commons on 2 November he declared himself willing to accept compulsion, though with the hope that it would come with general consent. Asquith's leadership, long attacked from without, might be repudiated by his own fellow Liberal ministers unless some adroit move should make it appear that neither he nor the discredited Kitchener was personally responsible for imposing conscription. Yet the compulsionists were becoming stronger every week.[3]

---

[1] Brig.-Gen. John Charteris, *At G.H.Q.* (1931), 116; *Private Papers of Douglas Haig*, 105–14; Nicolson, *George V*, 267; John Terraine, *Douglas Haig* (1963), 160–7.

[2] 'What is now going on is being engineered by men (Curzon and Lloyd George, and some others) whose real object is to oust you. They know well that I give no countenance to their projects, and consequently they have conceived the idea of using you against me.

'God knows that we should both of us be glad to be set free. But we cannot and ought not. So long as you and I stand together, we carry the whole country with us. Otherwise, the Deluge!'

[3] Letter from Lloyd George, 2 Nov. 1915 ('P.M. made a powerful speech and went far on recruiting. In fact he satisfied us on that score'), William George, *My Brother and I* (1958), 252; Hankey, *Supreme Command*, i. 425–8, 431–2; Randolph Churchill, *Lord Derby, King of Lancashire: the official Life of Edward Earl Derby, 1865–1948* (1959), 191; Letter, Asquith to Kitchener, 17 Oct. 1915, Kitchener Papers. Excerpts in Magnus, *Kitchener*, 352–3; 5 *Parliamentary Debates* (Commons), lxxv, 518.

The existing machinery for war direction was damned even in the eyes of those who operated it. On 21 October a Cabinet which met in Asquith's absence deputized Crewe to inform the Prime Minister that the War Committee was too large and divided to make decisions; a much smaller group was desirable. In the unanimous conviction of the Cabinet a drastic change was imperatively necessary. It was difficult to name the members of such a select and more powerful group without including the Secretary of State for War. But at the end of the month Lloyd George in a long philippic warned Asquith that 'unless there is a complete change in the War Office . . . I can no longer be responsible for the present war direction'. Lloyd George's threatened resignation, or so he claimed, would be accompanied by that of Bonar Law.

What now particularly aroused Lloyd George's ire was Kitchener's failure to have increased the carrying capacity of the single-track railway from Greece into Serbia. The War Council had directed Kitchener to see to this in February last. At the meeting of the War Committee of 11 October it was revealed that nothing had been done; hence, it was argued, the impossibility of giving Serbia effective help. The Asquith Government was now so feeble that the dismissal of Kitchener might well topple the whole edifice. It would require all of Asquith's ingenuity to avoid a crash. But this ingenuity was his in full measure.[1]

The preliminary condition both for reorganization and for the retention of Lloyd George and Bonar Law within the Cabinet was the removal of the Secretary of State for War. General Monro's 'unacceptable' report provided the opportunity. Asquith was able to persuade Kitchener to go out himself to Gallipoli to 'review the situation'. Once again a naval attack was being urged, this time by the Chief of Staff of the Mediterranean Squadron. Commodore Roger Keyes, long a proponent of a naval attempt on the Straits, had been allowed by Admiral de Robeck, now as always opposed to an 'adventurous' policy, to return to London to state his case personally. Keyes found Balfour and Jackson well disposed to a naval strike

---

[1] Crewe. Report to the Cabinet of 21 Oct. 1915, Asquith Papers; Lloyd George, *War Memoirs*, i. 307–9; *Riddell War Diary*, 90–92; Gollin, *Proconsul*, 312–14.

combined with a renewed military offensive. The Board of Admiralty not only ordered the Grand Fleet to release four battleships and four destroyers to the Aegean but also urged Admiral de Robeck to return on leave. He was ordered to choose as his successor an officer who would be willing to lead a naval attack.[1]

Kitchener left for the Peninsula on 4 November. The Cabinet had agreed to his departure in the hope that he could later be persuaded to return not to London but to his former barony in Egypt. Asquith immediately took over the War Office. But Asquith was no longer master of the Government.

Under the Constitution of the United States an American President is always Commander-in-Chief; thus strategy and policy are both under control of the head of state. The same end was attained by Churchill in the Second World War when he assumed the newly created office of Minister of Defence. It was toward a similar arrangement that Asquith was working in November 1915. But he was not strong enough to impose it on his Coalition Cabinet; his proposition to take over the War Office permanently was vetoed by Bonar Law as Leader of the Conservatives.[2]

Instead Asquith while in temporary charge of the War Office constituted a new and smaller War Committee, changed the commander-in-chief in France, and began arrangements to make the Chief of General Staff at G.H.Q., Chief of the Imperial General Staff at home. Direction of the British Army was transferred from the Secretary of State for War (in his capacity as President of the Army Council) to the Chief of the Imperial General Staff. Thus Kitchener's successor as war lord was not Lloyd George, by now less Asquith's subordinate than his rival, but a non-political 'neutral' staff officer, Lieutenant-General William R. Robertson.

The composition of the new and smaller War Committee was announced by Asquith to the House on 11 November. 'It will consist, in the temporary absence of Lord Kitchener, of five members': Asquith, Balfour, Lloyd George, Bonar Law, and McKenna. The exclusions are worth noting. The Foreign

[1] Lloyd George, *War Memoirs*, i. 311; *The Naval Memoirs of Admiral of the Fleet Sir Roger Keyes, 1910–1918*, ii (1935), 452–3, 523; Dardanelles Com. Final Rpt. 55–56; *Mil. Opns. Gallipoli*, ii. 412; *Naval Opns.* iii. 201–6; Hankey, *Supreme Command*, ii. 457.
[2] Blake, *Unknown Prime Minister*, 269.

Secretary, his reputation affected by the Balkan disasters, was not a member. The omission was in principle both regrettable and symbolic, for it implied the divorce of strategy from foreign policy that was to become so marked a feature of the conduct of the war. Churchill, the originator of the Dardanelles Expedition, was also left out. Deprived of useful occupation, he resigned his sinecure office and joined the Army in France.[1]

On 23 November the new War Committee recommended the evacuation of Gallipoli as advised by reports from Kitchener and the General Staff. Kitchener had not heard any further word from the Admiralty of a renewed naval attack. The only contribution of Admiral de Robeck, who had still not stirred from Lemnos, to the debate was to demand that Helles (at the tip of the Peninsula) be retained to prevent the Germans from using the Peninsula as an antisubmarine base. Kitchener had come reluctantly to the conclusion that in view of the likelihood of German assistance in men or munitions evacuation seemed inevitable. The General Staff was of the same opinion.[2]

Yet still the Cabinet could not bring itself to sanction a withdrawal. Lord Curzon requested and obtained a delay while he drew up memoranda of protest on grounds of the blow to Imperial prestige.[3]

In the course of this final delay Asquith called Lord Esher[4] from Paris and requested him to tell Sir John French that he must relinquish his command. It was not easy to elicit the letter of resignation, but Sir John on a visit to London discovered that he had forfeited his earlier political backing and

[1] *5 Parliamentary Debates* (Commons), lxxv, 1336; Letter, Churchill to Asquith 11 Nov. 1915 (The right decisions are dependent on efficient execution for results), Asquith Papers; Hankey, *Supreme Command*, ii. 442–3; Churchill, *World Crisis*, iii. 882–5.

[2] Dardanelles Com. Final Rpt. 57; Hankey, *Supreme Command*, ii. 459; General Staff. Action to be taken at Gallipoli. Telegram, Kitchener to Prime Minister, 22 Nov. 1915, Asquith Papers; Lord Kitchener's Report to the Cabinet on his East Mediterranean Mission in November 1915, 2 Dec. 1915 (de Robeck cannot recommend any naval action), Kitchener Papers.

[3] Report to the King on the Cabinet of 24 Nov. 1915. The Evacuation of Gallipoli I and II. C. of K. 25, 29–30 Nov. 1915, Asquith Papers.

[4] Reginald Baliol Brett, 2nd Viscount Esher (1852–1930). Lord Esher's position in 'Society', interested intelligence in Imperial affairs, and devotion to intrigue coupled with a determination not to bear the responsibility of office made him an important 'behind the scenes' figure in Edwardian England and war-time Europe. In November 1915 he was acting as an 'observer' in Paris, ostensibly on behalf of Kitchener.

could engineer no revolt. On 4 December he submitted his resignation.[1]

By then Kitchener had returned to England. He had dutifully obeyed instructions to call on the King of Greece with a warning not to join the Central Powers, but ignored repeated suggestions that he return to Egypt and by his presence counter the moral effect of evacuation. He insisted on coming back to London. On his return on 1 December he immediately offered Asquith his resignation, but this was rejected without ceremony. Asquith had in mind a less dangerous solution.[2]

But meanwhile the Gallipoli operation had finally to be liquidated. De Robeck had also at last returned to London, and his successor, Vice-Admiral Wester-Wemyss, promptly urged a renewed naval strike on the Narrows. But an unsupported naval attempt the Admiralty refused to sanction. Admiral Jellicoe from the Grand Fleet had protested that the passage of ships between his command and the Mediterranean made for 'constant changes in personnel'. It could 'no longer be pursued with safety'. All trained crews in the Navy, it appeared, must be under his personal command. Admiral de Robeck offered his discouraging counsels on the hazards of a naval attack. On the Peninsula winter had come. In the last days of November a blizzard claimed two hundred lives and five thousand casualties from sickness and frostbite—over a tenth of the total force. General Monro indicated that a renewed military offensive, even with the aid of troops from Salonika, would offer no prospects of success. The game was up. On 7 December the Cabinet decided to evacuate Suvla and Anzac. On the instance of the Navy the unfortunate troops at Helles were to continue to cling to the tip of the Peninsula.[3]

The stink of failure pervaded everywhere. In Mesopotamia the advance on Baghdad, begun on 11 November, was checked by

[1] *Esher Journals*, iii. 281–93; French, *Life of French*, 334; Nicolson, *George V*, 269.
[2] George Arthur, *Not Worth Reading* (1938), 234–5; Magnus, *Kitchener*, 366–7; *Riddell War Diary*, 134; *Rus. Dip. Docs.* ix. 232.
[3] Barrow, *Monro*, 88–89; Dardanelles Com. Final Rpt. 57–59; Hankey, *Supreme Command*, ii. 460–3; *Mil. Opns. Gallipoli*, ii. 431–9; *Naval Opns.* iii. 214–15, 219–20, 259–60; Admiral of the Fleet Lord Wester-Wemyss, *The Navy in the Dardanelles Campaign* (1924), 209, 218–24, 230–3; Report to the King on the Cabinet of 7 Dec. 1915 (Since Generals Monro and Birdwood believe a reinforced attack from Suvla would fail, there is no alternative to evacuating Suvla and Anzac, Helles being kept, at least for the moment).

the Turks in the battle of Ctesiphon thirteen days later, and the commander of the fourteen-thousand-man attack force, Major-General Charles Townshend, was forced to fall back on Kut. In the first week of December the Turks surrounded that town and began a siege.[1]

An operation undertaken to raise the prestige of the British Empire had brought only further humiliation.

In the Balkans the Allies had obtained but little more success. During November the British Government yielded to General Joffre's threat of resignation and disembarked three divisions from the Western Front at the port of Salonika. General Sarrail's advance into Serbia, in which General Mahon's Tenth Division had participated, had not succeeded in covering the Serb retreat. The remnants of the Serbian Army fled over the border into Albania, and General Sarrail fought his way back to Salonika. The British General Staff and Lord Kitchener now insisted in the strongest possible terms that all British troops must be withdrawn from Greece. The Government agreed with this decision and braced itself for the inevitable wrangle with M. Briand.[2]

Thus the British Government in the first week of December contemplated the wreckage of its hopes. All its prospects had been blasted. The ministerial direction of the war, thoroughly discredited, had failed to evolve a viable strategy. New men, new methods, a new policy were needed. The recall of Sir John French made it possible for Asquith to institute all three while still remaining Prime Minister.

There was little effective choice in the naming of Sir John's successor. No military reputations had survived among senior commanders outside of France, while on the Western Front no Wellington or Napoleon had unmistakably emerged. Hence only the three Army commanders and the Chief of the General Staff G.H.Q. St.-Omer were eligible, though Lieutenant-General Sir Henry Rawlinson, then commanding IVth Army Corps, would probably have been a better choice than any of

---

[1] Brig.-Gen. Sir James E. Edmonds, *A Short History of World War I* (1951), 383–4.
[2] *AF*, viii (1), Annexes, nos. 779, 785, 822; Hankey, *Supreme Command*, ii. 448, 450–3; *Mil. Opns. Macedonia*, i. 33–37, 45–84; Trevelyan, *Grey*, 287–8, 302; Report to the King on the Cabinet of 3 Dec. 1915 (Kitchener, in view of actual and impending disasters at Baghdad, Gallipoli, Egypt, and Salonika, will resign unless at least the last of these be averted by British withdrawal. Those present all concur).

these.[1] Of the three Army commanders only one, General Sir Douglas Haig, had been in command during all of 1915. It was his First Army that had played the major part in both the May and the September offensives. General Robertson, the Chief of Staff, had been recommended by Sir John as his successor, but he was not a gentleman, had spent all his career as a staff officer, and could be more usefully employed at home. So of course it must be Haig, Asquith concluded. On 19 December General Sir Douglas Haig became Commander-in-Chief of the British Armies in France.[2]

Robertson was to come back to London as Chief of the Imperial General Staff with greatly extended powers. General Sir Archibald Murray, who was unpopular with the French and lacked prestige with G.H.Q. St.-Omer, at Asquith's bidding —persevered in despite protests from Army commanders in the field—was offered a command in Egypt. His successor was a much stronger man. 'Wully' Robertson had while in France made an excellent impression on visiting politicians, Lloyd George included, and on the King, who urged, as did Esher and Haig himself, the benefits to be derived from Robertson as C.I.G.S. From this position Robertson could 'regularize' the conduct of the war and 'steady' the 'unstable' French. As for Kitchener, he was to be kept on only as a figurehead, and to ensure that he would indeed be one Robertson was encouraged to dictate conditions for assuming office.[3]

In a letter to Kitchener of 5 December, a copy of which was sent to the Prime Minister, Robertson demanded that:

1. The War Committee be relieved of responsibility to the Cabinet for the conduct of military operations.

[1] Rawlinson's friendship with Kitchener may have been a handicap.

[2] Note in Asquith's handwriting dated 6 Dec. 1915, Asquith Papers; *Private Papers of Douglas Haig*, 116–19; Terraine, *Haig*, 167–70.

[3] *Private Papers of Douglas Haig*, 112–15; Robertson, *Soldiers and Statesmen*, i. 193–206; Letters, Stamfordham to Bonham Carter, 1 Nov. 1915, Esher to Prime Minister, 29 Nov. 1915 (Robertson, not Murray, has Army's confidence). Stamfordham to Prime Minister, 3 Dec. 1915 (The King believes Robertson should be made C.I.G.S., responsible to War Council only), Asquith Papers; Letters, Asquith to Kitchener, 16 Dec. 1915 (Murray has accepted Asquith's offer to take Monro's place). Rawlinson to Fitzgerald, 18 Dec. 1915 (Murray must not be given a combat position, for which he is and knows himself to be incapable). Asquith to Kitchener, 20 Dec. 1915 (Murray must go to Egypt directly). Robertson to Kitchener, 20 Dec. 1915 (expresses surprise at Murray's nomination). Kitchener to Robertson, 21 Dec. 1915 (the decision is the Prime Minister's), Kitchener Papers.

2. All advice on military operations to the War Committee be made through the C.I.G.S.

3. All orders on military operations be issued by the C.I.G.S. under the authority of the War Committee, and not under that of the Army Council presided over by the Secretary of State for War. Theatre commanders would communicate henceforth directly with the C.I.G.S.

4. 'The Secretary of State for War . . . be concerned with actual military operations only on the same footing as any other Member of the War Council.'

'I hope you will not think that I have any desire to make a bargain for myself,' Robertson assured the unfortunate Kitchener, 'but I feel strongly that I cannot serve the War Council, and my King and Country as Chief of the Imperial General Staff unless the above conditions are fulfilled.'[1]

These were indeed formidable demands, and Kitchener's first reaction was to persist in his intention to resign. He and Grey, however, were about to proceed to Paris to inform M. Briand yet again that British troops could not stay at Salonika. On their trip they were joined by General Robertson, who consented to modify his letter. The new copy, dated 10 December, omitted the humiliating formal demand that Kitchener enjoy only the same position as other members of the War Council. The remainder of the document still effectively secured Kitchener's powerlessness. Since Kitchener remained formally head of the War Office, Robertson was prevailed upon to agree that the orders on military operations which the C.I.G.S. alone would issue would be made under the authority of the Secretary of State for War rather than the War Committee. Otherwise no important changes were made, although (as Curzon for one pointed out) neither Robertson nor Kitchener had any authority to relieve the War Committee of responsibility to the Cabinet.[2]

---

[1] The letter in Field-Marshal Sir William Robertson's *From Private to Field-Marshal* (1921), 239–43, is the revised and final version. The first draft is in the Asquith and Kitchener Papers. Magnus, *Kitchener*, 370, gives excerpts.

[2] Hankey, *Supreme Command*, ii. 453–4; Beaverbrook, *Politicians and the War*, 217–18; Magnus, *Kitchener*, 370–1; Robertson, *Private to Field-Marshal*, 237–9; *Esher Journals*, iii. 293–7; Letter, Esher to Asquith, 10 Dec. 1915 (Kitchener has after struggle conceded Robertson's demands, save for the responsibility of the

Kitchener also agreed to leave British troops at Salonika. M. Briand's government appeared in its turn to be tottering to its fall over the failure to help the Serbs and his most likely successor was Clemenceau, like Kitchener an opponent of the Salonika venture. But Clemenceau was also known as an enemy of the President of the Republic, M. Poincaré. Therefore, Kitchener wrote Asquith on 10 December,[1]

I think our visit here has done much good and perhaps has prevented a ministerial crisis which would be difficult to deal with as he [Clemenceau] hates the President of the Republic. . . . I met Robertson at Calais and brought him on here. We have had several long talks and have settled the difficulties raised by his letter, so it is allright about his being C.I.G.S. and I think he is the right man for the place.

On 23 December General Robertson assumed the office of Chief of the General Staff. His first act was to demand the evacuation of Helles in terms that were to express all his future military policy. 'Retention of Helles means dispersion, not concentration of effort.' The War Committee agreed, and on 27 December the Cabinet confirmed final evacuation of the Gallipoli Peninsula. The old system had been liquidated, the new established.[2]

That war by Cabinet government, after working well enough on the whole during the first months of the war, had quite collapsed during the course of 1915 was undeniable. The need for direction and co-ordination presented by the Gallipoli expedition and the harsh pressures engendered by the advances of the Central Powers in Russia and South-East Europe proved too much for a weakened and divided ministry.

The governmental direction of the war never entirely recovered from the discredit incurred in 1915. This was natural but unfair. British strategic policy that year was wrecked not

Secretary of State for War in issuing orders, to be given by Robertson under Kitchener's authority. Constitutionally Kitchener's views are correct, and Robertson has agreed); Letter, Curzon to Asquith, 18 Dec. 1915, Asquith Papers.

[1] *Esher Journals*, iii. 293–6; Letter, Kitchener to Asquith, 10 Dec. 1915, Kitchener and Asquith Papers.

[2] Barrow, *Monro*, 96–97; Callwell, *Experiences of a Dug-Out*, 106; Robertson, *Soldiers and Statesmen*, i. 145; Hankey, *Supreme Command*, ii. 463.

through having been conceived by statesmen rather than
soldiers; but because these statesmen as a group could neither,
in the absence of leadership from the Prime Minister, agree
among themselves, nor, for want of disinterested staff advice,
make decisions based on knowledge, nor, finally, obtain acceptance of their policy by the military and naval chiefs who had
to carry it out. Purely *conciliar*, rather than ministerial, direction
proved ineffective.

It was at the Dardanelles that England could most profitably
strike in 1915, and success there could have been ensured without endangering the security of either the Grand Fleet or the
Western Front. But for victory in that theatre two conditions
were indispensable. First, ministers required the ability and the
will to assess and control the claims of the nation's competing
military and naval commands. Second, they needed to regard
the Dardanelles expedition as a complex and major combined
operation demanding well-co-ordinated and continuous military, naval, and diplomatic action. At no time was either of
these requirements fulfilled.

At the beginning of the year an attack toward Constantinople was sanctioned as a purely naval venture that could be
broken off if unsuccessful. Concurrently the British forces in
France were regarded as at Joffre's disposal on his responsibility,
though never formally placed under his command. Hence the
Cabinet's surprise and misunderstanding at Sir John French's
isolated and frivolous attack at Neuve-Chapelle. Hardly had
one commander thus escaped from control than another, the
Admiral at the Dardanelles, successfully refused to persevere in
the naval attack. In consequence a miscellaneous group of military units concentrated for the exploitation of a naval success
was employed for the destruction of the Turkish Army on the
Gallipoli Peninsula, a task for which their limited numbers
were quite insufficient. This desperate gamble was accordingly
never submitted to the War Council for approval. Yet after
the first naval attempt the Navy was never more than an auxi-
liary at the Dardanelles.

The failure of Sir Ian Hamilton's first military attack on the
Peninsula brought down the Liberal Government, as the First
Sea Lord and the commander of the British forces in France
revolted against the policy of continuing with the Dardanelles

venture. The dominant ministers in the new Coalition Government, formed as a result of these uprisings, regarded Gallipoli less as an opportunity to be pursued than as a debt to be honoured if convenient and liquidated as soon as possible. In their view as to what new forces were needed to discharge this debt the new government was in the absence of staff advice all too willingly misled by Sir Ian Hamilton's optimism and willingness 'to make do'. The possibilities of naval and Greek assistance at Gallipoli were both neglected.

On the Western Front the Government vainly tried to dissuade General Joffre from undertaking what was already referred to derisively as yet another 'great offensive'. Six weeks later Russian discontent and French pressure made Kitchener agree and indeed insist on full British participation. Neither of these factors received a balanced evaluation, an omission for which it is difficult to avoid mentioning Sir Edward Grey.

By then the continuing Russian defeats, soon to lead to the entry of Bulgaria, rendered the Government and its councils incapable of any originative decisions, and from September onwards the Dardanelles Committee and its successor reacted feebly and inadequately to outside pressures. Only the disastrous permission for Nixon to 'march on Baghdad' indicated a will at the centre. Troops were sent and retained at Salonika only as a capitulation to French urgings; that the Government so capitulated was but another indication of its weakness and instability.[1]

The army at the Dardanelles, never adequately supported, was in effect allowed to moulder until threatened with destruction from either the enemy or the elements. Only then was evacuation undertaken. But ever since October the inevitability had been generally recognized. At that time Churchill circulated a long statement detailing some of the many diplomatic and military errors—already familiar to the reader—of policy on the Dardanelles. Sir Edward Grey commented thereon that the War Council had agreed to the enterprise on the understanding that it was exclusively a navy responsibility,

[1] Here, as in the decision to participate in Joffre's autumn offensive, it is Grey whom one must hold primarily responsible for the failure correctly to evaluate the political implications. Clemenceau and Poincaré somehow managed to work together during the last year of the war.

yet Churchill now blamed Kitchener and himself, neither of whom had been at the Admiralty![1]

In this attitude of mind lay the root cause of the failures of 1915. In the years to come there was to be greater concentration of force and devotion on less attainable goals.

[1] Memorandum by Churchill, circulated to the Cabinet 6 Oct. 1915. Excerpts in his *World Crisis*, iii. 820–4, 873–4. Grey's marginal notes and comments are on the copy in the Asquith Papers.

PART TWO

THE GENERALS' WAR

'I can give you no comfort. The soldier squareheads have got hold of the war solid and refuse to do anything except on the Western Front, damn it! . . . There is to be no shot fired, except in Flanders.'

Letter, JULIAN CORBETT to CAPTAIN RICHMOND, *c.* 13 March 1916.

IV

PRELUDE TO THE SOMME

At dinner L. G. said, "Bonar Law tells me that his people hate Asquith. I wonder why?" Colonel David Davies, one of L. G.'s secretaries, replied, "Because they cannot get him out".'

Diary, LORD RIDDELL, 16 July 1916.

A T the new year 1916 Great Britain and her Empire had been at war with Germany for a year and a half. During this period she had suffered, the Prime Minister announced to the House on 27 January, in casualties five hundred and fifty thousand officers and men killed, wounded, or missing.[1] For these substantial losses there were few gains to show. In 1914 the German thrust into France had been halted, and 'command' of the outer seas secured. In 1915 there had been nothing but disappointments and futile endeavour. On the Western Front three attempts at a breakthrough had utterly failed. At Gallipoli the last British troops had been withdrawn from Helles, at the tip of the Peninsula, on 8 January 1916. On the Eastern Front Bulgaria had joined the Central Powers, Serbia had been overrun, and all of Russian Poland and the Baltic coast south of Riga conquered by German troops. Yet though England had sustained mishaps and reverses, forfeited irrecoverable opportunities, and witnessed the defeat or collapse of her allies in Eastern Europe, she had none the less avoided any fundamental deterioration in her own strategic position. All members of the Triple Entente were still belligerents and resolved to continue the war to victory. The intervention of Italy was as great a threat to Austria–Hungary as the intervention of Bulgaria was a protection. The British economy had not yet been threatened. Unlike the French, Britain in 1916 could still dispose of her forces as she would.

[1] The exact figure given was 549,467, the casualties to 9 Jan. 1916. Of these 128,138 were killed, 68,048 missing. (5 *Parliamentary Debates* (Commons), lxxix, 1438.)

The country's lack of fortune had only, it appeared, strengthened its will for victory. On 23 February Asquith told the House,[1]

> I stated in clear, direct, explicit, and emphatic language what are the terms upon which we in this country are prepared to make peace, and I will repeat them . . . On the 9th November, 1914 . . . I used this language and I repeat it to-day:—
> 'We shall never sheath the sword, which we have not lightly drawn, until Belgium'—and I will add Serbia—'recovers in full measure all, and more than all, which she has sacrificed, until France is adequately secured against the menace of aggression, until the rights of the smaller nationalities of Europe are placed upon an unassailable foundation, and until the military domination of Prussia'—this is the language I used—'is wholly and finally destroyed.'

In a speech that April to visiting legislators, Asquith further explained,[2]

> As a result of the War we intend to establish the principle that international problems must be handled by free negotiation on equal terms between free peoples, and that this settlement shall no longer be hampered and swayed by the overmastering dictation of a Government controlled by a military caste. That is what I mean by the destruction of the military domination of Prussia—nothing more, but nothing less.

In spite of protestations to the contrary, Asquith's proclamation remained tolerably obscure. It was an expression of moral indignation, a means of fostering fervour for war, rather than a definition of policy. There was no policy; the Government had not yet decided why or for what the nation was fighting.

Britain had entered the war to prevent French defeat and Belgian occupation. In the latter aim she had been unsuccessful.

---

[1] Great Britain, 5 *Parliamentary Debates* (Commons), lxxx (1916), 736–7.

[2] Speech to French Senators and Deputies, 10 Apr. 1916. *War Speeches by British Ministers* (1917), 104–9. Cf. first leaders of *Westminster Gazette*—whose editor, J. A. Spender, was Asquith's only journalist confidant—for 24 Feb. ('Before we think of peace, we have to see that the military system which has inflicted this immeasurable calamity upon all Europe . . . is thoroughly discredited and destroyed. The Prime Minister does right to speak in his formula of the "military domination of Prussia". That is the enemy. When we have dealt with that we may be able to think of a tolerable way of living with the German people . . .') and 11 Apr. 1916 ('. . . The Prime Minister . . . means that we are determined to make an end of the State System . . .').

Hence the war continued, but through victory many individual statesmen and officials hoped, sometimes to change the German constitutional structure, but more often to weaken the German Empire in general and the Kingdom of Prussia in particular by British destruction of the German Navy and seizure of the German colonies, and by encouraging France, Denmark, and Russia to annex Alsace-Lorraine, Schleswig, and Prussian Poland respectively. Thus the threat of German hegemony in Europe would be suppressed, while British hegemony in Africa and much of Asia would be preserved.[1]

All these territorial, naval, and political desiderata could be included in the capacious, vague, and convenient phrase, 'destruction of the military domination of Prussia', or the still less discriminating, destruction of 'Prussian militarism'.

It was during the war of movement, when hopes were high, that Asquith first proclaimed the final destruction of Prussian military domination as Britain's basic war aim. After November 1914 a crushing military victory appeared less likely, and in the course of 1915 Sir Edward Grey from time to time implied that on the basis of a German evacuation of Belgium Britain might be willing to make peace. But during the spring of 1915 Haldane in a Cabinet memo on 'The Future Relations of the Great Powers' argued that 'the military hierarchy in Germany should be dethroned'. This could come, he argued, through Germany's being confronted with inevitable 'crushing defeat'. Asquith's exegesis of April 1916 appeared to confirm Haldane's view. Henceforth both 'Prussian militarism' and 'German domination', i.e. both the German Empire's internal constitution and her power in Europe and above all overseas, were to be destroyed. So Tory and Liberal, 'realist' and 'idealist', views as to the nature of the German menace were fused. In this process the modest aim of Belgian restoration was quite left behind.[2]

[1] 5 Parliamentary Debates (Commons), xcvi (30 July 1917), 1847–55 (Balfour, 'We entered this War . . . with little in our minds besides the necessity of defending Belgium and the necessity of preventing France from being crushed before our eyes'); Rus. Dip. Docs. vi (1) nos. 278, 329, (2) no. 484; C. Jay Smith, Russian Struggle for Power (1914–1917) (N.Y., 1956), 55–58; The Peace Settlement in Europe. Memorandum by Mr. Balfour, 4 Oct. 1916. Lloyd George, War Memoirs, i. 523–9; Foreign Office memo on War Aims, Aug. 1916. David Lloyd George, Truth About the Peace Treaties, i (1938), 131–50.

[2] Arthur S. Link, Woodrow Wilson and the Progressive Era, 1910–1917 (1954), 161, 198; Charles Seymour, The Intimate Papers of Colonel House (1926), i. 347–8, 353–4,

It was evident that within the then foreseeable future—for the spectre of European revolution had not yet re-emerged—only a crushing military victory over the German armies could secure these wider aims. But it was far from evident that such a victory was possible. Therefore a few key men within the British Government, and they alone—the Prime Minister, Grey, Balfour,[1] and Lloyd George—had on the day before Asquith's 'war aims' speech to the House of Commons contracted an insurance policy with the United States that, in default of an Entente victory, would at any rate guarantee either the restoration of Belgium or United States entry into the war on the side of the Entente.

On 22 February 1916 Colonel House, the confidential emissary of President Wilson, made the proposal, set down in writing and initialled by Sir Edward Grey, and confirmed by the President two weeks later, that

President Wilson was ready, on hearing from France and England that the moment was opportune, to propose that a Conference should be summoned to put an end to the war. Should the Allies accept this proposal, and should Germany refuse it, the United States would probably enter the war against Germany.

Colonel House expressed the opinion that, if such a Conference met, it would secure peace on terms not unfavourable to the Allies; and, if it failed to secure peace, the United States would [probably][2] leave the Conference as a belligerent on the side of the Allies, if Germany was unreasonable. Colonel House expressed an opinion decidedly favourable to the restoration of Belgium, the transfer of Alsace and Lorraine to France, and the acquisition by Russia of an outlet to the sea,[3] though he thought that the loss of territory incurred by Germany in one place would have to be compensated to her by concessions to her in other places outside Europe.

It will be noted that no mention was made of Serbia.

For the moment the War Committee, which—together with the Chief of Imperial General Staff and First Sea Lord—was alone informed of the Grey–House agreement, decided to take no action. The restoration of Belgium and the most

380; *Rus. Dip. Docs.* vii (1) no. 204; Dudley Sommer, *Haldane of Cloan: His Life and Times, 1856–1928* (1960), 332–3.

[1] The omission of Bonar Law is worth noting.

[2] The President's insertion.

[3] Constantinople.

cherished territorial aims of the two other members of the Triple Entente were not enough. They desired a crushing military victory and 'the destruction of the military domination of Prussia'.[1]

To what was this extreme policy due? Was it an expression of confidence in the success to be attained as a result of the British nation now for the first time devoting its energies and organizing power primarily to the business of war? So it would seem to the superficial observer. Munitions of war were pouring out in quantity if not in quality. The first step on the long and, as it developed, never fully trod road to universal national service was taken with the conscription of single men in the first Military Service Act in January 1916. In May compulsion was further extended to all men between the ages of eighteen and forty-one. The munitions and the men now regularly available in unprecedented quantities would be used, thanks to the new system of war direction, for one purpose: the defeat and destruction of the German armies.[2]

The genesis of this new system has already been described. Born in the disappointments of the last months of 1915, it consisted of an enlarged and reconstituted General Staff under General Sir William Robertson responsible to a War Committee made up of the Prime Minister, the two Service secretaries, the Chancellor of the Exchequer, the Leader of the Conservative party, and Lloyd George. The Cabinet retained nominal overall responsibility, but in fact were often kept in ignorance; they were not, for example, informed of the House–Grey memorandum until the end of the year.[3]

The new machinery was to concentrate Britain's, and the Empire's, waxing military strength on the Western Front, where the mass of the German armies was located. In December 1915 the mercurial and impressionable Sir John French had

[1] Lloyd George, *War Memoirs*, i. 408–13; Viscount Grey of Fallodon, *Twenty-Five Years, 1892–1916* (N.Y., 1925), ii. 123–37; Lord Hankey, *The Supreme Command* (1961), ii. 478–80; *Intimate Papers of Colonel House*, ii. 195–202; Link, *Woodrow Wilson and the Progressive Era*, 197–205, 219–22, 253–6; Ernest R. May, *The World War and American Isolation, 1914–1917* (Cambridge, U.S.A., 1959), 352–60, 371–81.

[2] Hankey, *Supreme Command*, ii. 471–7.

[3] Grey, *Twenty-Five Years*, ii. 130–3; Lord Crewe, The Conduct of the War, 5 *Parliamentary Debates* (Lords), xxii (31 May 1916), 222–49.

been replaced by a phlegmatic and determined Scot, Sir
Douglas Haig. Personal leadership was replaced by a vast
military bureaucracy. On 28 December the War Committee,
on the request of the C.I.G.S., recorded that[1]

From the point of view of the British Empire, France and Flanders
will remain the main theatre of operations.
Every effort is to be made for carrying out the offensive operations
next spring in the main theatre of war in close co-operation with the
Allies, and in the greatest possible strength.

Doubtless in the beginning of 1916 these indications of
national commitment to a war to be ended only by enemy
capitulation, no matter what the cost, corresponded to the
public mood. But so far as the governing instrument was concerned the proclamation of unlimited war aims and the adoption
of a Western military policy represented not determination,
but appeasement; not self-confidence, but abandonment. To
remain in the seat of power the Asquith Coalition ceased to
wield power. To stay in office one year longer they adopted the
policies of their opponents. For this complaisance they naturally
received no gratitude then or since.

The nation was now bereft of any real leadership. But important segments of the Government—one is tempted to write the
'soul' of Liberalism—were fundamentally opposed to both the
political and military strategy actually adopted in the course
of 1916.

Thus on conscription the impending decision to adopt compulsory service had at the end of 1915 led five members of the
original Liberal Cabinet—Simon, McKenna, Runciman, Grey,
and Birrell—to submit their resignations. England could not,
they argued, afford in addition to her other obligations the cost
of an Army on the Continental scale. The loss of human life and
deprivation of personal freedoms were also factors in their
reasoning. Of the five, however, all but Sir John Simon were
persuaded to remain at their posts.[2]

---

[1] Brig.-Gen. Sir James E. Edmonds, *Military Operations France and Belgium, 1916*, i
(1932), 10, *Appendices* 3; Hankey, *Supreme Command*, ii. 466–9.
[2] Hankey, *Supreme Command*, ii. 470–2; Stephen McKenna, *Reginald McKenna,
1863–1943* (1948), 255–9; J. A. Spender and Cyril Asquith, *Life of Herbert Henry
Asquith* (1932), ii. 201–4; G. M. Trevelyan, *Grey of Fallodon* (Longmans Library
edn., 326–7).

On military strategy, several members—led by Balfour—of
the War Committee (and how many others on both the War
Committee and the Cabinet must have shared their doubts?)
expressed scepticism on the utility of a large-scale offensive
in the West in 1916.[1]

But neither Liberals nor Easterners could now hope to
control strategy or policy. Their utmost ambition could only
be to act as a brake.

The fundamental reason for this powerlessness was that the
failures and procrastinations—real or apparent—of 1915 had
exhausted the Government's public and parliamentary support.
The unfortunate Prime Minister in particular was made the
scapegoat for Britain's inability to win the war. Only the fear
that Asquith's fall would disrupt Britain's own 'Union Sacrée',
her apparent unity of will to wage war, kept the Government
in office. How else, it was reasoned, could the 'Left'—Labour and
the Radicals—be persuaded to continue their support of the war?[2]

Through Lloyd George? The man of 'push and go' could not
bring himself to resign and lead an opposition, however much
he threatened to do so and whatever his expressed dissatisfac-
tions with the conduct of the war.

Through Churchill, who had returned to the House from 'the
trenches' in March? His speeches on naval and military strategy
were listened to with attention, but his identification with the
Dardanelles campaign and his pre-war belligerency on Irish
Home Rule made him particularly unacceptable to the Conservative party.

Through the moderate Bonar Law? The leader of the Conservatives was well aware of the Government's unpopularity and
lack of support in the House. In private he fully admitted, was
indeed 'convinced . . . that the Government might be beaten

---

[1] Hankey, *Supreme Command*, ii. 467, 469–70, 495; *Intimate Papers of Colonel House*,
ii. 128; *Lord Riddell's War Diary, 1914–1918* (n.d. but *c.* 1933), 154, 198; *The Private
Papers of Douglas Haig, 1914–1919* (1952), (ed.) Robert Blake, 122–3; Letter, Birrell
to Prime Minister, 29 Dec. 1915 (Agrees with McKenna and Runciman on two
far more important subjects than recruiting: (1) money, (2) strategic policy as
expounded in Murray's long, unconvincing, and frightening paper). Note by the
Secretary of State for War on a Memorandum by the First Lord of the Admiralty
dated 27 Dec. 1915. 8 Jan. 1916 (Balfour suggests that the very possible
failure of a major offensive in the West may involve Allied defeat), Asquith Papers.

[2] Blanche E. C. Dugdale, *Arthur James Balfour* (1936), ii. 156–7 (' . . . I know that
the Government is hated, discredited, distrusted. They hate Asquith').

at any moment in the House of Commons, and he was quite certain that, if there was anyone to lead an Opposition, they would be driven from office in a short time'.[1] But, he reasoned,[2]

If we broke up the present Government, it is obvious that a new Government could not exist in the present House of Commons. There would therefore be the immediate necessity of a general election; it would be fought, in spite of the war, with almost the usual amount of party bitterness, and if our Party succeeded in getting a majority we would be faced with an opposition of precisely the same nature as that at the time of the Boer War. This would really mean in my opinion that in a very short time we would have martial law all over the country; for not only would there be strong Opposition in the House of Commons but that Opposition would encourage any form of opposition outside . . . the first effect of such a change, when it was obvious that instead of even the appearance of unity the nation was bitterly divided, would be to discourage our Allies and make our enemies feel certain that we could not stay the course.

He therefore—like Asquith a prisoner of the need for unity—took no action.

Other Conservative chieftains were less responsible. In the absence of statesmen, the 'guerilla' leadership of the Parliamentary opposition fell by default to Sir Edward Carson. A small group, whose regular members included Carson, Milner, Geoffrey Dawson, the editor of *The Times*, Waldorf Astor, the proprietor of the *Observer*, and Leopold Amery, met weekly to discuss the war and political strategy. Lloyd George occasionally attended, as did Sir Henry Wilson on leave from his reduced status as a corps commander on the Western Front. 'Our one object', Amery artlessly recorded in his memoirs, 'was to work for the more effective conduct of the war and, above all, somehow or other, to secure a change of government.'[3]

Carson's role was his favourite—prosecuting attorney. In debate after debate, the Government was taunted for its inefficiency, for not having its heart in the war, for not waging

---

[1] Denis Gwynne, *Life of John Redmond* (1932), 466–8.

[2] Letter to Henry Wilson, 31 Mar. 1916, Robert Blake, *The Unknown Prime Minister* (1955), 280–1.

[3] Leopold Amery, *My Political Life* (1953–5), ii. 81–82; H. Montgomery Hyde, *Carson: The Life of Sir Edward Carson, Lord Carson of Duncairn* (1953), 397; A. M. Gollin, *Proconsul in Politics* (1964), 323–46. Carson's moves in the House were paralleled in the Lords by Milner, who wished to force a general election.

PLATE 6

Major-General Sir Frederick Maurice with General Sir William Robertson leaving
the Hotel Crillon after the Allied Conference, 26 July 1917

PLATE 7

Sir Douglas Haig leaving General Headquarters

the war with sufficient hate or blindness, for conciliating neutrals. Asquith was urged to extend conscription to Ireland, to prepare for economic warfare against Germany after the armistice, never to grant an armistice, to use the instrument of sea-power to enforce a complete blockade regardless of neutral rights and to coerce smaller neutrals like Greece. *The Times* and the rest of the Northcliffe Press joined at appropriate moments to hammer home the moral: the Asquith–Bonar Law régime would not win the war, because it had not, and could not, sufficiently dedicate itself to winning it.[1]

In July expressed parliamentary discontent was so strong that the Government was forced to permit a parliamentary inquiry into the Gallipoli and Mesopotamian expeditions. 'Side-shows' were now politically impracticable.[2]

Beset by this storm of jingoistic opposition, the Government could not hope to control the new military system it had created in December 1915. With the appointment of Haig and Robertson, G.H.Q. France had become an alien and unfriendly power, demanding and ungrateful. The territory under its control could only be approached through the proper diplomatic channels, as the Attorney-General, Frederick E. Smith, for one soon discovered. When 'F.E.', known to be—or to wish to be—a confidant of Kitchener, tried to visit Churchill in the front lines without proper authorization from G.H.Q., he was promptly taken into custody by the military authorities and sent back to British headquarters at St. Omer.[3]

The principal demands of G.H.Q. France were agreed on at a meeting between the new Commander-in-Chief and his

---

[1] Hyde, *Carson*, 406–7; *The Nation*, 22 and 29 Jan., 29 July 1916 ('The House of Commons is fast becoming a kind of multi-molecule. . . . There is Sir Edward Carson's following, declared . . . to number at least 120 members. Its most conspicuous support is the Khaki brigade. . . . In half-shy association with this group, is the Cawley party, a curious, half-revival of the Liberal League, basing itself on a "vigorous" conduct of the war. . . . Both are anti-Ministerial. . . . The Cawley group is being enlarged, and now contains sixty members').

[2] Hankey, *Supreme Command*, ii. 519–25; Sir Charles Petrie, *Life and Letters of the Right Hon. Sir Austen Chamberlain* (1939–40), ii. 71.

[3] Lord Beaverbrook, *Politicians and the War, 1914–1916*, ii (n.d.), 38–43 ('. . . the intention of the military . . . had been to send Birkenhead under escort to Boulogne, and deport him as one having no pass'); Birkenhead, *F. E.: The Life of F. E. Smith, First Earl of Birkenhead* (1959), 284–5; *Private Papers of Douglas Haig*, 126–7; General Macready, *Annals of an Active Life* (n.d.), i. 232–4; Lieut.-Col. C. à Court Repington, *The First World War, 1914–1918* (Boston, 1921), 121–2.

emissary in London, who was to take the post of Chief of the Imperial General Staff. Robertson later recorded:[1]

I had a long and earnest talk with Haig about the general situation, which was then as bad as it could well be, while measures for prosecuting the war were still being conducted in London, too much upon the principle of 'business as usual'. Naval, military, and all other essential war services continued to be dependent upon voluntary methods and there was great dispersion of force. Like myself, Lord Haig was convinced that success could be obtained only by the full development of our resources, and by their consistent concentration against the principal enemy. *It was therefore agreed between us* that I should urge the Government *to make every able-bodied man available for national service* in one form or another, *and to utilize our main resources on the Western Front.*[2]

Robertson took with him to London the heads of his Operations and Intelligence sections, who were given the same functions within the War Office. *Vis-à-vis* the Secretary of State for War and the War Committee the C.I.G.S. wielded exceptional powers. The provisions of the Kitchener–Robertson agreement have already been described.[3] In January an Order in Council made Robertson 'responsible for issuing the orders of the Government in regard to Military Operations'. The following month the operations in Mesopotamia were made a War Office responsibility. Communications between the General Staff and Commanders-in-Chief were so privileged that they were not shown even to the Secretary of State for War or to the War Committee.

'Wully' Robertson's powers were further increased by the support of the Northcliffe Press and the Carsonite opposition. With the Military Correspondent of *The Times*, Colonel Repington, he had continual confidential discussions; and the latter's pen was always at his service. Never did the Generals have a freer hand than in 1916. In the course of the year they pitilessly repressed the Easter revolt in Ireland, persuaded the War Committee to recommend universal national service, and threw all

[1] Field-Marshal Sir William Robertson, 'Relations with the Government, 1916–1918', British Legion *Journal*, vii. 9 (Earl Haig Memorial Number, March 1928), p. 236.
[2] Present author's italics.
[3] See above, pp. 113–14.

the weight of their influence against a negotiated peace. The strategy of 1916 was entirely their making.[1]

The first concern of the new C.I.G.S. was, he wrote, 'to get every possible man, horse and gun on the Western Front'.[2] Already the British troops in France numbered just under a million, but the 'side-shows' in Salonika and 'Mespot' were misusing, in Robertson's opinion, the services of one hundred and forty thousand soldiers of the Empire, while the evacuation of Gallipoli combined with the effects of unreasonable fears of a Turkish attack had increased the strength in Egypt to nearly two hundred thousand men.[3]

Of the fourteen divisions in Egypt nine were sent to France before the opening of the Somme campaign. All the Australian and New Zealand infantry were included, and those divisions left behind were considered to be of inferior quality. The commander in Egypt, Sir Archibald Murray, was enjoined to restrict his mission to the defence of Egypt west of the Suez Canal.[4]

[1] Hankey, *Supreme Command*, ii. 500; *Mil. Opns. Fr. and Bel. 1915*, ii. 409; *Riddell War Diary*, 177; Repington, *First World War*, entries for 1916, *passim*; Field-Marshal Sir William Robertson, *From Private to Field-Marshal* (1921), 243, and *Soldiers and Statesmen, 1914–1918* (1926), i. 178, 286 ('. . . throughout 1916, the General Staff were accorded suitable freedom of action. . . . To this fact, perhaps more than to any other, may be largely attributed the military achievements of the year, which left the position in all theatres of war infinitely more satisfactory and hopeful than it had been twelve months before'); Victor Bonham-Carter, *Soldier True* (1963), 144–5.

[2] Letter to General Maxwell, Egypt, Jan. 1916. Sir George Arthur, *General Sir John Maxwell* (1932), 240–1. Cf. Letter, Fitzgerald, personal military secretary to Kitchener, to Gabriel, 2 Mar. 1916 ('Steady preparation is continuing with the main object, of strengthening ourselves on the Western Front, and reducing our detachments in other theatres of war'), George Arthur Papers, National Register of Archives, Public Record Office, London.

[3] Troop distribution, 1 Jan. 1916:

France	987,200
Egypt	157,705
Gallipoli	39,206
Salonika	92,954
Mesopotamia	47,500
India	
British	78,468
Indian	196,500

(*Mil. Opns. Fr. and Bel. 1916*, i. 18–19).

[4] Hankey, *Supreme Command*, ii. 500–1; Capt. Cyril Falls and Lieut.-Gen. Sir G. McMunn, *Military Operations Egypt and Palestine*, i (1928), 98–100, 170–4; Field-Marshal Earl Wavell, *The Palestine Campaigns* (3rd edn., 1931), 40–42.

In Mesopotamia, too, a defensive policy would be followed, but first General Townshend and his troops had to be freed. 'Our chief anxiety', wrote Kitchener's personal military secretary, 'is the future of Kut-el-Amara and the beleaguered forces there.'[1]

At Salonika the British forces had been allowed to remain in order to keep M. Briand in power and thus avoid an expected clash between Clemenceau as Premier and the French President, Poincaré. The efforts of Robertson, seconded by Kitchener and the Cabinet, to withdraw entirely from Greece met with such protests from Briand that Asquith decreed that the British forces should continue in occupation. But British authorities declined to provide their troops in that area with artillery, or mules and equipment for mountain warfare; made the 'British Salonika Army' administratively and logistically dependent upon Egypt, which looked on 'Salonika's' requests without favour or understanding; and provided that army with a new commander, Lieutenant-General G. F. Milne, specially chosen because he was deemed to have the strength of character to resist the blandishments of General Sarrail. With the reconstitution of the Serbian Army and its transport to Greece in the spring the French began to urge the need for a renewed offensive, but Robertson and the War Committee, supported by a 'unanimous' Cabinet, returned a blunt refusal.[2]

Robertson further urged on the War Committee the desirability of making peace with Turkey or Bulgaria. Turkey would be allowed to retain Constantinople, or alternatively Bulgaria would be given the territory in Macedonia so often vainly promised her at the expense of Greece and Serbia during the summer and autumn of 1915.[3]

By the opening of the Somme battles Robertson's efforts had

[1] Letter from Fitzgerald cited above, p. 131, n 2. See also Hankey, *Supreme Command*, ii. 469, and Great Britain . . . *The Campaign in Mesopotamia, 1914–1918*, compiled . . . by Brig.-Gen. F. J. Moberly (1923–7), ii. 289.

[2] France. Ministere de la Guerre. Etat-Major de l'Armée. Service Historique. *Les Armées françaises dans la Grande Guerre*, [*AF*], vii (1), p. 499, Annexes nos. 1187, 1302, 1346; *Private Papers of Douglas Haig*, 148; Hankey, *Supreme Command*, ii. 501–3; Capt. Cyril Falls, *Military Operations, Macedonia*, i (1933), 96–136.

[3] Note prepared by the C.I.G.S. for the War Committee, on the Assistance that Diplomacy might Render to Naval and Military Operations, 12 Feb. 1916, Asquith Papers. Robertson's own summary is to be found in his *Soldiers and Statesmen*, i. 208–10.

increased the strength of the British Armies in France to one million four hundred thousand men organized into fifty-three fully staffed divisions.[1]

The employment of the increased British forces on the Western Front on a grand offensive in 1916 had been proposed by allied commanders and their representatives at a meeting held under General Joffre's patronage at his headquarters at Chantilly the previous December. On 8 December the conference had adopted a French proposal recommending simultaneous offensives on the Russian, Italian, and Western Fronts in the spring.[2]

Haig and Robertson had their own reasons for desiring the British share in these offensives to be big and spectacular. Nothing but a substantial British victory would convince the sceptics in the War Committee that the 'Western' policy was the correct and fruitful one. Nothing less would stop the flow of schemes by 'amateur strategists' to 'divert' men and material from France.

These conscientious objectors to an offensive in the west [a G.H.Q. apologia revised by Haig himself immediately after the war explained] were not amenable to argument. The only hope of convincing them . . . was to show that Germany was not invincible on the Western Front. A marked success there, even if not decisive, would surely encourage doubters to believe in the final possibility of final victory on the main front and to continue the effort to attain it.[3]

[1] The official figure on 30 June 1916 was 1,426,000 men. *Mil. Opns. Fr. and Bel. 1916*, i. 20 n. 2. See also Letter, Robertson to Joffre, 30 June 1916, in *AF*, iv (2), Annexe no. 1812; and George Dewar and Lieut.-Col. J. H. Boraston, *Sir Douglas Haig's Command, December 19, 1915, to November 11, 1918* (1923), i. 85 n.

[2] The Russian Commander-in-Chief, General Alexieff, had urged a combined attack directed at Budapest, 'the French, English and Italians, starting from Serbia and Albania, . . . the Russians attacking in Galicia and Bukovina'. This plan was rejected by General Joffre.

Mil. Opns. Fr. and Bel. 1916, i. 6–7. For Alexieff's proposal, see Telegram, Sazonov to Ambassadors at Paris, London, and Rome, 11/24 Nov. 1915, published in Emile Laloy, *Les Documents secrets des archives du Ministère des affaires étrangères de Russie* (Paris: Bossard, 1919), no. 28, pp. 122–3;*Mémoires du maréchal Joffre (1910–1917)* (Paris, 1932), ii. 166–7.

[3] Haig, 'Memorandum on Operations on the Western Front', deposited in the British Museum, the authorities of which as late as February 1961 refused access, as cited in *Private Papers of Douglas Haig*, 365. According to Robert Blake, editor of the Haig papers, 'the document was actually written by Haig's successive Chiefs of Staff . . . but Haig himself carefully revised it and added some notes of

At least as important a factor was professional and national pride. The British Empire had now finally developed the army its world importance warranted. 'There is no doubt to my mind', Haig confided in his diary, 'but that the war must be won by the Forces of the British Empire.' In London Robertson expressed similar sentiments to the War Committee. Only now were the British forces strong enough to be able *by themselves* to mount an attack on the enemy with hopes of success; it was time for the British to play their full part in the war and assume their rightful position of leadership within the Entente.[1]

The aim of this new British offensive would be the same as those of 1915: the destruction of the German Army. A year earlier Hankey and Churchill had argued that the static warfare in the West, the product of the defensive power of the machine-gun and barbed wire, demonstrated the need to develop new weapons systems. The infantryman, groaning under sixty-six pounds of pack, had become an exposed beast of burden; the mobile cavalryman's horse equally lacked protection. To introduce the lost factors of mobility and protection a new weapon was needed. The 'tank', or, as it was earlier more graphically described, the 'caterpillar', was eventually to introduce not only mobility and protection but also surprise to the battlefield. Its eventual success needs no emphasis here.[2]

But in early 1916 the British military authorities, perhaps naturally, drew no such adventurous conclusions from a year's further experience of consistent failure. What impressed them was the dual fact that the Allied offensives succeeded in making an initial break in the enemy line but could effect no further breach. 'The break-*in*', to quote Cyril Falls, 'could not be converted into a break-*through*.'[3] The higher commands and staff (battle units had fewer illusions) attributed this failure not to the machine-gun, but to the enemy's artillery and large resources

his own'. For confirming evidence on this motive see also Letters, Robertson to Haig, 5 and 13 Jan. 1916, ibid. 122–4, and Brig.-Gen. John Charteris, Haig's chief intelligence officer, *Field-Marshal Earl Haig* (1929), 189–90.
  [1] *Private Papers of Douglas Haig*, 125; The Question of Offensive Operations on the Western Front. Note by the Chief of the Imperial General Staff, 5 Jan. 1916. Note prepared by the C.I.G.S. for the War Committee . . . 12 Feb. 1916. Asquith Papers.
  [2] Winston S. Churchill, *The World Crisis, 1911–1918* (4-vol. Odhams Press edn.), ii. 508–26; Hankey, *Supreme Command*, i. 228–31, 244–54.
  [3] Cyril Falls, *The Great War* (N.Y., 1961), 83.

of man-power. To protect the attacking force from enemy artillery and thus attain a break-through it was concluded that the attack should be made on a wide front, perhaps 25 miles. The greatly increased rate of munitions production would make the 'break-in' a far easier task than before. The artillery would now first gain the ground, the infantry would then occupy it.

Once the 'break-in' had been achieved, the cavalry would enter the battle area and 'roll up the flanks'. The problem of enemy man-power resources could only be met by exhausting the enemy's reserves; if possible, through a series of preliminary attacks; otherwise, through continued infantry combat. When the enemy reserves had been 'used up', those Allied troops who remained could combine with the cavalry to make a final, and decisive, attack. Hence the need to bring in an indefinitely large number of troops to kill and be killed; hence the expectation of a 'prolonged' offensive lasting several weeks. If casualties were exchanged at an equal rate on the Western Front, the Germans, Robertson argued, would eventually have to shorten their lines. So, as it was frequently expressed in what ought to have been the most informed circles, 'killing Germans' would 'win the war'.[1]

G.H.Q. would have preferred to make its attack in Flanders, towards Ostend, but the desire to rely on Empire troops alone in an area of especial concern to British interests conflicted with the tactical need for a wide front. A visit of Haig and Lord Curzon to King Albert of the Belgians again demonstrated that monarch's opposition to an offensive on Belgian soil. So Joffre's

[1] Letter, Haig to Asquith, 25 Jan. 1915, Asquith Papers; *AF*, iv (1), Annexe no. 175; Letter, Haig to Kitchener, 19 Jan. 1916 (Decisive blow must not be delivered until the enemy reserves have been committed), Kitchener Papers; The Question of Offensive Operations on the Western Front. Note by the C.I.G.S. for the War Committee . . . 5 Jan. 1916 (Hitherto the exhaustion of the enemy's reserves has not been attempted. Moreover, even a limited success would use up enemy resources in men and material, thereby shortening military and national resistance), Asquith Papers; A note on the resources in men, of the Allies and of the enemy, and their effect on the duration of the War, General Staff, 31.3.16 (Equal casualties incurred on both sides of the Eastern and Western Fronts would work to Britain's and Russia's, though not to France's, comparative advantage, since neither the British nor the Russian Empire had as yet committed its full man-power resources. Therefore, (1) if comparative casualties can be kept equal, the Entente Powers should engage the Germans as heavily as possible, (2) important modifications on West and Russian/German Fronts may be expected by the beginning of winter 1916, (3) the intenser the fighting in the meantime, the sooner these changes will come), Kitchener Papers.

proposal for a joint offensive of the two armies along the river
Somme was accepted, even though the enemy's defences were
most strongly developed in this area.[1]

What this Western strategy for winning the war consistently
misinterpreted was the ability of the Central Powers constantly
to renew their source of reserves for the main army through
conscription of their own and subject populations and their
ability to supply that army by rail transport. (This last was a
curious omission on the part of men who continually exclaimed
at the Easterners' 'ignorance' of logistics.) Haig and Robertson
repeatedly underestimated Germany's ability to find new
recruits. They seem to have thought of the conduct of war in
Napoleonic terms: to engage in battle against the enemy army
with 'overwhelming' force would not only win that battle but
also thereby compel capitulation of the adversary state. Napoleon
had been justified in these views; supreme commanders in an
age of industrial democracy were not. G.H.Q., moreover, did
not even seek battle conditions in which its own casualties would
not exceed those of the opponent. It is, in fact, despite all the
apologias that have and will continue to appear, necessary
to agree with C. S. Forester's evaluation in his absorbing novel
The General, a study of a British senior commander on the Western Front. After depicting a headquarters debate on 'what had
gone wrong' in the offensive of autumn 1915, Forester comments:[2]

In some ways it was like the debate of a group of savages as to
how to extract a screw from a piece of wood. Accustomed only to
nails, they had made one effort to pull out the screw by main force,
and now that it had failed they were devising methods of applying
more force still, of obtaining more efficient pincers, of using levers

[1] *Les Carnets de guerre d'Albert Ier Roi des Belges* (Bruxelles, 1953), 71–74; Mission
to the King of the Belgians, Feb. 1916. Curzon of Kedleston, 8 Feb. 1916.
Asquith Papers; Letter, Joffre to Haig and Robertson, 10 Feb. 1916 (a joint attack
would permit 'un front de quelque 70 kilomètres, et c'est sur l'étendue du front
d'attaque qu'il faut compter pour empêcher l'ennemi de se rétablir après nos
premiers succès'), *AF*, iv (1), Annexe no. 172.

Capt. Liddell Hart, in his 'Notes and Queries' to the author on the manuscript
of this book, writes, 'In the autumn of 1915 [these defences] were very weak—as
I have good reason to know as I was serving there myself. By the following summer
the constant harassing policy of the British High Command led the Germans to
develop the defences intensively—thus in effect fortifying the front that their troops
were about to attack. But the defences on the French sector were not developed so
intensively—which partly explains the greater initial success of the French attack.'

[2] C. S. Forester, *The General* (Boston, 1936), 226–7.

and fulcrums so that more men could bring their strength to bear. They could hardly be blamed for not guessing that by rotating the screw it would come out after the exertion of far less effort; it would be a notion so different from anything they had ever encountered that they would laugh at the man who suggested it.

The generals round the table were not men who were easily discouraged—men of that sort did not last long in command in France. Now that the first shock of disappointment had been faced they were prepared to make a fresh effort, and to go on making those efforts as long as their strength lasted.

'As long as their'—that is to say, of the British nation and Empire —'strength lasted.' The tactics and concept of 'attrition' were faulty; it could not attain its aim. And even if 'attrition' could impose victory it was highly doubtful that 'the destruction of the military domination of Prussia' was worth the destruction of British manhood. The British military authorities never asked themselves the question, nor did the British Government until the end of the year. And then it was too late, because England was soon to be reduced to fighting for survival.

The French command, keenly aware of France's dwindling military man-power, and sobered by a year and a half of grand offensives in which the French had taken first the only and then the leading part, approached the Battle of the Somme in a very different spirit though with similar tactical doctrine. It was happy to leave the 'wearing-down' task to the other armies of the Entente; the most it expected on the Western Front was a series of limited attacks resulting, primarily through use of artillery, in limited territorial gains and a sufficient weakening of the enemy to prevent his launching another offensive on the scale of Verdun. This divergence between French and British conceptions was to have its effects on the course of the battle.[1]

On 14 February Haig and Joffre agreed that the campaign in the West would begin on 1 July. Haig, fearing the effects of an apparently fruitless preliminary assault on British opinion, refused to make a separate attack in April to draw off the German reserves. He did, however, agree to make a preliminary attack the week before the main offensive for that purpose.[2]

---

[1] AF, iii, Annexe no. 2793, iv (2), Annexe no. 494, vii (C1), Annexe no. 736; Mil. Opns. Fr. and Bel. 1916, i. 33–34.
[2] AF, iv (1), Annexes nos. 147, 221, 222; Private Papers of Douglas Haig, 129.

138   PRELUDE TO THE SOMME

One week later the Germans began their own, somewhat more thoughtfully conceived, 'war of attrition' against the French with an attack on Verdun. This stroke was welcomed by the British command, for the longer the German offensive went on the greater the extent to which the enemy was bound to exhaust his own reserves. He would be so much more the weaker when the decisive counter-attack was launched at the Somme.

It seems to me [Robertson wrote Joffre] that we can desire nothing better than that the enemy should continue his attacks, as they will use up his troops to a much greater extent than the operations of 'usure' which you had proposed that we should employ against him. I am strongly of opinion that, by attacking, the enemy is playing our game.[1]

The continued agony at Verdun also furnished an argument for the Somme offensive the logic of which the sceptics on the War Committee could not deny. Surely England could not refuse to relieve her faithful ally! In January 1916, at Mr. Balfour's insistence, the War Committee had resolved that 'it must not be assumed . . . offensive operations . . . are finally decided on'. On 12 March a conference of Commanders-in-Chief at Chantilly agreed that the Russian and Italian participation in the combined offensives would begin 'at the earliest possible date', which meant May. Robertson on 31 March informed the War Committee 'It is now necessary . . . to decide, at once and definitely, whether they do or do not approve'. On 7 April the Government finally authorized Sir Douglas Haig to concert an offensive with Joffre. The British commander was made independent of the C.I.G.S. for the actual conduct of the forthcoming military operations.[2]

As spring wore on and the pressure at Verdun intensified Haig, supported by a lukewarm Robertson, urged that the British share in the attack be further delayed, in order to prolong the process of German attrition and to accumulate the maximum number of artillery and men. A really 'decisive' success could thus be assured, and this was all the more necessary because anything less would lead to a 'victory of the "peace-

[1] AF, iv (1), Annexe no. 593.
[2] Hankey, Supreme Command, ii. 494–5; Mil. Opns. Fr. and Bel. 1916, i. 12–13, Appendixes no. 4; AF, iv (1), p. 620, and Annexe no. 1212; Private Papers of Douglas Haig, 124, 137–8; Robertson, Soldiers and Statesmen, i. 259–60.

mongers" who argued that the Germans could not be beaten', as Haig told Joffre's representative at his court. But at a meeting with Joffre on 26 May Haig agreed to revert to the date originally agreed on. According to Haig's diary,[1]

General Joffre explained the general situation . . . the Russians intended to attack on the 15th June. . . . The French had supported for three months alone the whole weight of the German attacks at Verdun. . . . If this went on, the French Army would be ruined. He, therefore, was of the opinion that the 1st July was the latest date for the combined offensive of the British and French. I said that, before fixing the date, I would like to indicate the state of preparedness of the British Army on certain dates and compare its condition. I took 1st and 15th July, and 1st and 15th August. The moment I mentioned 15th August, Joffre at once got very excited and shouted that 'The French Army would cease to exist if we did nothing till then'. The rest of us looked on at this outburst of excitement, and then I pointed out that, in spite of the 15th August being the most favourable date for the British Army to take action, yet, in view of what he had said regarding the unfortunate condition of the French Army, I was prepared to commence operations on the 1st July or thereabouts. This calmed the old man.

The Brusilov offensive in fact started with glorious effects on 4 June, followed by an Italian counter-offensive on the 17th. The Germans had been 'using up' their reserves at Verdun without stint for over four months. On the Western Front the Allies were estimated to have a superiority of thirty divisions. The British Army was at its peak in men, material, and morale. Never before, and never again till the fall of 1918, were the prospects of a military victory over the German Army so attractive. Haig, tactically independent of both Joffre and the C.I.G.S., had worked out the details of the attack with his customary dull thoroughness. At the Cabinet of 27 June Asquith informed his colleagues that a simultaneous Allied offensive was being pursued on all fronts—Russian, Italian, and British in the West.[2]

This announcement was welcome, for in the months of preparation for the Somme the British nation had endured an uninterrupted series of defeats and disappointments.

In Mesopotamia General Townshend's twelve-thousand-man

---

[1] *Private Papers of Douglas Haig*, 144–5. See also *AF*, iv (2), Annexes nos. 128, 194, 301, and *Mémoires du maréchal Joffre*, ii. 236.
[2] Report to the King on the Cabinet of 27 Jan. 1916, Asquith Papers.

force at Kut-el-Amara had surrendered to the Turks on 29 April. A series of rescue attempts and a proffered bribe of a million pounds to the enemy commander had failed to secure their release. Many of the British troops, though not their egotistical commander, were never to be heard from again.

Map 5: The English Channel, North and Baltic Seas.

After Townshend's capitulation a defensive policy in Meso-potamia was reaffirmed.[1]

In the North Sea the long-expected battle between the British and German war-fleets had taken place off the Danish coast of Jutland on 1 June. The outcome, though strategically inconclu-sive, was a bitter disappointment to the British general public, political world, and naval profession. British sea-power had not performed the one mission for which Fisher had toiled to transform

---

[1] *Campaign in Mesopotamia*, iii. 3–4; C. R. M. F. Cruttwell, *A History of the Great War, 1914–1918* (2nd edn., Oxford, 1936), 347–9.

the Navy ever since 1904—the destruction of the German fleet. The Grand Fleet had lost fourteen ships, the High Seas Fleet eleven, and those mostly of lesser tonnage. The German gunnery had shown itself clearly more effective than the British. An Admiralty conference at the end of June decided in consequence that no general fleet action would be sought unless the German Navy began action against the British coast or was used in an invasion attempt. Sir John Jellicoe redoubled his caution, and after in August missing an encounter with the High Seas Fleet which he believed would have led him to a submarine ambush he determined that 'the fleet ought not to operate south of Lat. 55° 0' N. and the east of Long. 4° E.' About one-half of the North Sea (including almost all of the waters south of Scotland) was thus excluded from the Grand Fleet's 'zone of effective action', and the most powerful naval force that Britain had ever wielded had assumed a defensive posture which it would not succeed in abandoning for the remainder of the war.[1]

Four days after Jutland the North Sea claimed the life of the Englishman whose prestige probably still stood highest in the estimation of the general public. In the 'inner circle' that prestige had vanished. Even Asquith had turned against his Secretary of State for War. Longing to get away, Kitchener had succeeded in extracting an invitation from the astonished Emperor of Russia. On 5 June the cruiser *Hampshire*, detached from the Grand Fleet to convey Kitchener to Archangel, struck a mine. All but some dozen passengers and crew were drowned. The great soldier-statesman of the war had vanished; reconciliation to the fact of his death was so difficult that rumours of his survival long continued to circulate. None of the statesmen or military leaders left in public life filled the vacuum. The absence of leadership at the centre, long existent, became henceforth glaringly evident.[2]

---

[1] Falls, *Great War*, 217–18; Hankey, *Supreme Command*, ii. 492–3; Sir Henry Newbolt, *Naval Operations*, iii (2nd edn., 1940), 313–14, Appendixes E, F, and G, iv. 1–16, 24–26, 47–49.

[2] Sir George Arthur, *Life of Lord Kitchener* (1920), iii. 349–60; Hankey, *Supreme Command*, ii. 505–9; Maj.-Gen. Sir Alfred Knox, *With the Russian Army, 1914–1917* (1921), ii. 419–20; Donald McCormick, *The Mystery of Lord Kitchener's Death* (1959), *passim*; Philip Magnus, *Kitchener: Portrait of an Imperialist* (1958), 374–81; *Journals and Letters of Reginald Viscount Esher* (1934–8), iv. 32.

Who was to be the new Secretary of State for War? Robertson and the Army Council desired either Milner, then known as a prominent leader of what the radical *Nation* called the 'Junker' opposition; the genial Lord Derby, who would serve as figurehead; or Asquith himself with Derby as Under-Secretary. Asquith inclined, as he had the preceding November, to this last solution, but Bonar Law once again thwarted him and forced Lloyd George's claim. The promotion marked a further decline in the Prime Minister's authority, but there were compensations. As Edwin Montagu, currently Financial Secretary of the Treasury—and long a protégé of the Prime Minister, who had made his career—wrote to Asquith,[1] 'it would . . . be clearly advantageous to have L.G. at the War Office during the announcement of heavy casualties and a possibly unfruitful offensive'.

All possible precautions were taken to prevent Lloyd George 'interfering' with strategy. His desire for a return of the Munitions Ministry to War Office control and the abrogation of the Kitchener–Robertson agreement was not satisfied. Lord Derby, who was known for his 'loyalty' to the Army, was brought into the War Office as Under-Secretary of State for War and in addition given the position of President of the Army Council, a place hitherto reserved for the War Minister himself. Despite his advisers' pleas to the contrary Lloyd George, after a routine letter of refusal, took the office, fenced in as it was, cheerfully enough. As he took the oath of office the Clerk of the Privy Council remarked, 'I never saw him so radiant with satisfaction, positively inundating the atmosphere with a glow of conscious pride.'[2]

---

[1] Frank Owen, *Tempestuous Journey: Lloyd George His Life and Times* (N.Y., 1955), 319.

[2] Sir Almeric Fitzroy, *Memoirs* (Hutchinson, n.d.), ii. 630. Also Christopher Addison, *Politics from Within, 1914–1918* (1924), i. 261–3; Lord Beaverbrook, *Politicians and the War, 1914–1916* (N.Y., 1928), 225–37; Robert Blake, *The Unknown Prime Minister: The Life and Times of Andrew Bonar Law* (1955), 288–90; Randolph Churchill, *Lord Derby, King of Lancashire* (1959), 211–15; Owen, *Tempestuous Journey*, 316–19; *Riddell War Diary*, 189–95; Petrie, *Austen Chamberlain*, ii. 50–51. Munitions were given to Montagu, after a refusal from Austen Chamberlain, and Montagu in that capacity became a member of the War Committee. The appointment of such a lightweight indicates the real importance of this body.

V

THE SOMME

'L.G. burst out once, and said that we were all asked to keep silent
and bow the knee to this military Moloch.'

Diary, COLONEL REPINGTON, 25 October 1916.

A T 7.30 in the morning of 1 July, a hot sunny day, some one
hundred and forty thousand Imperial troops emerged
painfully from their trenches and, weighed down by their
packs, walked slowly upwards toward their destination for the
day—the second 'line' in the German defence system, two miles
away along the heights. For seven days the British guns had
artlessly sprayed sixteen hundred thousand shells into the enemy
lines, crippling the enemy's artillery. General Rawlinson, whose
Fourth Army made the main attack, had planned to launch the
infantry assault at dawn with only the enemy's first line as the
day's objective; but these precautions, in G.H.Q.'s opinion,
neglected both the overpowering effect of the Allied artillery
and the need for continued observation of that artillery's
targets. The British attack was delivered along fifteen miles of
a combined Franco-British twenty-three-mile front. All other
sectors along the British line were ordered to facilitate the
'break-in' by raids on the enemy lines and similar diversionary
tactics. For some three weeks all of G.H.Q.'s efforts were
directed to a successful penetration; the so-called 'wearing-out'
battle came later, and as second best.

At the end of the first day the results were clear. Along the
northern two-thirds of the British line of attack there had been
absolutely no progress. On the remaining six miles of the British
front the troops had succeeded only in puncturing the enemy's
first line. The infantry, which had advanced as on parade,
keeping carefully 'dressed', had been slaughtered by machine-
gun fire. At least fifty-seven thousand had fallen, some 60 per
cent. of the officers and 40 per cent. of the men engaged.

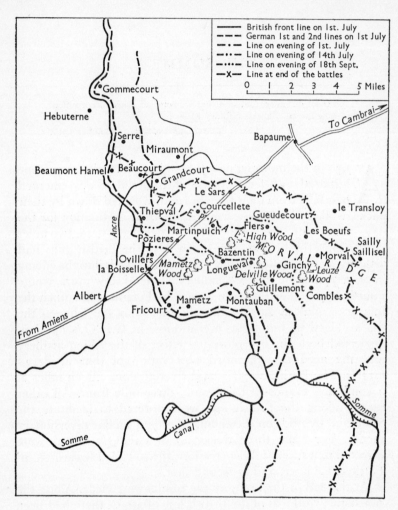

Map 6: The Somme Campaign.

The British Army had sustained the greatest loss in its history.[1]

If General Haig was discouraged he did not show it. He gave directions for renewal of the offensive and wrote the C.I.G.S. that[2]

It has not been possible to push on fast enough to deprive them [the Germans] of the possibility of bringing up reserves. . . . We have to be prepared for a struggle lasting for several weeks, and very exhausting to both sides . . . signs of serious demoralization are evident in many of the enemy's units.

On 14 July Rawlinson tried again. This time his forces attacked at dawn, in hopes of evading machine-gun fire, and under cover of a 'creeping' barrage. The enemy's second 'line' —along a ridge running between the villages of Morval and Thiepval, some two hundred feet above the British forces— was finally captured, but only along a three-mile front, two narrow for exploitation. A third assault, launched the night of the 22nd, failed to widen the breach.

Thereupon Haig changed, not his tactical objectives, but (at any rate 'for the record') their strategic basis. Battle was to continue 'to secure the whole of the MORVAL–THIEPVAL ridge', some nine miles wide, but 'as a basis for further operations, while at the same time wearing down the enemy's strength'. A renewed general assault to effect a breakthrough would be made in late September; in the meantime attacks would be made only with 'careful and methodical' preparation. 'We must practise such economy of men and material as will ensure our having the "last reserves" at our disposal when the crisis of the fight is reached.'[3]

[1] The literature on the battle of the Somme is extensive. The following works are of particular value: *Official History of Australia in the War of 1914–1918*, vol. iii. *The Australian Imperial Force in France, 1916* (1929 and subsequent edns.); *Les Armées françaises dans la Grande Guerre* (hereinafter cited as *AF*) t. iv., *Verdun et la Somme*; Great Britain. *History of the Great War*. Brig.-Gen. Sir James E. Edmonds, *Military Operations France and Belgium, 1916* (1932, 1938); C. R. M. F. Cruttwell, *A History of the Great War, 1914–1918* (2nd edn., 1936), 255–79; Cyril Falls, *The Great War* (N.Y., 1961), 195–208; Liddell Hart, *A History of the World War, 1914–1918* (1934), 303–31. A recent popular account is Brian Gardner, *The Big Push: A Portrait of the Battle of the Somme* (1961).   [2] *AIF in France, 1916*, 318.

[3] The Commander-in-Chief's Instructions to the Fourth and Reserve Armies, 2nd August. *Mil. Opns. Fr. and Bel. 1916*, ii, Maps and Appendixes, no. 13, pp. 34–36. See also *AIF in France, 1916*, 529.

It is hopeless to dignify this farrago or its application on the
field of battle with the term 'attrition'.[1] The intent at this stage,
though hardly the result, was less the 'wearing-out' of the enemy
than a temporary conservation of the British Army's own
resources.

The French contribution to the theoretically joint attack had
been more fruitful. On the first day the Sixth Army, one of a
Group of Armies under the command of General Foch, had
reached the German second line in one bound. Its losses were
on the fifth estimated at less than eight thousand men. The
C.I.G.S., observing these results, suggested to the French Army
representative at the War Office that Haig might well devote
his energies to further exploitation of the French breach. When
Joffre was informed he sharply rebuked his envoy, ordering him
to refuse discussion and warning him of the dangers of debate.
Joffre also recalled Foch to his headquarters at Chantilly and
reminded him of his task: to '*support the British forces on the north,*
our offensive on the south remaining secondary and always
subordinate to the results obtained on the north'.[2]

The French and British Commanders-in-Chief were, for
different reasons, equally determined that the Somme should
be in the main a British battle, and so it remained.

The C.I.G.S. continued to have difficulties. G.H.Q. France
was furnishing the War Office with no analysis of the progress
of the battle, and General Robertson complained that he had
'to depend almost entirely upon Press communiques'. The relief
of Verdun, on which the C.I.G.S. had laid so much stress in
his presentations to the War Committee, had already been
achieved. The German forces opposite that fortress had been
reduced in number the moment the preliminary bombardment
at the Somme had begun; the last German attack in the area,
on 11 July, had failed, and thereafter the German commander
was ordered to stand on the defensive. By the beginning of
August the General Staff reported to the Cabinet that the French
military authorities were no longer anxious about Verdun. It
added, moreover, that total losses of Empire troops in the Somme

---

[1] 'The Somme—Battle of Attrition', reads a chapter heading in Cyril Falls's
recent (1959) *The Great War*.
[2] *AF*, iv (2), Annexes nos. 2100, 2106. See also Maj.-Gen. Sir E. Callwell,
Field-Marshal Sir Henry Wilson: His Life and Diaries (1927), i. 287.

offensive had already mounted to 155,000 men. Concurrently, the Attorney-General, 'F. E.', circulated to the Cabinet an analysis of the battle written by Churchill. The memorandum stated that the British casualties were greater than the German, and expressed scepticism on the claim that many German divisions were being 'used up':[1]

We have not advanced 3 miles in the direct line at any point. We have only penetrated to that depth on a front of 8,000 to 10,000 yards. Penetration upon so narrow a front is quite useless for the purpose of breaking the line. It would be fatal to advance through a gap of this small size, which could be swept by a cross-fire of artillery. . . .

In *personnel* the results of the operation have been disastrous; in *terrain* they have been absolutely barren. . . . From every point of view . . . the British offensive *per se* has been a great failure. With twenty times the shell, and five times the guns, and more than double the losses, the gains have but little exceeded those of Loos.[2] And how was Loos viewed in retrospect?

Haig, apprised of this critique, arrived at the over-all conclusion that Churchill's judgement, always weak, had further deteriorated. A few days earlier Robertson had pleaded for a secret statement of Haig's achievements and objectives, on which the C.I.G.S. confessed himself unclear, and added that the War Committee might summon Haig to London. Haig's confidence remained unshaken. Not only had Verdun been relieved and the Russian successes in the East made possible, but, in the words of Haig's own summary,

Proof given to world that Allies are capable of making and maintaining a vigorous offensive and of driving enemy's best troops from the strongest positions has shaken faith of Germans, of their friends, of doubting neutrals in the invincibility of Germany. Also impressed on the world, England's strength and determination, and the fighting power of the British race.

[1] Letter, Robertson to Haig, 1 Aug. 1916. Field-Marshal Sir William Robertson, *Soldiers and Statesmen, 1914–1918* (1926), i. 270–1; Summary of the Military Situation . . . for the Seven Days ending 3rd Aug., with Comments by the General Staff. 3rd Aug. 1916. Asquith Papers; Memorandum. W. S. C. 1 Aug. 1916. Winston S. Churchill, *The World Crisis, 1911–1918* (4-vol. Odhams Press edn.), iii. 1054–9.
[2] The name of the village captured by the British forces in the offensive of the preceding autumn.

The only possible future action was 'maintenance of a steady offensive pressure'. Any less heroic course would weaken the faith of Britain's allies and her own army. 'In another six weeks, the enemy should be hard put to it to find men. . . .' However, 'It would not be justifiable to calculate on the enemy's resistance being completely broken by these means without another campaign next year.'

With this mishmash, which Robertson circulated to the War Committee and Cabinet, the Government had to remain content. Haig was assured by the War Committee 'that he might count on full support from home'. There was no further interference or inconvenient questioning from London. G.H.Q. was left undisturbed to prepare its second attempt at a breakthrough.[1]

During the whole of August and the first two weeks of September the 'wearing-out' battle was relentlessly pursued. This prolonged struggle did not secure the whole of the Morval–Thiepval ridge, but the capture of the villages of Guillemont and Ginchy in the first days of September widened the British front to seven miles.

Haig refused, in spite of repeated urgings from Joffre, to deliver a second general offensive along the original broad front of 1 July. Consequently the French attacks during the beginning of September were tactically unrelated to the British effort. But by mid-September G.H.Q. was confident that the enemy's defences and reserves had been so worn down and his morale so shaken as to warrant a second 'push' in full force, to be delivered from the British-held sector of the ridge. General Rawlinson's Fourth Army was again to make the main attack. 'The Chief', he noted in his diary, 'is anxious to have a gamble with all the available troops.' The danger, however, as Rawlinson went on to observe, was the effect of the preceding 'wearing-out' battle on the British Army's own effectives. 'We shall have no reserves in hand save tired troops.'[2]

[1] *The Private Papers of Douglas Haig, 1914–1919* (ed.) Robert Blake (1952), 157–9; Duff Cooper, *Haig* (1935), i. 345–6; *Mil. Opns. Fr. and Bel. 1916*, ii. 232; *Journals and Letters of Reginald Viscount Esher* (1934–8), iv. 40–43.

[2] Maj.-Gen. Sir Frederick Maurice, *The Life of General Lord Rawlinson of Trent* (1928), 170; *AF*, iv (3), Annexes nos. 2864, 2942, 3005, 3073, 3116; *Mil. Opns. Fr. and Bel. 1916*, ii. 300, Maps and Appendixes, App. 16, pp. 46–47 ('The general plan . . . will be . . . to press the main attack south of the Albert–Bapaume road with the object of securing the enemy's last line of prepared defences between Morval

For the battle G.H.Q. could now, it hoped, rely on some fifty models of the caterpillar, that 'somewhat desperate innovation', to quote the C.I.G.S.[1] This new instrument of war had been developed within the Admiralty under Churchill's inspiration and protection. He had informed Haig of its existence in December 1915. In February 1916 the 'tank', as it was now called for reasons of security, had undergone its first inspection in England for the benefit of a number of cabinet ministers and other Very Important Persons. Its trials there had been most successful.

Should such a revolutionary and promising weapon be employed at so early a stage in its development? Lloyd George, Churchill, Hankey, and others thought not, and they pressed their views on the Prime Minister, who so informed the Commander-in-Chief. Haig, however, aware that the forthcoming attack would be his last serious attempt of the year, was understandably convinced that all possible measures must be taken to make it a real success. By 15 September thirty-six tanks, the survivors of the original fifty-nine sent over, were employed in detachments of two or three as spearheads for the assault.[2]

During the two attacks of 15 and 25 September only nine of the tanks pushed ahead with the infantry. Another nine fell behind but helped to clear captured ground. The remainder either broke down or were ditched. Even so, the few tanks uncrippled by mechanical deficiencies helped by the end of September to clear the entire ridge of German troops.

By then, however, the Germans had erected new lines of defence; and when the British troops reached the valley below they discovered that, to quote General Charteris, Haig's Director of Intelligence, 'the Germans are now able to put their artillery at such ranges that we cannot reach them behind the ridge, whereas they can reach our infantry in front of it'. On

and Le Sars, with a view to opening the way for the cavalry'); Liddell Hart, *History of the World War*, 327–8. [1] Cooper, *Haig*, i. 359.

[2] The 'destroyer' or 'male' tanks carried two six-pounder guns; these were flanked and protected by 'man-killing' or 'female' tanks carrying four heavy machine-guns. Each tank had a crew of seven and moved at three miles an hour, less than an infantryman's pace. Churchill, *World Crisis*, iii. 1052–3; Cruttwell, *History of the Great War*, 271; *War Memoirs of David Lloyd George* (2-vol. Odhams Press edn.), i. 385; Lord Hankey, *The Supreme Command 1914–1918* (1961), ii. 513–14; Liddell Hart, *The Tanks* (1959), ii. 47–70; *Mil. Opns. Fr. and Bel. 1916*, ii. 232–5, 237–41, 245–9.

2 October the weather broke, and there began a steady down-pour, turning the battleground to mud. Nine days later Charteris belatedly remarked that 'I have been studying the weather records of this area for the last hundred years and find that October is the wettest month of the whole year'. The British troops, dispirited and exhausted, could not, as Rawlinson had earlier feared, effect any discernible progress under these con-ditions. Battle continued, but reflected no consistent plan or objective.[1]

So far, despite titanic efforts, the stalemate on the Western Front had remained unbroken. In the East, however, the Russians had assumed the offensive for the first time since the winter of 1914 and had penetrated into enemy territory. The Brusilov offensive, launched in early June from the Russian 'South-West Front' in response to an Italian appeal, was in-tended only as preliminary to a major attack to be delivered further north; but it crumpled the Austrian resistance, equal in physical strength but not in fortitude to the Russians. In spite of Brusilov's lack of ammunition or transport, his forces by mid-August had reached the slopes of the Carpathians and occupied the Bukovina, adjoining Rumania's north-west frontier.[2]

This success, combined with extreme French and Russian pressure, finally emboldened the Rumanian Government to declare war against Austria-Hungary. In exchange, however, Rumania demanded from the Entente not only extensive terri-torial concessions but also three hundred tons of munitions a day and, in order to 'contain' the Bulgarians, on whom Rumania refused to declare war, a preliminary offensive by the inter-national army at Salonika under General Sarrail.[3]

The British authorities in London, both military and govern-

---

[1] Brig.-Gen. John Charteris, *At G.H.Q.* (1931), 171–2; Cruttwell, *History of the Great War*, 274; Hart, *History of the World War*, 328–9; *AIF in France 1916*, 895–6; Lord P. C. Newton, *Retrospection* (1941), 228; *Mil. Opns. Fr. and Bel. 1916*, ii. 457–8.

[2] Falls, *Great War*, 220–7; Hart, *History of the World War*, 298–301; General Golovine, 'Brusilov's Offensive', *Slavonic Review* (April 1935), 571–96.

[3] Almost no diplomatic documents on the Rumanian intervention have been published. See, however, Albert Pingaud, 'L'intervention de la Roumanie dans la guerre européenne', *Revue d'histoire de la Guerre Mondiale* (1935), 117–51; *Mémoires du maréchal Joffre* (1932), ii. 313; Maurice Paléologue, *La Russie des tsars* (Paris: Plon, 1921–2), ii. 315–29; Cruttwell, *History of the Great War*, 293.

mental, watched the long negotiations with Rumania, which
were carried on principally by Russia, with scepticism and
detachment. The attempt to entice the Balkan powers into the
conflict, on which the British Government had so concentrated
its hopes and efforts throughout most of 1915, now appeared to
statesmen disillusioned by these past experiences futile and almost
irrelevant. Sir William Robertson made quite clear to the War
Committee his continued conviction that any serious operations
at Salonika would do more harm than good. 'Until the Bulgars
reduce their forces', he wrote to Grey, 'we have no prospect of
doing any good, and if we came to grief or failed to achieve
sufficient success to satisfy Rumania she might after all not
come in.'[1] Besides, War Office policy in Eastern Europe, as
Lloyd George reminded the editor of *The Times*, remained one
of attempting to persuade Bulgaria to change sides. Robertson's
observations to the War Committee and his orders to General
Milne faithfully reflected the C.I.G.S.'s conviction that there
should be no offensive until Rumania definitely entered the war,
if she ever did, and that even then the 'offensive' must be purely
demonstrative—bluff.[2]

At Rumanian insistence, the Entente Powers, Great Britain
included, agreed by a military convention signed 17 August to
the delivery of the three hundred tons of munitions a day. In
addition, 'The Allies undertake that a definite offensive ["offensive affirmée"] from Salonika shall precede by at least eight
days the entry of Rumania into the war, in order to facilitate the
mobilization and concentration of all the Rumanian military
forces. The offensive will begin on 20 August 1916.'[3]

How could these obligations be reconciled with Sir William
Robertson's expressed intentions? As to the nature of the military operations to be undertaken, the British civil authorities
experienced no difficulty. Lord Hardinge of Penshurst, Permanent Under-Secretary of State for Foreign Affairs, wrote

[1] Robertson, *Soldiers and Statesmen*, ii. 120.
[2] Capt. Cyril Falls, *Military Operations, Macedonia*, i (1933), 169–70; *AF*, iv (2),
Annexe no. 1812, viii (1), Annexes nos. 1369, 1370, 1384; Hankey, *Supreme Com-
mand*, ii. 533, which refers to 'obscure negotiations' with Bulgaria even after the
Rumanian declaration of war against Austria-Hungary; Joffre, *Mémoires*, ii. 309–10;
Georges Suarez, *Briand: Sa Vie — Son Œuvre*, iii (Paris: Plon, 1939), 358–60; Evelyn
Wrench, *Geoffrey Dawson and His Times* (1955), 137.
[3] *AF*, viii (1), Annexe no. 1457. Excerpts from the English translation are in
Mil. Opns. Macedonia, i. 139. See also Hankey, *Supreme Command*, ii. 532–4.

Robertson two days before the signing of the military convention that[1]

> After your very clear explanation at the War Committee a few days ago of the extent of offensive that our forces are prepared to take at Salonika as their immediate objective, Lord Grey and I both considered that the Rumanian text 'offensive affirmée' expresses sufficiently clearly the intentions of our military authorities.

As to the date, Bulgarian foresight and General Sarrail's dilatoriness ensured that the Salonika Army would not begin offensive operations until Rumania had been thoroughly committed. On 18 August Joffre telegraphed Sarrail ordering him to begin his offensive two days later. But on the same day as Joffre's telegram the Bulgarians moved first in an attack on the flanks of the Salonika Army. In the west they seized the town of Florina, which commanded the mountain pass into Serbia, and in the east that of Kavalla, which the Entente Powers had proposed to turn over to Bulgaria themselves to procure her adhesion to their cause. General Sarrail thereupon vented his fury on the Greeks, who had ceded Kavalla without resistance, rather than on the Bulgars, and postponed offensive action until 10 September, over two weeks after the Rumanian declaration of war. In the meantime he sponsored a Venizelist revolution at Salonika which eventually through Allied armed support would develop into the government of Greece. In the lukewarm operations which then ensued the British contingent guarded Sarrail's right flank and 'demonstrated' their presence through a series of raids and occasional local attacks. None of these operations, however, affected Bulgarian action against Rumania.[2]

Even before the Salonika 'offensive' began it was evident that Rumania was in peril. Germany, Bulgaria, and Turkey promptly declared war in support of their ally. At the end of August the replacement of Falkenhayn by Hindenburg as Chief of Staff was rightly interpreted as heralding a renewed German thrust to the East. It was not long in coming. Already in the first days of September a German–Bulgarian–Turkish force

---

[1] Robertson, *Soldiers and Statesmen*, ii. 121.

[2] *AF*, viii (1), Annexe no. 1462, (2), pp. 100–39; Cruttwell, *History of the Great War*, 300; Falls, *Great War*, 238–41; Asquith Papers.

under General Mackensen crossed the Bulgarian frontier and invaded the Dobrudja.

Rumania was ill-prepared to meet the danger. The bulk of her forces were in Transylvania; the Brusilov offensive had ground to a halt, and General Alexiev refused to give the Rumanians any further assistance; while the promised munitions had not and would not arrive. They had to be delivered through Russia, whose transport facilities were primitive and officials unhelpful. But it will not do to put all the blame on the Tsarist Empire. As Dr. Addison, a follower of Lloyd George and currently Parliamentary Secretary to the Office of Munitions, noted:[1] 'Everybody had a good deal of scepticism about Roumania actually coming in until the final step was taken and ... we were holding off doing much in the way of munitions for them.' From Britain she never did receive more than what the official history of the Ministry of Munitions calls 'miscellaneous stores'.[2]

Lloyd George as Secretary of State for War asked the C.I.G.S. in a memorandum on 4 September what now could or should be done for Rumania. The answer, given to the War Committee five days later, was predictable. The continuance and intensification of the offensive upon the Somme might so threaten the security of the German lines as to prevent the execution of the plan to attack Rumania. Any other strategy would be a flagrant, inexcusable, surrender of the initiative to the enemy.[3]

The September 'push' in the West came and went, however, with no discernible effect on the Balkans. Between the beginning of the Brusilov offensive and the 'tank' attack in the West the German headquarters transferred fifteen divisions from the Western Front to the East.[4] In October the forces under General Falkenhayn repulsed the Rumanian invasion of Transylvania and drove the invaders back to their border along the South

[1] Christopher Addison, *Politics from Within, 1911–1918* (1924), i. 266.

[2] *History of the Ministry of Munitions*, vol. ii, pt. viii, pp. 58–59, 68, 70, 88–99 (from which appendix it appears that in 1916 Rumania received from England in all 400 machine-guns and 100 tons of high explosives). See also Hankey, *Supreme Command*, ii. 534; Pingaud, 'L'intervention de la Roumanie', *Revue d'histoire de la Guerre Mondiale* (1935), 146; and Suarez, *Briand*, 358–60.

[3] Possible Action of the Central Powers during the Autumn and Winter of 1916. General Staff, War Office, 9 Sept. 1916, Asquith Papers. Summarized in Robertson, *Soldiers and Statesmen*, ii. 123–4; Lloyd George, *War Memoirs*, i. 324–5.

[4] According to Cruttwell, *History of the Great War*, 288.

Carpathians. Meanwhile General Mackensen's troops captured Constantsa, Rumania's chief seaport, and rapidly occupied all of the country east of the Danube.

The impending collapse of Rumania could only be averted, Robertson continued to assert, committed as he was to operations in the West, through Russian action and renewed pressure at the Somme. How irritating proposals for change in the Empire's 'fixed' strategy must have been! Within the War Committee Lloyd George urged that the British, French, and Italian Governments should between them promptly send reinforcements of eight divisions to Salonika for a concentrated attack on Sofia. Such a force, General Milne reported, might secure at any rate a limited success. Robertson was enraged at his Secretary of State's 'interference', all the more dangerous because it coincided with the urgings of the French and Russian Governments and military authorities. He personally threatened Lloyd George with resignation; the General Staff would refuse to issue orders for reinforcements. The next day, 10 October, Robertson sent for Colonel Repington and told him what had transpired. Repington in his turn informed Lord Northcliffe, who, 'much exercised', stormed into Lloyd George's office and threatened to 'destroy' the Secretary of State for War by means of all the powerful resources of his newspapers.[1]

Lord Northcliffe could not, however, ward off the pressure from France and Russia. British and French ministers met at a conference at Boulogne on 20 October, and once again the British were informed that Briand's government would fall unless something were done for France's allies in Eastern Europe. Thereupon the War Committee decided to reinforce its contingent in Greece by one second-line Territorial Force division, currently in France. The division had not yet experienced any action beyond a trench raid, and, in the words of the official historian of the 'Macedonian' campaign, 'was not yet at its best'. Robertson reluctantly agreed that the Government really had no other choice. The reinforcement was meant only as a symbol of unity; it was not expected to—and did not—have any

---

[1] Lord Beaverbrook, *Politicians and the War, 1914–1916*, ii (n.d. but 1932), 121; *Esher Journals*, iv. 58; Frank Owen, *Tempestuous Journey: Lloyd George His Life and Times* (N.Y., 1955), 324–5; Lieut.-Col. C. à Court Repington, *The First World War, 1914–1918* (Boston, 1921), 358–61; Robertson, *Soldiers and Statesmen*, ii. 127–9. Lloyd George's omission of this incident from his *War Memoirs* is curious.

military value. The 60th (London) Division assembled at Salonika on Christmas Day. By then operations from that city had ceased and the Rumanian capital of Bucharest had fallen.[1]

During all the summer and autumn of 1916 the prolonged slaughter on the Western Front had had as yet no evident military effect other than the relief of Verdun, long since attained. The round-up of the Rumanian armies had not been prevented. Nor was the balance sheet of 'attrition' at all encouraging. Germany, according to the Imperial General Staff's own estimate of 26 October, had recently *increased* her effective military manpower by three hundred thousand. Behind the 5,470,000 troops on active service she had in addition two million reserves still available. Meanwhile, the British casualties on the Western Front in the four months from July through October had mounted to the horrifying total of over four hundred and fifty thousand, of which more than one hundred thousand had died.[2]

These unavoidable facts necessarily rendered General Robertson's position as the supreme arbiter of British strategy insecure. During the autumn of 1916 he had to contend with a number of attempts by the 'politicians' to evade what Robertson considered to be the indispensable implications of Western strategy. The C.I.G.S. was forced to keep an alert eye, and on occasion even adopt a rearguard action, on operations not only in the Balkans, but also in Egypt, Mesopotamia, and even the Red Sea. In addition he had to cope with personal manœuvres designed, or so he concluded, to weaken his authority. And finally he had—though only briefly—to counter an attack against the overall strategic policy for which he stood.

The internal struggle with reference to operations in the Balkans has already been described. South of the Aegean further

---

[1] *Mil. Opns. Macedonia*, i. 201–2, 220; Telegram, Foreign Office to Lord Granville, Paris, 24 Oct. 1916 ('Despatch of the division must not be regarded as in any way modifying the opinion hitherto held by the War Committee that a decision must be sought on the Western Front and that therefore all detachments of troops from that front to the Balkans or elsewhere should be reduced to the minimum'). *AF*, viii (2), Annexe no. 1185; Hankey, *Supreme Command*, ii. 535–7; Sarah Gertrude Millin, *General Smuts* (1936), ii. 28; Repington, *First World War*, 371–2, 376–7.

[2] Lloyd George, *War Memoirs*, i. 536–9; Robertson, *Soldiers and Statesmen*, i. 274–9; 'Approximate Casualties by Months in the Expeditionary Force, France', *Statistics of the Military Effort of the British Empire during the Great War, 1914–1920*, The War Office, March 1922 (H.M.S.O., 1922), pp. 258–9.

trouble for the C.I.G.S., if also for the Ottoman Empire, had been precipitated by the 'natives' under nominal Turkish overlordship.

In June 1916 Sherif Hussein, Amir of Mecca, had proclaimed the, or rather an, Arab revolt against the Turkish rule in the Hedjaz. Several days later the Turkish garrison in Mecca surrendered. The War Committee thereupon pressed the desirability of an advance of the Egyptian Expeditionary Force across the Sinai Peninsula to improve the prospects of a widespread Arab rebellion and generally to stir up trouble for the Turks. Sir Archibald Murray henceforth justified his proposed march to the small coastal town of El Arish, on the peninsula just west of Palestine, both in terms of the security of Egypt and the Suez canal (which made sense to Robertson) and in terms of 'harassment' of the Turks in Syria (which did not).

The defeat of a Turkish raiding party under the leadership of a German officer at the 'Battle' of Romani on 4 August indicated that the E.E.F. could well afford to think in offensive rather than in defensive terms. During the autumn little action took place, but with the aid of conscripted Egyptian labour a standard-gauge railway and 12-inch pipe line were laid across the Sinai desert. No such effort was of course ever devoted to Salonika. By the end of October the railway was within striking distance of the Turkish position at Arish. What the policy for Murray's command would be after it fell had not been decided.[1]

The War Committee, supported within the Cabinet notably by Lord Curzon, from time to time also pressed Robertson to dispatch one brigade of troops to the Red Sea to secure Mecca, the Holy City of Islam, from Turkish recapture. The C.I.G.S. as often declined and in November finally flatly refused to issue the requisite order.[2]

With regard to the operations of the Salonika Army and the

---

[1] *AF*, viii (2), Annexe no. 503, ix (1), Annexes nos. 72, 113; Capt. Cyril Falls and Lieut.-Gen. Sir G. McMunn, *Military Operations Egypt and Palestine*, i (1928), 178, 230–2, 245–7, 258; *Mil. Opns. Macedonia*, i. 202; Field-Marshal Earl Wavell, *The Palestine Campaigns* (1931 edn., numerous printings), 46–63 ('the . . . British . . . turn the desert into a workshop and call it war', p. 59); Hankey, *Supreme Command*, ii. 531–2.

[2] *Mil. Opns. Egypt and Palestine*, i. 232–4; Robertson, *Soldiers and Statesmen*, ii. 153–63; Wavell, *Palestine Campaigns*, 55.

Egyptian Expeditionary Force Robertson during the fall of 1916 at any rate held his own against the politicians of the War Committee. But on 'Mesopotamia' he encountered his first—small but definite—setback.

After the surrender of Townshend's forces at Kut a defensive policy in the Mesopotamian theatre had been reaffirmed. But what did this imply? There was no real question of complete evacuation; the control of the entire Persian Gulf—achieved earlier as a result of the original expedition to Basra and of Russia's subsequent agreement to cede central Persia to British control as a *quid pro quo* for Constantinople—would not be so easily yielded. During the summer and autumn of 1916 British rule in the hinterland of the head of the Persian Gulf was in no way menaced. On the Tigris only minor operations were taking place. Surely, Robertson argued, the Mesopotamia Expeditionary Force should at least withdraw to Amara (still one hundred miles north of Basra on the river Tigris), which had been taken in June 1915. The War Committee would not agree. Several of its members saw no reason why the force should not again prepare to take Baghdad.

The new commander in Mesopotamia, Robertson's own choice, Lieutenant-General Sir Stanley Maude, a very capable, experienced, and energetic officer, who had revitalized the hitherto bedraggled force, was averse to any retreat. The Government and Robertson compromised. On 28 September the War Committee resolved that railway construction and other improvements in communication would continue to be undertaken 'in view of a possible future advance on Baghdad, which is, however, not at present contemplated'. Two days later the C.I.G.S. wired Maude that his mission was 'to maintain our occupation of Basrah Vilayet'. It was also 'the desire of His Majesty's Government, if and when possible, to establish British influence in the *Baghdad*[1] Vilayet'. Several weeks later the Commander-in-Chief in India, General Monro, wired that General Maude's forthcoming operations would ensure that 'greater control would be exercised by us over all tribesmen, and confidence in our prestige and intention to stay would be greatly increased'.[2]

[1] Author's italics.
[2] Robertson, *Soldiers and Statesmen*, ii. 74.

For the first time in the history of the war British military operations were being undertaken for the expressed principal purpose of extending the British Empire. It would not be the last.[1]

These compromises on policy in minor theatres—which did not affect the main strategic theme—were bearable. But there were in addition vexatious personal disputes. The Secretary of State for War was continually urging Robertson to go to Russia to confer with General Alexieff on that country's needs. The success of the Brusilov offensive, with inferior material and numbers only equal to the enemy, had presented an unpleasant but hopeful contrast to the Somme. It was true that the Russian advance had been at Austrian and not at German expense, but even this was not a negligible accomplishment. What might not Russia do if she were only equipped with ammunition and in particular heavy artillery!

Robertson could not in principle deny the desirability of furnishing Russia with material; and in October told Haig that heavy artillery originally intended for the British armies in France was being sent to Russia before the winter closing of its ports.[2] The C.I.G.S., however, suspected, and perhaps with reason, that if he did not drown on the way like Kitchener he would, again like Kitchener on an earlier occasion, find himself deposed in all but name upon his return. He would not go, and in his refusal was supported by the King, who affirmed, 'I will not hear of it'.[3]

Meanwhile Lloyd George had dispatched Field-Marshal Sir John French, now Viscount French of Ypres, on a visit to the French sector of the Western Front to study their artillery tactics. This sign of independence aroused the strongest resentment and suspicions at G.H.Q. Already Lloyd George had asked Foch how the latter had succeeded in keeping his casualties down at the Somme. 'I would not have believed', Haig then noted, 'that a British Minister could have been so ungentlemanly as to go to a foreigner and put such questions regarding his own subordi-

---

[1] C. E. Callwell, *Life of Sir Stanley Maude* (1920), *passim*; Hankey, *Supreme Command*, ii. 530–1; Brig.-Gen. F. I. Moberly, *The Campaign in Mesopotamia, 1914–1918* (1923–7), iii. 42–56; Field-Marshal Sir William Slim, *Unofficial History* (1959), 42.

[2] *Private Papers of Douglas Haig*, 172.

[3] Randolph Churchill, *Lord Derby, King of Lancashire* (1959), 222–4. See also Beaverbrook, *Politicians and the War*, ii. 115–17; *Private Papers of Douglas Haig*, 171; Lloyd George, *War Memoirs*, i. 461–4; Hankey, *Supreme Command*, ii. 556–7.

nates.' And now,[1] 'this employment of F.M. French . . . by the S. of S. coupled with the desire which he expressed of sending Robertson to Russia for two months, seems to indicate a definite desire to have a puppet like French in the War Office as C.I.G.S. instead of Robertson'. Robertson told Lord Esher that the appointment of Sir John French as acting C.I.G.S. during the proposed visit to Russia had already been arranged.[2]

These skirmishes were mere incidents, serving only to increase the military's suspicions of their Secretary of State. But at the beginning of November Lloyd George made his first attempt within the War Committee to change Britain's over-all strategic policy. The Prime Minister's eldest son, the brilliant and attractive Raymond Asquith, had been killed in Haig's second attempt at a breakthrough, on 18 September. According to Lloyd George it became 'almost impossible' to discuss the tactics upon the Western Front thereafter with the Prime Minister. 'You can see how it hurts him.' In late September, as a matter of fact, Asquith still seemed to think the German lines might be broken, opening the way to the cavalry.[3]

Two memoranda by Robertson, elicited by Lloyd George, finally served to clear the air. These expressed the C.I.G.S.'s conviction that the continuance of the 'Western' policy was essential.

We must make available for the Army all men fit for military service who can by any expedient be released; and having got the men we must place them where they can best make their might felt: there must be no mistakes in our grand strategy. . . . Our forces in France should be at the greatest possible strength by next spring . . . all the resources of the Empire, and all demands for men for whatever purpose, should be examined from that point of view.

He could not however say when or even precisely how this concentration would bring about Germany's defeat. After all, he reminded the War Committee on 3 November, 'we are not fighting for some comparatively minor object which we might

[1] *Private Papers of Douglas Haig*, 170.
[2] Ibid. 167–70; R. Churchill, *Derby*, 227; *Esher Journals*, iv. 66–67; Major the Hon. Gerald French, *The Life of Field-Marshal Sir John French* (1931), 344; Hankey, *Supreme Command*, ii. 555.
[3] *Esher Journals*, iv. 55; *Lord Riddell's War Diary, 1914–1918* (n.d. but c. 1933), 214; Asquith Papers.

hope to attain after giving the enemy a sound beating, but we are to continue the war "until the military domination of Prussia is wholly and finally destroyed" '. What was needed was 'more men and more guns and munitions' in the West, where 'a moral and material ascendency' over the enemy was being 'steadily' gained.[1]

If we do this, and if we do not fritter away our efforts in non-vital theatres, and if Russia can be supplied with a reasonable amount of heavy artillery and other necessary war material, we may hope that in the future the pressure upon the enemy on both fronts will be not less severe than it has been in the past. . . . [Even so] I think we shall be well advised not to expect the end at any rate before the summer of 1918. How long it may go on afterwards I cannot even guess.

This was certainly not very encouraging. The War Committee thereafter held a series of meetings at which, to Robertson's mystification, military and naval advisers were excluded; and Lloyd George, no longer fearful that Lord Northcliffe might be listening, castigated the Western policy. In its place he recommended that the forthcoming conference of Allied commanders at Chantilly to settle the strategy for 1917 be postponed by a week, and that the French, British, and Italian Governments hold a conference of *ministers only* beforehand. This would be followed by a military conference in Russia, 'preferably at the Russian General Headquarters', to 'be attended by the principal generals from the West, preferably Generals Robertson, Joffre, Castelnau and Cadorna'. There would also be a governmental conference in Russia, to which the Allies would send their most eminent statesmen. Grey, forsaking the habits of a lifetime, was to be the British representative. These proposals, Lloyd George later stated, 'were approved in principle'. The continuance of the Somme offensive into 1917 was deprecated. Appropriate telegrams to Paris and Rome were immediately dispatched; and both the French and Italian Governments agreed to the preliminary conference of Governments in Paris. Robertson was informed that his presence in Russia was essential; but, once

[1] C.I.G.S. Memoranda of 26 Oct. and 3 Nov. 1916. See Lloyd George, *War Memoirs*, i. 536–41; *Mil. Opns. Fr. and Bel. 1916*, ii. 533; Robertson, *Soldiers and Statesmen*, i. 274–9.

PLATE 8

b. General Sir Hubert Gough Commander, Fifth Army

a. Arthur J. Balfour, First Lord of the Admiralty (with General Rawlinson), at G.H.Q., October 1916

again declining argument, simply refused to leave. In this refusal he was backed by the titular leader of the Conservative party, Mr. Bonar Law.[1]

These moves certainly implied at the minimum the intention on the part of the War Committee to support the demands of the Russian at the expense of the Western Front.

How far G.H.Q. in France divined the Government's novel assumption of initiative is uncertain, but there could be no doubt of the dissatisfaction in England with the lack of progress at the Somme. In the House of Commons the Prime Minister on 11 October had been able to announce no more than that 'By these operations we have since 1 July advanced a distance of some seven miles on a front of nine miles'; and Sir Edward Carson in reply had underlined the fact that this progress, 'won at considerable cost', showed that 'it is no use concealing either from ourselves or from the country that we still have before us a Herculean task'. Some ten days later Mr. Balfour on a visit to G.H.Q. had remarked to the officer accompanying him 'that in view of the losses sustained since July 1st, if the Battle of the Somme ended on the present line and we failed to break through, it would be looked upon by the public as a defeat'.[2]

There were rumours at G.H.Q. that F. E. Smith, Churchill, and others had 'banded together' in an effort to have Haig removed from his command, as Sir John French had been after an equally unsuccessful, but far less costly, campaign season the year before.[3]

The Somme campaign was visibly dying. Haig had long given up hopes of any breakthrough. The cavalry had been ordered returned to the rear. The battlefield was a sea of mud; the troops could not advance and the high-explosive shells, piercing deep into the earth before bursting, merely churned up the terrain. The extreme exhaustion of the troops and the

---

[1] Beaverbrook, *Politicians and the War*, ii. 116–17; *AF*, v (1), Annexe no. 88; R. Churchill, *Derby*, 226–7 (Letter to Lloyd George, 12 Nov. 1916, 'If Grey and Kiggell go with planning powers, he, Robertson, will have to accept whatever decisions they may come to . . .'); Lloyd George, *War Memoirs*, i. 541–4; Viscount Grey of Fallodon, *Twenty-Five Years, 1892–1916* (N.Y., 1925), ii. 130; Hankey, *Supreme Command*, ii. 556–7; Repington, *First World War*, i. 386–7.

[2] *Esher Journals*, iv. 62–64.

[3] Great Britain. *5 Parliamentary Debates* (Commons), xxxv (11 Oct. 1916), 102–6; *Private Papers of Douglas Haig*, 170.

state of the ground, Lieutenant-General Sir Launcelot Kiggell, Haig's Chief of Staff, informed General Joffre's representative, quite prevented the broad-front attacks the French commander continued to demand. Eventually Haig wrote Joffre a letter telling him in no uncertain terms to mind his own business.[1]

The morale of the British and Imperial troops, so high in early summer, had descended to a low point. Before the Somme the supreme punishment in the Australian Imperial Force was to be sent home in disgrace. The 'wearing-out' battle in August had made, according to the Australian 'Eyewitness' and subsequent Official Historian, a permanent impression on this exceptionally fine body of men, and henceforth imprisonment had to be introduced. In October there were cases of desertion to the enemy among the British troops, hitherto a very rare occurrence, and the Germans had even been informed of an oncoming attack. The first officer to be tried and shot for desertion since Haig's assumption of command was ordered executed in December. 'No one', a corps commander pointedly protested to G.H.Q. against a scheduled attack, 'who has not visited the Front can really know that state of exhaustion to which the men are reduced.'[2]

Under these conditions the prospects for G.H.Q. at the forthcoming Allied Commanders' Conference at Joffre's headquarters at Chantilly on 15 November were not encouraging. The French during the first days of November had mounted a counter-offensive in the Verdun area and, making an advance of some two miles, recaptured Forts Douaumont and Vaux. What trophies could the British command offer? Surely none in their present battlefield. 'The mud in front was quite terrible', Haig noted on a visit to H.Q. Fifth Army. Yet just north and west of the Morval–Thiepval ridge, in the valley of the river Ancre, he added (hopefully?), 'the ground is fit to attack over'.[3]

The commander of the Fifth Army was General Sir Hubert

[1] *AIF in France, 1916*, 894–6; Newton, *Retrospection*, 228–9; *AF*, iv (3), Annexes nos. 1052, 1094, 1137 (Letter, Haig to Joffre, 19 Oct. 1916. 'I must remind you that it lies with me to judge what I can undertake and when I can undertake it'), 1541; *Private Papers of Douglas Haig*, 172–4.

[2] Liddell Hart, *History of the World War*, 330; *AIF in France, 1916*, 862–73, 894, 918, 940; *Private Papers of Douglas Haig*, 183.

[3] *Private Papers of Douglas Haig*, 174.

de la P. Gough, an officer noted for his dash and 'cavalry spirit'. On 8 and 10 November Gough was paid a visit by Haig's Chief of Staff. General Kiggell first reminded Gough of the forthcoming conference at Chantilly, and added,[1]

the heavy losses entailed by the fighting at the Somme and elsewhere were making their effects felt at home, and sorrow, suffering and anxiety were undoubtedly weakening the resolution of some people. Murmurs were heard in the country. Mr. Lloyd George, always sensitive to the breath of public opinion, was already feeling a lack of confidence in Haig and was no longer giving him his whole-hearted support; in fact, it is not too much to say that he was already intriguing against him. Talk of the responsibility of finding another Chief was in the air, and suggestions were seriously made that we should fight our main battles in some theatre of operations other than against the principal and, in fact, the only enemy which counted —the Germans.

A change in the strategy which had so far guided the British and Allied Councils, might have far-reaching and disastrous consequences, but if it were possible for the Fifth Army to win some success before the date of the conference, the Chief's position in maintaining the right policy would be materially strengthened, and an atmosphere of greater confidence created.

The Commander-in-Chief himself visited Gough on Sunday the 12th. He entered into no details on his own personal position, but, reminding Gough of the Conference to meet on Wednesday, said, according to Haig's own diary, that: 'The British position will doubtless be much stronger (as memories are short) if I could appear there on the top of the capture of Beaumont Hamel for instance, and 3,000 German prisoners.'[2]

Gough was more than willing, and the next morning the attack was launched. The first day's work appeared a brilliant little success. By 1 p.m., Haig noted, 'it was reported that the whole of the ridge from Beaumont Hamel to Beaucourt was in our possession. . . . After lunch I went to H.Q. Fifth Army and thanked Gough. . . . The success has come at a most opportune moment.'[3] The next day's operations were less spectacular and Haig upon his departure for Chantilly ordered them shut down.

[1] General Sir Hubert Gough, *The Fifth Army* (1931), 155-6.
[2] *Private Papers of Douglas Haig*, 176.
[3] Cooper, *Haig*, i. 365.

Gough, confident of the prospects, succeeded in having this instruction countermanded, and the attack continued for two days more, when the first blizzard of the winter brought it, and the whole Somme campaign, to an end.[1]

The 'Battle of the Ancre' had advanced a mile or so and captured a German salient which, to quote the British official history, 'had few merits as a defensive position for the winter'. General Gough later recorded that 'I was glad to know that the result of the battle was not confined to the very severe defeat we had inflicted on the enemy'. Mud had hampered the operations after all, and some men drowned in it. The casualties incurred for this trophy, on which the Prime Minister, General Joffre, and others of the great congratulated Haig in Paris, were over twenty-three thousand human beings.[2]

[1] *Private Papers of Douglas Haig*, 176–7; *Mil. Opns. Fr. and Bel. 1916*, ii. 509–24.
[2] George A. B. Dewar assisted by Lieut.-Col. J. H. Boraston, *Sir Douglas Haig's Command: December 19, 1915, to November 1, 1918* (1923), i. 190; *Esher Journals*, iv. 65–67; Gough, *Fifth Army*, 159; *Private Papers of Douglas Haig*, 179; *Mil. Opns. Fr. and Bel. 1916*, ii. 524.

VI

THE LEAP IN THE DARK

'The responsibility of those who needlessly prolong such a War is not less than that of those who needlessly provoke it.'
LORD LANSDOWNE, Memorandum for the Cabinet, 13 November 1916.

THE campaign season for 1916 was over, and 'victory' was further off than ever. Rumania was being overrun, food supplies were running low, and the menace of submarine warfare appeared for the first time as a mortal danger to Britain's survival. It was natural that, during the last phases of the Somme campaign, men in the cold, damp, foggy gloom of a London winter should wonder if they must continue on the path they had chosen to tread.

In early November the War Committee, it will be recalled, had proposed a ministerial conference at Paris between the French, British, and Italian Governments for the purpose of placing greater emphasis henceforth on the Russian front; and had concurrently urged postponement of the inter-allied military conference due to meet at General Joffre's headquarters at Chantilly. The Chantilly conference convened on schedule none the less. A copy of the War Committee telegram to the French foreign minister conveying the aforementioned proposals had somehow fallen into Robertson's hands. The C.I.G.S. promptly sent this information as a 'Personal and Secret' telegram to General Joffre, who refused Briand's request for postponement. Consequently on 15 November the military and governmental conferences on the future strategy of the Entente opened simultaneously, and in conflict, at Chantilly and Paris respectively.[1]

[1] France. *Les Armées françaises dans la Grande Guerre* [hereinafter cited as *AF*], v (1), Annexe no. 88; *War Memoirs of David Lloyd George* (2-vol. Odhams Press edn.), i. 543-4; Lord Hankey, *The Supreme Command, 1914-1918* (1961), ii. 556; Georges Suarez, *Briand: Sa Vie — Son Œuvre*, iv (Paris: Plon, 1940), 3; Report, Prime Minister to the King, 13 Nov. 1916 (Asquith and Lloyd George are going to France to discuss with Briand an Allied Great Power conference in Russia on war strategy and diplomacy), Asquith Papers.

Lloyd George had prepared for the occasion a very long memorandum—to be submitted to M. Briand, the French *Président du Conseil*—written in his best prosecuting attorney style. The Prime Minister omitted a number of the more strident passages and made a number of minor changes which revised the tone and squeezed some of the juice out of the document. Even so it remained a formidable indictment. In over two years of war none of the major operations undertaken by either England or France had been successful. The Entente was about to lose all of south-east Europe. Further blunders would mean 'throwing away the chance of final victory'. German military man-power had actually increased, and every year a further million young men came of military age. Conquered Poland offered a further source of man-power of which Germany was preparing to take full advantage. The strategy of attrition, which now appeared to be the Allies' only policy for winning the war, not only ignored these facts but also the possibility of declining Allied morale on the home front (this section Asquith deleted) and the actual dangers of lack of credit and the submarine war against shipping.

'The importance of this [last] cannot be exaggerated.' Till a few weeks since the Allies had been holding their own against this new kind of warfare, but undoubtedly

during the last few weeks the destruction of Allied and neutral tonnage has [been most] alarming . . ., and unless effective steps can be taken to check it the consequences may be of the most serious character to the armies of the Allies. . . . Time is no longer in our favour. . . . But so far as the British Government can judge, the operations in the west, if continued on the present footing, hold out no hope of our inflicting on the German armies in 1917 a defeat sufficiently crushing to put an end to the War, unless we are able to reinforce them by much greater efforts in the other theatres of war.

What could be accomplished in these other theatres? The stalemate on the Italian front offered little hope of progress. The Russian fronts showed far more promise, but 'there will be great difficulties to overcome before serious progress can be made'. In south-east Europe 'the elimination of Bulgaria . . . would isolate Turkey, which would then be compelled to die of exhaustion, and would bring the Entente Powers markedly nearer to final victory'. 'The object of the conference [in Russia] must be to determine what it is possible to do on the Eastern Front, and what is the nature and importance of the help which the west ought to give to the east for those operations which are judged to be necessary.'[1]

When Asquith read this memorandum to Briand the French Premier, who had just returned from a mauling in the Chamber by Clemenceau, appeared harassed and inattentive. But in his welcoming speech to the delegates Briand too, who now had his own reasons for being dissatisfied with General Joffre's direction, urged that the time had come for the ministers of the Entente to take the strategy of the war into their own hands. The British proposal for a conference in Russia was accepted by the French and Italian Governments. Lloyd George then urged:[2]

We have got to help Russia and Roumania, not by taking from the surplus of our production, but by drawing if it must be upon what is necessary for ourselves;

and proposed that

The Governments represented at the present conference shall enter into an engagement to furnish in the fullest possible measures to their Allies the full military equipment asked for by the conference, which will be held in Russia, even if this should result in a certain slowing down in the equipment of their own Armies, and Russia shall on its side enter into an engagement to conform to the decisions adopted by this conference.

These proposals commanded general but verbal assent, and the Russian conference was agreed to 'in principle'.[3]

That same day, however, the military conference at Chantilly drafted resolutions drawn up by General Joffre's staff. These were not in harmony with the agreements reached in Paris, though in the event the decisions of both conferences proved equally abortive. Haig and Joffre had already agreed that during the spring of 1917 the French and British Armies

---

[1] Statement drafted by Mr. Lloyd George as a Basis for the Prime Minister's Statement at the Paris Conference on 15 Nov. 1916. Arthur Henderson Papers, Library of the Trades Union Congress, London. The version printed in Lloyd George, *War Memoirs*, i. 545–55, which also indicates Asquith's omission, is almost but not quite identical. The summary and quotations in the text are from the unexpurgated version. See also Hankey, *Supreme Command*, ii. 557–8.

[2] Lloyd George, *War Memoirs*, i. 562–3.

[3] Ibid. i. 555–66; Hankey, *Supreme Command*, ii. 559–61.

would undertake two separate broad-front offensives: the French
between the rivers of the Oise and the Somme, the British some
twelve miles north between the villages of Bapaume and Vimy.
Thus all pretence of tactical co-ordination between the two
armies was abandoned. The French infantry strength was due
to decrease by a third in the course of 1917. At a subsequent
conference of British Army Commanders Haig gave a 'briefing',
and, as summarized by General Rawlinson, indicated that 'The
French can put up one more big battle, and thereafter we shall
have to take the chief part.'[1]

Joffre and Robertson wanted the 1917 offensive to take place
in February or March to avoid the Germans' forestalling the
Allies as at Verdun. Haig, however, insisted that the new
offensive could not be undertaken till May, by which time his
troops would be rested and his armies again brought up to
strength. The resultant compromise, as expressed in the Chantilly resolutions, was feeble. Over the winter, offensive operations
would continue in so far as climate permitted. The Armies of the
Coalition would undertake *to be ready* to undertake general
offensives 'from the first fortnight of February 1917'. At that
time or thereafter the decision on the actual dates of the various
offensives would be made. All the offensives on the various
fronts would be launched within a three-week interval.[2]

As for the Rumanian theatre, the Chantilly resolutions
grandiloquently announced that Bulgaria must be put 'out of
action'. For this purpose the Russians would attack from the
north, seconded by the army at Salonika, which would be
increased to twenty-three divisions from the current eighteen.
The figure of twenty-three was conveniently arrived at by
drawing on British, Italian, and Serbian resources which were
known at the time to be non-existent or unavailable.[3]

---

[1] Maj.-Gen. Sir Frederick Maurice, *The Life of General Lord Rawlinson of Trent*
(1928), 178; *AF*, v (1), Annexes nos. 73, 129; *The Private Papers of Douglas Haig,
1914–1919*, (ed.) Robert Blake (1952), 175–6.

[2] *AF*, v (1), Annexes nos. 32, 46. The resolutions passed by the Chantilly
Conference are printed in ibid., Annexe no. 119, and, in translation, in Cyril
Falls, *Military Operations, France and Belgium, 1917*, i (1940), Appendixes Volume,
Appendix no. 1. For the background and discussions of the conference see *AF*, v
(1), pp. 67–68, and Annexes nos. 104, 114, 115; *Mil. Opns. Fr. and Bel. 1916*, ii.
530–3, and *1917*, i. 1–11.

[3] *Mil. Opns. Fr. and Bel. 1916*, ii. 533 n. 1, *1917*, i. 10; *Mémoires du maréchal Joffre*
(Paris: Plon, 1932), ii. 358–61.

These resolutions were presented to the *Paris* governmental conference on the 16th by Generals Joffre, Haig, and Robertson as a *fait accompli*. Briand and Asquith, as was their custom, acquiesced and proposed acceptance by the conference pending the decisions to be made at the later meetings in Russia. Lloyd George rightly challenged the estimate of twenty-three divisions for Salonika, but, as General Joffre pointed out, the railway construction which would have made the deployment of so large a force feasible had not been undertaken.[1]

In any event it was all much too late to save Rumania. As the Paris and Chantilly conferences dispersed, Von Falkenhayn's troops finally forced the Vulcan Pass to the South Carpathians and began the invasion of Wallachia. All that could be done was to limit the benefits to the Central Powers of the conquest of Rumania. On 23 November Asquith reported to the King that, after consideration of the news from Rumania, the Cabinet desired that grain and oil stores in that country be destroyed. John Norton-Griffiths, a tough adventurer, who also happened to be a Member of Parliament, was sent to Rumania for this purpose. He burned or wrecked as many oil-fields and destroyed as much standing corn as possible; the resultant damage has been estimated at fifty-six million pounds and, according to Cruttwell, the oil-fields yielded 'nothing to the enemy for several months'. For these exploits Norton-Griffiths was created a Knight Commander of the Bath and, after his suicide following a financial scandal in Egypt, awarded several paragraphs in the *Dictionary of National Biography*.

Meanwhile from Salonika the Serbian troops under General Sarrail's overall command had advanced across the Serbian frontier and on 19 November captured the town of Monastir. With this widely heralded little success the Salonika campaign ended. The Russian forces gave the Rumanians no active help until the troops of the Central Powers had overrun all of Wallachia and the Dobrudja and advanced to the river Sereth and to Moldavia. The Rumanian Government and King retired to Jassy, just south of the Russian frontier, and the retreating Rumanian Army was able under Russian protection to remain in Moldavia to recover and refit. All of Rumania south of the river Sereth was under the occupation of the enemy. So ended

[1] Lloyd George, *War Memoirs*, i. 568–71; Hankey, *Supreme Command*, ii. 561–3.

the Allies' services to that unhappy country in 1916. By way of *envoi* Robertson commented to the editor of the *Daily Chronicle* that 'He never thought that they [the Rumanians] ought to come in, and he always considered that they would not be much good when they did join.'[1]

Scarcely had Asquith and Lloyd George returned to London from their disappointing journey to Paris than they were confronted by a still more fundamental—though closely related—issue than war strategy. Lord Lansdowne, the original architect of the Anglo-French Entente and currently Minister without Portfolio, reviewed the same discouraging facts as Lloyd George but had arrived at a different conclusion. In a memorandum written on 13 November and circulated to the Cabinet, Lansdowne not only asked if the military and naval leaders were confident they could defeat Germany but, should the answer be in the negative, went on to suggest that 'we ought at any rate not to discourage any movement, no matter where originating, in favour of an interchange of views as to the possibility of a settlement'.[2] The reference to possible American mediation was plain.

From May 1916 onwards Colonel House had been dispatching a series of telegrams to Grey imploring him to accept American mediation on the terms of the House–Grey memorandum of 22 February, an agreement, the reader will recall,[3] altogether favourable to the interests of the Triple Entente. The Foreign Secretary remained firm, however; and finally on 28 August, the day after Rumania's declaration of war, returned (in the words of Professor Link, the most recent and most scholarly biographer of President Wilson) 'a rather brutally firm' refusal.[4] Grey's statement, however, was too discreet to

[1] H. A. Taylor, *Robert Donald* (1934), 109. Report to the King on the Cabinet of 22 Nov. 1916. 23 Nov. 1916, Asquith Papers; Christopher Addison, *Politics from Within, 1911–1918* (1924), i. 266–7; C. R. M. F. Cruttwell, *A History of the Great War, 1914–1918* (2nd edn., 1936), 296–8; Hankey, *Supreme Command*, ii. 535; 'Norton-Griffiths, Sir John', *D.N.B. 1922–1930*; Robert Keith Middlemas, *The Master Builders* (1963), 277–85.

[2] Lord Lansdowne's Memorandum of 13 Nov. 1916, Earl of Oxford and Asquith, *Memories and Reflections, 1852–1927* (Boston, 1928), ii. 173.

[3] See above, pp. 124–5.

[4] Arthur S. Link, *Woodrow Wilson and the Progressive Era, 1910–1917* (1954), 219, *President Wilson and His English Critics* (Oxford, 1959), 14; Charles Seymour (ed.),

suit Lloyd George's purposes. A month later it was clear that
the Somme offensive had failed, the Brusilov offensive exhausted,
and that Rumania was in great danger. The Allied plans for
victory in 1916 had not borne fruit, and the question of satisfying the national interests of the Triple Entente rather than
their wildest dreams naturally engaged more interest than
before.

It was this moment that Lloyd George chose to deliver,[1] to
the distress of the Foreign Secretary, a public warning to
President Wilson not to interfere in the affairs of others. On
29 September the Secretary of State for War declared in an
interview with an American press proprietor that[2]

The fight must be to a finish—to a knock-out. . . .
The whole world—including neutrals of the highest purposes
and humanitarians with the best of motives—must know that there
can be no outside interference at this stage. Britain asked no intervention when she was unprepared to fight. She will tolerate none
now that she is prepared until the Prussian military despotism
is broken beyond repair.

Grey protested—and it is an indication of how low the political power of the Foreign Secretary had fallen that he could do
no more—that[3] 'it has always been my view that until the
Allies were sure of victory the door should be kept open for
Wilson's mediation. It is now closed for ever as far as we are

---

The Intimate Papers of Colonel House, II. From Neutrality to War, 1915–1917 (1926),
278–9, 282–3, 286–92, 318–19.

[1] Lloyd George may have been prompted by a warning of a public armistice
proposal by President Wilson from Cecil Spring Rice, British Ambassador to
Washington. See following note.

[2] The Times, 29 Sept. 1916. The Diary of Chandler P. Anderson, formerly legal
adviser to the American Ambassador to London, for 15 Sept. 1916, reads:

At a conference . . . with Spring Rice . . . today, he told me his Government
[had information the President would make an armistice proposal] on behalf of
the German Government . . . they would express a willingness to withdraw their
troops from Northern France and part of Belgium . . . his Government . . . were
confident of their power to drive the German forces out of Northern France. . . .
He said that he hoped . . . it could be forestalled in some way.
I suggested . . . perhaps the simplest solution would be to have a member of
his Government make public in London a general statement of their attitude
toward the question of intervention, and peace proposals at this time.
He said that that struck him as the wisest course to pursue, & he was going to
recommend it to his Government. (Library of Congress, Washington, D.C.)

[3] Lloyd George, War Memoirs, i. 509–12.

concerned.' Lloyd George in reply rudely expressed his 'callous impenitence'.

At that time England could still have accepted American mediation or indicated a willingness to negotiate peace without giving the impression of acting under duress. During the following six weeks, however, the strategic security of the British Isles was for the first time in the war dangerously threatened. This was due partly to submarine attacks against shipping, partly to the apparent beginnings of cruiser warfare in the Channel. Since the end of March British merchant ships had been sunk at the rate of from twelve to twenty a month. In September the sinkings increased alarmingly, and in November were at a rate of forty-two ships. A letter from Jellicoe to the Prime Minister warned that the losses in merchant shipping might force peace by early summer. Viscount Grey wrote Mr. Balfour that 'the submarine danger seems to me to be increasing so rapidly that unless in the next two months or so we can do something about it, the Germans will see their way to victory'.[1] These fears were more than confirmed by the minister in a position to know, the President of the Board of Trade. Mr. Walter Runciman prophesied a 'complete breakdown in shipping . . . much sooner than June [1917]'.[2]

No less alarming, though ignored by subsequent historians, was the threat to the 'command' of the English Channel. The reader will recall how the Grand Fleet, with all its attendant vessels, had excluded itself from the waters between the Continent and the English Coast after an unexpected near-encounter with the High Seas Fleet in August.[3] The only British naval vessels in the Channel were in the Dover Patrol. As yet no German surface vessels had dared to enter the Channel. But on the night of 26 October a German destroyer force from Zeebrugge, diverted from the High Seas Fleet, had successfully raided the vessels of the Dover Patrol, sinking several small craft and one empty transport, and returned to its base on the Belgian coast without loss or hindrance. Admiral Bacon, the

[1] Blanche E. C. Dugdale, *Arthur James Balfour* (1937), ii. 163.
[2] Christopher Addison, *Politics from Within, 1914–1918* (1924), ii. 10; Joseph Davies, *The Prime Minister's Secretariat, 1916–1920* (Newport, Mon., 1952); Hankey, *Supreme Command*, ii. 553–4; Lloyd George, *War Memoirs*, i. 506–15; Sir Henry Newbolt, *Naval Operations*, iv. 323–4.
[3] See above, p. 141.

commander of the Dover Patrol, had immediately stopped troop transport across the Channel. This action, he informed the Admiralty, was his only recourse against 'a raid that cannot be prevented'. 'No attempt was made to provide for a defence of the Straits, nor could such defence be attempted with the vessels then at my disposal.'

> The German sailors . . . recent raid [Admiral Bacon informed Haig several weeks later] has opened their eyes to the fact that they can interfere with our communications without much danger or difficulty. He [the Admiral] cannot prevent these raids . . . our command of the Channel is precarious, and . . . our ports may be closed oftener in the future than in the past.

The isolation of the British Isles from the Continent, leaving the British Army stranded, was now a possible operation of war. Even the invasion of England from Belgium could now reasonably be feared.[1]

The impact of submarine warfare was further increased by the poor harvest of 1916 and the conscription of agricultural labour into the Army. During 1916, the President of the Board of Agriculture reported, the reduced crop had amounted to a loss of ten to twelve weeks' supply. Henceforth it was in some areas 'no longer a question of maintaining a moderate standard of cultivation, but rather whether cultivation will cease'.[2] To these woes were added the increasing difficulty of obtaining credit for munitions and other purchases in the United States.[3]

The course of the war had not only gravely affected England's ability to carry on the struggle but had also weakened the war-will of her major Allies. France's governing instrument, though not her population, was as yet unaffected. But in Italy and

---

[1] Adm. Sir Reginald Bacon, *The Dover Patrol, 1915–1917* (Hutchinson, n.d.), ii. 343–4, 600–1, 605; Robert Blake (ed.), *The Private Papers of Douglas Haig, 1914–1919* (1952), 180–1; *Naval Opns.* iv. 53–66; Lieut.-Col. C. à Court Repington, *The First World War, 1914–1918*, i. 393–6, and esp. 395 ('The public, said Balfour, were under the impression that the Straits of Dover were mined and netted and so forth, but the storms and currents swept all away, and the marvel was that the Germans had done so little all this time').

[2] As cited in Lansdowne's Memorandum, Asquith, *Memories and Reflections*, ii. 167.

[3] Basil Collier, *Brasshat: A Biography of Field-Marshal Sir Henry Wilson* (1961), 253 ('Bonar Law . . . said ominously that "if America liked to refuse us money and ammunition, then we must make peace" '); Link, *Woodrow Wilson and the Progressive Era*, 258–9.

Russia new governments had been formed containing men whose devotion to the *guerre à l'outrance* was questionable. In the Tsarist Empire Sasanov had been replaced as Foreign Minister by the equivocal Stürmer, despite the protest of the British Ambassador. The Government that had brought Italy into the war against the wishes of its legislature had been overthrown. The failures of the repeated Italian offensives upon the Isonzo and the million-man loss incurred by Russia in the Brusilov offensive had failed to break the military stalemate, had quenched popular ardour, and had stirred up parliamentary discontent.[1]

The professional historian, with his occupational bias in favour of the influence of reason in history, is liable to wonder why views similar to the Lansdowne memorandum had not been urged in the councils of the British Government long before November 1916. That document, like Lloyd George's philippic of the same date, reviewed the discouraging crises in shipping, food, and Allied morale. It also for the first time emphasized the cost to Britain not only in money but in young life.

In the matter of man-power we are nearing the end of our tether. . . . Our own casualties already amount to over 1,100,000. . . . There is no reason to suppose that, as the force at the front in the different theatres of war increases, the casualties will increase at a slower rate. We are slowly but surely killing off the best of the male population of these islands.

All this [Lansdowne continued] it is no doubt our duty to bear, but only if it can be shown that the sacrifice will have its reward. . . . Our forces and those of France have shown a splendid gallantry on the Western Front, and have made substantial advances; but is it believed that these, any more than those made in 1915 with equally high hopes and accomplished by not less cruel losses, will really enable us to 'break through'? . . . Can we afford to go on paying the same sort of price for the same sort of gains? . . . The responsibility of those who needlessly prolong such a War is not less than that of those who needlessly provoke it.

The real problem, concluded this searching analysis, was whether the crushing military victory that Asquith and Lloyd George had publicly demanded could in fact be obtained. The

---

[1] Frank P. Chambers, *The War Behind the War, 1914–1918* (1939), 296–300, 328–32.

first step was to ascertain what England could realistically hope
to attain. 'Let our naval, military and economic advisers tell us
frankly whether they are satisfied that the knock-out blow can
and will be delivered.' If not, though 'the interview given by the
Secretary of State for War in September last to an American
correspondent has produced an impression which it will not be
easy to efface' some other war aims besides a victory in battle
ought to be evolved.[1]

The Prime Minister, complaisant as ever, agreed to this
sensible suggestion and invited opinions from the Admiralty
and the General Staff. Lloyd George in transmitting this request
to the C.I.G.S. urged, according to the latter's memoirs, that
Lansdowne's views needed to be peremptorily stamped upon.
He suggested that, in framing a reply, 'I should speak out quite
plainly and not "be afraid to let yourself go".'[2]

Robertson's statement, submitted on 24 November, has never
been published in its entirety. It must be the most bellicose and
offensive document ever inflicted on a British Cabinet. It failed,
however, to supply any reasoned answer to Lord Lansdowne's
question. The Empire could not cease fighting until it had
exerted its greatest efforts. These had not been undertaken
earlier due to the failure of the Liberal Government to introduce
compulsory service before the war. The General Staff's view was
that any peace terms which conserved the military domination
of Prussia would estrange the Dominions and Allies and dis-
honour the memory of those soldiers who had already given
their lives. Peace would be an 'insult to [the] fighting services'.
Only 'cranks, cowards, and philosophers' (this last a hit at
Balfour) could doubt the necessity of going on with the war. 'In
short, we need to have the same courage in London as have our
leaders in the North Sea and in France. . . . My answer to the
question is: "I am satisfied that the knock-out blow can and
will be delivered if only we take the necessary measures to give
us success, and take them in time. We shall win if we deserve
to win".' Robertson appended a note from Haig which once
again emphasized the decline in the German Army's morale

[1] Lord Lansdowne's Memorandum of 13 Nov. 1916, Asquith, *Memories and
Reflections*, ii. 165–75.
[2] Field-Marshal Sir William Robertson, *Soldiers and Statesmen, 1914–1918* (1926),
i. 280. See also Lloyd George, *War Memoirs*, i. 521–2, and *Private Papers of Douglas
Haig*, 181–2.

and promised victory if all resources continued to be poured into his command on the Western Front.[1]

The Lansdowne–Robertson interchange naturally provoked no little stir. Sir Robert Cecil, Minister of Blockade, confirmed Lord Lansdowne's fears on the stability of the Allies. 'France is within measurable distance of exhaustion. The political outlook in Italy is menacing. In Russia there is great discouragement. She has long been on the verge of revolution.' Even so, he pointed out, 'peace would be known by the Germans to have been forced upon us by their submarines', and would be an admission of weakness. 'I feel, therefore, that we are bound to continue the War.'[2]

Lord Grey belatedly informed his Cabinet colleagues of the agreement he had signed with Colonel House the preceding February, and gravely reproved the C.I.G.S. for his emotionalism. Lord Lansdowne had performed 'a faithful and courageous act'. It would be 'premature to make peace' as long as 'the position of the Allies is likely to improve'. It was likely that it would so improve 'provided the Allies can continue the war with full vigour through next year, or even for the first eight months of next year'. But could they? It was uncertain whether Russia or France would persevere in a *guerre à l'outrance*. The shipping position was becoming progressively graver.

If the time arrived when . . . the situation would change in the course of the next few months to the disadvantage of the Allies and would progressively deteriorate, then it would be incumbent on the Government of the Allies to wind up the war at once on the best terms obtainable, *presumably through the medium of not unsympathetic mediation*, and, if they did not do so, they would be responsible for future disaster to their countries.

Let, therefore, the naval authorities now be heard.[3]

The conclusion of the Secretary of State for Foreign Affairs was ominous, because the helplessness of the Admiralty before

[1] Robertson, *Soldiers and Statesmen*, i. 281–4; Maj.-Gen. Sir C. E. Callwell, *Field-Marshal Sir Henry Wilson* (1927), i. 299; Lloyd George, *War Memoirs*, i. 521; Lansdowne, Memorandum of 27 Nov. 1916, Asquith Papers.

[2] Robert Cecil, Memorandum, 27 Nov. 1916. Asquith, *Memories and Reflections*, ii. 147–9.

[3] Memorandum, 27 Nov. 1916. G. M. Trevelyan, *Grey of Fallodon* (Longmans Library edn., 1940), 322–4. The italics have been added. See also Grey's *Twenty-Five Years, 1892–1916*, ii. 130–3.

PLATE 9

b. The Marquess of Lansdowne
Minister without Portfolio 1915–16

a. H. H. Asquith
Prime Minister 1908–16

the menace of the submarines was known, and indeed admitted.[1] But Lord Grey's views, cogent as they were, no longer commanded assent. The following day, the 28th, the Military Members of the Army Council submitted a memorandum asking for what Robertson four days earlier had called 'the necessary measures to give us success'. The Army needed, the Military Members reported, another nine hundred and forty thousand men in 1917. The first draft of the memorandum made no comment on how these men were to be obtained. According to Robertson, Lloyd George desired such a recommendation, and 'eventually, in order to meet his wishes', the Military Members suggested that the military age be raised from forty-one to fifty-five and that 'all men up to that age . . . be utilized for such national service as H.M. Government deem to be essential to the "effective prosecution of the war" '.

The War Committee met two days later, on 30 November, and made unconditional surrender to the Generals', the radical right's, and Lloyd George's long-standing demand. They approved of compulsory *national* service for all men to the age of *sixty*, and noted that they 'attached great importance' to the enactment of the necessary legislation before Christmas. The advisability of extending compulsion to women would be considered by an interdepartmental committee. 'Certain members of the Cabinet', Robertson wrote Haig four days later, 'objected to the Industrial Compulsion Scheme we got through the War Committee', and before they could once again reconcile their consciences to yet another authoritarian measure the Government had fallen.[2]

On 7 December Lloyd George became Prime Minister with a mandate to 'win the war'. How could the partisans of the knock-out blow logically formulate anything other or less than the continuance of a Western strategy? How could an Easterner deliver the knock-out blow? How could one be an Easterner and

---

[1] Hankey, *Supreme Command*, ii. 553–4; *Naval Opns.* iv. 324.

[2] Hankey, *Supreme Command*, ii. 551–2; *Private Papers of Douglas Haig*, 183; Robertson, *Soldiers and Statesmen*, i. 302–4; History of the Ministry of Munitions, vi (1), 43–44; Supply of Men for the Army: Memorandum by the Military Members of the Army Council to the Secretary of State for War, 28 Nov. 1916, Asquith Papers. Lloyd George had proclaimed the need for conscription of individual labour since June 1915, and had then instructed his subordinates at the Ministry of Munitions to draft 'a measure of industrial compulsion and discipline'. See Lord Beveridge, *Power and Influence* (1952), 127–8.

expect to win the war? These questions Lloyd George could never satisfactorily answer to his own or others' satisfaction; and the disparity between his aim and his proclaimed methods, between his national policy and his military strategy, accounts for much of his subsequent failure to put that strategy into effect.

. If the year 1915 was a period of ministerial control and formulation of strategy, 1916 was one in which the pattern of military operations was dictated by the high command.

Both the strategies of 1915 and of 1916 proved unsuccessful, but for different reasons. The failures of 1915, this writer has earlier argued (and, hopefully, shown), were due to errors in execution rather than conception. The Dardanelles campaign was wrecked less by the enemy than by the rebellion of the naval command in the Mediterranean and the military command in France and by the inability of the various ministers responsible for this complex combined operation to agree on its scope and nature and supply adequate support. The strategic failures of 1916, however, were irremediable. The mistake was one of conception. There was, *for the British Army as it existed in 1916*, no reasonable prospect of defeating the German Armies in battle upon the Western Front. 'It has been suggested', reads the official, and virulently Western, British history of military operations during the war, 'that the troops which fought on the 1st July were not sufficiently well trained or led to defeat the Germans.[1] . . . Possibly it is as well that the break-through did not succeed, and leaders and troops were not tested against the Germans of 1916 in open warfare.'[2]

This lack of realism could hardly have been unsuspected by those then in positions of power. Yet the high command was permitted not only to begin battle upon the Somme but to continue a series of onslaughts long after there was any rational basis for belief in ultimate success, however defined. Professional and national pride and the belief that some kind of victory could be obtained largely explain the determination of the high command to launch the Somme offensive; the French demand for the relief of their own armies before Verdun and the general expectation that Britain contribute her share to the offensives

[1] The bias of the Regular officer against Kitchener's armies is evident.
[2] *Mil. Opns. Fr. and Bel. 1916*, ii. 490–2.

begun by all major nations of the Entente in the summer of
1916, were in themselves sufficient and not unreasonable induce-
ments for the Government to sanction the battle. But for the
continuance of the offensive a different type of explanation
must be sought.

As far as the High Command is concerned the answer is plain.
Both Haig and, more significantly, the Chief of the Imperial
General Staff, were committed, prejudiced, and partisan.
Neither of them would admit defeat. Neither the failure of the
first Somme attack, nor the entry of Rumania, nor that country's
defeat, nor the failure of the September tank attack caused
anything but a hardening of view and an increasingly defensive
attitude. In 1916 both Haig and Robertson were men of faith.
The Commander-in-Chief remained convinced that the enemy
army's morale was on the point of collapse; the C.I.G.S., ten
years later, recorded in his analysis of the war that 'the military
achievements of the year . . . left the position in all theatres of
war infinitely more satisfactory and hopeful than it had been
twelve months before'.[1]

The ability of the High Command to impose its policy, with
the minor exception of Mesopotamia, throughout 1916 upon
the Government against the latter's better judgement was due,
it is here suggested, to the Generals' alliance (1) with the
unofficial but most effective opposition in the Commons and the
Lords under the respective leadership of Carson and Milner;
and (2) with the Secretary of State for War, Mr. Lloyd George.
These men were allied in a common struggle for three separate but closely related aims: a *guerre à l'outrance*,[2] a Western
strategy, and compulsion for industrial labour. The 'radical
right' political opposition in the House under Carson was eager
to use any stick to beat the Government, desired Germany's complete defeat to end once and for all that country's challenge to
the hegemony of the British Empire outside Europe, and was inspired by men eager not only to control but to subjugate labour.

Support of the High Command's demands was a means to
attainment of these diverse ends. Lloyd George, who in 1916
became identified with the 'knock-out' blow, had entered into

[1] Robertson, *Soldiers and Statesmen*, i. 286.
[2] There was once, significantly enough, no English-language equivalent; 'all-out'
war had not been coined.

political alliance with the Conservatives and espoused the cause of industrial conscription as a means 'to win the war' ever since the formation of the First Coalition. On the basic political issues of 1915 and 1916 he had at every crucial stage aligned himself with the High Command—on 'shells', on the *guerre à l'outrance*, and on strategy. In 1915 he had fought for withdrawal from Gallipoli, and in 1916 he made no official criticism of the Somme offensive until November,[1] however much he unburdened himself to friends and others not in a responsible position.

The manner in which Lloyd George and Robertson combined in the last days of the Asquithian régime in an attempt to have the *guerre à l'outrance* continued as official policy and to fasten industrial compulsion upon the nation has been described. Support of the Generals' conduct of the war, however fruitless or illogical that conduct might be, was the price paid by Lloyd George and the radical right for the attainment of their own political aims. For this they obtained their reward. 'The present Government', Sir Henry Wilson told Lloyd George on 26 November, 'stank in the nostrils of the whole army . . . if he was to break away and raise the standard of victory he would have a unanimous army behind him.'[2]

Neither Lloyd George nor the High Command nor the radical right was hampered in these struggles by any particular sense of responsibility. Lloyd George was not yet Prime Minister. The radical right was not yet represented in the government. Haig and Robertson believed that the function of the country and the Government was to serve, support, and sustain the Western Front. Both political and military questions were examined in the light of that assumption.

The policies of 1916—war, military, and domestic—had by the end of the year become extremist, because they were imposed by extremists. The responsibility for these policies was of course the Government's—a front-bench Coalition made up largely of moderate and sensible men under the moderate and sensible Asquith. There is no doubt that the strategy of 1916 and its political results—the introduction of compulsory military service and the impending imposition of industrial compulsion —ran counter to the expectations and principles of the

---

[1] As indicated by the documents (including those cited by Lloyd George himself) now available. [2] Callwell, *Henry Wilson*, i. 299.

Government's leading Liberal members (Lloyd George excepted). It may be that the Government in adopting these measures had little alternative. Its political opponents were too strong. In addition, the great reliance of both Liberals and Easterners, the Royal Navy, had in the course of the year become increasingly unable to play any active part in the war or even to protect the United Kingdom. Such was, as has been traced in these pages, the aftermath of Jutland.

The approval of policies in which the Government had no real faith none the less sapped its confidence and lessened its moral strength. It could have accepted defeat in the Commons and passed on to its critics the moderating burden of responsibility along with the privilege of power before the crisis of December 1916. Alternatively, it could have called a general election. It did neither, but lingered on, an object of anger and contempt, a sad deflexion from the great Cabinets of 1906 and afterwards. The artful dissemination of the Casement diaries was not the only example of men of stature lowering their own dignity. The course of the Somme campaign reflected the political weakness of the Asquithian régime's last hopeless months.[1]

With the advent of the Lloyd George régime the 'old gang', the 'last of the Old Romans', departed. The Asquith–Haldane–Grey trio, which had come to power in time to consolidate and shape the pattern of a close alignment with France, had gone. Haldane, removed from the centre of affairs by his assumption of the office of Lord Chancellor in 1912, had been excluded from the First Coalition in punishment for his pre-war attempts to reach a naval understanding with Germany. Grey and Asquith remained, beyond the period of their most effective functioning.

On Asquith as war leader opinions have, justly, crystallized. His function had been to 'unify the nation', i.e. to attract acquiescence, if not loyalty, across the political spectrum. For this role colourlessness was a positive asset. The ferocious defiance of Churchill in 1940–2 applied to a different strategic posture, and to a far more unified society and nation. But as the conflict wore on, passions on each side of the spectrum—pacifist

[1] Fitzroy, Memoirs, ii. 630–1; Letter, Graham Wallas to Samuel, 8 Oct. 1916. John Bowle, Viscount Samuel (1957), 141–2; Letter, Robert Cecil to Asquith, 2 Nov. 1916, Asquith Papers.

and authoritarian—mounted. Meanwhile Asquith's virtues appeared less relevant, his faults more glaring. His conciliatoriness seemed weakness, his bluff good sense an irritating façade, his lawyerly acumen a means of evasion from reality. His real defects were increasingly perceived as intolerable. Asquith's lack of creative imagination, his inability to furnish new ideas or a fresh point of view, had always been there; but now, with the war going badly, the Prime Minister appeared positively wooden. Besides, the psychic and personal toll of the war on Asquith was heavy, draining his resilience and will. By 1916 the Prime Minister had become the passive spectator of events, fundamentally unwilling—despite the occasional compelling pressure—to steer the course of the juggernaut he had helped set in motion. Consequently the war brushed him aside, destroying his career as it destroyed so much else.

To Asquith's colleague and kindred spirit,[1] Edward Grey, the end of office and his public career, after eleven years as Foreign Secretary, must have come as a release. During the war years his eyesight and general health had steadily deteriorated. Unable any longer to face the stress of the Commons debates, in July 1916 he had been made a peer and transferred to the House of Lords. The war witnessed a steady decline in his authority vis-à-vis the service ministers and especially Lloyd George. The latter's 'knock-out blow' speech made evident how far the process had gone. Still, unlike the Foreign Secretary's fellow Liberal ministers, Grey kept an open mind about Asquith's displacement. The change in régime, he suspected, marked an improvement.[2]

The advent of war was to Grey, as to Neville Chamberlain twenty-five years later, a personal disaster to the conduct of which it was impossible to devote a whole-hearted participation. The hesitancy on the conduct of the negotiations for Italian entry into the war (in which affair Asquith for a time took over), the repeated rejections of Greek offers to join the Entente, the ineffectual blandishments to Bulgaria, the lack of any action on the House–Grey memorandum and on the 'war and peace'

---

[1] Asquith's 'relations with Grey', Lord Beaverbrook wrote, 'were of that distant but friendly type which an ocean might have with a contiguous mountain peak' (Politicians and the War, 1914–1916 [N.Y., 1928], 245–6).

[2] G. M. Trevelyan, Grey of Fallodon (Longmans Library edn., 1940), 271–3, 281, 327–8, 330–3.

issue generally—all these are susceptible of explanation; but they none the less convey an impression of confusion and lack of pondered decision. Like many other statesmen who continued to hold office in altered conditions, the Prime and Foreign Ministers were no longer at 'the height of events'.

It cannot, however, be said that in 1916 strategy was formally divorced from policy, because in that year the Government reaffirmed its war aim to be the whole and utter 'destruction of the military despotism of Prussia'. Yet the 'Generals' who imposed the strategy had no sympathy with the policy. Formal discussion of British war aims was begun within the War Committee in August 1916, and in a memorandum submitted at the end of that month the Chief of the Imperial General Staff implicitly attacked the Asquith formula. On the basis of a strict and narrowly balance-of-power theory of international relations Robertson expressed the view that the interests of the British Empire demanded that after the war Germany be conserved as a strong military power to counterbalance French and particularly Russian expansion. To this end Austria should be incorporated into the German Empire after the war. 'It is hard to believe', Robertson remarked, 'that Germany will ever be so crushed as to consent to the transfer of Posen to Poland', thus casually contradicting the entire basis of the Western strategy he so tenaciously expounded and defended.

At no time did either Haig or Robertson express any interest in the demilitarization of Germany or in changes in her constitutional structure. 'Few of us feel', Haig later told the King, 'that the "democratising of Germany" is worth the loss of a single Englishman!' Yet in 1916 both military chiefs were appalled at the possibility of the British Government's consenting to any peace before they had won victory in battle. To them, as to so many Commanders-in-Chief, victory in battle was the essence of war. It was also its only real purpose. No other aim was meaningful or worthy. Under the heading 'Objective' Haig in July 1916 emphatically wrote (in his diary) that the war must go on till Germany was obliged to accept whatever terms (who cares what they would be!) the Allies might dictate to her.[1]

[1] W. R. Robertson, General. Chief of the Imperial General Staff. War Office, 31 Aug. 1916. Lloyd George, *War Memoirs*, i. 497–503; *Private Papers of Douglas*

This narrow view excluded statesmanship, but in human terms was very understandable. The policy of Lloyd George on the *guerre à l'outrance* is more puzzling. In September he publicly proclaimed his faith in the 'knock-out' blow. If words mean anything, he thus said that the German armies must be defeated in battle, and this interpretation he elsewhere confirmed to anyone who would listen.[1] Did he really believe the Russians would do it for him? Could the 'Prussian military despotism' be so easily 'broken beyond repair'? Lloyd George's view, too, appears either irrational or irresponsible.

Of course nearly all public leaders and the bulk of the population *desired* the destruction of the German armies, a peace through victory. In 1916 the mounting casualty lists probably increased the public determination 'to see the business through'. One could not betray the cause for which so many had either died or laid waste their lives, that is to say that the 'cause', heretofore disputable or capable of change, a political aim, was henceforth transformed into something sacred and unquestionable. Nor could, in hundreds of thousands of homes, the thought that one's love had given up or marred his life in vain be endured or tolerated. Such an outlook could not last indefinitely, but in the autumn of 1916 it helped Lloyd George into power and kept England to its grim self-chosen path.

Doubtless Lloyd George shared in the feelings we have just sketched. His 'knock-out' blow interview stressed the need for punishment of those he believed responsible for the carnage in France. It may be that to this erstwhile radical Jacobin the war really was a crusade, while to aristocrats like Lansdowne it was primarily an instrument of policy. These are the imponderables of history. What is certain, however, is that once Lloyd George became Prime Minister and assumed the responsibility as well as the delights of supreme power Great Britain and America heard no more from him of 'knock-out' blows.

Haig, 277; Harold I. Nelson, *Land and Power: British and Allied Policy on Germany's Frontiers, 1916–19* (1963), 8–14.

[1] For example, Letter, Lloyd George to Robert Donald, 8 Jan. 1916 ('A peace imposed on Germany exhausted in food and materials only would not be durable. It would be a moral defeat for the Allies. . . . Only a crushing military victory will bring the peace for which the Allies are fighting, and of which Germany will understand the meaning. That victory we shall have; it will be complete and final'), as cited in *Current History* (N.Y., July 1916), 733.

It is, of course, far from sure that the German Government, even under extreme American pressure, would have consented to a negotiated peace in 1916 on the basis even of the one vital British interest, the evacuation of Belgium, to say nothing of the cessation of Alsace-Lorraine. All one can say is that the Entente in 1916 actively discouraged any attempt to exert or stimulate such pressure, from within Germany or without. What the effects of such pressure would have been, one cannot say, but the German Empire of 1916 was no dictatorship, military or otherwise.

Wisely or not, in 1916 the Entente, with Britain in the lead, decided to continue the *guerre à l'outrance* no matter what the cost. The costs were staggering, and the whole Western world continues to bear the effects of the commitments assumed in 1916.

In terms of human life, fighting on the Western Front during the period of the Somme campaign cost the British Army just under half a million (498,054) casualties, of which well over a hundred thousand (115,364 according to one official table, 108,684 according to another) were deaths. During the entire Second World War the British Army in the war against Germany suffered no more than the same number of both total casualties (494,930) and deaths (121,484). The French Army suffered a loss of two hundred thousand (204,253), and the German half a million (almost 500,000) against both its antagonists.[1] In order to avoid the intricacies of varying methods of compilation it may be useful for purposes of comparison to disregard the wound casualty figures. The War Office statistical digest on the war indicates that on the British sector of the Western Front from July to the end of the year Empire troops suffered one hundred and twenty-five thousand casualties (124,775) in killed, missing, and prisoners of war. Opposite this same sector the Germans suffered a total loss of eighty thousand men (79,880) in these same categories. These casualty figures, though they show that the enemy losses were indeed a terrible

---

[1] Capt. Liddell Hart, in his 'Notes and Queries' to the author on the manuscript of this book, writes, 'For the Somme you can take it . . . that the German figure of 465,000 casualties is as close to the mark as it is possible to get, while the Allied casualties were 623,000 (419,000 British and 204,000 French). But of the German casualties barely half were suffered on the British sector, as the French tactics were more economical and the artillery methods then superior to ours.'

burden to Germany and her army (a burden in part imposed
by the German High Command's insistence on a rigid defence
system), clearly demonstrate that the Entente was winning no
war of attrition. It is a pity that this fact has been obscured by
the uncritical acceptance by recent writers of the manipulation
and omission of casualty figures by the editor and principal
author of the British official history, Brigadier-General J. E.
Edmonds.[1]

The Somme offensive, however, may have saved the French
Army from collapse, certainly imposed a terrible strain upon
the German Army, and served as an effective schoolmaster in
the craft of battle to elements of the British command and staff
and to those troops who survived tuition. Henceforth British
tactics and fighting skill, if not ardour, steadily improved.

The strain on the German Army and nation imposed by a
continued defence against greater man-power and material
resources led First Quartermaster General Ludendorff, according to his memoirs, to the conclusion that 'If the war lasted our
defeat seemed inevitable.' The transient sense of desperation
played its part in the German decision to launch unrestricted
submarine warfare; the continued depression on the German
'home front' over losses in men contributed to the outbreak of
revolution and the eventual decision to sue for peace. Such, in
retrospect, appears to have been the limited contribution of the

[1] *Statistics of the Military Effort of the British Empire during the Great War* (The War
Office, March 1922), pp. 258–9, 324, 360; *Statistical Digest of the War* (1951),
13; *Mil. Opns. Fr. and Bel. 1916*, ii. pp. xiv–xvi; *Reichskriegsministerium, Der Welt-
krieg 1914 bis 1918, Die militärischen Operationen zu Lande*, xi (Berlin, 1938), 103.
For a criticism of the British official history's estimate of *enemy* casualties see
Capt. B. H. Liddell Hart, 'The Basic Truths of Passchendaele', *Journal of the
Royal United Service Institution*, civ, no. 616 (Nov. 1959), 436–8. The compilation
of British casualties is equally questionable; Edmonds was careful to include
those incurred on the actual Somme battlefields (left undefined), not on the
British front as a whole. The casualties estimates were thus lowered from
498,054 to 416,654. The French and German figures were left as they were, and
in the latter case increased. See *Mil. Opns. Fr. and Bel. 1916*, i. 496–7. M. J. Williams,
'Thirty Per Cent: A Study in Casualty Statistics', *Journal of the Royal United Service Institution*, cix, no. 633 (Feb. 1964), 51–55, effectually demolishes Edmonds's
arguments. Observers on the battlefield itself were impressed by the obvious disparity between British and enemy dead, and by the comparatively low numbers of
German troops used for counter-attacks. See *The Australian Imperial Force in France
1916* (1929), 943–5. The entry in Repington's *First World War* for 8 Jan. 1917,
pp. 424–5, reads, 'Saw the A.G., Sir Nevil Macready, at the War Office. . . . Our
losses on the Somme had been 460,000.'

strategy of attrition in general and the Somme campaign in particular to Germany's defeat.

In terms of general history, the continuance of the war after 1916, as is well known, broke the political and social structure of pre-war Europe, a process which began with the Russian Revolution and ended—perhaps—with the communization of Eastern Europe after the Second World War.

On Great Britain the effect of the decision to continue the *guerre à l'outrance* can be simply stated. From the formation of the Lloyd George Coalition until the summer of 1918 she fought on the strategic defensive. None the less, she of course eventually won the war, though the German Army was not and—in Haig's and Lloyd George's opinion as expressed in October 1918—could not be defeated in battle. That victory proved barren for Britain, though perhaps it need not have been so. The peace settlement imposed on Germany was unviable, due not least to Lloyd George's own share in its making. The consequence of a negotiated peace we cannot know, but how could the political structure have survived the nation's execration of those who led Great Britain into such a war? By the end of 1916 the British Government and nation were hardly free agents; England had become caught and captured in the undercurrents of the war, knew neither how to withdraw nor how to win, but could only, more or less wisely, endure. Lloyd George did so, more craftily and with more daring than most. The fall of Asquith must therefore be considered a good fortune, if not for Europe, at any rate for England and the British Empire.

Note: The anti-labour bias of the 'radical right' is strikingly emphasized by the following letter by F. S. Oliver (a member of the weekly cabal described on p. 128 above) to Austen Chamberlain (A. M. Gollin, *Proconsul in Politics* (1964), 540).

The nation . . . has been (as I see it) like a man engaged in defending his house against thieves. Behind him is a dog of his own household—an ill-tempered brute, who . . . is quite ready to fix his teeth in his master's throat. . . . I am for turning sharply on the dog, daring him to fly at my throat, and beating his bones to a jelly if he does. . . . Believe me, *yov will have to have it out with that Dog sooner or later*. . . . By the dog of course I mean Labour, not Ireland. And of course only a minority of Labour. . . .

PART THREE

LLOYD GEORGE'S WARS

'I back the little man to win.'
Letter, LORD HALDANE to his mother, July 1917.

VII

THE NEW IMPERIALISM

'I am an Imperialist and not a Little Englander, because I am a British Race Patriot.'

MILNER, 'Credo'.

A FTER a week of intense negotiation, intrigue, and conflict, fitfully illumined for the public and Parliament by in-spired and biased stories in the Press, Lloyd George became Prime Minister. Only two days later, on 9 December 1916, the great administrative innovation of the new régime, the sovereign War Cabinet, whose proclaimed function it was to run the war, met for the first time, and continued to convene daily. Its membership was small enough to permit efficiency and dispatch. Only five men were in the new supreme council: Lloyd George, Bonar Law, and Arthur Henderson, and Lords Curzon and Milner. Arthur Balfour frequently attended its sessions, but bore no responsibility.

The number of its members who had no other major duties was smaller still. The Prime Minister's burdens were innumerable. Bonar Law was not only Leader of the Conservative party but now Chancellor of the Exchequer and Leader of the House of Commons as well. In the last capacity he would act, Lloyd George explained, as 'sentry' for the War Cabinet to defend it against attacks, and this task occupied most of his time. Arthur Henderson, Leader of the Labour party, was an unhappy and ineffective member, serving primarily as spokesman for the labour movement. Eventually his colleagues succeeded in ousting him altogether. Only George Curzon, with his less pressing responsibilities as Lord President of the Council and Leader in the House of Lords, and to a greater degree Alfred Milner, as Minister without Portfolio, were really free to devote themselves to the conduct of the war.[1]

[1] Robert Blake, *The Unknown Prime Minister: The Life and Times of Andrew Bonar Law, 1858–1923* (1955), 344–5, 357–8; *War Memoirs of David Lloyd George* (2-vol.

Both Curzon and Milner were former proconsuls of Empire, in India and in South Africa respectively. Both were staunch imperialists. Milner's was the stronger personality, and he soon became the mainstay of the War Cabinet. Milner's influence was further increased by the appointments of his followers and disciples to key positions within the central machinery of government. 'A good part of the old Milnerian Kindergarten', the Radical *Nation* bitterly commented, had 'transferred from Pretoria to the more spacious playground of Downing Street.' Waldorf Astor, Lionel Curtis and Philip Kerr all became members of the Prime Minister's personal secretariat, the much disliked 'Garden Suburb'. Kerr left the editorship of the *Round Table*, a journal devoted to Imperial 'unity', to become the Prime Minister's 'expert on imperial and foreign affairs'. The novelist John Buchan became deputy director of the newly created Ministry of Information. Leopold Amery and Mark Sykes were appointed to the War Cabinet Secretariat as experts on European–Far Eastern (a significant if implausible juncture) and Islamic affairs respectively. They were given the rank of Under-secretary of State and the special duty of preparing weekly intelligence summaries for the information of ministers, a function previously performed only by the General Staff. For the first and last time in British history, the 'New Imperialism', repudiated by the electorate in 1906, had captured the citadel of power.[1]

The fundamental tenet of the New Imperialism (unlike the Liberal imperialism of Grey and Haldane, which was content to work within the existing political, economic, and social structure) was the *supreme* and overriding need for an Imperial polity which would dominate the formulation of both foreign *and internal* policy. 'Milner said', Professor Hewins noted in April 1917, 'the one thing he was anxious about was that we

Odhams Press edn.), i. 634; Mary Agnes Hamilton, *Arthur Henderson* (1938), 117; Lord Hankey, *The Supreme Command, 1914–1918* (1961), ii. 578–82, 594.

[1] Leopold Amery, *My Political Life* (1953–5), ii. 92, 98; Hankey, *Supreme Command*, ii. 588–91 ('we issued two weekly reports, . . . the Eastern Report and the Western Report'); Shane Leslie, *Mark Sykes* (1923), 288–9; Christopher Sykes, *Two Studies in Virtue* (1953), 177; Leonard Stein, *The Balfour Declaration* (1961), 474 ('Speaking of George's eccentric War Cabinet', Scott writes in his journal [27 Feb. 1917], '[Carson] said that of course Milner and Curzon were the only two, besides G. himself, who counted, and of these Milner was by far the most useful and influential'); A. M. Gollin, *Proconsul in Politics* (1964), 376–81.

PLATE 10

b. Viscount Milner
Member, War Cabinet, December 1916–April 1913
Thereafter Secretary of State for War

a. David Lloyd George
Prime Minister, December 1916–1922

PLATE II

a. Andrew Bonar Law
Leader, Conservative and Unionist Party 1911–21

b. Lord Northcliffe

should get out of the War a really consolidated Empire.' In that Empire the United Kingdom was conceived, not as the 'mother country', but rather as the eldest sister. Those of British, or in any event 'Teutonic', race throughout the Empire must combine to control and guide the dependent peoples within their jurisdiction. Hence the need for some form of federal union free from the control of the 'parochial parish pump' politics of the British House of Commons; for an Imperial citizenship and Imperial compulsory service; for a common external tariff. Thereby might be attained that final withdrawal from European affairs, that 'splendid isolation' which imperialist statesmen had long desired without ever having achieved. 'We are not a part of Europe,' one of them had written in May 1915, 'even if the most important unit of the British community lies off the European coast.' Only the failure of 'Britons' to make the Empire strong and cohesive enough to ignore the balance of power in Europe had required war against German domination of the Continent.[1]

The war offered an opportunity to achieve that unity and strength. Hence the immediate convening of an Imperial War Cabinet which met in March 1917, attended by the Prime

---

[1] W. A. S. Hewins, *The Apologia of an Imperialist: Forty Years of Empire Policy* (1929), ii. 136; *The History of The Times*, iv (1952), 1067; Maj.-Gen. Sir C. E. Callwell, *Field-Marshal Sir Henry Wilson: His Life and Diaries* (1927), i. 323. L. S. Amery's *My Political Life* and Milner's *The Nation and the Empire* are revealing on the imperialist ethos, while the article, 'All in a Garden Fair', in *The Nation* of 24 Feb. 1917 is an amusing parody, still well worth reading. Recent discussions of the British imperialist outlook include A. P. Thornton, *The Imperial Idea and its Enemies* (1959), and *The Cambridge History of the British Empire*, vol. iii, *The Empire-Commonwealth, 1870–1919* (1959), 344–9. See also Gollin, *Proconsul, passim*.

No intensive analysis of the spectrum of British imperialism is here attempted. For one attempt at defining the spectrum, see the essay by A. F. Madden in *The Cambridge History of the British Empire*, vol. iii, *The Empire-Commonwealth, 1870–1919* (Cambridge, 1959), pp. 338–54. In the 'Prologue' to the present work, attention has been called to the importance of the imperialist–Little Englander split for British home and foreign policy before the war. The 'New Imperialism', as the word is here used [Madden prefers 'Radical Imperialists', among whom he lists Chamberlain, Rosebery, and Milner], refers to the doctrinaire wing—those men for whom the political and strategic requirements of the Empire should dominate and shape domestic [e.g. trade and tariffs, 'national' service] as well as foreign policy. The note of religious faith with this group is unmistakable, and was, indeed, from time to time proclaimed. Haig (of all people!) told the Archbishop of York (William Lang) that 'we ought to aim at organising a great Imperial Church to which all honest citizens of the Empire could belong'. [*Private Papers of Douglas Haig*, p. 246.]

Ministers of the Dominions, and the subsequent invitation to General Smuts, the South African delegate, to join the War Cabinet. Smuts accepted and remained a member for the rest of the war, imploring his colleagues and the public not to give undue attention to European affairs. Germany, he declaimed, much to General Robertson's annoyance, was already beaten. Had she not lost her colonies?[1]

The Imperialist polity had clear implications for the future aims of British strategy. 'We have battled and will continue to battle our hardest for the common cause in Europe', Amery wrote the Prime Minister,[2]

But on behalf of that cause, as well as in defence of our existence, we shall find ourselves compelled to complete the liberation of the Arabs, to make secure the independence of Persia, and if we can of Armenia, to protect tropical Africa from economic and military exploitation. All these objects are justifiable in themselves and don't become less so because they increase the general security which will enable that *Southern British World which runs from Cape Town through Cairo, Baghdad and Calcutta to Sydney and Wellington* to go about its peaceful business without constant fear of German aggression.[3]

That 'Southern British World' did not, however, as yet exist. The Empire had not yet been 'consolidated', even territorially. In Africa, 'from Cape Town through Cairo', German East Africa remained unconquered, despite sporadic fighting ever since the ill-fated landing at Tanga. The campaign under the leadership of General Smuts in 1916 had not succeeded in bringing the enemy commander-in-chief to action, and the south-eastern section of the colony remained under German control. Until the new régime came to power this far-distant theatre had been virtually ignored by the Government, the General Staff, and the Press. But under the New Imperialism pressure was exerted to extend the limits of British occupation over the entire German territory.[4]

---

[1] Amery, *My Political Life*, ii. 91 ; Hankey, *Supreme Command*, ii. 657 ff.; Sarah G. Millin, *General Smuts* (1936), ii. 41–49, 96–102, 138; Lieut.-Col. C. à Court Repington, *The First World War, 1914–1918* (Boston, 1921), ii. 53–54, 107; *Lord Riddell's War Diary, 1914–1918*, 277.   [2] Amery, *My Political Life*, ii. 160–1.
[3] Present writer's italics.
[4] Cyril Falls, *The Great War* (N.Y., 1961), 252–4; W. O. Henderson, 'The Conquest of the German Colonies', *History* (September 1942), 136–7; Hankey, *Supreme Command*, ii. 638, 685.

In the 'Middle East', between Cairo and Calcutta, General
Maude's troops had conquered much of 'Mesopotamia', but
Palestine and Southern Persia were still outside the confines of
the British Empire. Tighter control over the new greatly enlarged British zone of Persia was recommended by a Cabinet
committee under Lord Curzon appointed in March 1917.
The Basra 'vilayet'[1] would be incorporated directly into the
Empire, while in the Baghdad 'vilayet' indirect British rule
would be established under a 'resident . . . behind an Arab
façade'. The requisite instructions by the War Cabinet were
sent to British local authorities. The solution to the Palestine
problem was less easy to find; the area must first be wrested from
the Turks, after which the French would have to be persuaded
to release the British Government from its obligations made
the year before to place the Holy Land under international
administration. In April Lloyd George told the British Ambassador to Paris that in Palestine 'the French will have to accept
our Protectorate; we shall be there by conquest and shall
remain, we being of no particular faith and the only Power fit
to rule Mohammedans, Jews, Roman Catholics, and all
religions'.[2]

Amery in his memoirs states that a draft he prepared in
January urging 'the special importance of securing continuity of
territory or of control both in East Africa and between Egypt
and India . . . was adopted with little alteration'. It was obvious
that the best way of securing such control was through force
of arms during the war itself. Indeed the increasing success of
the German submarine campaign emphasized the need to
acquire the territory the Empire required before peace was
forced upon the homeland.[3]

The above sketch of the New Imperialist war aims is not
meant to imply that a strategy designed primarily to achieve
them had become formal governmental policy. What Lloyd
George's view was it is difficult to say. 'As a strategist you
agreed, I think' [on the importance of the Turkish War] Amery

---

[1] The basic local Turkish administrative unit, established in imitation of the
French in the 1860's and after.   [2] *Diary of Lord Bertie* (1924), ii. 122–3.

[3] Amery, *My Political Life*, ii. 102; *Robert Laird Borden: His Memoirs* (Toronto,
1938), ii. 695; Philip Graves, *Life of Sir Percy Cox* (1941), 219–20; Sir Charles
Petrie, *Life and Letters of the Right Hon. Sir Austen Chamberlain* (1939–40), ii. 80; Sykes,
Two Studies in Virtue, 204–5; Stein, *Balfour Declaration*, 316–17, 321, 334, 365, 387–8.

wrote to the Prime Minister in the letter already quoted.[1] 'But as a Welshman you put in a caveat against that predatory Saxon instinct which would once again see us emerge from a defensive war with vastly increased territories.' Lloyd George consistently avoided commitment on the ultimate fate of the German colonies, wishing to keep them as bargaining counters for eventual peace negotiations. Arthur Henderson told the Imperial War Cabinet that the Labour party would not tolerate an annexationist policy, but it must be added that no one paid any attention to his views.[2]

None the less an imperialist strategy, as Amery pointed out, suited the Prime Minister's own oft-expressed desire for a way round and for 'knocking off the props'. Similarly, Milner and Curzon were sceptical of the possibilities of 'success' in the West, and were anxious to look elsewhere on strategic as well as on political grounds. The failure of the Somme campaign had disillusioned many. Milner almost from the beginning of his service on the War Cabinet in fact believed an eventual nego-tiated peace with Germany to be irresistible. In their dis-satisfaction with the previous conduct of the war and the desire for some way out—other than that of ending the struggle—imperialists and Easterners were agreed.[3]

The entry of the New Imperialism, with its urge to domi-nance, also greatly increased, though it did not create, the determination of the British Government to control the conduct of the war. This will to power and control, rather than any decision to continue a *guerre à l'outrance*, was the real significance of the change in government. The changing political environ-ment of 1916–17 favoured the claims of He-men. Not only the Empire, but the other members of the Entente, must submit to direction from London. After two and a half years of war England considered herself, with some justification, to be Germany's principal and most dreaded foe. She was now, in the words of General Smuts, 'the financial, naval and, to a large extent, the military mainstay of the Entente'. It was time she assumed the war direction.

[2] Lloyd George, *War Memoirs*, i. 1037, *Truth About the Peace Treaties* (1938), i. 63–64; Amery, *My Political Life*, ii. 160–1; Hankey, *Supreme Command*, ii. 599.
[3] Callwell, *Henry Wilson*, i. 298, 311, 322; Basil Collier, *Brasshat: A Biography of Field-Marshal Sir Henry Wilson* (1961), 243.

This outlook would affect all facets of British war policy, but its implications were particularly clear for the Balkan theatre, where British troops remained in deference to French policy and under nominal French control. There, as Smuts pointed out,[1] military success would contribute to French, and not to British, prestige in the Balkans. A French proposal in December that Britain reinforce her contingent at Salonika by two more divisions was rejected.[2]

The installation of the New Imperialism in the seat of power was paradoxical. As a movement it despised parliamentary government; and the new administration was hailed by an imperialist publicist in close touch with Milner as owing no responsibility to the House. The War Cabinet was rather the first step to an Imperial executive responsible only to an as yet uncreated Imperial legislature. Lloyd George himself soon made known his intention not to waste his or his Ministers' time on the Front Benches. 'That mob . . . this rotten assembly at Westminster', in Milner's earlier phrase, was to be 'managed' by the parliamentary talents of Mr. Bonar Law while the gentlemen of Balliol College attended to Imperial policy.[3] The appointment of Milner who had, though not by name, been formally censured by the House ten years before over 'Chinese slavery' in South Africa, appeared a deliberate affront to Parliament.[4] He had, Lord Esher wrote in congratulation, come to power 'in spite of the terrible slum of democracy through which your way has lain and lies'. Yet the Lloyd George Government owed its formulation to the House, and Milner and Curzon their positions in the War Cabinet, to

---

[1] J. C. S. The General Strategic and Military Situation and Particularly That on the Western Front, 29 April 1917, Arthur Henderson Papers, Library of the Trades Union Congress, London. Most of the memorandum is reprinted in Lloyd George, *War Memoirs*, i. 909–16. See also W. K. Hancock, *Smuts: The Sanguine Years, 1870–1919* (Cambridge, 1962), 449–52.

[2] Amery, *My Political Life*, ii. 121; Hankey, *Supreme Command*, ii. 597; *Journals and Letters of Reginald Viscount Esher* (1934–8), iv. 46–47, 72–75, 114; Capt. Cyril Falls, *Military Operations, Macedonia*, i (1933), 256–7.

[3] For an American historian working in the first years of the Kennedy administration, the comparison between the bright young men of 1917 and the Harvard brain trusters of 1961, and indeed between the two governments, in relation to their predecessors, was inescapable.

[4] Lord Milner's decision, approved by the British Cabinet, to import indentured Chinese labour to the Transvaal to work the Rand mines had been an important feature of the 1905 election campaign.

Lloyd George's political requirements. The Government could make no major decision without constant anxiety over the effects on Parliament. This was very natural, for neither Lloyd George nor the New Imperialism commanded any solid political support, and an adverse vote in the House could smash the entire imposing, top-heavy 'Imperial' edifice.[1]

At this point a sketch of the political background of this government of adventurers is in order. The reader will recall the mention of Sir Edward Carson's wrecking activities within the House in 1916. On 8 November of that year Carson's talent for destruction finally led Bonar Law to smash the First Coalition for the same reason he had imposed its creation—to conciliate the Party of which Law was the ostensible leader. On that day a debate took place on the sale of German properties, primarily firms handling palm kernels, in Nigeria. Since Bonar Law was then Secretary of State for the Colonies, the matter affected his personal prestige. Carson, in an unseemly speech, had introduced a motion that the sale should be made only to British firms. 'Why not do it?' he asked. 'What is the answer? Ah, we must hurry up and get money for the Germans!'[2]

Carson's motion was defeated, but sufficient Conservatives voted for it to convince Law, who had declared the issue to be one of confidence in the Government, that he had lost his control over the Conservative party.[3] That same night Asquith told a friend, 'Bonar Law came to me with his teeth chattering. He had once said that unless he was entirely backed by his own people, he would resign. Now he was in opposition to the

---

[1] *Esher Journals*, iv. 80; Denis Gwynne, *Life of John Redmond* (1932), 466–8; Hankey, *Supreme Command*, ii. 660; Sidney Low, 'The Cabinet Revolution', *Fortnightly Review*, vol. 101 (Feb. 1917), 205–17; *The Milner Papers*, Cecil Headlam (ed.) (1931–3), ii. 291; *Cambridge History of the British Empire*, iii. 347 ('Instinctively repelled by inefficiency and waste, and preferring leadership to democracy, they believed that immediate benefits would flow only from a British paternal administration, impeded as little as possible by "that mob at Westminster" '), 347 n. 4 ('Curzon, Rosebery and Froude shared with Milner this antipathy towards parliamentary institutions').

[2] Great Britain. *5 Parliamentary Debates* (Commons), lxxxvii, 351. The fall of the First Coalition is the principal subject of Lord Beaverbrook's fascinating *Politicians and the War, 1914–1916*, ii (n.d., but *c.* 1932).

[3] 65 Unionists supported Carson and 73 Bonar Law, out of a total representation in the House of 286. (Robert Blake, *The Unknown Prime Minister: The Life and Times of Andrew Bonar Law, 1858–1923* [1955], 299.)

majority of his own people.'[1] Thereafter Bonar Law for the first time became willing to collaborate with Lloyd George to oust Asquith from the premiership. The pressure of the two men several weeks later to displace Asquith from the chairmanship of the Cabinet War Committee brought down the Liberal Coalition.

The Government which was formed in its place, however, was not what Carson or the dissident Unionists had expected. Carson had hoped for a seat in the War Cabinet, and in this ambition had been encouraged by Lloyd George. Once in office, however, the new Prime Minister, anxious to avoid such a *mauvais coucheur* as his colleague, tried to appoint Carson Lord Chancellor and finally compromised on the position of First Lord of the Admiralty. In Carson's stead Lloyd George at the last minute appointed to the War Cabinet Lord Milner. Milner enjoyed, as Lloyd George later observed, the support of the two very separate groups of Tory Die-hards and Tory intelligentsia. The last included the very influential Geoffrey Dawson, once a member of the *Kindergarten* and now editor of *The Times*, who had pressed Milner's claims. Milner was himself however not a political leader. Thereby Lloyd George for the moment (and he was a man who lived for the moment) gained the best of both worlds.

Lord Curzon, whose personal ambition was well known, was offered a seat in the War Cabinet in order to gain the support of the Conservative 'elder statesmen' in the First Coalition—the 'three C's' (Cecil, Chamberlain, and Curzon himself) and Walter Long—though it is only fair to add that the new Prime Minister also valued Curzon's industry and encyclopaedic knowledge of the Empire. The accession of the 'three C's', together with Arthur Balfour's agreement to take the Foreign Office, made possible the formation of a new Government which was presented to the House as a *fait accompli*.[2]

With the exception of the premiership, all the key governmental posts were held by Conservatives. Conservative support for the Government would now be a primary responsibility

[1] Asquith Papers. The extract in John Bowle, *Viscount Samuel* (1957), 40, is wrongly dated. See also Bonar Law's memorandum of 30 Dec. 1916, in Blake, *Unknown Prime Minister*, 304.

[2] *The History of The Times*, iv. *1912–1948* (1952), i. 301–6; H. Montgomery Hyde, *Carson* (1954), 413–14; *Riddell War Diary*, 213, 345; Gollin, *Proconsul*, 370–5.

not only of Bonar Law but also of Sir Edward Carson. 'The combination of L. G. and Carson', the editor of the *Observer*, J. L. Garvin, wrote to Fisher, 'is an indispensable part of the Parliamentary basis.' The Tory rank and file were, as Lloyd George said, 'suspicious and distrustful'.[1]

The Conservative party was of course still in a minority in the House of Commons.[2] All of the Liberal leaders, with the exception of the proscribed Churchill, were resentful of their erstwhile colleague and had refused to accept office in the new Administration, preferring, in Sir Herbert Samuel's words, to 'form a possible alternative Govt. which it was to the interest of the country to have'. The Liberal party machinery within the House remained in those Leaders' hands. Almost one-half of the Liberal members had indicated they would support the new Government, but could these long resist the pressure of the Whips and their own chief? The Irish Nationalist Party were, Lloyd George later commented, 'on the whole Asquithian'.[3] Perhaps they, if not the Irish nation, still hopefully awaited Home Rule. 'More than half the Labour Party [were] bitterly hostile.'[4]

The new Government therefore faced a still disgruntled House of Commons in which the old party lines and loyalties had been changed out of recognition by the stresses of war. The

[1] Blake, *Unknown Prime Minister*, 341; *Fear God and Dread Nought: The Correspondence of Admiral of the Fleet Lord Fisher of Kilverstone*, iii (1959), 424; Lloyd George, *War Memoirs*, i. 596; Hankey, *Supreme Command*, ii. 664–5.

[2] Seats of Parties in the House of Commons, 1 Jan. 1917:

Liberals	261
Labour	37
Nationalists	84
	382
Unionists	287
Independent	1
	288

(*Dod's Parliamentary Companion for 1917*, p. 240.)

[3] See, however, the comments in A. J. P. Taylor, *Politics in the First World War*: The Raleigh Lecture on History, British Academy, 1959, p. 81.

[4] Viscount Samuel, *Grooves of Change* (N.Y., 1946), 153; Lloyd George, *War Memoirs*, i. 596–621. See also Christopher Addison, *Politics from Within, 1911–1918* (1924), i. 270–1; Letter, Lloyd George to Derby, 15 Mar. 1917 ('Neil Primrose tells me that we can depend upon the support of anything between 150 and 100 Liberals and Labour men, and that there are only about fifty or sixty Liberals and Labour men who are out-and-out opponents of the Government'), Randolph Churchill, *Lord Derby, King of Lancashire* (1959), 259; Winston S. Churchill, *The World Crisis* (4-vol. Odhams Press edn.), iii. 1112; Gwynne, *Redmond*, 536.

House, now in a perpetual state of flux, awaited only leadership
and another in the fast recurring series of crises to bring down
the Lloyd George régime, that 'leap in the dark'. To stave off
revolt the Government had to remain constantly on the alert.
Eighty members of Parliament, 12 per cent. of its total strength,
were given office. The leader of the Labour party was awarded
a seat in the War Cabinet. Industrial compulsion, over which
so much fuss had been made during the past twenty months,
was shortly dropped in deference to Labour objections. The
Conservative 'elder statesmen', fearful of change, were assured
that no new appointment would for the present be made in
the command in France. At the end of December the King was
able to inform Sir Douglas Haig of his decision to promote the
Commander-in-Chief to the rank of field-marshal. 'I hope you
will look upon it as a New Year's gift from myself and the
country.' Lloyd George, however, continued to refer to Haig
as General.[1]

To these difficulties with the House there was one drastic
remedy—a general election. Lloyd George, generally distrusted
in the narrow world of politics, was reputed to be popular in
'the country', where the news of his accession was generally
greeted with relief. It was for fear of the results of a general
election that Asquith told his followers to refrain from an
immediate parliamentary challenge. The King and the officials at the Royal Court repeatedly advised Haig and Robertson
not to provoke Lloyd George too far, lest the latter call an
election from which he would emerge as dictator rather than
prime minister and liquidate the last remnants of the British
constitution. Why didn't Lloyd George take this step? Once
the Government had been forced to meet an issue in the House
and thereby discovered its own strength, an event which did
not occur until the Maurice debate of May 1918, it immediately
and enthusiastically began preparations for an election.[2]

[1] *The Nation*, 10 Mar. 1917, p. 759; Duff Cooper, *Haig* (1936), ii. 14. See also
Beaverbrook, *Politicians and the War*, ii. 325; R. Churchill, *Derby*, 285; Lloyd George,
War Memoirs, i. 633, 805–16; *5 Parliamentary Debates* (Commons), xcviii (29 Oct.
1917), 1237–49. The King had urged Haig's promotion the preceding August.
Asquith Papers.
[2] Addison, *Politics from Within*, i. 270; *Bertie Diary*, ii. 79; Georges Suarez, *Briand:
Sa Vie—Son Œuvre*, iv (Paris, 1940), 180–2; *The Private Papers of Douglas Haig,
1914–1919* (1952), (ed.) Robert Blake, 208–9; The Countess Haig, *The Man I Knew*,
(1936), 185.

Before then the obstacles to a general election must have seemed too great, if not to Lloyd George, doubtless to Bonar Law. Lloyd George had no party machine behind him—only an unorganized section of the Liberal party—and was dependent on Conservative party support. The leader of that party, and now also Leader of the House, was Andrew Bonar Law. The latter was 'before everything a party man, deeply concerned for his party, obedient to its instincts, and at each crisis the nominee of its machine'.[1] Law's commitment of the Conservative party to a war policy on 2 August 1914, his ultimatum for a Coalition on 17 May 1915, and his demand for the Prime Minister's resignation on 5 December 1916—each expressed in the form of a personal letter to Asquith—were, to an increasing degree, the result of party pressures. Law's opposition while in the Government to the Dardanelles campaign, and his repeated thwartings of Asquith's attempts to take over the War Office, faithfully reflected party views.

This acquiescence fitted in with Bonar Law's curiously attractive character: sombre, unpretentious, diffident—a natural fighter who battled for others and not himself. (Perhaps that is why, once in harness, he and Lloyd George worked together so well.) By nature a follower rather than a leader, one might suspect. He had in fact been a compromise choice for the position of leader of the Conservative party, not the best basis for independence of direction. When the time for decision came Bonar Law was in the position of 'I am their leader, therefore I must follow them'. So it had been on the three dates just mentioned; so it was to be again.

The political result was predictable. The Conservative party survived the war; the Liberal party was destroyed by Government decision in the 'coupon' election of December 1918.

The determination of the new Government, however, in imitation of the old, to appease a disaffected House continued seriously to affect the conduct of the war.

Five days after the formation of the Lloyd George Government the Central Powers made a public peace proposal. No specific provisions were revealed, but, stated the German Imperial Chancellor, Bethman Hollweg, 'the propositions . . .

---

[1] Keynes, *Essays in Biography*, as cited in Blake, *Unknown Prime Minister*, 532.

would be such as to serve as a basis for the restoration of a lasting peace'. This was rather disingenuous, but the Allied leaders did not pause to inquire for specific terms. The Entente flatly rejected 'a proposal which is empty and insincere'. The Allied Governments, if not their peoples, had made their choice. Now they must abide by it.[1]

On 20 December President Wilson asked all the belligerent powers to state the terms on which they would be willing to bring the war to an end. This request could not be so lightly disregarded; the President was gradually strangling off the supply of credit for the Allies and preparing counter-measures against the Allied blockade. It even seemed possible that Britain and America were heading toward a break in relations. The Entente reply, communicated to the United States on 10 January, added up all the desiderata of the members of the Entente. Among the aims listed was 'the enfranchisement of populations subject to the bloody tyranny of the Turks'. No mention, however, was made of the destruction, whether wholly or otherwise, of the military domination of Prussia.[2]

The change of government was generally welcomed by the High Command, for it symbolized the decision to continue the war and promised greater concentration of national resources to its conduct. The will to exercise greater control in war direction at the expense of the French was heartily shared by Robertson and Haig's staff at G.H.Q.—so long, of course, as that will to power did not manifest itself in weakened support for the Western Front. Already in the last stages of the Somme campaign Joffre's representative at G.H.Q. had noted with anxiety the increasing determination of the British staff to free itself from the unwelcome suggestions of 'Chantilly'.[3]

If the fall of Asquith was welcomed by G.H.Q. and the War Office Staff as a decision to exercise greater determination and control over the war, they none the less viewed his successor with trepidation. In retrospect Asquith appeared the more

[1] Lloyd George, War Memoirs, i. 653–67; Hankey, Supreme Command, ii. 599–600.

[2] Lloyd George, War Memoirs, i. 659–66; Arthur S. Link, Woodrow Wilson and the Progressive Era, 1910–1917 (1954), 253; Reply of the Allies to the President of the United States. Paris, 10 Jan. 1917. The War Cabinet. Report for the Year 1917 [Cd. 9005, 1918], App. I.

[3] France. Les Armées françaises dans la Grande Guerre [AF], v (1), Annexes nos. 134, 332.

congenial statesman. The General Staff had been able to rely
on his support for its strategic policy ever since the liquidation
of the Dardanelles. From Lloyd George they knew not what to
expect; but they feared the worst.

The potentialities for further disagreement between 'soldiers'
and 'statesmen', or, as it became less high-mindedly expressed,
between 'brass-hats' and 'frocks', were greatly increased by the
nature of the chief personalities concerned.

General Sir William Robertson was, like Lloyd George, a
self-made man—a rare phenomenon in the higher ranks of the
British Army of that day.[1] He had enlisted in the Army at
seventeen, spent twelve years in the ranks before winning his
commission, and thereafter occupied a succession of increasingly responsible staff (never line) positions. His native shrewd-
ness, which had helped lift him so far, prevented him from
accepting all the claims or sharing the self-deceptions of G.H.Q.
But he had come to London as an emissary from the Western
Front, and it was as such that he consistently interpreted his
functions. Impervious to blandishments or reason, graceless,
'aitchless', and chilling, he continued to defend the claims of
the Western Front against the 'slippery' politicians—while his
primary loyalty was reserved for Haig, a 'gentleman' who
throughout the war outranked him.[2]

Field-Marshal Sir Douglas Haig, unlike Robertson, was
invariably cool, courteous, and dignified. His long command
experience, comfortable means, and social connexions (he had
married one of Queen Alexandra's ladies-in-waiting) gave him
a personal prestige and ascendancy—even a kind of dull lustre—
that few of his fellow officers could match. But he was not one
of those who try to understand or reach their fellow men; like
Louis XIV, he was content to be the centre around which his

[1] 'Robertson is of a burly type physically. The face shows strength of expression.
He is fresh-complexioned, the eyes are keen and steady, the eyebrows dark and
bushy. He has a thick grey moustache and a powerful jaw and chin. In civilian
dress I should say he would be taken for a country gentleman of agricultural
pursuits rather than for a soldier.' (Michael MacDonagh, *In London During the
Great War: The Diary of a Journalist* [1935], 192.)

[2] Lord Beaverbrook, *Men and Power, 1917–1918* (1956), p. xxiii; Lloyd George,
War Memoirs, i. 466–9; Liddell Hart, ' "Wully" Robertson', *Through the Fog of War*
(1938), 110–15; Field-Marshal Sir William Robertson, *From Private to Field-Marshal*
(1921), *passim*; E. L. Spears, *Prelude to Victory* (1939), 33–35; Victor Bonham-Carter,
Soldier True (1963), *passim*.

world revolved. In brief, his was a reserved, perhaps even closed, personality—and he had long decided not to trust Lloyd George.[1]

What else can one say about the Commander-in-Chief? Thorough, decent, without a trace of imagination, he incarnated an age, a society, and a way of life the war itself was destroying almost day by day. The family motto of the Haigs, 'Tyde What May', was appropriate. Sir Douglas Haig forced the pace of destruction with imperturbability, obstinacy, and blindness.

If Robertson did not know the meaning of tact, or Haig that of personal understanding—Lloyd George knew both almost too well. Asquith, wrote Haig's Director of Intelligence, General Charteris, had been 'a Sahib . . . a tired-out Sahib', but none the less a gentleman. Lloyd George was not. He was only the most successful, the least reserved, demagogue the British people have ever known. His championing of the under-dog, his jibes at the landowning classes and the privileged ('Ah, those Dukes!), were remembered, and resented.

Lloyd George was of course Welsh, not English. Asquith, Churchill, Haig, Law, Robertson—these are all unmistakably men of British character, they fit only into the British social and spiritual climate, so matter-of-fact yet so unique. Lloyd George seems out of place in this northern environment, a Latin not a Saxon type.

The Prime Minister's personal life (he was known in some circles as 'the Goat') was rumoured to be expansive but indiscriminating. He had been the country's leading 'pro-Boer'. When he had visited G.H.Q. the preceding autumn his unmannerly behaviour had been minutely noted. His entourage of hangers-on and attendant gentlemen of the Press and screen made no favourable impression. He had 'sat with his arms on the table', and had been late for interviews. Sir Douglas Haig had been 'terribly disappointed with him'. If Lloyd George was of humble Welsh origin, Haig and his circle, who had long served with him, were predominantly Scotch or Irish gentry. An overwhelming proportion of the general officers in the British Regular Army had aristocratic background or connexions.

[1] *Private Papers of Douglas Haig*, Introduction, 15–30; W. S. Churchill, *Great Contemporaries* (Fontana, 1959), 180–90; Brig.-Gen. John Charteris, *Field-Marshal Earl Haig* (1929), *passim*, but see esp. pp. 204–7; John Terraine, *Douglas Haig*, (1963), *passim*, and his essay on Haig in *The Western Front, 1914–1918* (1964), 182–93.

Haig's Chief of General Staff, Lieutenant-General Sir Laurence Kiggell, to whom Lloyd George soon unveiled his griefs, was the son of an Irish J.P. He cut the Prime Minister short. 'He ruffled me so thoroughly that I argued vehemently with him and I fear without displaying the respect due to his high office. I told him he had better make peace at once if England was trying to take up the line that heavy losses could not be allowed.' Lloyd George, of whom it was said he cashed one's mental cheques before one had time to present them, was impatient with slower-minded associates. The incompatibility of temperament and mutual distrust were complete; and misunderstanding further increased by class prejudice on one side, by an arrogant sense of mental superiority on the other.[1]

The High Command was determined to keep the new Government on the straight and narrow path to salvation. They had no lack of allies, natural or otherwise, with whom close touch was maintained. The new Secretary of State for War, Lord Derby, felt obligated by his 'loyalty' to the Army chiefs. Above all the fluid state of Parliament offered constant opportunities for outside pressure.

The newspaper press was one source of such (indirect) pressure. In an age of a literate public—as yet inaccessible by radio or television—the Press was a valuable if (as it proved) dangerous and unreliable instrument. Newspapers could exert influence on Parliament, partly through the display and exploitation of carefully selected 'leaked' information. Thus the downfall of Asquith had been widely, though inaccurately, ascribed to the pressure of the Northcliffe and Beaverbrook Press; while, more truthfully, to the Repington telegram had been credited the creation of the First Coalition and the consequent slow strangulation of the Dardanelles campaign.[2]

[1] Charteris, *At G.H.Q.*, 180; Cooper, *Haig*, ii. 23; Earl Lloyd George, *Lloyd George* (1960), *passim* (a sad little book by the Prime Minister's eldest son); Elie Halévy, *Imperialism and the Rise of Labour* (Ernest Benn, 1961), 96–99; Hankey, *Supreme Command*, ii. 575–7; Reginald Pound and Geoffrey Harmsworth, *Northcliffe* (1959), 506; The Countess Haig, *The Man I Knew*, 170–1 ('Mr. Lloyd George arrived at the Western Front accompanied by a crowd like a lot of Cook's tourists. . . . Lloyd George's visits always gave Douglas the impression of being joy-rides. He was followed round by groups of photographers and cinematograph operators').

[2] R. Churchill, *Derby*, 268–9; *Esher Journals*, iv. 70 ('I pressed upon Henry the vital necessity of holding the narrow Calvinistic doctrine—so to speak—that salvation can only be found between Dunkerque and the Vosges').

The Northcliffe stable, owned and dominated by the dictatorial, capricious, and indeed incipiently insane Lord Northcliffe, claimed a total of half the circulation in London. To the 'quality', it offered *The Times*; to the 'man in the street', the *Daily Mail*—and both pressed the claims of the generals against the 'wiles of Downing Street'. Lord Northcliffe believed his mission in the war to be the protection of the soldiers from the politicians. How else could one assure the 'permanent cessation' of the 'German menace to civilization'? How else might the politicians whose careers he was convinced he had made be kept up to the mark? Northcliffe, Haig noted after a conversation with the great man, 'is determined to keep L.G. on right lines or force him to resign the Premiership'. The fashionable, extreme Tory *Morning Post* followed suit. The Liberal *Westminster Gazette*, well known in the political world of London if not elsewhere, continued the Asquithian line of supporting the generals, this time against the former Prime Minister's leading political opponent. The radical *The Nation*, fearful of the influence of the New Imperialism on strategy, abstained from criticizing the military leadership on that particular issue. The *Manchester Guardian* was equally alienated by the Milner and Curzon influence. The *Daily Telegraph* and *Daily Chronicle*, the friendship of whose editors or proprietors the Prime Minister was careful to cultivate, were more partial to the Government's case, but they had neither the mass circulation of the *Daily Mail* nor the prestige of the quality journals.[1]

Finally there was in, however ambiguously, the very centre of power His Majesty King George the Fifth. The Royal family, by tradition interested in the higher military appointments, had long helped Sir Douglas Haig in his career. It is probable that royal pressure obtained Haig's entry into the Staff College, in spite of his inadequate academic achievements and medical rejection on the grounds of colour-blindness. Now the Commander-in-Chief and the sovereign were in constant communication. Any move affecting Haig's personal position might prove awkward to the Government, already beset by so many ill-wishers. Moreover George V regretted Asquith's

<hr>

[1] Beaverbrook, *Politicians and the War*, ii. 331, *Men and Power, 1917–1918*, 55–63; J. L. Hammond, *C. P. Scott of the Manchester Guardian* (1934), 210–11; Repington, *First World War*, i. 427; Suarez, *Briand*, iv. 180–2. Files of the newspapers mentioned.

ouster and, like the rest of the Establishment of which he was the head, then disliked and feared Lloyd George. Ahead of the new Prime Minister—'the little man', as his social superiors half-patronizingly, half-admiringly, called him—lay a task of immense proportions.[1]

[1] Liddell Hart, *Through the Fog of War*, 39–57; Charteris, *At G.H.Q.*, 133; Harold Nicolson, *King George the Fifth* (1952), 276–7; Stanley Morison, 'Personality and Diplomacy in Anglo-American Relations, 1917', *Essays Presented to Sir Lewis Namier* (1956), 466.

PLATE 12

The Imperial War Cabinet, 1917

In the front row, from left to right, are seated: Mr. Arthur Henderson, Lord Milner, Lord Curzon, Mr. Bonar Law, Mr. Lloyd George, Sir Robert Borden, Mr. W. F. Massey, and General Smuts. In the middle row are: Sir P. Sinha, the Maharajah of Bikanir, Sir James Meston, Mr. Austen Chamberlain, Lord Robert Cecil, Mr. Walter Long, Sir Joseph Ward (Finance Minister, New Zealand), Sir George Perley (Minister of Canadian Overseas Forces), Mr. Robert Rogers (Canadian Minister of Public Works), and Mr. J. D. Hazen (Canadian Minister of Marine). In the back row are: Capt. L. S. Amery, M.P., Admiral Jellicoe, Sir Edward Carson, Lord Derby, Major-General F. B. Maurice (Director of Military Operations), Lieutenant-Colonel Sir Maurice Hankey, Mr. Henry Lambert (Secretary to the Imperial Conference), and Major Storr (Assistant Secretary)

VIII

PERIL

'The Navy is losing the war as fast as the Army is winning it.'
Letter, ADMIRAL BEATTY to SIR EDWARD CARSON, 30 April 1917.

THREE main strategic themes faced the new Government in the first few months of its existence: the French demands for a new offensive in the West, the beginnings of a new effort against the Turks, and the naval isolation of the British Isles. These consequently provide the framework for this chapter.

Lloyd George's first formal initiatives in the conduct of the war, made at the Rome (5–7 January 1917) and Calais (27–28 February) conferences, were maladroit and failed miserably. The Calais manœuvre in particular had lasting and unfortunate consequences. It must however be remembered that the obstacles confronting him made the surprise and secrecy, and consequent lack of support, of these moves difficult to avoid. Perhaps they, unlike his later forays, failed for want of preparation.

The first intervention was almost too dramatic to be taken seriously. At the end of December the Prime Minister pressed upon the French an immediate conference with the Italian Government, ostensibly to discuss the question of reinforcements for Salonika. The plenipotentiaries duly assembled at Rome on 5 January, to be startled by a memorandum and speech by the British Prime Minister advocating a general Italian offensive against the Austrians, to be supported by British guns. The British General Staff were not amused. The French representatives wanted all material staked upon their last desperate gamble, the forthcoming offensive on the Western Front. The Italian commander, General Cadorna, manifested no enthusiasm. The British proposal was referred to the three governments' 'military advisers', thus giving it a quiet burial.[1]

[1] Minutes and Conclusions, Anglo-French Conference, 10 Downing Street,

P

Obviously nothing very substantial could be accomplished by these methods. 'Personal diplomacy' had been ineffective. The Prime Minister, returning glumly through France, quarrelled with General Kiggell[1] and was greeted by a booming leader in *The Times*, entitled THE DECISIVE FRONT, reminding him

It is on the West . . . that the main decision must take place. . . . It is all-important, therefore, that our superiority upon the front should steadily increase. . . . The German armies must be broken up, captured, or destroyed. . . . We trust [these considerations] . . . are constantly present in the minds of those who are responsible for the conduct of the war.

Meanwhile the grand inter-Allied political and military conference at Petrograd had been postponed at the urgent request of the Russian Government, which, wracked with internal conflicts, desired only a peaceful passage into what its Bolshevik successors were fond of calling the 'dustbin of history'. It had become increasingly clear that the Entente would be lucky if Russia even stayed in the war. The great majority of her population, the officer in charge of British Intelligence in that country had reported, wanted nothing but peace.[2]

It was under these discouraging circumstances that on 15 January General Nivelle came over to London.

The new French commander and his staff had neither the weight nor the independent status of his predecessor. In mid-December General Joffre, 'Buddha', had disappeared from the scene, having been made Marshal of France and put out to pasture. The ramified staff organization at Chantilly was broken up. The overseas theatres directorate (Théâtre d'Opérations Extérieures) was placed under the Ministry of War, that is to say the 'politicians', at Paris. The new and diminished French staff lodged not in a luxury hotel but in a technical

---

26–28 Dec. 1916, Arthur Henderson Papers; Conférence du 6 janvier 1917 (à Rome, Palais de la Consulta), France. *Les Armées françaises dans la Grande Guerre [AF]*, v (1), Annexe no. 403; Callwell, *Henry Wilson*, i. 308–10; Collier, *Brasshat*, 256–8; Hankey, *Supreme Command*, ii. 605–11; Lloyd George, *War Memoirs*, i. 838–59.

[1] See above, p. 206.

[2] Beaverbrook, *Men and Power*, 46–47; Charteris, *At G.H.Q.*, 188–9; *The Times*, 8 Jan. 1917; Cooper, *Haig*, ii. 23; Repington, *First World War*, i. 449; Addison, *Politics from Within*, ii. 76; Callwell, *Henry Wilson*, i. 299, 311–13; Sir Samuel Hoare, *The Fourth Seal* (1930), 118; Lloyd George, *War Memoirs*, i. 648, 928–31.

PERIL   211

agricultural college at Beauvais. At its head—no longer
commander-in-chief of all French armies at home and overseas,
but simply commanding the armies of the North and North-
East—was an officer entirely unknown before the autumn of 1916.
General Nivelle, a mere colonel at the beginning of the war,
'ce tout petit jeune homme', in Foch's words (he was, in fact,
sixty), had no prestige in the eyes of G.H.Q.'s xenophobic
staff. The British Army's opportunity had come. Nivelle's first
request of his ally (or rival)—to take over enough of the line to
enable the French to constitute a 'mass of manœuvre' for
exploitation of the hoped-for breakthrough—was met with a
refusal. 'General Haig cannot accept in the present circumstances a situation which would deprive his Armies of all
offensive capacity.'[1]

General Nivelle had crossed the Channel to explain to the
War Cabinet his plans for the new offensive upon the Western
Front and to plead that the British Army be instructed to
accede to his request to relieve the French troops between the
Somme and Oise rivers. The new commander made a most
favourable impression. Already in a surprise attack in mid-
December at Verdun he had been reported as taking prisoner
about one-third of the total fighting strength of the enemy, an
unprecedented total. Unlike either Joffre or Haig or Robertson,
he was capable of reasoned and fluent speech, and that in
English! Of perhaps even greater importance, he presented, in
plausible terms, the case for the 'knock-out' blow Lloyd George
had earlier promised and for the delivery of which the Entente,
and most of all Great Britain, now stood in such desperate
need. Through surprise and a concentrated artillery barrage
a quick breakthrough would be effected, to be followed by (a
genuinely novel feature) a great specially constituted infantry
mass of exploitation. Unlike the Somme, the whole operation
would be a matter of days rather than weeks. General Nivelle
warned his hearers that from now on the French effectives
would steadily decline and that the French people, in the face
of further disappointments, might make peace. The French

---

[1] Cyril Falls, *Military Operations, France and Belgium, 1917*, i (1940), Appendix 3.
See also Brig.-Gen. John Charteris, *At G.H.Q.* (1931), 185; Randolph Churchill,
Lord Derby, King of Lancashire (1959), 265; *The Private Papers of Douglas Haig, 1914–
1919* (1952), (ed.) Robert Blake, 183–4; Jean de Pierrefeu, *G.Q.G. Secteur I* (Paris,
1920), i. 209–41.

Government and nation, it appeared, were resolved to place all their resources, emotional as well as material, into this great, and possibly final, effort.

Haig and Robertson, who were both present, urged the desirability of delaying the offensive, in which the British Army would perform the ungrateful task of 'containing' the enemy reserves, until the Russian and Italian armies could also attack, as had been the case the year before. But the French would brook no delay. Surprise, obtained through 'violence, brutality and rapidity', would be the key to victory.

The War Cabinet not only agreed to British participation and the requested relief but also provided Haig with the reinforcements, six divisions, one of them from Egypt, he requested. He would now have sixty-four divisions. It is difficult to see how the Government could have done otherwise. The responsibility for the offensive lay with France; and both Government and people appeared irrevocably committed. The French national temper at this stage of the war was greatly strained; the British could not afford to have it said that the offensive, which would be made in any event, had failed for want of Allied support. It was possible, though not probable, that the 'pitched battle' might even be successfully fought. Such were probably the considerations which led the War Cabinet to agree to Nivelle's proposals. In any event the result would soon be known: 'In case these operations do not achieve the success which is to be expected and must be very rapidly attained ('qui doit être obtenu très rapidement'), the battle will be broken off by [mutual] agreement.'[1]

A month later, on 15 February, while the Inter-Allied Conference at Petrograd was still in progress, the London morning newspapers reproduced some highly coloured accounts of an interview given by Field-Marshal Haig to a group of French correspondents at the end of January. It had been the first time the British commander had seen any representatives of the French Press, who had certainly given their readers what they, but hardly the War Cabinet, wished to hear. There would be a great offensive upon the Western Front, and the

---

[1] *AF*, v (1), Annexes nos. 447, 455, 456; Charteris, *At G.H.Q.*, 190; Churchill, *World Crisis*, iii. 1122–30; *Private Papers of Douglas Haig*, 200–1; Lloyd George, *War Memoirs*, i. 873–91; Hankey, *Supreme Command*, ii. 613–14.

German lines would 'undoubtedly be broken'. 'The war of
trenches must make way for a war of movement.' 'Our cavalry
is ready to turn his defeat into a rout.' Haig also made several
allusions to the undesirability of sending war material to any
but the 'decisive' front. 'What we still need in larger quantity
are guns and railways. We shall never have too many guns.' The
Field-Marshal had observed that 'we are supplying our friends,
especially Russia [and] Italy . . . with all kinds of material. This
is an obligation we cannot evade. . . . [But it] must not be lost
sight of . . . that the Western front is and will remain the principal front of operations.'[1]

The interview. moderate and harmless enough by the
standards of controversy which then prevailed, provoked an
extraordinary reaction. In London Haig's boastful, 'un-English'
tone (as it appeared in translation from the French) was
generally deplored. A question was raised in Parliament if the
interview had been approved by the Government. A memorandum was issued to the Press warning of the lack of hope for
a military decision in the West in the near future; the war of
attrition would continue. The officer at G.H.Q. responsible for
foreign correspondents, Major Neville Lytton, was summoned
to render explanation to the War Cabinet. His appearance only
made matters worse. 'Lloyd George', Lytton wrote in retrospect, 'appeared to be in a towering passion. . . . The Prime
Minister seemed unwilling to believe a word of what I said, and
I, in turn, getting angry, very nearly left the room . . . if what I
said was not believed, I was better back in France, where I had
important work to do.' Major Lytton was, however, sufficiently
alarmed first to get in touch with Lord Northcliffe. Northcliffe
saw the Prime Minister and warned him not to make too much
of the affair. 'A Storm in a Tea-Cup', *The Times* leader of 21
February was justly headlined. The blame was placed on
Lytton's superior, General Charteris.[2]

This trivial incident was an indication of the extraordinary
sensitivity of both the Government and G.H.Q. Its significance

[1] Charteris, *At G.H.Q.*, 192; *Private Papers of Douglas Haig*, 194; Neville Lytton,
Press and General Staff (1920), 66; *Morning Post* and *The Times*, 15 Feb. 1917.

[2] Beaverbrook, *Men and Power*, 361–3; Charteris, *At G.H.Q.*, 193–6; Lytton,
Press and General Staff, 70–71; Repington, *First World War*, 460–4; 5 *Parliamentary
Debates* (Commons), xc, 808–9, 1163, 1199, xcvi, 1535; *The Nation*, 14 and 24
Feb. 1917; *The Times*, 21 Feb. 1917.

was that it provided Lloyd George with an excuse to attempt to lessen Haig's prestige, or even procure his dismissal, while also ensuring that the French would have no subsequent basis for recrimination over the conduct of the forthcoming offensive.

The same day that the Haig Press interview appeared Lloyd George talked at length to the French representative at the War Office, Commandant Bertier de Sauvigny. The War Cabinet, he said, had been greatly impressed by the new French Commander-in-Chief and was convinced that the forthcoming operation must proceed according to Nivelle's, and not Haig's, plans. To this end they were willing to subordinate the British to the French commander and, in case of need, even replace Haig. Several days later Arthur Balfour formally proposed an Anglo-French governmental conference at Calais to be attended by the two Commanders-in-Chief. 'The British Government', the French Ambassador, M. Paul Cambon, reported, 'fears the erratic behaviour of its chief commander who appears a little carried away by his recent good fortune [an allusion to Haig's promotion to Field-Marshal] and has recently allowed himself to give some very unfortunate interviews.'[1]

The story of the ensuing Calais Conference has been often told, usually in suitably shocked tones. On 24 February the War Cabinet, at a meeting to which Derby was not invited and Robertson told he need not attend, authorized the Prime Minister to ensure 'the adoption of such measures as might appear best calculated, as the result of the discussion at the Conference, to ensure unity of command both in the preparatory stages of, and during, the operations'. Lloyd George wrote a personal letter to Briand urging a prior meeting between the two and a small attendance. 'We should invite each of [the two supreme commanders] to express his opinion freely and without reserve on the plans of the other.'

The conference, which Haig was informed would be devoted to railway allocation, began 26 February. After the railway question had been brought up, only to be set aside, Nivelle at Lloyd George's request produced a draft proposal on the future command relationships of British and French headquarters. This document, which appeared to remove any right of

---

[1] *Journal d'Alexandre Ribot et Correspondences Inédites, 1914–1922* (Paris, 1936), 42, 48 n. 2; Suarez, *Briand*, 150–4, 180–2; *Mil. Opns. Fr. and Bel. 1917*, i. 536–8.

communication between G.H.Q. and the British Government for an indefinite period, was generally recognized as being too drastic, and a compromise, drawn up by Hankey, was adopted. The War Cabinet would direct Haig to adapt both his preparations and operational plans to General Nivelle until, by Cabinet decision, the British participation in the joint offensive had come to an end.

So the great army of the British Empire—still fresh, yet now sufficiently strong and experienced for its commanders to aspire to the military leadership of the Entente—was, in Haig's words, to come under 'a junior *foreign* commander'. The humiliation could not and would not be borne. No sooner had the Conference dispersed than Haig, aided by the Germans, began to nullify its resolutions. The German Army had already begun its slow and painstaking withdrawal from the sixty-five mile salient between Arras and Soissons to the newly constructed *Siegfried-Stellung*, known to the British as the 'Hindenburg Line', thus shortening the German front and confronting the perplexed British and French commanders with a new and improved tactical barrier. Their troops proceeded painlessly to occupy all of the old Somme battlefields. 'We walk', Sir Henry Wilson noted, 'slowly and solemnly after the Boches.'[1]

To Haig his future action was clear. 'I don't think "the Nivelle Battle" is at all likely to come off, so the War Cabinet agreement then falls to the ground', he wrote Derby on 3 March. The British Army must now prepare itself for a possible German attack upon Ypres and the French channel ports. Meanwhile preparations for the recapture of Vimy Ridge proceeded, notwithstanding General Nivelle's remonstrance against this operation at the Calais Conference.[2]

Nivelle and the French Government did not agree with Haig's interpretation of the German intentions, and pressed the War Cabinet to call Haig to order. Not only did they get no satisfaction, but a series of telegrams and a long letter from the British Government bade the French to a new conference, to be held this time not in the comparative isolation of Calais

[1] Callwell, *Henry Wilson*, i. 330. The Calais and London conferences are described in detail in Spears, *Prelude to Victory*, 199–203. See also R. Churchill, *Derby*, 247; *Private Papers of Douglas Haig*, 196, 203; Hankey, *Supreme Command*, ii. 615–18; *Mil. Opns. Fr. and Bel. 1917*, i. 537, Appendix 19; Suarez, *Briand*, iv. 157, 159–75.
[2] R. Churchill, *Derby*, 250; Spears, *Prelude to Victory*, 549–67.

but in London. A memorandum from Haig had stimulated War Cabinet fears of a German attack upon Ypres and the French Channel coast, the success of which would be ascribed to the actions of the British Government.

My centre of gravity has been shifted southwards by the extension of my line recently ordered and now completed. The railways on which I should be so dependent in an emergency are not under my control and it has become evident that I can place no reliance upon them. By the recent decision of the War Cabinet at the Calais Conference I may find myself deprived of the disposal of my reserves at the critical moment. . . .

The King, who had not been notified of the War Cabinet resolution of the 24th until after the Calais Conference had dispersed, supported his Commander-in-Chief. The Dardanelles Commission had published its report on 9 March, condemning that campaign and by implication the civilian 'interference' in strategy that had brought it about. Perhaps other influences were brought to bear.

The London Conference (12–13 March) ended in an 'Agreement . . . on the Application of the Calais Convention', consisting of a series of qualifications, introduced at Haig's insistence and supported by the War Cabinet, nullifying in practice any control over G.H.Q. by the French command. The 'Nivelle offensive' became in fact, save for the time factor, two separate and uncoordinated major operations. The British Army undertook precisely those operations, notably the attack on Vimy Ridge, it had decided upon in agreement with Joffre the preceding year. The only modification was in the date, April instead of June, and this advance was better suited to the newly formed projects of the High Command for a subsequent offensive in Flanders in the course of the summer.[1]

---

[1] *AF*, v (1), 421–2, Annexe no. 865; R. Churchill, *Derby*, 253–4; Cooper, *Haig*, ii. 63–74; *Private Papers of Douglas Haig*, 203–12; Hankey, *Supreme Command*, ii. 618–20; *Mil. Opns. Fr. and Bel. 1917*, Appendix 20; Field-Marshal Sir William Robertson, *Soldiers and Statesmen, 1914–1918* (1926), ii. 220–1; Spears, *Prelude to Victory*, 255, Appendixes XII, XIX, XX; Suarez, *Briand*, iv. 178–9; *The Times* second leader, 9 Mar. 1917 (Asquith and Churchill are blamed for the Dardanelles venture; the Lloyd George Government is far superior; for 'In both the great fighting departments there is the true combination of a wise political chief, who recognizes his limitations, and a first-rate technical adviser, who is not afraid to speak his mind'). See below, pp. 243–5.

However Lloyd George's ultimate intentions be interpreted, the first effort at 'unity of command' ended in failure, and in a failure with consequences. Military resentment at the Prime Minister was deep and lasting. It still affects the literature of the war. 'So ended', reads the most recent British general history of the war, written by one with long service on the official history, 'one of the most unsavoury episodes in British political–military relations.' The personal breach between the High Command and Lloyd George, and for that matter the entire War Cabinet, was complete. Henceforth the Lloyd George Government was looked upon by the High Command as personal enemies. In any future government proposal, be it strategic or organizational, the soldiers looked first for the suspected hidden motive. Lloyd George had never made a more fateful error. Henceforth he forsook his previous rashness for caution, perhaps too great caution.[1]

While the French were forced to accept the independent status of the British Armies in the West the dying Russian Empire was constrained to witness, on 11 March, the unopposed entry of British and Indian troops into the fabled city of Baghdad. The British Empire had obtained the first striking success in the new general war, the one waged against the Ottoman Empire. To the British would go the prestige, and, they trusted, the solid gains to be derived from this new and promising struggle against a weaker antagonist.

For the first time in the history of the war the British Government now viewed the forces under the command of General Murray in Egypt and General Maude in Mesopotamia, as well as the Russian Army of the Caucasus, as armies engaged in a common task. That mission was first of all to conquer the outlying territories of the Ottoman Empire. It was hoped, and with considerable reason,[2] that through these operations Turkey would be forced to accept defeat, and in consequence Bulgaria as well. The end of the war would then be in sight.

1 Falls, *Great War*, 267; Cooper, *Haig*, 57; Maj.-Gen. Sir Frederick Maurice, *Life of General Lord Rawlinson of Trent* (1928), 189; Robertson, *Soldiers and Statesmen*, ii. 214. Calais was to Lloyd George as the Cuban invasion attempt was to Kennedy.
2 The effective strength of the Turks by March 1917 had fallen to four hundred thousand.

(218)

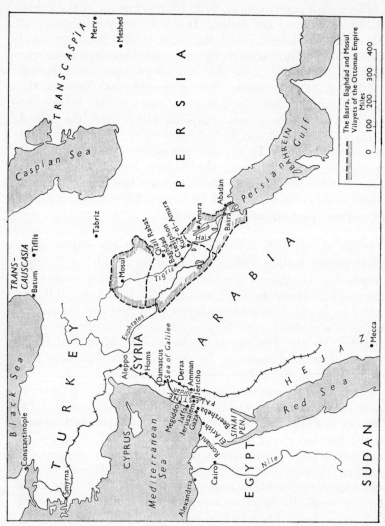

Map 7: The 'Near East'.

Even if these larger objectives were not obtained, all of the
Ottoman Empire south of Asia Minor would in one form or
another come under British control.[1]

Several days after the Lloyd George Government was formed
the Chief of the General Staff and General Murray were
requested to give their 'appreciation' of the possibilities of an
offensive into Palestine culminating in the capture of Jerusalem.
General Murray reported he would need a reinforcement of
two divisions for operations beyond Egypt. General Robertson
raised this estimate to three, refused Murray's suggestion that
he be sent a cavalry division from France, and stressed the
difficulties to be encountered due to lack of shipping and transport facilities across the desert sands. He however held out
hopes for a more extensive effort by Murray's forces in the
autumn, after the offensive in France had run its course.
Robertson's views were formally accepted by the War Cabinet,
and when they decided to participate in the Nivelle offensive
they also withdrew a further division from the Egyptian
Expeditionary Force.[2]

Robertson's new instructions to both Egypt and Mesopotamia, however, enjoined the British commanders to take what
aggressive action they could with the forces at their disposal.
In each theatre the British in fact enjoyed an enormous preponderance of force (perhaps five to one) over the enemy. The
Russian High Command for its part agreed, both at the Petrograd Conference and in telegraphic communication with the
C.I.G.S., that the Army of the Caucasus would manœuvre in
accord with the British. A trilateral attack would thus be
mounted from Armenia, Palestine, and Mesopotamia. The
prospects were surely encouraging.[3]

The anticipation of Russian aid was soon to exert an

[1] W. E. D. Allen and Paul Muratov, *Caucasian Battlefields: A History of the War
on the Turco-Caucasian Border, 1828–1921* (Cambridge, 1953); D. Chapman-Houston,
The Lost Historian: A Memoir of Sir Sidney Low (1936), 267–70, 438–9; Repington,
First World War, i. 484; Telegram, C.I.G.S. to Hanbury-Williams and Knox, 14
Apr. 1917, Arthur Henderson Papers.
[2] Lloyd George, *War Memoirs*, ii. 1081–4; Robertson, *Soldiers and Statesmen*, ii.
164–7; *Mil. Opns. Egypt and Palestine*, i. 250–1, 259–61, 272–3; *Mil. Opns. Macedonia*,
i. 252; *Campaign in Mesopotamia*, iv. 3.
[3] *Mil. Opns. Egypt and Palestine*, i. 260–1; *Campaign in Mesopotamia*, iii. 79, 86–90;
Robertson, *Soldiers and Statesmen*, ii. 79, 227; Falls, *Great War*, 251; Callwell, *Henry
Wilson*, i. 316.

influence upon British movements in Mesopotamia. On 12 December General Maude had begun a series of cautious operations which in the course of the next two months ejected the Turks from their positions along the river Tigris and its tributary, the Hai, below the meeting of the two streams at Kut-el-Amara, where Townshend's forces had been forced to surrender ten months before. Kut itself was recaptured on 24 February.

These siege-warfare actions had been encouraged by General Robertson, who had authorized Maude to incur a casualty rate of 25 per cent. In early February the Russians jolted the British into more hurried action. The Grand Duke Nicholas, now commanding the Army of the Caucasus with headquarters at Tiflis, informed the War Office that some of his forces would shortly move through Persia and on to Mosul and Baghdad. But the British had no intention of letting the Russians get to Baghdad. Robertson told Maude that he need no longer feel himself hampered by a fixed casualty rate and informed him that it was now also 'the policy of H.M. Government to establish British influence in the Baghdad Vilayet'.[1] 'You are required by this decision to press enemy in direction of Baghdad.' By private telegram General Maude was warned not to let the Russians get there first. The unopposed entry into Baghdad on 11 March was quickly followed by British occupation of the surrounding area. Maude, so far the only successful field commander in the British Army, was promoted to lieutenant-general. The Russian forces, still making their way through Persia, did not, save for an isolated detachment, advance beyond that nation's boundaries.[2] No offensive had yet been made from Armenia.[3]

In Egypt the forces under the remote and uninspiring command of General Murray had, in the slowest military movement ever recorded in that area's unrivalled long history, crossed the Sinai Peninsula as far as El Arish, only to find, in their advance on that town, that the Turks had departed. By

[1] Cf. the instructions of 30 September 1916, above, p. [157].
[2] Russian and British detachments met at the village of Qizil Rabat, west of the Persian border, on 2 Apr. 1917.
[3] Brigadier Dillon, Memories of Three Wars (1951), 81; Campaign in Mesopotamia, iii. 125–6, 157, 199 n.; Robertson, Soldiers and Statesmen, ii. 77; Arnold Wilson, Loyalties, Mesopotamia (1930), i. 210, 225–7.

early January all of the Sinai Peninsula was cleared of Turkish troops.[1]

Almost two months later, on 26 March, the British Egyptian command finally launched its first major attack against the Turks. A combined foot and mounted infantry assault was made upon the greatly outnumbered Turkish forces at the Biblical city of Gaza, on the Palestine coast. The Turks were hard pressed, and a wireless message indicating their intention to surrender was intercepted by British headquarters in Cairo and forwarded to the British command post before the beleaguered city. Through the mistake of a staff officer the message was not given to the 'Eastern Force' Commander until he had ordered withdrawal lest the horses of the cavalry suffer from thirst. None the less Sir Archibald Murray, who had not been present, wired the news back to London that a great victory had been won. The 'victory' was made much of in the British Press, and General Murray received congratulations from the King, the Imperial War Cabinet, Lord Derby, and General Robertson. He was also, however, presented with an unexpected directive, issued on the initiative of the General Staff: he was to exploit his 'success' and proceed directly to the destruction of the Turkish armies and the capture of Jerusalem. Further employment of his victorious armies would depend on the achievements of the Russian Army of the Caucasus. Trapped by his own complacency, General Murray prepared for a renewed assault on the now reinforced and fully prepared Turkish positions at Gaza.[2]

The Turkish war had the additional effect of temporarily changing the British attitude toward operations in Greece. The French commander of the international army there, General Sarrail, had been ordered by his government to make another attack in April in support of the simultaneous Nivelle offensive in France. The British War Office, left uninformed of his plans, was no more enthusiastic than it had been the preceding autumn. But then came reports that the Turkish command

[1] Field-Marshal Earl Wavell, *The Palestine Campaigns* (3rd edn., 1931), 58–67.
[2] *Mil. Opns. Egypt and Palestine*, i. 320–5; Repington, *First World War*, i. 502; Robertson, *Soldiers and Statesmen*, ii. 171; Wavell, *Palestine Campaigns*, 67–84; *The Times*, 30 Mar. 1917 ('British troops have fought and won a great battle in Palestine. . . . Whether we shall continue our advance now—"Gaza is not in plight to say us nay"—or defer it, remains to be seen').

had withdrawn a division from the Bulgarian front and Constantinople for service against General Maude in Mesopotamia. 'Salonika' thereby came to be viewed in an entirely different light, and the British not only authorized General Milne to participate in the forthcoming offensive but also urged on General Sarrail the need to advance its date. At the same time Lloyd George warned the French that this was the Salonika army's last chance. If definite success were not achieved the British would proceed to withdraw.[1]

The concept of a Turkish war had none the less revitalized all three 'side-shows'. These were rapidly becoming the focal point of attention.

Hardly, however, had the operations of the new Turkish war begun than military defeat and the first stages of the Russian Revolution combined to doom the efforts of the British Empire in the Middle East to the same stagnation that had so long prevailed on the Western Front.

In Greece the British forces on 24 April made what was supposed to be a preliminary attack in the heavily fortified region of Lake Doiran. This had been completely repulsed, and to General Milne's surprise the other armies under General Sarrail's command made no move against the enemy for another fortnight, and then with no success.[2]

In Palestine the Egyptian Expeditionary Force made a frontal assault in the grand 'Somme' style, complete with tanks and gas, against the now greatly strengthened Turkish positions. 'Second Gaza' (17–19 April), unlike the First, was an unmistakable British defeat which no dispatch could palliate. The Egyptian command's principal concern was now the construction of defensive positions. General Murray reminded London of his previous statement that he would need reinforcements amounting to two infantry divisions with field artillery and siege howitzer batteries for a successful invasion of Palestine, but pleaded that they be refused him. Information had already reached the War Office that the Turks with German assistance meant to recapture Baghdad.[3]

These reverses were serious enough, but of even greater

---

[1] *AF*, viii (a), Annexes nos. 1744, 1745; *Campaign in Mesopotamia*, i. 301–2.
[2] *AF*, viii (2) Annexe no. 1581; *Mil. Opns. Macedonia*, i. 305–17, 328–38, 342–5.
[3] *Mil. Opns. Egypt and Palestine*, i. 354–6; *Campaign in Mesopotamia*, iii. 301.

significance were the first effects of the Russian Revolution. What was already being referred to as the Russian defection had entirely removed one of the principal strategic bases of the general offensive against the Ottoman Empire. Shortly after the outbreak of the revolution in Petrograd in early March the Army of the Caucasus, of which so much had been hoped, had lapsed into inactivity. The war against Turkey, so recently begun, appeared to have ended.[1]

What of the implications of the revolution in Russia for the war against Germany? War-weariness in the Tsarist Empire had already affected all sections of society. The Inter-Allied mission to Petrograd (1–20 February 1917), with Lord Milner and General Sir Henry Wilson as chief British delegates, had met with apathy and obstruction. A Munitions Mission had been left behind to supervise the distribution and use of Allied material. Milner on his return, however, recommended to the War Cabinet that the Russians be given aid primarily in the hope that they would thereby be induced to remain in the war. It was no longer to be expected that the Russians would win it. Their morale was too low. In April the British Ambassador to Russia and agents of the War Office warned London not to expect any further offensives from the Eastern Front.[2]

All the more need, then, for the Nivelle offensive to have real and lasting effects. On 9 April Field-Marshal Haig's armies had begun the preliminary 'containing' operations. They captured Vimy Ridge and advanced from two to five miles on their twenty-mile front. By the prevailing standards this was a notable achievement. It could have been far greater had the initial advance been pressed with determination. The

---

[1] Christopher Addison, *Four and a Half Years: A Personal Diary from June 1914 to January 1919* (1934), 356; *Mil. Opns. Egypt and Palestine*, i. 355; *Campaign in Mesopotamia*, iii. 297–302, iv. 3–4; Stein, *Balfour Declaration*, 338; Telegram, Hanbury-Williams to C.I.G.S., 16 Apr. 1917, Arthur Henderson Papers.

[2] Addison, *Four and a Half Years*, 339, *Politics from Within*, ii. 76; Sir George Buchanan, *My Mission to Russia and Other Diplomatic Memories* (1923), 114; Maj.-Gen. Sir John Hanbury-Williams, *The Emperor Nicholas II as I Knew Him* (1922), 214; *History of The Times*, iv. 1912–1948 (1952), 1, 250 n.; Hoare, *Fourth Seal*, 205–6; Memorandum by Lord Milner, *National Review*, vol. 115 (Nov. 1940), pp. 653–64; Telegrams between the C.I.G.S. and Generals Hanbury-Williams and Knox, 14–16 Apr. 1917, Arthur Henderson Papers.

British command, however, was satisfied. 'We have', Charteris noted, 'done our share', and 'secured every tactical point that we intended to take'. Preparations for the Flanders offensive could now proceed. 'We are still attacking,' General Charteris wrote on the fifteenth, 'just to prevent the Germans from moving their troops from our front to the French front, but practically our task here is over.'[1]

On the next day the French made their great effort. Surprise had been altogether forfeited, and the original tactical plan dislocated by the German withdrawal in the north. After the fall of Briand in March, the new Minister of War, M. Paul Painlevé, had expressed extreme scepticism on the prospects of the proposed offensive. Nivelle had been allowed to continue his preparations only after an unprecedented meeting, attended by his army group commanders and key figures in the French Government, to discuss whether the operation should take place at all.

Nivelle had persevered, but the operations on 16 April belied all hopes. The thirty-division attack reached the enemy second defence position in a few places, but could effect no further tactical gain. The territory, guns (150), and prisoners (20,000) taken in the first few days bore no relation to the emotional capital invested by the French in this gambler's throw. It was more than the 118,000 or so casualties that were lost. The French nation's reactions against the hopes built up over the preceding months were to prove almost fatal to France and to the cause of the Entente. At the end of April the recently formed and very weak government of Alexandre Ribot dismissed the discredited Nivelle and in his place appointed General Pétain, known to favour a military policy of 'limited liability'. The operations in the West had succeeded only in weakening the will of the French to victory.[2]

[1] Charteris, *At G.H.Q.*, 214–15; *Mil. Opns. France and Belgium 1917*, i. 550; 5 *Parliamentary Debates* (Commons), xciii, 1093–6 (9 Mar. 1917. Bonar Law, 'We have taken, in fact, four times the amount of territory here which was taken on the Somme'); Spears, *Prelude to Victory*, 430–3.

[2] Jere Clemens King, *Generals and Politicians* (1951), 147–68; Callwell, *Henry Wilson*, i. 338–44; Lloyd George, *War Memoirs*, i. 916–19; Note by Lieut.-Gen. Sir H. H. Wilson, 30 Apr. 1917, Arthur Henderson Papers; C. R. M. F. Cruttwell, *A History of the Great War* (2nd edn., Oxford, 1936), 410–13; Pierre Renouvin, *La Crise européenne et la première guerre mondiale* (3rd edn., Paris, 1948), 429–35, 453.

Yet at the end of April it was neither the collapse of the
Turkish war nor even the possibility of Russian and French
withdrawal from active participation in military operations
against Germany that most disturbed the authorities in London.
What inspired real dread was the German submarine offensive
against shipping.

This threat had been long postponed. Pressure within
Germany for a submarine war against Allied commerce had
begun during the first winter of the war. In February 1915 the
Germans declared that the waters surrounding the British
Isles constituted a war zone, and the first submarine campaign
began. At that time, however, the Germans had only some
twenty-four 'U'-boats fit for commerce destruction, and it was
only beginning to be realized that these craft could venture
out into the open seas.

A variety of counter-measures were then undertaken. 'At
this date there were only four known methods of dealing with
the submarine. A patrol vessel could sink it by ramming; she
could blow it up with the explosive sweep; she could sink it by
gunfire; or she could entrap it by means of nets, which were
then being evolved.'[1] The submarine, however, had first to be
located, and it was on the last two measures, which offered
opportunities for concealment and decoy manœuvres, that
attention concentrated. The 'Q-Ship', an armed vessel camou-
flaged as a merchant carrier, was developed. Large nets
were placed in the English Channel, festooned with inefficient mines and topped by specially marked buoys. The
Dover barrage, patrolled by 'drifters'[2] supported by armed
trawlers and small war-vessels, came into being. The existence of this barrier for a time served as a sufficient deterrent,
and German submarines were ordered not to traverse the
Channel.

What really thwarted this first submarine campaign, however,
was not British counter-measures, but United States protests
following the loss of American lives owing to the sinking of the
Lusitania in May and the *Arabic* in August 1915. In September

---

[1] Archibald Hurd, *The Merchant Navy*, i (1921), 368–9.
[2] These small fishing vessels, manned by crews closely linked by family or
neighbourly ties, are described in ibid., 372 ff.

1915 German submarines concentrated on naval—not merchant
—targets in the Mediterranean.[1]

In October 1916 the German Admiralty limitations on their
submarines' freedom of action were reduced, by which time
the submarines themselves had increased in numbers and
improved in quality and tactical direction. In February 1917
the Germans finally threw off all self-imposed restrictions and—
rather imprudently—publicly embarked on unlimited submarine
warfare. The immediate effects were startling. Neutral shipping
generally, save for that of Norway, declined to approach
British waters. The tonnage and number of ships sunk rose
steadily—in March alone 317 merchant vessels were lost. These
sinkings were due to an active submarine fleet of 110 vessels,
of which only one-third were operating at any particular
time.

There now appeared to be no effective counter-measures.
The submarines' increased range posed insuperable problems
of detection. The seas were too wide for patrolling, mines and
nets under the new conditions were largely ineffective, and
when an occasional destroyer did sight a submarine it almost
never succeeded in effecting any damage.

Why not then seek to evade the enemy, or, should this prove
impossible, accept battle under the most favourable conditions?
Why not adopt the tried expedient of convoys? Sir John
Jellicoe—who had been transferred in the last days of the
former government on Asquith's direction to the position of
First Sea Lord for the express purpose of directing the anti-
submarine effort—resolutely refused to consider a convoy
system. Jellicoe persevered in this stance despite a prescient
memorandum by Hankey and intermittent pressure by the
War Cabinet and the newly created Ministry of Shipping.
Convoys were essentially a defensive measure. They offered
too large a target, made too great a demand on the merchant-
men's skill in navigation, and, a far greater objection, would
require destroyers on service with the Grand Fleet. There were,
after all, Admiralty statistics showed, an average of 2,500 to
2,600 ships entering British ports every week. The Admiralty,
however, in spite of repeated statements that it was 'consider-

---

[1] The discussion in the text is largely based on Hurd, *Merchant Navy*, i and ii,
and C. Ernest Fayle, *Seaborne Trade*, ii (1923), both *passim*.

PERIL 227

ing the problem', had not made any systematic study of the convoy system.[1]

The opposition of the senior naval officers in the Admiralty even to giving convoy a trial was not, Lloyd George relates, shared by the First Lord. Sir Edward Carson supported them none the less. On taking office he had declined to attend meetings of the Naval Staff. He would only, he explained, get in their way. As First Lord his function would be to protect the Admirals from any outside criticism. In a speech at a meeting at the Aldwych Club, under the chairmanship of Lord Northcliffe, he had defined his position.[2]

I advise the country to pay no attention to amateur strategists, who are always impatient and always ready for a gamble. We cannot afford to gamble with our Fleet.

As long as I am at the Admiralty the sailors will have full scope. (Cheers.) They will not be interfered with by me, and I will allow no one else to interfere with them! (Cheers.)

From the politician who appeared to have the strongest personal following in the House, the man who had destroyed the First Coalition, this was a formidable warning.

Even so the challenge must be met. In the last fortnight of April the sinkings increased sharply. The total losses that month were 412 ships totalling 870,824 tons. The average life of a merchant vessel coming to or leaving Great Britain had long been ten round voyages. Now of every one hundred steamers leaving the British Isles twenty-five never returned. No construction could replace the losses. It was difficult to believe that the morale of the civilian crews could endure indefinitely.

Disaster and defeat could now be measurably predicted. Great Britain might live, but it could not wage war after October. The country, Jellicoe warned in two urgent memoranda for the War Cabinet, was facing starvation. 'The situation

[1] Cruttwell, *A History of the Great War* (1936), 382 n. 1; C. Ernest Fayle, *Seaborne Trade*, iii (1924), 42 ff., 99, 128–9; Hankey, *Supreme Command*, ii. 639–49; Admiral of the Fleet Viscount Jellicoe of Scapa, *Crisis of the Naval War* (1920), 112–15, and *The Submarine Peril: The Admiralty Policy in 1917* (1934), 111–12; Sir Henry Newbolt, *Naval Operations*, iv. 346, 380; Rear-Admiral William Sowden Sims, *Victory at Sea* (1920), 28.
[2] Beaverbrook, *Men and Power*, 150–3; Ian Colvin, *Life of Lord Carson*, iii (1936), 217; Lloyd George, *War Memoirs*, i. 684; *The Times*, 9 Mar. 1917, p. 9.

calls for immediate action.' All imports save those 'essential to the life of the country' must be 'immediately stopped'. Foodstuff reserves should be built up while shipping still remained. Mammoth, 'unsinkable' vessels should be constructed, and the hull of one such vessel was laid down in Belfast that month. A withdrawal from Salonika, a theatre of which Jellicoe had been informed the War Office disapproved, must be effected. The country must prepare to withstand a prolonged siege.[1]

It was an intolerable position, and the War Cabinet declined to tolerate it. They nerved themselves to overrule Sir Edward Carson and attempt the desperate expedient of convoys. The new Commander-in-Chief of the Grand Fleet, Admiral Sir David Beatty, favoured a trial,[2] and one had already been made in the North Sea on the Scandinavian run.

Meanwhile the Ministry of Shipping in conjunction with a junior naval officer was investigating the Admiralty statistics on shipping and ascertained that these included coastal and short sea (primarily cross-Channel) transport. There was, it now for the first time became clear to the Admiralty, only a total of from 120 to 140 ships entering British ports each week. For such a number the seventy or so destroyers considered requisite might after all be obtained from the total strength in home waters of 279 without endangering the security of the Grand Fleet, the more so since the submarine campaign had just swept America and its navy into the war. Finally, the Ministry of Shipping had devised a comprehensive scheme for convoy control.[3]

---

[1] Fayle, *Seaborne Trade*, iii. 91, 104–5; R. H. Gibson and Maurice Prendergast, *German Submarine War, 1914–1918* (1931), 146; Jellicoe, *Submarine Peril*, 118; *Naval Opns.*, iv. 370–1, 379–82, 385, v. 17, 21–24; Sims, *Victory at Sea*, 8, 39, 318–20.
[2] So did Admiral Sims, representing the American Navy Department at the Admiralty.
[3] Fayle, *Seaborne Trade*, iii. 99–100, 128–9; Jellicoe, *Submarine Peril*, 130–1; *Naval Opns.* v. 18–20; J. A. Salter, *Allied Shipping Control* (Oxford, 1921), 123–4 ('Every one in an official position knew of course that there were not 2,500 ocean-going ships arriving each week, but only a very few in control of merchant, not naval, ships realized that the real number was anything like as small as 140. This wrong impression had two bad results. It disguised, until April 1917, the real rate of loss. Not many men realized that for some time past the average life of a ship had been only ten round voyages. It also exaggerated the magnitude of the administrative task involved in a convoy system. The escort of thousands of vessels a week would have been an impossible effort—twenty arrivals a day was a manageable problem').

On 25 April the War Cabinet empowered the Prime Minister to make a personal visit to the Admiralty and preside over a meeting of the Board. He would summon whom he pleased. The Press, Lord Beaverbrook states, was informed that fifty-five merchant ships had been sunk in seven days. 'It is vital', the Prime Minister then wrote Carson, 'that we should settle this infernal question. Otherwise we might sink.' On the thirtieth the Prime Minister and Curzon descended upon the Admiralty, where Lloyd George took the First Lord's chair. He was informed that the Admiralty would agree to attempt the experiment of a convoy system.[1]

Lloyd George had won. He had defied Carson and, though this was as yet far from evident, saved the United Kingdom from surrender.

The political risk thus incurred, however, had been very great. No further political danger could wisely be assumed if at all avoidable. What was now to be done about the Western Front? Haig and Robertson urged, in response to inquiries from the Prime Minister, that the French be pressed to continue their offensive. A passive stance would, Robertson argued, at this time be an admission of defeat. Already Haig had renewed the British operations, though only with tired and depleted units. This offensive 'on the cheap' was designed partly to encourage the French, but also to disguise the movement of large numbers of troops for the forthcoming operations on the Belgian coast. These attacks were tactically bitter failures. 'It was as if', a German regimental history reports, 'doors into great reception rooms had been opened and then closed again as soon as sufficient guests had entered.'[2]

The War Cabinet met on 1 May to discuss the situation in France. Lloyd George according to his memoirs deprecated exerting pressure on the French to continue, but his colleagues

---

[1] Beaverbrook, *Men and Power*, 154–6; Rear-Admiral W. S. Chalmers, *Life and Letters of David, Earl Beatty* (1951), 314; Colvin, *Carson*, iii. 257; Lloyd George, *War Memoirs*, i. 690–2; Hankey, *Supreme Command*, ii. 649–51.

[2] *Das. Inf. Regt. Bremen*, as cited in Capt. C. G. Wynne, 'Pattern for Limited Nuclear War', *Royal United Service Institution Journal* (Nov. 1957), pp. 496–7. See also Cooper, *Haig*, ii. 89–90; Lloyd George, *War Memoirs*, i. 916–19; Falls, *Great War*, 274–5; General Sir Hubert Gough, *The Fifth Army* (1931), 189–90; *Mil. Opns. Fr. and Bel. 1917*, i, pp. xi, 411–12, 428, 550–2.

thought otherwise and their views prevailed. 'Let the armies fight while time remained', was perhaps the dominant consideration. Lloyd George and Robertson went over to Paris and on 4 May urged the French Government to continue the joint offensive. He would, he told Robertson and Haig on the 3rd, recommend whatever they proposed. The French Government agreed to go on fighting, but, in the words of General Robertson's report of a meeting held that morning with Generals Pétain and Nivelle,[1]

It is no longer a question of aiming at breaking through the enemy's front and aiming at distant objectives. It is now a question of wearing down and exhausting the enemy's resistance, and if and when this is achieved, to exploit it to the fullest extent possible. In order to wear him down we are agreed that it is absolutely necessary to fight with all our available forces with the object of destroying the enemy's divisions. . . . We are all of opinion that our object can be obtained by relentlessly attacking with limited objectives, while making the fullest use of our artillery.

The British, it had been informally agreed upon, were to make the main attacks. The Prime Minister pressed that this resolution be adhered to, and urged that the generals keep their plans of operations to themselves. Ministers needed to know neither place, nor time, nor numbers engaged.

On his return to England the Prime Minister found that the House of Commons was up in arms. On Churchill's, and perhaps others', advice, a secret session was held on 10 May. Asquith had been opposed to this novel procedure, so Churchill opened the debate. He stressed the perils of the general and shipping situation and urged an end to the ceaseless offensives on the Western Front, lest Britain's and France's remaining man-power be cast away. Let us, he implored, wait for 'the American millions and meanwhile maintain an active defensive on the Western Front'. Was it true, he asked, that the French had suffered a great disappointment?

Lloyd George made no promise for the future. He replied that[2]

---

[1] Lloyd George, *War Memoirs*, i. 925–6. See also ibid. 921–7; Churchill, *World Crisis*, iii. 1137; Commandant de Civrieux, *L'offensive de 1917 et le commandement du général Nivelle* (Paris, 1919), 187–93; *Private Papers of Douglas Haig*, 227–8; Hankey, *Supreme Command*, ii. 625–30; *Mil. Opns. Fr. and Bel. 1917*, i. 429–30.

[2] Walter Roch, *Mr. Lloyd George and the War* (1920), 196–7. See also Churchill,

...our military leaders, and those of the French, are satisfied that this battle is proceeding according to their plans. .... In the battle of the Somme the Germans sold ground, they sold villages at very high prices. Therefore we were not sure that our losses were not heavier than those of the Germans. That is not so in this battle, owing to the heavy German counter-attacks. Our superiority of ammunition is considerable. By hammering, hammering, the time comes when armies crack. Our military leaders feel confident that is the only strategy by which we can win.

The British Government had by implication adopted and approved a military policy of pure attrition. Lloyd George, though he had overborne the admirals, had for the moment yet again aligned himself with the generals. The powers given to Robertson by the Order in Council of January 1916 were reaffirmed on 20 April 1917. The Nivelle offensive and the Turkish operations had largely failed. The general strategic situation had never been so grim. It was no time to take unnecessary chances.

Yet, if the power of the new Goverment *vis-à-vis* the House and the military command had never been so low, the control over the policies of the Entente which British authorities, both civil and military, had long desired was now thrust upon them. France and Russia were steadily weakening factors; the United States, with the aid of British naval intelligence,[1] had just been unwillingly pulled into the maelstrom. American military plans were uncertain; and preparations barely begun. Britain had not only obtained control, she must exercise it or see the entire Entente cause collapse. How would she wield her new power? On 4 May Lloyd George informed the French that the British would make a general withdrawal from Salonika beginning 1 June. Shortly afterwards the British Government requested the dismissal of General Sarrail, recalled General Murray, and appointed General Allenby to the Palestine command. At the

---

World Crisis, iii. 1112–14; 5 *Parliamentary Debates* (Commons), vol. xciii, 1270–1, and ciii, 268.

[1] The Zimmermann telegram, offering Mexico 'the best territories in Texas, New Mexico, and Arizona', had been intercepted by the Admiralty before the declaration of unlimited submarine warfare and transmitted to the American Government on 24 February (Arthur S. Link, *Woodrow Wilson and the Progressive Era, 1910–1917* [1954], 271; Ernest R. May, *The World War and American Isolation, 1914–1917* [Cambridge, Mass., 1959], 421).

end of May Haig wrote Robertson that 'for the last two years most of us soldiers have realized that Great Britain must take the necessary steps to win the war by herself, because our French Allies had already shown that they lack both the moral qualities and the means for gaining the victory'.[1]

The pattern for the remainder of the campaign season was already fixed.

[1] *Private Papers of Douglas Haig*, 234. See also Charteris, *At G.H.Q.*, 216; *Esher Journals*, iv. 103–5; Lloyd George, *War Memoirs*, ii. 1913–14; *Mil. Opns. Macedonia*, i. 317–18; Note by Lieut.-Gen. Sir H. H. Wilson, 30 Apr. 1917, Arthur Henderson Papers.

IX

PASSCHENDAELE

'The Generals won't make peace and the Admirals won't fight.'
Saying attributed to CHURCHILL, September 1917.

IN the summer and autumn of 1917 the British Government was forced to envisage a negotiated peace with the German Empire. The war-weariness of her Continental allies, the revival of international socialism, and the German submarine warfare against merchant shipping made such a mental adjustment, however painful, unavoidable.

From France, from Italy, and above all from Russia came reports of a popular demand for peace which the weak Governments of these three nations appeared unable long to resist.

In Italy enthusiasm for the war, never widespread, had almost died away.[1]

In France, the failure of the Nivelle offensive had had dire repercussions. Generals Foch and Pétain, now Chief of General Staff and Commander-in-Chief respectively, admitted in private conversation that 'La Grande Guerre est finie'. Pétain was clear that his army could not endure another winter of war. The attempt to carry out 'limited offensives' in accordance with the Anglo-French Paris agreement of 4 May had led to widespread mutinies continuing through June.[2] Analysis of these almost unprecedented revolts showed that a general peace was the mutineers' primary demand. Thereafter General Pétain's first care was to prevent the French Army from falling to pieces in his hands. French politics were dominated partly by the 'war aims' controversy—an indication of the weakening of the will to victory—but also by a series of messy financial scandals

---

[1] *War Memoirs of David Lloyd George* (2-vol. Odhams Press edn.), i. 505; Pierre Renouvin, *La Crise européenne et la première guerre mondiale* (3rd edn., Paris, 1948), 465–6; Sir James Rennell Rodd, *Social and Diplomatic Memories (Third Series), 1902–1919* (1925), 337–45.

[2] And, in isolated cases, into the autumn.

involving German funds. M. Briand, now out of office, eagerly
prepared to initiate peace talks in Switzerland through the
former German counsellor of embassy at Paris, Baron de
Lancken. An excited chamber and two very weak governments
proclaimed their determination to make peace only after the
return of Alsace-Lorraine, but how long would this last-ditch
defence against immediate peace negotiations remain tenable?[1]

The Russian situation aroused even more serious concern. In
Russia 'peace', the British Ambassador reported, 'is the universal desideratum'. On 18 May the new Provisional Government
called for 'the re-establishment of a general peace . . . without
annexation or indemnity'. Events, however, soon made it clear
that for Russia the end of the world conflict was most likely to
come through a German victory. In the beginning of July the
Minister of War, Alexander Kerensky, had succeeded in launching an offensive against the Austrians, but a German counter-
attack in the middle of the month proceeded to wreck the old
Tsarist Army as a fighting force. Thereafter the Germans proceeded to conquer Riga, Latvia, and the Baltic Islands with
little resistance from the Russians. The failure in September
of the attempt by the new Commander-in-Chief, General
Kornilov, to overthrow the Kerensky Government and re-
establish military discipline was much regretted by official
circles in Paris and London. Thereafter the Entente lost patience
and ceased to look for any further aid from her eastern ally. An
Inter-Allied military conference in Paris in mid-July concluded
that Russia might well leave the war entirely before the end of
the year. In that event, the generals recommended, the forces
in all theatres save the Western Front should be reduced to the
minimum required for defence; and the Allies should proceed
to re-define their war aims.[2]

---

[1] *Les carnets de guerre d'Albert Ier Roi des Belges* (Bruxelles, 1955), 155;
France. *Les Armées françaises dans la Grande Guerre* (Paris, 1922–39), *AF*, v (2), 192;
Journals and Letters of Reginald Viscount Esher (1934–8), iv. 122–3, 145–9; *Some War
Diaries, Addresses and Correspondence of Field-Marshal the Right Honourable the Earl of
Ypres*, (ed.) Gerald French (1937), 291; Renouvin, *La Crise européenne*, 482–4;
Lieut.-Col. C. à Court Repington, *The First World War, 1914–1918* (Boston, 1921),
i. 574; Alexandre Ribot, *Lettres à un ami* (Paris, 1921), 295; *Official Statement of War
Aims and Peace Proposals*, (ed.) James Brown Scott (Washington, D.C., 1921),
103, 136.
[2] *Diary of Lord Bertie of Thame, 1914–1918* (1924), ii. 173–4, 177, 180–1; Sir George
Buchanan, *My Mission to Russia and Other Diplomatic Memories* (1923), 151, 185;

The military exhaustion of the principal European combatants was exploited by the emergence of the international
socialist movement as a politically significant factor in a new
context of widespread social unrest which affected even the
British Isles. The continuing Russian revolution had not only
deposed the Tsar and (temporarily) despotism but increasingly
challenged the whole European political and social order. The
bureau of the 'evolutionary' Second International, dormant
since 1914, called for a conference of socialist groups at Stockholm to examine the international situation. The Petrograd
Soviet, more desirous of social revolution, issued a similar but
more militantly worded appeal. The British Labour Party Conference, which in January 1917 had overwhelmingly endorsed
the policy of a *guerre à l'outrance*, in August voted 'to go to Stockholm' by 1,846,000 to 550,000. In April and May a series of
engineering strikes brought out two hundred thousand workers
over the greater part of the country. And in June a conference
in Leeds convened by the extremist Independent Labour Party
and British Socialist Party not only welcomed the revolution
in Russia but called for its extension to Britain. To that end it
urged the establishment of 'local Workmen's and Soldiers'
Councils' in the Russian manner. For the first time since Queen
Victoria's middle years republicanism had acquired popularity.[1]

To these 'disintegrating forces' as Lloyd George called them,
the entry of the United States might furnish a counterbalance.
Could, in the state of comparative exhaustion of the major
belligerents, millions of fresh American troops on the Western
Front turn the scale? The first preoccupation of both the British
and French Governments was to urge the United States to
permit and encourage the enlistment of Americans by the

Paul Cambon, *Correspondance, 1870–1924*, iii (Paris, 1946), 196; Maj.-Gen. Sir Alfred
Knox, *With the Russian Army, 1914–1917* (1921), 677–8; *Mil. Opns. Fr. and Bel. 1918*,
i. 3–5; Constantin Nabokoff, *Ordeal of a Diplomat* (1921), 165; *Lord Riddell's War
Diary*, 272.
    [1] Carl F. Brand, *British Labour's Rise to Power* (Stanford, 1941); G. D. H. Cole, *A
Short History of the British Working Class Movement, 1789–1947* (1952), 360; Merle
Fainsod, *International Socialism and the World War* (Cambridge, Mass., 1935) *passim*;
Stephen R. Graubard, *British Labour and the Russian Revolution* (Cambridge, Mass.,
1956), 36–38; Hildemarie Meynell, 'The Stockholm Conference of 1917', *Inter-
national Review of Social History* (Amsterdam), Parts 1 and 2 (1960), 1–25; Lloyd
George, *War Memoirs*, ii. 1148–54; *Fear God and Dread Nought: The Correspondence
of Admiral of the Fleet Lord Fisher of Kilverstone*, (ed.) Arthur J. Marder, iii (1959),
463, 475–6, 484–5; A. M. Gollin, *Proconsul in Politics* (1964), 540–50.

hundreds of thousands in their respective armies. To this, however, the American Government would not agree. The Entente was now assured of unlimited credit, and the British Admiralty of American destroyers for convoy and of yet another battleship squadron for service with the swollen and inactive Grand Fleet. For the immediate future, however, American military co-operation would be limited to a one-division American Expeditionary Force to serve in the *French* sector of the Western Front. Marshal Joffre, whom the French Government had sent post-haste to the United States in rivalry to a British mission under Balfour, had performed his last service to France by persuading the American Government so to bolster French morale. The 'psychology of the plea', the Secretary of State, Mr. Robert Lansing, recalled, had 'appealed strongly to the American authorities'. Preparations for dispatch of a larger force with more ambitious objectives proceeded at what appeared to the Entente to be an excessively leisurely pace, and it was the opinion of British military authorities, and above all of General Robertson, that the American decision to form an army independent of the British and French military commands meant that American troops would be unable to effect any serious military operation on the Western Front for 'a very long time', if at all. Why indeed should the Americans in this theatre ever find the secret which had so long eluded the French and British forces?[1]

Besides, would the losses in shipping permit England to continue the war in the meantime? Throughout the summer and early autumn of 1917 the sinkings went on at a prohibitive rate. An estimate prepared by the Shipping Controller in August indicated that England could not supply the needs of her own population and overseas expeditions after the end of the year. Not until the end of 1917 was it clear, and then only to the unprejudiced observer, that the introduction of the convoy system had conquered the U-boat menace. Not until March 1918 did the construction of British shipping exceed the losses.[2]

---

[1] Lloyd George, *War Memoirs*, ii. 1299; *War Memoirs of Robert Lansing* (N.Y., 1935), 275–7; Frederick Palmer, *Newton D. Baker, America at War* (N.Y., 1931), i. 154–5; U.S. Department of State, *Papers Relating to the Foreign Relations of the United States*. Supplements. *The World War, 1917* (1932–3), i. 71; John J. Pershing, *My Experiences in the World War* (N.Y., 1931), i. 17–18, 30–33.
[2] C. Ernest Fayle, *Seaborne Trade*, iii (1924), 465, 470; Admiral Jellicoe, *The Submarine Peril* (1934), 94–95; Sir Henry Newbolt, *Naval Operations*, v (1931), i. 128.

That the submarine peril remained mortal so long was due
in large measure to the policies and attitudes of the Board of
Admiralty. Not until September was the convoy system generally used for ocean transport. It proved an unqualified success,
due mainly to evasion from the enemy. Out of 2,095 merchant
vessels in convoy, only twenty, less than 1 per cent., had been
lost. None the less the Admirals continued to regard convoys as
defensive, and therefore in principle unsound. They persisted
in overestimating the number of sailings for which escort would
be required; the First Sea Lord was clear that the necessary
escort could not be provided. Once again the Government
intervened, and a few sloops and destroyers were wrested even
from the Grand Fleet. The United States Navy was found willing
to provide escort for the New York convoy.[1]

Yet the mistrust of the Admirals remained fixed. As late as
the end of September the naval Commander-in-Chief in the
Mediterranean, Admiral Calthorpe, expressed his distaste and
regret at the employment of such an unorthodox method of
naval warfare. Nor was this view confined to the British Navy.
At an inter-allied naval conference in September Admiral
Jellicoe expounded the Admiralty's plans for anti-submarine
operations: a blocking operation against all the German har-
bours with old battleships and cruisers; or, alternatively, the
laying of an immense minefield in all the northern entrances to
the North Sea. Neither of these proposals was greeted with
enthusiasm. To cite but one objection, the British Admiralty
had still not devised an efficient mine. The other delegates, however, had little to suggest. Then the American representative,

---

[1] The first two experimental ocean convoys left Gibraltar and Newport News, Va.,
on 10 May and 24 May respectively. Regular convoys from these two ports and from
New York and Sydney, Nova Scotia, began in July. Outward-bound convoys were
introduced in mid-August. By September 1917 there were 120 to 130 sailings so
escorted each way every eight days, covering the greater part of the Atlantic and
Gibraltar trade. The convoy system was not extended to the Mediterranean until
October and afterwards.

Meanwhile the Admiralty made energetic but misdirected efforts at alternative
methods of combating the submarine menace. None of these—'Q-ships', 'dazzle'
painting, aircraft 'hydrophonic' squadrons, the raiding and blocking of the Zeebrugge and Ostend submarine bases, the laying of minefields and barrages on a
gigantic scale in the North Sea and Dover Straits—were successful in their aim.
How the Royal Navy could have benefited from application of the techniques of
operations analysis! (E. Ernest Fayle, *Seaborne Trade*, iii (1924), and Henry Newbolt,
Naval Operations, v (1931).)

Admiral Sims, surprised—but also impressed—his fellow admirals by remarking that the answer to the submarine had already been found, and that the problem was now one of improving an existing system. When the Germans realized the success of the convoy system and began to devise counter-attacks, the Allies, Admiral Sims stressed, would have two alternatives: either to use their Dreadnought battleships for convoy, or make the best terms of peace they could.[1]

Allied war-weariness, the socialist ferment, and the naval war thus forced the War Cabinet to consider a peace without victory. But no British Government could conclude such a peace without ignominy unless the terms included the German evacuation of Belgium and its coastline. Could the Germans be induced to agree? Lloyd George in a series of speeches attempted without success to elicit a statement on the subject from the German Chancellor. 'No German statesman', he noted at Glasgow on 28 June, 'has ever said they would restore the independence of Belgium.' 'The Kaiser', he said at the Queen's Hall on the third anniversary of the declaration of war, 'had not yet learned the alphabet of peace. The first letter in that alphabet is restoration. Then we will talk.'[2] Later that month the Vatican made an appeal to the belligerents for a negotiated peace. The British reply was that no progress could be made until the points of difference between the combatants were clearly known; the Central Powers, Balfour wrote, 'have never definitely intimated that they intend . . . to restore [Belgium] to her former state of entire independence'. A German declaration on Belgium, the British envoy to the Vatican, Count de Salis, informed the Papal Secretary of State, 'appeared to be desirable', as it was 'a point . . . of especial importance to us'. A direct German approach to England was finally made through the Spanish Foreign Office

[1] Fayle, *Seaborne Trade*, iii. 132–47, 188; Lloyd George, *War Memoirs*, i. 693–9; *Naval Opns.* v. 81–82.

[2] On 24 October 1917 Smuts told a National War Aims Committee at Sheffield that

> He did not think it worth while to pursue the war until we had got rid of the Kaiser and all the other evils with which we were oppressed. . . . Until we knew in advance that there would be complete evacuation and restoration of Belgium, we were not even going to talk about peace. . . . The German people could have peace tomorrow from the Entente, but the initiative rested with them.

(Source: *The Times*, 25 Oct. 1917.)

in September. The British decision, delayed[1] until 8 October, was that the Government would 'receive any communication' Germany might 'desire to make . . . and . . . discuss it with their Allies'. No answer from Germany was received. By the end of 1917 the strategic stalemate had ended. It was now Germany that desired peace through victory.[2]

In the summer of 1917 Great Britain's will to victory was stronger than that of her Continental allies. She was now indeed the real mainstay of the alliance. But for this very reason it was less easy for the British Government to be flexible in approaching the question of peace negotiations. This government, moreover, was characterized by continued increasing weakness and lack of self-confidence vis-à-vis the House of Commons. In May and July 1917 the Russian Government, the Petrograd Soviet, and the German Reichstag had passed resolutions pleading in principle for a peace of reconciliation. The statement voted by the French Chamber of Deputies on 5 June, despite a parenthetic ritual reference to 'Prussian militarism', betrayed rather than proclaimed a similar spirit. But no such conciliatoriness reigned in the House of Commons. The British parliamentarians resolutely refused to make any 'weak-kneed' resolution on war aims. Motions welcoming the Reichstag resolution and the Russian Government proposals and calling on the British Government to restate their peace terms were rejected by overwhelming majorities.[3]

Meanwhile party politics continued to be a source of

---

[1] Perhaps in hopes of victory in Flanders.

[2] Lloyd George, *War Memoirs*, ii. 1211–20; 1231–44; Lloyd George, *The Great Crusade* (1918), 104, 125; Correspondence relative to the Peace Proposals made by His Holiness the Pope to the Belligerent Powers on 1 August 1917. August–October 1917. Parliamentary Paper 'Miscellaneous, no. 7 (1919)', *British and Foreign State Papers, 1917–1918*, vol. cvi (1921), 575–89; Renouvin, *La Crise européenne*, 486–92.

[3] G. Lowes Dickinson, *Documents and Statements relating to Peace Proposals and War Aims* (December 1916–November 1918), xvi. 145; Great Britain, *5 Parliamentary Debates* (Commons), xciii (16 May 1917), 1625–1734 (a resolution moved by Snowden, welcoming a Russian Government proposal repudiating imperialist conquest and aggrandizement, and calling on the British Government to restate their war aims accordingly, defeated by 238 to 32), xcvi (26 July 1917), 1479–1590 (a resolution moved by Snowden, expressing agreement with the Reichstag resolution, calling on the Allies to restate their war aims accordingly, and accepting a Russian proposal that a forthcoming conference on war aims comprise representatives of peoples as well as government, defeated by 148 to 19); Arno J. Mayer, *Political Origins of the New Diplomacy, 1917–1918* (New Haven, 1959), 80–81, 133, 179–80.

anxiety to the War Cabinet. The Liberal chiefs had remained implacable, and in May Asquith rejected an overture to enter the new administration. In mid-July a reorganization brought Churchill into the Government as Minister of Munitions and shunted Carson upstairs from the Admiralty into the War Cabinet, where, as Lloyd George told the King's private secretary, he would be 'very useful and especially in making speeches in the country'. Milner hoped that 'part of the bargain' would be 'that Carson helped B. L. in the House of Commons, where I think the Govt. lacks fighting power'. Both these moves greatly increased the Government's efficiency; while the appointment of Sir Eric Geddes as First Lord of the Admiralty introduced a degree of common sense in the naval administration of the war. Reorganization of the Admiralty, seriously undertaken in mid-1917, was almost a prerequisite to British survival; and could not be other than superficial without the removal of Carson and Jellicoe as well.[1]

Yet, however necessary, the cabinet changes of 18 July 1917 seriously if temporarily weakened the Government. 'Ll. G.', Haldane wrote, 'is out to liberalize his Government. Curzon, I am told, is kicking, but I back the little man to win.' Curzon, however, was not the only one to protest. Churchill's appointment aroused particular fury in the ranks of the Tories. The National Unionist Council had carried a motion that Churchill's return to office would be 'an insult to the Navy and the Army'. Sir George Younger, Chairman of the Unionist Party, had warned the Prime Minister that 'his inclusion in the Government would prove disastrous to its fortunes'. Now the man many of the Tories believed responsible for the Ulster 'pogrom' and the Antwerp and Dardanelles 'fiascos', that 'floating kidney in the body politic', had been brought back into power. The resulting uproar, Lloyd George recalled, for a brief period seriously threatened the life of the Government.[2] As for Carson, disgruntled at his so-called promotion, he made speeches to the country, but ones that attacked War Cabinet policy. While

---

[1] Lord Beaverbrook, *Men and Power, 1917–1918* (1956), 169–71; Letter, Crewe to Asquith, 31 May 1917, Asquith Papers; Gollin, *Proconsul*, 436–42.

[2] 'The Unionists protested, from Bonar Law downwards; but they could do nothing, short of going over to Asquith. It was safer to offend them than to run the risk that the Liberals might reunite.' (A. J. P. Taylor, *Politics in the First World War*: The Raleigh Lecture on History. British Academy, 1959, p. 92.)

Lloyd George put out feelers on Belgium Carson proclaimed
that if the Germans wanted to negotiate they must first withdraw
their troops behind the river Rhine, well east of the German
border. On a visit to G.H.Q. in September he urged Sir Douglas
Haig 'to talk freely with Mr. Asquith'. The latter the next day
himself told Haig that the 'present Government is very shaky';
and both men of state assured Haig of their support of his plans
to win the war despite governmental doubt or hesitations.[1]

The House of Commons, lacking confidence in Asquith and
bereft of Churchill, became even further liable to the influence
of irresponsibles like Pemberton Billing and to the simple
xenophobia of Brigadier-General Henry Page Croft's tiny
'National Party', formed in September with a platform of
'complete victory in the war and after the war' and 'the
eradication of German influence'. The Government tacked
accordingly and adopted more cautious procedures. In May
the War Cabinet had favoured allowing British Labour and
Socialist delegations to travel to Stockholm; but at the beginning of August they refused to issue the requisite passports.
Arthur Henderson, who was in favour of 'going to Stockholm',
was manœuvred out of the War Cabinet and replaced as
Labour representative by George Barnes, a trade unionist
official and politician of long standing, but a comparatively
unknown personality. On the 16th Mr. Kennedy Jones, the
creator of the *Daily Mail*, made his maiden speech; 'the war
aim of the Allies', he said, 'is perfectly well known . . . we were
out to beat the German to his knees and then to skin him alive'.
He was followed by the Prime Minister who remarked that it
was 'a very interesting speech. I congratulate him upon it.'[2]

Opposition to a negotiated peace was of course not confined
to irresponsibles. There had always been plenty of counter-

---

[1] Christopher Addison, *Four and a Half Years* (1934), ii. 411; Beaverbrook, *Men
and Power*, 120-40, 156-79; Carson, Speech at Belfast, 20 July 1917. *The Times*,
21 July 1917, 3a; Brig.-Gen. John Charteris, *At G.H.Q.* (1931), 251-2; Lloyd
George, *War Memoirs*, i. 636-8; 5 *Parliamentary Debates* (Commons), xcvi. 1443;
Private Papers of Douglas Haig, Robert Blake (ed.) (1952), 254-5; Frank Owen,
Tempestuous Journey: Lloyd George His Life and Times (N.Y., 1955), 410-15; Dudley
Sommer, *Haldane of Cloan: His Life and Times, 1856-1928* (1960), 346.

[2] George Barnes, *From Workshop to War Cabinet* (1924), *passim*; 'Barnes, George
Nicoll', *D.N.B. 1931-1940* (1949); Brig.-Gen. The Lord Croft, *My Life of Strife*
(Hutchinson, n.d.), 129-35; Lloyd George, *War Memoirs*, 1121-39; 5 *Parliamentary
Debates* (Commons), xcvii (16 Aug. 1917), 1465-71.

arguments: such a peace would only be a suspension of arms; it would be regarded by the Dominions, the Allies, and the services as a betrayal; the only way to ensure a lasting peace was to make manifest the failure of aggression. Now a new and even more powerful factor had arisen: in the revolutionary situation of 1917 victory was the only way to avoid domestic upheaval. How else could Great Britain's continued participation in a war the relevance of which to British vital interests was so debatable be fully justified?

If we really defeat the enemy England will recover her balance quickly enough [Viscount Esher wrote the King's private secretary on 24 August].[1] If we fail to beat the enemy and have to accept a compromise peace, then we shall be lucky if we escape a revolution in which the Monarchy, the Church and all our 'Victorian' institutions will founder . . . the institutions under which a war such as this was possible whether monarchical, parliamentary or diplomatic, will go under. I have met no one who, speaking his inmost mind, differs from this conclusion.

On 2 August the protectionist W. A. S. Hewins proposed an amendment to a bill defining the powers of the new Ministry of Reconstruction. The Minister, Dr. Addison, a Liberal, would be excluded from advising on matters of 'commercial, industrial and agricultural policy'. The amendment was defeated by only 89 to 64 votes. Hewins noted in his diary that

We were beaten by only 25. An enormous number abstained. The Government were horribly frightened. I saw Bonar Law afterwards. . . . If we had won he said he would have immediately resigned. I said, 'I suppose so.' He said it was a dangerous game. He did not see who could take their place. I said I was not anxious about that. . . . I told [Walter Long] the Government would be fortunate if they lived till Monday week. . . . At present it seems to me that the proper course is to get rid of the Government as quickly as possible. . . . This Government will certainly lose the war, *make a bad peace and produce a revolution,* and must be ended.[2]

---

[1] *Esher Journals,* iv. 137.
[2] Present writer's italics. W. A. S. Hewins, *The Apologia of an Imperialist* (1929), ii. 159–66. See also *5 Parliamentary Debates* (Commons), xcvi. 2367–2414; *The Nation,* 22 Sept. 1917, p. 632 ('The appointment of Mr. Hewins . . . the Mullah of Tariff Reform, is too much . . . a really gratuitous insult to Liberal sentiment . . . one must assume powerlessness to resist a Tory demand. Is that really the measure of Mr. George's position in his Cabinet?').

Hewins was soon propitiated by the Government's favourite device and became Under-Secretary of State for the Colonies, but the threat to the Government's existence remained. It had become too dangerous, the Government presumably concluded, to cross Haig or upset in too direct a manner his plans to 'win the war'. How else could domestic upheaval be avoided?

The apparent imminence of peace and the weakness of the British Government during the summer of 1917 formed the background against which the War Cabinet and its newly formed Committee on War Policy discussed, reluctantly sanctioned, and impotently witnessed the fruitless course of the campaign in Flanders long advocated by both the Admiralty and General Headquarters in France. The Committee on War Policy was constituted on 8 June in response to a memorandum by Lord Milner urging the need to counter the current drifting by a fresh stock-taking. The Prime Minister was chairman; Curzon, Milner, and Smuts members; and Bonar Law a frequent participant. Their principal task was to consider a plan pressed by both their naval and military 'advisers' for the clearance of the Belgian coast that same summer. As an alternative Lloyd George, who had no belief that such an attempt could succeed, advocated an operation of much smaller scope but comparable advantage: an Italian offensive, supported by some three hundred British guns, with the aim of capturing Trieste and perhaps Trentino. The Prime Minister had good reason for believing that a separate peace could then be made with Austria-Hungary, with a consequent 'isolation' of Germany.[1]

The project of an advance along the Belgian coast had been pressed ever since the great debate on British strategy had begun at the end of 1914. But in 1915 and 1916 the High Command's desire to attempt such an ambitious task had been subordinated to the different plans of General Joffre. At the end of 1916, however, the unforeseen course of the naval war had prompted the Admiralty to urge the Flanders operation again, and this time as a matter of extreme urgency. This initiative was due in part to the German submarine offensive, but more to the beginning of cruiser warfare in the English Channel. The alarm roused

[1] Lord Hankey, *The Supreme Command, 1914–1918* (1961), ii. 672–3; Evelyn Wrench, *Alfred Lord Milner: The Man with no Illusions* (1958), 335.

by the destroyer raid of 26 October 1916 has been described.[1] The Admiralty thereafter formally proposed a military operation to occupy the Belgian coast with the double object of lessening the submarine danger and avoiding the possibility of German control of the English Channel. On the former point the Admiralty's reasoning was faulty. Rather less than a third of the shipping losses were due to the submarines on the Belgian coast, and there was no reason to believe that compelling these vessels to work from Wilhelmshaven or Kiel instead would have seriously affected the total U-boat effort. But intelligent staff-work was not, as the debate on convoy was abundantly to illustrate, then an Admiralty characteristic. Their fears for loss of control of the Channel, however, were more justified; for the Grand Fleet and its attendant eighty destroyers were stationed far to the North, off the Scottish coast.[2]

Robertson and Haig both welcomed the Admiralty initiative. If the Channel were lost their armies in France would be stranded. Conversely, a substantial British advance along the coast would result not in the creation of yet another exposed salient but would 'fix' the German forces and result in either their defeat or withdrawal from the entire coast: a 'rollback' with incalculable consequences. And doubtless Haig and his staff were glad of the opportunity to undertake operations in a region whose importance to British security had long been axiomatic and to be able to conduct them in substantial independence of the French.

The 'Belgian coast' proposal was accordingly agreed upon at a conference in Robertson's room in the War Office on 23 November 1916 attended by the C.I.G.S.; the First Sea Lord, then Admiral Jackson; General Haig; and Admiral Bacon. They were in possession of an unsigned draft letter from Asquith stating that 'There is no operation of war to which the War Committee would attach greater importance than the successful

---

[1] See above, pp. 172–3.

[2] Combined Strategy in Connection with Submarines. Note by the First Sea Lord of the Admiralty and the Chief of the Admiralty War Staff, 16 November 1916, Asquith Papers; Brig.-Gen. James E. Edmonds, *Military Operations, France and Belgium, 1917*, ii (1948), 1–7, Appendixes I–IV; Capt. S. W. Roskill, 'The U-boat Campaign of 1917 and Third Ypres', *Journal of the Royal United Service Institution*, civ, no. 616 (November 1959), 440–2; Jellicoe, *Submarine Peril*, 93, 115 (according to which, in June 1917, there were 80 destroyers with the Grand Fleet, 59 on convoy and trade protection, and but 33 on the Dover Force).

occupation, or at least the deprivation to the enemy, of Ostend, and especially Zeebrugge.' On 1 December Robertson wrote Joffre that 'my Government desire the occupation of these two towns to form one of the objectives of the campaign next year'. The proposed operation, which met the British Army's obligations under the Chantilly agreement of two weeks before, was accepted by the French commander, whose staff proceeded to draft a plan of campaign. But then Joffre had been superseded by Nivelle, and the Flanders operations fell again into the background, though the operations of the British Army during the 'Nivelle offensive' were designed by their commander to serve as preparation for the ensuing British effort. Now the camouflage had been removed, and G.H.Q. needed to wrest final approval from a new and unsympathetic government.[1]

In the meantime the naval situation had gravely deteriorated, and it appeared unlikely that the war could be much further prolonged. The shipping losses appeared prohibitive and irremediable. The overwhelming preponderance of these losses was of course due to the German submarine campaign. Once again, however, it was to the threat of German cruiser warfare in the Channel that the Admiralty reacted most strongly. The German destroyer forces based on the Belgian coast had made three further raids on the Channel between February and April. That of 17 March resulted in the loss of two British destroyers and one merchant ship. Less than a week later came news of the transfer to Belgium of yet another destroyer flotilla from the High Seas Fleet. On 24 April German naval raiders bombarded Dunkirk and sank a French warship.[2]

The Admiralty, and in particular the new First Sea Lord, Admiral Jellicoe, were now at their wits' end. Admiral Bacon's Dover Patrol could only be reinforced at the expense of the Grand Fleet (whose needs were liberally interpreted by its commander, Admiral Beatty) or of the nascent convoy system. 'There seemed every reason to suppose [the Germans] would go on and turn these raids . . . into a regular destroyer war of attrition.'[3]

[1] *AF*, v (1), Annexes nos. 207, 239; Lloyd George, *War Memoirs*, ii. 1250–2; *Mil. Opns. Fr. and Bel. 1917*, i. 21, ii. 8–10; *Private Papers of Douglas Haig*, 245.
[2] Cyril Falls, *The Great War* (N.Y., Capricorn, 1961), 294; Newbolt, *Naval Opns.* iv (1928), 352–68.
[3] Newbolt, *Naval Opns.* iv (1928), 365–8. See also ibid. 352.

It was hardly conceivable that the enemy's ignorance of his favourable naval position across the Channel could long continue. Once their mental blinkers were removed ('at any one selected moment the Germans could bring a very superior destroyer force for raids into the Channel')[1] the Straits of Dover would probably be swept clear of British forces. It was therefore absolutely necessary to turn the Germans out of Belgium at the earliest possible moment.

The supposed advent of peace further reinforced the arguments for the coastal operation. If Germany would not agree to evacuate Belgium she must be forced to withdraw. Otherwise Great Britain's security would be permanently jeopardized. 'Such a situation', wrote Jellicoe for the War Cabinet, 'would be a menace to the existence of Great Britain.' For the failure to protect or recover that coast after almost three years of major military operations it was difficult to believe that responsible officials, be they military or civilian, would escape a public demand for accounting (and possibly retribution) which would make the Dardanelles and Mesopotamia controversies seem tame.[2]

The desperate state of the naval war and the prospect of peace through mutual exhaustion were powerful arguments for undertaking the proposed offensive. The implications to be drawn from the dispiritedness of the French nation and troops were less obvious, and reasoned discussion rendered more difficult by ignorance as to the degree of the demoralization within the French Army.[3] The basic factors, however, were clear. On the one hand, the general discouragement made a British offensive all the more desirable to encourage the French and keep them in the war; this view was pressed on the War Cabinet with great vigour by General Sir Henry Wilson, who had just returned to

[1] Jellicoe, *Submarine Peril*, 94. See also ibid. 93, 115; Hankey, *Supreme Command*, ii. 679, 701; Lloyd George, *War Memoirs*, ii. 1292; Field-Marshal Sir William Robertson, *Soldiers and Statesmen, 1914–1918* (1926), ii. 243–4.
[2] Robertson, *Soldiers and Statesmen*, ii. 243–4; C. E. W. Bean, *The Australian Imperial Force in France, 1917* (1933), 552 n.
[3] Haig had been told directly by Pétain's Chief of Staff of the outbreak of mutiny, but had not given this information to the War Cabinet. Even he, however, was not aware of the mutinies' extent, concerning which much remains obscure to this day. Lloyd George and the War Cabinet well knew that the French troops had become unamenable to discipline and were so informed by the Head of the British Military Mission to the French Government, Brig.-Gen. Sir E. L. Spears.

London from his now meaningless position as Chief Liaison Officer between the British and French commanders. On the other hand, the French abstention from serious operations made the success of a British offensive less likely. The need to protect the demoralized French Army from a possible German attack, in retrospect the only strategic justification for the Flanders campaign, was also noted.[1] The French command, though as sceptical as Lloyd George himself on the wisdom of the Flanders campaign, was of course relieved to see the British forces kept occupied; and insisted that G.H.Q. accept, however unwillingly, the support of six French divisions under General Anthoine, made directly responsible to Field-Marshal Haig.[2]

Lloyd George for his part had once again returned to the plan for support of an Italian attack against Austria, first proposed by him at the Rome conference in January. But in the interval Austria had indicated her war-weariness in the most explicit manner.

The new Emperor, Charles, had given his brother-in-law, Prince Sixte of Bourbon, a French national serving in the Belgian Army, a letter proposing peace negotiations, whether general or separate being left undetermined. Prince Sixte had proceeded to show this and a subsequent communication to the French Prime Minister and President and to Lloyd George and

[1] As Capt. Liddell Hart has pointed out (in 'The Basic Truths of Passchendaele', *Journal of the Royal United Service Institution*, Nov. 1959, 438), 'Hindenburg and Ludendorff never for a moment considered the idea of attacking the French front in 1917, even after the obviously shattering collapse of the French offensive in the spring. Their minds were concentrated on finishing the war on the Eastern Front. . . . Moreover, the logistical difficulties of a large-scale shift of German forces from East to West for a knock-out blow against the French between August and autumn would have been immense.' Authorities in London, however, could not read the Germans' minds or afford to underrate their efficiency.

[2] It is possible that in May and June Pétain urged on Haig the need for continued British attacks, but unlikely that he did so thereafter. *Diary of Lord Bertie*, ii. 153; Maj.-Gen. Sir C. E. Callwell, *Field-Marshal Sir Henry Wilson* (1927), i. 360–4, ii. 1–3; Duff Cooper, *Haig*, ii (1936), 134; George A. B. Dewar, assisted by Lieut.-Col. J. H. Boraston, *Sir Douglas Haig's Command*, i (1923), 352 ('French participation in the Flanders had not been sought and was not desired by the British'); Sir Sam Fay, *War Office at War* (1937), 77; Hankey, *Supreme Command*, ii. 671; *Private Papers of Douglas Haig*, 234–58, 368–9; Lloyd George, *War Memoirs*, ii. 1258–70; Repington, *First World War* (Boston, 1921), 585; *Lord Riddell's War Diary* (1933), 258; Ribot, *Lettres à un ami* (1924), 184; Letter, Gen. Davidson to the Editor, *The Times*, 14 Nov. 1934, p. 5 (5); Capt. B. H. Liddell Hart, 'The Basic Truths of Passchendaele', *R.U.S.I. Journal* (Nov. 1959), 433–42; Letter, E. L. Spears to Paul Guinn, 30 May 1961.

the King. Lloyd George had leapt at the opportunity, but in
the absence of any territorial concessions to Italy these preliminary soundings bore no fruit. The Italian Foreign Minister,
Baron Sidney Sonnino, had assured Lloyd George on 19 April
that any peace that did not secure to Italy all the 'unredeemed'
territories promised her by the Treaty of London two years
before would provoke revolution. 'The people would sweep [the
Government] away, would rise in revolution, banish their King
and set up a Republic.'[1] The British Prime Minister felt no
obligation to continue the war against Austria until all of
Italy's claims were met. However, if General Cadorna's forces
were supported by artillery and ammunition, of both of which
they were short, they might finally succeed in the capture of
Trieste, only eight miles from the Italian lines. As Prince Sixte
more than once asked the Prime Minister, why, if the Italians
desired the adjoining territories so much, did they not themselves proceed to conquer them?

Italian pride being assuaged by the success of their armies
and Austrian morale correspondingly shaken, peace negotiations
with the Austrian Empire might be undertaken with greater
chance of success. Robertson appeared to have been distinctly,
if briefly, attracted by this scheme, for on 9 June Haig noted[2]

I had a long talk with Robertson. He wished me to realize the
difficult situation in which the country would be if I carried out
large and costly attacks without full co-operation by the French.
When autumn came round, Britain would then be without an Army!
On the other hand it is possible that Austria would make peace, if
harassed enough. Would it not be a good plan, therefore, to support
Italy with guns? I did not agree. Altogether I thought Robertson's
views unsound. I told him that I thought the German was now at his
last resources, and that there was only *one sound* plan to follow, viz.,
without delay to

    1. Send to France every possible man.
    2. ,,   ,,   ,,   ,,   ,,   aeroplane.
    3. ,,   ,,   ,,   ,,   ,,   gun.

---

[1] Lloyd George, *War Memoirs*, ii. 1189.
[2] *Private Papers of Douglas Haig*, 236. See also Philippe Amiguet, *La vie du prince
Sixte de Bourbon* (Paris, 1934), 128–30; Lloyd George, *War Memoirs*, 1175–1204;
Hankey, *Supreme Command*, ii. 674–6; Harold Nicolson, *King George the Fifth* (1952),
314; *Journal d'Alexandre Ribot* (Paris, 1936), 67–70, 88.

Thereafter Robertson supported Haig's project, perhaps out of loyalty rather than conviction. The C.I.G.S. was beginning to appear not so much firm as obstinate.

On 19 June the Cabinet Committee met with their 'advisers' and Haig to discuss the proposed offensive. Field-Marshal Haig arrived in London with his prestige enhanced by an indisputable tactical success. In the Battle of Messines (7–14 June), General Plumer's Second Army—by means of the explosion of nineteen large underground mines followed by intense artillery fire—had taken the opposing ridge from a temporarily demoralized enemy. Subsequent German counter-attacks had entirely failed in their purpose and the British now held the former dominating southern flank of the Ypres salient. The way was clear for an attack further north.[1]

That attack appeared all the more desirable in view of still another threat to the homeland—that of German air-power. On 13 June a squadron of German aeroplanes based on the Belgian coast had made their first great raid on London. The casualties were some 590, an enormous figure for the 'home' if not the 'fighting' front; and intense excitement was aroused in the London populace, the Press, and in government circles. Two squadrons of aircraft were ordered to be transferred from the Western Front: one to England, the other to Calais.[2]

The formal discussions between navy, army, and government took place from 19 to 25 June. The Prime Minister informed Haig and Robertson that he and they were at the parting of the ways. He had no belief, nor did his colleagues, that the proposed offensive could succeed where so many preceding ones had failed. The total Allied man-power on the Western Front, including not only the British and French but also Russians, Portuguese, and Belgians, was only 15 per cent. superior in numbers to the Germans. Since the French and Russian troops were inactive, Sir Douglas Haig would be fighting the entire German Army. In number of guns there was equality, and the Germans now had more reserves.

The basic strategy, Lloyd George commented, should now be to await the Americans, but in the meantime some seventy-five

[1] *Mil. Opns. Fr. and Bel. 1917*, ii. 32–90; Liddell Hart, *A History of the World War, 1914–1918* (1934), 417–22 ('The Siege-War Masterpiece').
[2] H. A. Jones, *The War in the Air*, v (1935), 26–32.

batteries should be lent to General Cadorna, whose forces had
a 50 to 80 per cent. superiority of man-power over the Austrians
but who lacked artillery. No peace with Austria could be
possible without satisfying the legitimate claims of Italy and no
Italian statesman would be allowed to make peace without
securing both the Trentino and Trieste. Austria-Hungary could
be persuaded to concede the Trentino, but Trieste would have
to be conquered before a separate peace could be arranged.
Now Sir Douglas Haig would have to advance an average of
twenty to thirty miles before capturing Zeebrugge and Ostend,
but Trieste was only eight miles from the Italian lines. The
Austrian troops were inferior to the Germans, and had had no
experience of bombardment on the Western Front scale.

Jellicoe, however, stated emphatically that England could
not afford to wait for the Americans. The shipping losses would
not permit Great Britain to continue the war into 1918. In the
meantime, if the army could not get the Belgian ports, the Navy
could not hold the Channel, and the war was lost. The Belgian
coast must be cleared *now*. Every day the threat both from the
sea and the air became greater.

Robertson's views were also gloomy. If a standstill policy were
instituted in the west the Germans might advance further along
the coast and take Dunkirk. The only safe action was to continue the present plan, wear down the enemy further, and even
if for nothing more, hope to improve the air and naval situations
and so increase British staying power.

Haig, by contrast, remained sanguine. He was the only
authority who was really convinced he knew how to win the
war. The German Army was steadily deteriorating and had
already lost much of its moral force. These statements were
supported by the usual (and notoriously fanciful) calculations
on enemy reserves by Haig's Chief of Intelligence, General
Charteris. The defeat of the enemy was merely a question of
time and of perseverance.[1]

Wearily, the Cabinet Committee surrendered. On the 25th

---

[1] Lloyd George, *War Memoirs*, ii. 1272–1304, 1461–6; *Private Papers of Douglas
Haig*, 238–41; Hankey, *Supreme Command*, ii. 676–82; Sarah Gertrude Millin,
General Smuts, ii (1936), 68–70; Robertson, *Soldiers and Statesmen*, ii. 241–7. For an
example of the 'Charteris treatment' see Historical Division, Department of the
Army, *United States Army in the World War, 1917–1919*, vol. ii, *Policy-Forming Documents,
American Expeditionary Forces* (Washington, 1948), 32–35.

Haig was authorized to continue his preparations. Thereafter the Government procrastinated. Another sizeable air raid took place on 7 July, causing great stir, and on 18 July, the same day as the Cabinet changes which caused so much trouble, the committee concluded that the offensive must be allowed to proceed. It could not, however, be allowed to degenerate into the protracted, costly, and indecisive operations such as had occurred in the offensive on the Somme in 1916. If a degree of success commensurate with the losses were not achieved, the offensive should be dropped. The War Cabinet accepted this conclusion at a 'rough and tumble meeting' on the 20th, and the next day Haig noted that[1]

> An official letter arrived by King's Messenger to-night from C.I.G.S. stating that the Cabinet had at last approved of my plan, but wished arrangements made to send troops to Italy if the plan does not succeed. In my opinion, it would be the act of a lunatic to detach troops from France to any theatre at this stage.

Ten days later the offensive began.

The War Cabinet, subject to joint military and naval pressure and to the arguments just described, had once again subscribed to the type of operation of which it was justifiably so sceptical. Within the War Cabinet Haig's plans were supported only by Smuts and—half-heartedly—Curzon. The most powerful members of the Government—Lloyd George, Milner, and Bonar Law—believed that the offensive must again fail, and with possible dire effects on Army morale. Outside the prejudiced ranks of the British General Staff the certitude that the operation would not succeed was generally shared by those in positions of responsibility or otherwise knowledgeable. King Albert of the Belgians stated that there was no chance of success and firmly declined to have his troops participate. The decision to commit the British Army to the bogs of Flanders had been generally deprecated: by Pétain, by Foch, by Sir Henry Wilson ('futile, fantastic, dangerous'), by Colonel Repington, by Haig's divisional if not his Army Commanders. The German forces in the West had never been so strong. The enterprise was hopeless. The British Government was not formally apprised of these

---

[1] *Private Papers of Douglas Haig*, 246. See also ibid. 241, 245; Hankey, *Supreme Command*, ii. 683–4; Robertson, *Soldiers and Statesmen*, ii. 17, 247–9.

opinions. Sir Henry Wilson, desirous of succouring France, and concerned about his own future, may have been guilty of deceit in not reporting those of the French command as well as his own. But with all the sources of information at its disposal, need the Government have remained in ignorance?[1]

The decision of the War Cabinet to let this hopeless offensive proceed has, unlike the similar decision with regard to the Somme, led to much debate. That there were many arguments for the offensive, should it prove successful, has been demonstrated. The War Cabinet, however, did not believe that the offensive could clear the Belgian coast; and they were proved right. There remained the opinions that even a tactically unsuccessful operation might contribute to German 'attrition' and French 'staying power'. Neither of these views appears to have been generally shared within the War Cabinet.

The War Cabinet acquiescence has none the less been labelled 'unavoidable',[2] since the alternative would have been the fall of the Government.

Whether the Government would have fallen by forbidding the offensive is, however, a matter of opinion; in 1916 there had been more than one obvious alternate Prime Minister, in 1917 there was none. The consequences in terms of 'national unity', that is to say of willingness to wage the war, of a break-up of the Government would of course have been more serious in 1917 than the year before. That the War Cabinet actually evaluated these consequences, however, is far from evident.

Even so one is reluctant unequivocally to condemn, however much one may regret, the sanctioning of the Flanders offensive.

[1] Maj.-Gen. Sir E. L. Spears, in the summer of 1917 Head of the British Military Mission to the French Government, has informed the present writer that 'It was not the function of my Mission to advise the British Cabinet or the War Office upon such matters as the efficacy and desirability of the projected Flanders campaign' (Letter, 30 May 1961). *AF*, v (2), Annexe no. 289; Lieut.-Gen. Sir Tom Bridges, *Alarms and Excursions* (1938), 194; Callwell, *Henry Wilson*, i. 349–63, ii. 1–3; Lloyd George, *War Memoirs*, ii. 1265–70, 1292–8, 1304; *Private Papers of Douglas Haig*, 242; *Mil. Opns. Fr. and Bel. 1917*, ii. 27; Repington, *First World War*, i. 571, 588–9.

[2] Hankey, *Supreme Command*, ii. 702. See also ibid. 701 ('There is no doubt that [Lloyd George] was absolutely convinced that the attack in Flanders had not the remotest prospect of success. . . . All his colleagues, too, had grave doubts about the offensive's prospects . . . Jellicoe's . . . extreme pessimism on what would happen in the narrow seas if the coast of Flanders was not cleared of the enemy . . . produced an almost decisive effect').

The compulsion to attempt to avert the consequences of defeat in 1917 was stronger than to gamble on victory in 1916; perhaps one must deplore, not the War Cabinet's lack of political courage, but rather their understandable reluctance to veto an operation which of course just *might* succeed, uniquely because of their own doubts.

Perhaps the principal conclusion to be drawn from the perplexity of the War Cabinet in June 1917 is that they should earlier have insisted on professional 'advisers' in whom they had more confidence.

The course of the Flanders campaign need be only briefly described. The first attack, begun by the dashing General Gough on 31 July, was a dismal failure. Heavy rainfall began in the evening and continued through the month of August. The rain and guns together turned the battlefield, as General Charteris noted, into 'a sea of mud, churned up by shell-fire'. Further attacks in mid-August were repulsed, and depression and discouragement spread throughout the Army. Gough recommended cancellation of the entire operation; Haig instead on the 25th transferred operational control to General Plumer, a slow but steady general, who demanded and obtained a three weeks' delay before continuing the offensive on a limited 'Messines' basis.[1]

Reports of the discouragement of the Army came back to England, where the numbers of wounded and crippled were accumulating. At the base depot of Étaples there were 'republican' riots. Hankey, and later Bonar Law, suggested that the time had come to review and perhaps cancel the entire operation. Robertson was sent out in the hope that he would so recommend. He found Haig still confident. His generals were less so, but, in spite of Haig's invitation, the C.I.G.S. did not believe it would be proper to ask the Army commanders their opinions in the absence of the Commander-in-Chief. He did not feel justified in carrying his doubts so far as to recommend the cessation of the attacks. But he returned to London sorely puzzled.[2]

[1] Bean, *AIF in France, 1917*, 727–9; Charteris, *At G.H.Q.*, 243; General Sir Hubert Gough, *Fifth Army* (1931), 205; *Mil. Opns. Fr. and Bel. 1917*, ii. 183, 206–9, 384–5.
[2] Robertson, *Soldiers and Statesmen*, ii. 255. See also ibid. 262; Robert Blake, *The Unknown Prime Minister: The Life and Times of Andrew Bonar Law, 1858–1923* (1955),

My views are known to you [he wrote Haig on 27 September]. They have always been 'defensive' in all theatres but the West. But the difficulty is to *prove* the wisdom of this now that Russia is out. I confess I stick to it more because I see nothing better, and because my instinct prompts me to stick to it, than because of any good argument by which I can support it.

The Prime Minister, however, would not take the responsibility of hampering Haig in any way. This stance was manifested by his policy toward the Italian campaign. In late August General Cadorna's operations showed more promise than usual, and the French command proposed that a hundred guns be sent to Italy from General Anthoine's First Army, on service in Flanders. At a conference in London on 4 September Carson expressed his opposition to the transfer; and it was finally agreed that, subject to Haig's approval, Anthoine should release fifty guns only on the express proviso that the French themselves provide the remaining fifty from other sectors of the front! A few days later Haig agreed to 'liberate' all one hundred, subject to Pétain's willingness to replace them if or when needed. Two weeks later Cadorna went on the defensive, upon which the British and French Governments promptly agreed to withdraw immediately and simultaneously all their heavy artillery units from the Italian Front.[1]

On 20 September, several days after Asquith's and Carson's personal assurances of support, General Plumer launched the first of his 'new style' attacks. A well-planned and extremely dense artillery barrage was followed by small-unit infantry actions—using grenades rather than rifles—aimed primarily at eliminating resisting machine-gun units in their 'pillbox' forts. The 'Battle of the Menin Road' and the subsequent blows of 'Polygon Wood' (26 September) and 'Broodseinde' (4 October) met with entire success; the German resistance was ineffective. The Allies were now using their superiority in material in a way which, granted fine weather, made 'success' certain. Haig's hopes rose once more, and he told the sceptical

362; Hankey, *Supreme Command*, ii. 693; Repington, *First World War*, ii. 30–31; Brig.-Gen. E. L. Spears, *Prelude to Victory* (1939), 342.

[1] *AF* v (2), 309–10, 1130–1, Annexe no. 1050, vi (1), Annexe no. 5; Callwell, *Henry Wilson*, ii. 13–14; *Private Papers of Douglas Haig*, 252–4; Hankey, *Supreme Command*, ii. 695–6, 699 n. 1; Robertson, *Soldiers and Statesmen*, ii. 252.

Gough and Plumer that the need for caution had now passed. The cavalry were ordered to be brought within a day's ride of the battle-front, and the French were urged to attract the German reserves. But on 4 October the weather broke again, and in several days the rain became torrential. The meteorologists offered no hope of improvement. The drainage system of the fields had been destroyed by the incessant bombardments, and the battlefield became a quagmire. A number of men were drowned in the water or smothered in the mud. The British artillery was no longer effective. The Army and divisional commanders, and even some of Haig's 'yes'-men at G.H.Q., generally very ill-informed on battle conditions, favoured shutting the offensive down. The French Military Mission to G.H.Q. and General Anthoine marvelled at the Field-Marshal's persistence. The French President, Poincaré, asked Haig when the operations would stop. Only Haig remained unpersuaded, and, overruling his Army Commanders, ordered on the 17th and again on the 28th that operations continue. A persistent offensive, he believed, was the secret to victory. Sooner or later, given the supposed deterioration in the German Army, that victory would come. G.H.Q. statistics were now changed to indicate the exhaustion of German man-power by May or June 1918. Only a direct order from London, as the French Mission had reported, would induce Haig to end the campaign.[1]

No such order was forthcoming. Lloyd George continued to be of the opinion, as he informed French and Italian statesmen on 8 August, that 'we had put our money on the wrong horse'.[2] In early September he had retired to Wales in his only prolonged period of nervous depression throughout the war. He had certainly been placed in a very difficult position. On his recovery he went to France and on the 25th, a day of victory for the British, visited G.H.Q. The Prime Minister was shown a group of prisoners specially chosen to illustrate Charteris's opinion on the physical deterioration of German troops. Thereafter he

---

[1] *AF*, v (2), Annexes nos. 929, 1140, 1214, 1216, 1286, vi (1), Annexe no. 12; Bean, *AIF in France, 1917*, 761–2, 790, 875–85; General Charles Bonham Carter, personal memoirs, in Victor Bonham-Carter, *In a Liberal Tradition* (1960), 166–7; Charteris, *At G.H.Q.*, 258–9; Falls, *Great War*, 303; *Private Papers of Douglas Haig*, 258–60; *Mil. Opns. Fr. and Bel. 1917*, ii. 296–7, 325, 346; Repington, *First World War*, ii. 82–84.
[2] *Journal d'Alexandre Ribot*, 174 n. 1.

devoted his energies to the military plans for the winter and spring, operations which were to be planned and approved by a different set of military advisers. As far as the 'Supreme Command' was concerned the Flanders campaign required no further attention. On 16 October the Prime Minister sent Haig the War Cabinet's congratulations on the achievements of his Armies since the end of July. 'I am personally glad to be the means of transmitting this message, and desire to take this opportunity of renewing my assurance of confidence in your leadership.'[1] This was the first such message Haig had received from the War Cabinet. Lloyd George's abdication was now no less complete than Asquith's. On 23 October the French Army won a victory at Malmaison, signalizing its reparation as an effective fighting force. And still the British troops floundered hopelessly in the ooze and slime.[2]

During this summer and autumn of 1917 the Flanders campaign—the outcome of Haig's stubbornness, the Admiralty's fears and mental inertia, and the Government's weakness and indecision—was naturally the dominant theme in British military policy.Events in Greece and Palestine, and Lloyd George's tentative gropings toward a new military system equally exemplify both the Government's desire to reconstruct a new strategy from the ruins and its unwillingness to accept the correlating political risks.

From Greece two of the six British infantry divisions, the bulk of the cavalry, and a large proportion of the heavy artillery were withdrawn despite the agonized protests and delaying actions of the French Government—supported by all the other Allies—and the despair of the Serbs. As a *quid pro quo* for the withdrawal of the first division the British Government agreed to French demands for the seizure of the Greek harvest in Thessaly and for the deposition of King Constantine. The consequent entry of Greece into the war under the premiership of Venizelos was viewed as an additional commitment rather than an aid but was borne with philosophy. The withdrawal of the second division was the principal business of a grand conference

---

[1] *Private Papers of Douglas Haig*, 261.
[2] Lloyd George, *War Memoirs*, ii. 1315–16; Gough, *Fifth Army*, 211–12; Hankey, *Supreme Command*, ii. 694–703; Repington, *First World War*, ii. 98–99; *Riddell War Diary*, 271–4.

of all the Allies (the United States, being an 'Associated Power', did not attend) held in Paris on 25 and 26 July. The British delegation, confronted with unanimous opposition, agreed to postpone action a little longer but at a session with the French Government in London on 6 and 7 August finally wrenched these troops free. No further withdrawal would be made without consultation.[1]

Lloyd George had not gone to all this trouble with the French merely to feed the two 'free' divisions so obtained into what he regarded as Sir Douglas Haig's slaughterhouse. He proposed that they be sent to Palestine to revive the Turkish war. The General Staff agreed. The reinforcement of the Egyptian Expeditionary Force might divert the threatened German-Turkish offensive directed at Baghdad and Maude's troops in Mesopotamia. This proved to be the case. Perhaps fears of yet another humiliation in 'Mespot' played their part in the final decision, for the report of the Mesopotamia Commission, a dreadful document, had been published in June, causing much anxiety and mental suffering in sections of the public, and considerable flurry in the political world. The War Cabinet had been forced to hold numerous meetings on disciplinary action to be taken, and the Secretary of State for India, Austen Chamberlain, had resigned.

The 60th (London) and 10th (Irish) divisions were accordingly dispatched across the Mediterranean, where they participated in the victorious battles of 'Third Gaza' and the capture of Jerusalem at the end of the year. These victories, however, were due primarily to the change of command in the E.E.F. effected by the War Cabinet in June.[2]

After the fiasco of 'Second Gaza' the War Cabinet had decided to relieve the colourless and fussy Sir Archibald Murray

[1] Fears that the British departure would provoke a general dissolution of the 'Allied Armies in the East' and Painlevé's trust in General Sarrail perhaps explain the tenacity of French opposition to even this limited disengagement. *AF*, viii (2), 501, Annexes nos. 1841, 2007; Cambon, *Correspondance*, iii. 181; Hankey, *Supreme Command*, ii. 636-7, 687-90; Cyril Falls, *Military Operations Macedonia* (1933), ii. 2-3, 13, 291; *Journal d'Alexandre Ribot*, 158, 172-3; Ribot, *Letters à un ami*, 314-18, 339-40.

[2] Hankey, *Supreme Command*, ii. 527-9; Cyril Falls, *Military Operations Egypt and Palestine* (1928), ii (1), 4-7; Robertson, *Soldiers and Statesmen*, ii. 142-3; Liman von Sanders, *Five Years in Turkey* (Annapolis, 1927), 179; Field-Marshal Earl Wavell, *The Palestine Campaigns* (1931 edn.), 89-91; 98-100, 108-10.

of his command. His appointment to Egypt, at a time when the policy in that theatre was purely defensive, had been one of the many service appointments made by Asquith to keep the administration happy at the expense of rendering it effective. Lloyd George had afterwards offered the Egyptian command to General Smuts. The latter ascertained from Robertson that he would receive little support from the War Office and, fearing that the campaign would therefore remove him indefinitely from the centre of affairs, leaving him 'stranded' in Palestine, declined. Robertson was thereupon asked to recommend a suitable leader. He made an excellent, almost inspired, choice: General Edmund Allenby, then commanding the Third Army on the Western Front.[1]

Allenby was a large, bluff, strong man with a terrible temper, a gift for leadership, independence of spirit, and willingness to make use not only of his but others' brains. His relations with Haig had long been unhappy. Even so he was chagrined at his new appointment, regarding it as a demotion, until his interview with the Prime Minister. Lloyd George unveiled some of his dreams, told Allenby to ask for all he needed, and in turn demanded Jerusalem as a Christmas present for the British nation. Allenby, in conspicuous contrast to his predecessor, immediately made his presence felt and revitalized a rather dispirited and aimless force. The dispatch of new aeroplane squadrons enabled the British for the first time to achieve 'command of the air' in Palestine. Throughout the autumn the new commander made preparations for a renewal of the offensive, with plans actively designed to take advantage of the nature of the terrain, the special capacities of the troops under his command, and the Turks' own hitherto well-justified views on British tactics.[2]

Meanwhile Lloyd George perplexedly shopped around for new men and new policies. It was now obvious that the effective adoption of a strategy different from the one that had so long prevailed would require the elimination of the Haig–Robertson combination from the key position in the Government's system

[1] L. S. Amery, *My Political Life*, ii (1953), 136; Lloyd George, *War Memoirs*, ii. 1087–9; Millin, *General Smuts*, ii. 37–41.

[2] Lloyd George, *War Memoirs*, ii. 1089–91; Liddell Hart, *Through the Fog of War* (1938), 95–102; General Sir Archibald Wavell, *Allenby* (1940), 15–19, 183–91, 201–6, 294–301, *Palestine Campaign*, 96, 103–7.

of war direction. The direct removal of both, or even of Robertson, the weaker link, Lloyd George ruled out because he feared the resultant furore would overturn his government. Yet perhaps Robertson's position, too strong for direct attack, could be either neutralized or outflanked?[1]

It was toward neutralization, otherwise known as the 'alternate advisers' scheme, that Lloyd George's thoughts first turned. On 14 August Lord Riddell, proprietor of the sensationalist *News of the World* and an old friend of the Prime Minister, arranged a meeting between Lloyd George, Sir Henry Wilson, and Sir John (now Viscount) French, since December 1914 Commander-in-Chief Home Forces. At this and subsequent meetings the Prime Minister suggested that henceforth Robertson's proposals be reviewed for the War Cabinet by a military 'triumvirate' consisting of French, Wilson, and one other. Sir Henry Wilson had no difficulty in demonstrating the futility of such a scheme and instead proposed a more ambitious change which could be justified as a major advance in the conduct of coalition warfare, while actually serving to 'outflank' the C.I.G.S. 'I then disclosed my plan of three Prime Ministers and three soldiers, to be over all C.I.G.S.'s and to draw up plans for the whole theatre from Nieuport to Baghdad.' The British 'soldier', needless to say, would be Sir Henry Wilson who in the meantime was rescued from unemployment and given the Eastern Command with headquarters in London. Further to tempt the Prime Minister, 'I rubbed in the five months of mud and snow ($\frac{1}{2}$ November–$\frac{1}{2}$ April) during which we (and Italy) can do nothing, though the weather a little farther down the line in Asia Minor and Egypt is perfect.'[2]

Lloyd George was 'distinctly taken'. The 'Supreme Council' scheme was obviously far preferable in itself and might be used to eliminate Robertson's influence entirely. The 'Supreme Council' would also be an agency whereby, as Amery for one stressed, Great Britain could increase her influence with the Allies and direct the general conduct of the war. Yet the difficulties were also formidable. The French were pressing for an inter-allied *military* staff since the appointment of Foch as their

---

[1] Lloyd George, *War Memoirs*, ii. 1370–1.
[2] Callwell, *Henry Wilson*, ii. 7, 10. See also Amery, *Political Life*, ii. 125, and *Riddell War Diary*, 265.

Chief of General Staff in May. But to the French such an inter-allied organization was a means of re-establishing French influence and a supreme command on the Western Front under a French general, perhaps even the notorious Sarrail, who enjoyed Painlevé's entire confidence. British and French ambitions proved ultimately reconcilable, but in the summer of 1917 the British Government could not afford to repeat the experiment in 'unified command' that had been ruined by the Nivelle fiasco and probably would not have agreed to accept any foreign limitations upon its own freedom of action even on the Western Front. Besides, why should the French and Italians support an offensive against Turkey the success of which would establish British hegemony throughout the 'Middle East'? Negotiations on a 'Supreme Council' were undertaken with M. Painlevé in September and October, but Lloyd George could not bring himself to make any commitment.[1]

Meanwhile the Prime Minister reverted to the 'alternate advisers' scheme. General Cadorna's decision to assume the defensive eliminated hopes of imposing peace on Austria through attacks from Italy. The War Cabinet turned with relief to the Turkish war, now being waged solely by 'Empire' forces. Could not Turkey be eliminated altogether by a sustained offensive from Palestine, inquired Lloyd George on 5 October?[2]

The C.I.G.S. was sure such an attempt would be mistaken policy, and said so in a memorandum of 8 October. Allenby, however, was informed that the War Cabinet wished to remove Turkey from the conflict, and was asked his requirements 'to make certain' the occupation of Palestine up to a line between the port of Jaffa and the town of Jerusalem. It was hoped that after British interests had been thereby secured and the Turkish forces given a sound beating the Ottoman Empire could be induced to leave the war. A new division could be sent him every sixteen days. The General Staff estimated Allenby would need at least five more divisions. These might be furnished, but

---

[1] Amery, *Political Life*, ii. 125–6; *Private Papers of Douglas Haig*, 251, 255; Hankey, *Supreme Command*, ii. 713–14; Paul Painlevé, *Comment j'ai nommé Foch et Pétain* (Paris, 1923), 241, 244–6, 256.

[2] Callwell, *Henry Wilson*, ii. 15–16; Hankey, *Supreme Command*, ii. 697–8; Robertson, *Soldiers and Statesmen*, ii. 256.

Allenby's own estimate was then received. He would require a reinforcement of thirteen divisions![1]

On 11 October the War Cabinet met as a 'Council of War' on the precedent of 5 August 1914 with not only Robertson but also John French and Henry Wilson in attendance. The Prime Minister reviewed the strategic situation. Once again the Allies were ending yet another unsuccessful campaign season. Russia and France had ceased to fight, the United States would not afford serious assistance until 1919. What should Great Britain do in 1918? Continue the Haig–Robertson strategy of concentration and a ceaseless offensive on the Western Front? Concentrate on the Western Front but make active use of the forces already in being in Palestine and Mesopotamia? Remain generally on the defensive save for minor attacks (the 'Pétain policy'), while awaiting American participation? Or 'knock out the props' through an offensive against Turkey?[2]

Wilson and French were requested to submit their advice in writing, and given access to the War Office files. That same day the C.I.G.S. wrote Haig, 'I do not much care what advice is tendered, as I shall not budge an inch from my paper and do not suppose that you will budge from yours.' After interviews with Foch and Rawlinson and receipt of the usual glum memorandum from Jellicoe, this time on the difficulties of transport in the Mediterranean, Sir Henry Wilson no longer talked of an offensive on Turkey during the 'mud months'. Both 'alternate advisers' had written their reports by 20 October. Of Viscount French's twenty-six pages, twenty were devoted to an attack on Haig. He had lost over a million men to no particular purpose. For the immediate future Britain could only remain generally on the defensive. Both he and Wilson now clearly advised against a Turkish offensive. It would be impossible 'this winter' and 'wrong' 'next spring or summer', according to Wilson. Both papers declined to offer any specific advice for the future but

---

[1] Callwell, *Henry Wilson*, ii. 14–15; *Mil. Opns. Egypt and Palestine*, ii (1) 26–27; Robertson, *Soldiers and Statesmen*, ii. 178–82; Wavell, *Allenby*, 204–5 ('The real explanation of the size of [Allenby's] request lies in the wording of the War Office telegram which required him to say what force he required to "make certain" of reaching Jaffa and Jerusalem, and in the estimate of twenty divisions, including two Germans, which his Intelligence produced as the maximum force which the enemy might bring against him'), *Palestine Campaigns*, 108.

[2] *Esher Journals*, iv. 142–4; *Mil. Opns. Fr. and Bel. 1918*, i. 17–18.

both in conclusion urged that this function be accomplished through the establishment of a 'Superior Council of the Allies'.[1] But having requested alternate advice Lloyd George was now afraid even to let its nature be known.

Curzon [told] me [Hankey noted on 10 October] that, if the Prime Minister drove out Robertson, Robert Cecil, Balfour, Derby, Carson, and he himself, probably, would leave the Government, which would then break up. [The next day], . . . I walked round St. James's Park with Lloyd George. . . . I repeated Curzon's warning in very straight terms and He (Ll. G.) took the hint very quickly. I told Curzon what I had done and he said I had rendered a very considerable public service. . . . I lunched today with Montagu who told me that Asquith had got hold of Ll. G.'s difficulties with the soldiers and thinks he may get back.

At Robertson's demand the War Cabinet had agreed that the French–Wilson papers should be sent to him through the Secretary of State for War for comment. On the 20th they were first handed in to Hankey.

The reports confirmed my worst anticipations. They both recommended a central council, including a staff of generals in Paris, to be independent of the national General Staffs. This alone is enough to drive Robertson into resignation. They both condemned the continuance of the Flanders offensive next year, which is the course that Robertson and Haig recommend.

Several days passed in discussions on how to handle these explosive documents. 'After lunch [on 22 October] I discussed the French–Wilson memoranda with Milner, who had just been reading them—the P.M. having directed me to show him a copy. His view was that Robertson must see them at once—but he agreed with me that the Government would very likely come down over it.' Lloyd George persuaded Viscount French to tone down parts of his document and on the 25th Hankey 'went to Derby to hand him French's revised report and to notify to him the War Cabinet's decision that he should communicate the French–Wilson memoranda to Robertson'. By then the threat of disaster had once more come to the War Cabinet's rescue.

---

[1] Callwell, *Henry Wilson*, ii. 17–18; Lloyd George, *War Memoirs*, ii. 1425–35; *Mil. Opns. Fr. and Bel. 1918*, i. 18–20; Robertson, *Soldiers and Statesmen*, ii. 259–60.

An Austro-German force had broken through the Italian lines
near the village of Caporetto. The period of hesitation and
indecision was over. A new chapter had begun.[1]

[1] Hankey, *Supreme Command*, ii. 712–16. See also Callwell, *Henry Wilson*, ii. 18–19;
Letter, Robertson to Carson, 20 Nov. 1917 ('I knew nothing about the proposal
to set up a Council until November 2nd, when our Ambassador at Rome received
a telegram from the Foreign Office on the subject'), Ian Colvin, *Life of Lord Carson*,
iii (1936), 284–5.

X

THE WAY ROUND

'Let us return to the faith of our forefathers, and recognize that on the sea and by the sea we live.'
SIR AUCKLAND GEDDES, Minister of National Service, to the House of Commons, 14 January 1918.

THE joint Austro-German offensive against Italy began on 24 October at Caporetto. Two days later a breakthrough was achieved, the Italian Second Army dissolved into prisoners and stragglers, and the High Command lost control of the troops and the situation. For two to three weeks thereafter the fate of Italy was uncertain. It was generally believed that Venice would be lost, and with it the control of the Adriatic. The new Italian Prime Minister, Signor Orlando, talked of carrying on the war from Sicily. But by 10 November the Italian forces had regrouped and formed a defensive line along the Piave river. Italy remained a belligerent, having lost some seven hundred thousand men through surrender and desertion, and most of the province of Venezia. The prospects for luring or forcing Austria-Hungary out of the war had disappeared, and the Entente had sustained a major strategic reverse.[1]

The Caporetto disaster affected British military policy in two ways. The five English divisions dispatched from the Western Front to Italy's aid finally forced Field-Marshal Haig to cease offensive operations in Flanders. The dismay caused by Italy's collapse, so reminiscent of Rumania's defeat the preceding year and of Serbia the winter before that, provided a suitable

[1] Maj.-Gen. Sir E. Callwell, *Field-Marshal Sir Henry Wilson* (1927), ii. 26; C. R. M. F. Cruttwell, *A History of the Great War, 1914–1918* (2nd edn., Oxford, 1936), 460–5; Maréchal Foch, *Mémoires pour servir à l'histoire de la guerre de 1914–1918* (Paris, 1931), ii, p. xxxvii; *War Memoirs of David Lloyd George* (2-vol. Odhams Press edn.), ii. 1398; *Intimate Papers of Colonel House* (1926), iii. 223, 235; Pierre Renouvin, *La Crise européenne et la première guerre mondiale* (3rd edn., Paris, 1948), 497–500.

atmosphere for Lloyd George to launch his project for a new military system—the Allied Supreme War Council.[1]

On 26 October the Prime Minister instructed the reluctant Robertson to order the still more reluctant Haig to send two divisions to Italy. Whatever hesitation Lloyd George may have had in overriding the C.I.G.S. was overcome by the news that M. Painlevé was sending six French divisions and General Foch to the Italians' rescue. 'Ll. G. wrote a letter to Robertson,' Hankey noted, '. . . warning him that, if we are to get control of our Allies (as Robertson is always pressing we should do), we must give them substantial assistance when in difficulties. . . . Lloyd George is anxious to utilize the occasion to strengthen our hold on the Allies.' 'In view of the continual friction between French and Italians I consider it important', wrote Smuts to the Prime Minister, 'that the reinforcements should be only under British command.'[2]

Robertson was sent off to Italy to get him out of the way and to prevent Foch from taking over control of the Italian Army.

A War Office press campaign minimizing the extent and dangers of the Italian defeats was called off; and General Kiggell, who came over to London with a message from Haig urging the continuance of the offensive on the Western Front as the best means to help Italy, failed to prevail. Two more divisions from the British Armies in France were sent on 8 November, and General Plumer left the next day for Italy as commander of the British contingent. There was talk of sending Sir Douglas Haig to Italy as supreme commander of all forces, including Italian, in that theatre. Haig, whose forces on the 6th had finally captured the village of Passchendaele, a little less than five miles from the original trench line, was forced to close down his operations. On the 20th the Flanders campaign was formally ended.[3]

[1] Brig.-Gen. J. E. Edmonds (ed.), *Military Operations, France and Belgium, 1917*, ii (1948), 352, *Italy, 1915–1919* (1949), Appendix I, 389–97.

[2] Lord Hankey, *The Supreme Command, 1914–1918* (1961), ii. 717, 719; Sarah Gertrude Millin, *General Smuts*, ii (1936), 124.

[3] *Diary of Lord Bertie of Thame, 1914–1918* (1924), ii. 210; Callwell, *Henry Wilson*, ii. 19–21; Brig.-Gen. John Charteris, *At G.H.Q.* (1931), 266; *Private Papers of Douglas Haig* (1952), Robert Blake (ed.), 262; *Mil. Opns. Fr. and Bel. 1917*, ii. 360, iii. 10, *Italy 1915–1919*, 58, 352, 358; Paul Painlevé, *Comment j'ai nommé Foch et Pétain* (1923), 258–9; Henry Wickham Steed, *Through Thirty Years* (1924), ii. 146–7.

By then much had happened, and the Field-Marshal's operations for the first time were publicly criticized by the Prime Minister. At the end of October M. Painlevé and M. Franklin-Bouillon came over to London yet again. After discussions with the French the War Cabinet decided on the 2nd of November:[1]

To accept in principle the proposal for the establishment of a Supreme Inter-Allied Council consisting of the Prime Minister and one other Minister, who would meet at frequent intervals together with a Permanent Inter-Allied Advisory General Staff composed of one General Officer from each of the principal Allies.

The British general officer would be Lieutenant-General Sir Henry Wilson.

So once again, and for the first time since some of his activities were described in the Prologue to this narrative, this glib, voluble Irishman found himself at the very centre of affairs. His quick and superficial intelligence, his 'gift of the gab', and his eye for the main chance were to be exerted on behalf of the British Government and not against it.

Since the fall of Sir John French, Wilson's fortunes had been uneven. No longer a member of the G.H.Q. staff, as a corps commander on the Western Front in 1916 he failed to 'fit in', and was unable to prevent or to revenge a successful local enemy attack. His mission to the Tsarist government and his liaison position with General Nivelle had been unfruitful, thwarted by developments no man could have affected. The Supreme War Council, which was in large measure his brain-child, offered Henry Wilson another opportunity and rescued him from half-pay status. He seized it eagerly and found himself at home, perhaps for the first time since his pre-war service as Director of Military Operations. Lloyd George's Government, for its part, had found the military adviser it desired and could—so long as the war lasted—most easily work with.

The British pressed for London or Boulogne as the site of the new War Council, the French for Paris. The British in effect ceded the substance of French demands by the compromise choice of Versailles. Doubtless Lloyd George and Milner

---

[1] Lloyd George, *War Memoirs*, ii. 1438.

concluded they might have a freer hand outside of the parliamentary and newspaper pressures of the British capital.[1]

Three days later the French and British Prime Ministers, General Foch and both General Robertson *and* General Wilson met with the Italian Government and High Command at the seaside resort town of Rapallo. The British and French Governments promised the Italians all necessary aid and demanded the dismissal of General Cadorna. On the 7th the three Governments constituted a Supreme War Council 'to watch over the general conduct of the War'. 'Each Power delegates . . . one Permanent Military Representative whose exclusive function is to act as technical adviser to the Council.' It was essential, Mr. Lloyd George stressed, that this officer hold no other appointment. Sir William Robertson stamped out of the conference and told Hankey to enter his departure in the minutes.[2]

Five days later the British Prime Minister, in Paris on his return trip, made a public arraignment of Allied strategy during the preceding three years at a luncheon banquet attended primarily by French dignitaries. Mr. Winston Churchill sat near by. Contrary to his usual procedure, Lloyd George had spent two whole days carefully preparing his text. Doubtless he remembered the lack of attention given his confidential memorandum to the French the preceding November. This time his complaints would not pass unheard.[3]

There had never been, the Prime Minister began, real unity in Allied strategy. Up to the current time the 'great generals' from 'many lands . . . all sat at the same table and metaphorically took thread and needle, sewed [their] plans together and produced them to a subsequent civilian conference as one great strategic piece'. But the enemy had always torn the result to ribbons. 'Stitching is not strategy.' This war, he continued, was

[1] Ibid. 1437; Hankey, *Supreme Command*, ii. 718–19; *Mil. Opns. Fr. and Bel. 1918*, i (1935), 30; Painlevé, *Foch et Pétain*, 260–6; U.S. Historical Division, Department of the Army, *United States Army in the World War, 1917–1919*, vol. ii. *Policy-Forming Documents American Expeditionary Forces* (Washington, 1948), No. 72.

[2] France. *Les Armées françaises dans la Grande Guerre [AF]*, vi (1), Annexe ii. 58; Callwell, *Henry Wilson*, ii. 21–23; Hankey, *Supreme Command*, ii. 719–23; Lloyd George, *War Memoirs*, ii. 1439–41; *Mil. Opns. Fr. and Bel. 1918*, i. 30–32; Minutes, first session, Allied Supreme War Council, 7 November 1917, Rapallo. *Records of the Supreme War Council*, National Archives, Washington, D.C.

[3] Hankey, *Supreme Command*, ii. 724–7; Frank Owen, *Tempestuous Journey: Lloyd George His Life and Times* (N.Y., 1955), 435; Painlevé, *Foch et Pétain*, 275.

really a siege, a blockade of 'two huge Empires'. Yet the implications of this fact had been consistently overlooked. The Allies,
instead of striking at the enemy's weakest points, had attacked
the strongest bastions. Of course, 'We have won great victories.
When I look at the appalling casualty lists, I sometimes wish it
had not been necessary to win so many.' Half the men who fell
in the futile attempt to break through on the Western Front—in
September [1915]—would have saved Serbia, would have saved
the Balkans, and completed the blockade of Germany. A year
later, 'the siege of the Central Powers was once more raised . . .
once again France and England had the whole of their strength
engaged in the bloody assaults of the Somme'. And why was
this allowed to happen? Because 'there was no authority whose
concern it was to prepare measures in advance for adverting the
doom of Roumania'. Now the same fate threatened Italy.

It is no use minimizing the extent of the disaster. If you do then
you will never take adequate steps to repair it. When we advance a
kilometre into the enemy's lines, snatch a small shattered village
out of his cruel grip, and capture a few hundreds of his soldiers we
shout with unfeigned joy. And rightly so, for it is a symbol of our
superiority over the boastful foe, and a sure guarantee that we can
and shall win. But what if we advanced fifty kilometres behind his
lines, made 200,000 of his soldiers prisoners, and taken 2,500 of his
best guns, with enormous quantities of munitions and stores?

Yet

The Italian disaster may yet save the Alliance, for without it I
do not believe that even now we should have set up a real Council.

His present complaints were therefore designed to awake 'public
opinion' to the 'real danger' caused by the pre-existing want of
an inter-Allied military system. Now that 'This Council has
been set up', the need was to 'keep those narrow instincts, and
interests . . . from reasserting their dominance'. After all, he
concluded,[1]

We shall win, but I want to win as soon as possible. I want to win
with as little sacrifice as possible; I want as many as possible of that
splendid young manhood which has helped to win victory to live
through to enjoy its fruits.

[1] Reuter's report on Lloyd George's speech, 12 Nov. 1917, *Daily Telegraph*,
13 Nov. 1917. Extracts are given in Lloyd George, *War Memoirs*, ii. 1442–5.

These were terrible words, and when a week later (the 19th) Asquith opened a debate in the House on the innovation of the Allied Supreme War Council it was generally felt that the Prime Minister had achieved a remarkable personal victory. Asquith's speech, which weighed up the pros and cons of the new Council with emphasis on the disadvantages, struck its hearers as lifeless and dull. Lloyd George's reply by contrast, fiery and combative in tone, appeared more in tune with the perils of the hour, though in substance it was rather conciliatory. The Council, he had already stressed, was a purely advisory body, and in correspondence with the Secretary of State for War he conceded the C.I.G.S. the right both to accompany the Prime Minister to all meetings of the Council and to advise the War Cabinet on all recommendations the Council might make prior to a final decision.[1]

The fact was that the series of shocks administered to the British public, parliament, and Press in November and December of 1917 altogether favoured Lloyd George's efforts to free himself from the High Command.[2]

[1] Randolph Churchill, *Lord Derby, King of Lancashire* (1959), 291-2; Great Britain, 5 *Parliamentary Debates* (Commons), c, 27-29, 224, 389-90, 893-939; *Lord Riddell's War Diary, 1914-1918* (n.d.), 292; Lieut.-Col. C. à Court Repington, *The First World War, 1914-1918* (Boston, 1921), 292; *The Times*, 20 Nov. 1917, p. 9 (1) ('A TRIUMPHANT VINDICATION').

[2] *Press Opinions of the Allied Supreme War Council*: The *Manchester Guardian* welcomed the new Council unreservedly in its editorial of 14 Nov., entitled *Mr. George's Speech*, and again the following day ('If war were decided "on points", the decision would have gone in favour of our army on the west. But war is decided by results'). The Asquithian *Westminster Gazette*, an evening paper, wrote on the 15th that

It is doubtful in our opinion whether such a body can exercise supremacy over sovereign and responsible Government, and the use of a word borrowed from the terminology of Prussian militarism is liable to misunderstanding and misrepresentation.

After Lloyd George's Commons speech, however, it felt constrained to state that

We have already expressed our opinion that an Allied Council, rightly constituted, is highly desirable and should prove a most useful part of the machinery of war.

The Times on the 12th welcomed the Council in principle, but not as a vehicle for 'amateur strategists' or as affecting the positions of Haig or Robertson. The following day it commented that the Prime Minister in his speech had 'let himself go . . . we are not altogether sorry that he has done it'. The *Evening Standard* on 10 Nov. [welcomed], 'as a step of the first importance, the creation of supreme political and military control for the whole of the Western Allies . . . there is little doubt that if the Board of Control now constituted had existed some months ago we should not be confronted by the present Italian situation. Such a Board would no doubt have decided to accept Cadorna's plans for a blow at Austria through Laibach.'

The last phases of the Flanders campaign and the Caporetto defeat had already stirred some sections of the Press into expressing their uneasiness at the soldiers' conduct of the war. Even *The Times*, in welcoming THE FRENCH VICTORY ON THE AISNE, had commented in its first leader that 'both the British and French who are floundering in the sea of mud beyond Ypres will hear with envy of a battle fought at a well-drained altitude of six hundred feet'. The *Manchester Guardian* and the *Evening Standard*, the journal with a 'Larger Circulation Than All Other Penny Evening Papers Combined', were more outspoken. That same day (25 October) the former in its first leader commented that

the muscle of the army has been developed disproportionately to the power of the Staff work, divisional and headquarters, which is the brain of the army. Our military critics have sometimes talked as though endurance and sacrifice were ends in themselves, whereas the business of war is to win cheaply, to attain the maximum of results with the minimum of effort—in other words to be lavish of the things of the mind and economical of bodily suffering and life. What strikes one about recent French victories is that they seem to be dominated by these ideas.

Caporetto caused the *Manchester Guardian* to lose patience:

It is the third time this has happened [read the leader of the 29th], and each time through precisely the same cause. The first time was with Serbia, the second with Rumania and if we add the failure of the Dardanelles expedition, this is the fourth time. The cause has been the same every time—the apparent inability of the War Office to take a sufficiently broad view of the war as a whole . . . the concentration of effort on Flanders . . . has been carried to the length of an obsession and has been allowed to shut out the view of the war as a whole, which it is the duty of the General Staff as distinguished from the generals in the field to take.

On 1 December the voice of Northern liberalism returned to the attack:

. . . about the military conduct of the war . . . we dare not be silent. It is profoundly unsatisfactory . . . perhaps the most pernicious [of cant phrases] are that civilians ought not to interfere in military affairs and that it is always best to trust the man on the spot. . . . To set up such a distinction in this country, where the army normally

attracts so small a part of the ability of the country, is especially
absurd, for it would mean that the direction of our wars was being
entrusted to a class normally not distinguished for its intellectuality.
We might wage war with the Afridis successfully on such conditions,
but not with the Germans.

. . . the general has been running the war instead of the General
Staff running the generals. Every one of our mistakes in this war
has been due to these causes. If it had not been for the excessive
preponderance in their counsels of the vested military interest of
Flanders . . . we should long ago have won this war in the East. The
men on the spot in Flanders dominated the General Staff, and the
General Staff dominated the statesmen who alone were able to take
a wide view of the whole of our national needs in this war.

. . . two practical counsels. . . . Strengthen the political control,
which at any rate makes some attempt to see the war as a whole. . . .
Strengthen the General Staff so that it is capable of governing its
generals and seeing more campaigns than the one in Flanders,
more of the world than the lines between the sea and St. Quentin.

These 'attacks' were immediately interpreted by the General
Staff's adherents as 'inspired' by Downing Street, and doubtless
this view was correct, but the 'inspiration' could not have succeeded had the doubts not already been present.[1]

It was, however, neither the Flanders campaign, with its
losses of some three hundred thousand, nor the Caporetto
disaster that really shook the faith of 'public opinion' in 'the
generals'. It was the boomerang effect of an attempt by G.H.Q.
to refurbish its faded prestige.[2]

In November 1916 Haig had asked General Gough to 'take'
Beaumont-Hamel and thereby improve the standing of the
British Armies in France at the forthcoming Allied military con-
ference at Chantilly. On 13 October 1917, when it was evident
that no visible success would soon come to British arms in
Flanders, the Field-Marshal approved preliminary preparations

[1] *Evening Standard*, 16, 30–31 Oct., 1, 3, 6, 8, 12 Nov. 1917; *Manchester Guardian*,
25 Oct., 1 Nov. 1917; *The Times*, 25 Oct. 1917; *Sunday Times*, 14 Oct. 1917.¦See
also Repington, *First World War*, 127. Colonel Repington in his dispatches from 'the
front' had given a true picture of the 'unspeakable' battle conditions at Passchendaele. See *The Times*, 26 Oct. 1917. Lloyd George warned Haig of 'retaliation' on
the 'Press question' at the beginning of November (Duff Cooper, *Haig* [1936],
ii. 203; Hankey, *Supreme Command*, ii. 719).
[2] Capt. B. H. Liddell Hart, 'The Basic Truths of Passchendaele', *Journal of
the Royal United Service Institution*, civ, No. 616 (November 1959), 438.

for an operation designed 'to restore British prestige and strike a theatrical blow against Germany before the winter'. On 20 November, as the Flanders campaign expired, a tank attack was launched in the direction of Cambrai.[1]

The battle of Cambrai is known to military historians as the first clear demonstration of the revolution in land warfare brought about by the tank. But the original conception of the action, as held by G.H.Q., and for that matter the Tanks Corps, was of a raid without serious military object. General Pétain's offer of infantry support for exploitation was ignored. To G.H.Q.'s critics, now growing in numbers, the issue of the battle afforded visible proof of the High Command's incapacity.[2]

On the first day all went far better than planned. A force of over three hundred tanks—haltingly followed by five infantry divisions still groaning under the seventy-two pound weight of their packs—advanced four miles at one bound on a six-mile front, an advance as great as that achieved in the three and a half months at Passchendaele. The two enemy divisions opposite were shattered.[3]

This amazing success took G.H.Q. quite by surprise. The cavalry, on which the command's hopes for strategic exploitation after the 'breakthrough' were still pinned, were belatedly brought up but failed to survive the scattered pockets of enemy machine-gun fire. Still, in G.H.Q.'s view, the necessary prestige victory had already been attained. General Pétain was told his forces would not be required. Was not Cambrai to be remembered as a *British* Army success, designed to vie with Malmaison?[4]

The applause from London was overwhelming. At the orders of the War Office the church bells were rung for joy, and flags displayed in celebration, for the first time in the course of the war. Congratulations were poured on to the command of the British armies in France. Haig's private secretary, Sir Philip Sassoon, M.P., assured his electorate that the victory at Cambrai more than made up for the Russian defection. 'A good comment',

---

[1] Charteris, *At G.H.Q.*, 268; Maj.-Gen. J. F. C. Fuller, *Memoirs of an Unconventional Soldier* (1936), 170; *Mil. Opns. Fr. and Bel. 1917*, iii. 9, *1918*, v. 603.

[2] *AF*, vi (1), 137–8, Annexe 90; *Mil. Opns. Fr. and Bel. 1917*, iii. 24.

[3] *Mil. Opns. Fr. and Bel. 1917*, iii. 285; Liddell Hart, *The Tanks* (1959), i. 128.

[4] *AF*, vi (1), Annexe 112; *Mil. Opns. Fr. and Bel. 1917*, iii. 233.

PLATE 13

b. General Sir Edmund Allenby
Commander-in-Chief (from June 1917) Egyptian
Expeditionary Force

a. Lieutenant-General Sir Laurence Kiggell
Chief of General Staff, G.H.Q. British Armies in France

Colonel Repington noted in his diary, 'upon L. G.'s sarcastic references to the Western Front.'[1]

The plaudits must have been very satisfying, but the applause did not last long. On 30 November a German counter-attack took Third Army's staff entirely by surprise and demonstrated that the German Army's morale was not as shaken as believed. Major-General de Lisle, commanding the Twenty-Ninth Division of Gallipoli and other fame, was surprised in his pyjamas. There were tales of heroic resistance in undress, and more of general disorder and confusion. When a week later the German counter-attack in its turn came to a halt, the British Army had lost to the south but a little less territory than it had gained in the north.[2]

The publicity had been too great to avoid backfire. Questions were asked and criticisms voiced in Parliament. An inquiry was demanded and accorded. Held at G.H.Q., it naturally blamed the 'undertrained' troops for the setback. This conclusion, however, carried little conviction. The Times began openly to criticize both G.H.Q. and the C.I.G.S. Its proprietor, Lord Northcliffe, on his return from America in November had found one of his nephews—mortally wounded at Cambrai—inclined to ascribe his forthcoming death to the bullheadedness of the High Command. Northcliffe reminded Haig's personal secretary that, 'There is the memory of a dead man, or the knowledge of a missing or wounded man, in every house. Outside the War Office, I doubt whether the Higher Command has any supporters whatever.' The Times, in an oft-quoted editorial entitled A CASE FOR INQUIRY, contended that[3]

we can no longer rest satisfied with the fatuous estimates, e.g. of German losses in men and moral, which have inspired too many of the published messages from France. . . .

We must not be misunderstood. The merest breath of criticism on any military operation is far too often dismissed as an 'intrigue' against the Commander-in-Chief, and therefore we would say at

[1] Repington, First World War, ii. 140. See also Mil. Opns. Fr. and Bel. 1916, i. 148 n. ('the correspondents were advised that it would be opportune to make the most of any British success obtained') ; 5 Parliamentary Debates (Commons), ic. 1326 (21 Nov. 1917), 1624 (17 Dec. 1917); Daily Telegraph and The Times (22 Nov. 1917).
[2] AF, vi (1), Annexe 156; Paul Cambon, Correspondance, iii (Paris, 1946), 202; Mil. Opns. Fr. and Bel. 1917, iii. 293; Daily Chronicle, 7 Dec. 1917, The Times, 10 Dec. 1917. [3] The Times, 12 Dec. 1917.

once that SIR DOUGLAS HAIG, in our sober judgement, possesses the undiminished confidence both of the Army and of the Government at home. [But] His weakness . . . is his inveterate devotion to those who have served him longest—some of them perhaps too long . . . the Germans took advantage of a brilliant British success to strike back unexpectedly at a wholly unready part of the line. . . . To judge only from our Correspondent's account . . .—of Brigade Headquarters raided, of generals fighting in their pyjamas, of doctors interrupted in their dressing stations—we may agree that they are all magnificent, but they should never have occurred.

A month later a new M.P., Mr. Smallwood, distressed the House by an account of the death of his two sons. In each case he held the War Office procedures partially responsible—for the death of one son, for not being allowed to visit with the other the night of his death. In the tug-of-war over man-power in the winter of 1917–18 the Press were no longer overly eager to feed more men to the command in France. 'I am certainly left almost alone to fight the case of the Army for men', Colonel Repington now complained. 'It is a public misfortune that the Northcliffe press does not support me. Only the *Morning Post* and *Globe* are playing the game by the Army.'[1]

Neither Passchendaele, nor Caporetto, nor Cambrai, to be sure, dismaying as these reverses were, really changed the fundamental conditions that had governed the conduct of the war ever since the winter of 1914. What finally broke the military stalemate was the Russian armistice signed at Brest-Litovsk on 5 December.

The Russian withdrawal from the war, long feared, was now a fact, and Germany set free to devote her military efforts to the West. All the repeated onslaughts in the past of both the French and British Armies appeared to have been in vain. The chilling effects of the realization of what might soon come upon the Western Front compelled a radical—and public—re-evaluation of the entire meaning of the war. In the spring and summer of

---

[1] Repington, *First World War*, 165; Reginald Pound and Geoffrey Harmsworth, *Northcliffe* (1959), 598, 620–1. See also *Les carnets de guerre d'Albert Ier Roi des Belges* (Brussels, 1953), 172; *Mil. Opns. Fr. and Bel. 1917*, iii. 293–300; 5 *Parliamentary Debates* (Commons), c. 1329–32, 2247–51 (12, 20 Dec. 1917), ci. 539–44, 1099–1103 (19, 23 Jan. 1918); *Daily Chronicle*, 10 Dec. 1917; *Evening Standard*, 11 Dec. 1917.

1917 Great Britain's position had been more dangerous, but knowledge of the deadliness of the submarine threat—now passed away—had been confined to a small inner circle. Now the pending danger was clear to all. The task henceforth, both Colonel Repington and Mr. Asquith agreed, though they assured each other they could not afford to say so publicly, was not to achieve victory, but to avoid defeat. Asquith now ruminated over taking the lead in the movement for a negotiated peace. 'He said that he did not like to take up a line until . . . there was likely to be a general response.' Lord Milner did not share these scruples; the British were now, he declared in one of his rare public speeches, 'fighting for our lives'.[1]

Of course, if they did not have to, all the better. Lord Lansdowne in a letter refused by *The Times* but published in the *Daily Telegraph* on 29 November had finally brought the 'peace question' into the open. The war had, he said, already lasted too long. Could not the two opposing groups somehow find agreement on the principles of the peace settlement?[2]

The reception of the Lansdowne letter made it clear that statesmen would have to tread warily. Even so, in view of the disappearance of the Eastern Front, the British Government would perhaps now have greeted a general peace with something like relief, always providing that the Germans would agree to evacuate Belgium. Nor does it appear that either the War Office or G.H.Q., and certainly not Haig, would have interposed any objection, always provided that Mr. Lloyd George took the responsibility.[3] Neither Liberal nor Conservative statesmen

[1] Lord Milner. *Fighting for Our Lives*. Speech . . . Plymouth, 21 Feb. 1918 (Constable, 1918) ('It is not now a question of destroying Prussian militarism. The question is, whether Prussian militarism should destroy us . . . neither America nor this country is fighting in order to dismember the German people or to interfere with their clear right to decide for themselves under what constitution they choose to live'); Repington, *First World War*, ii. 248. See also J. L. Hammond, *C. P. Scott* (1934), 225, and *Autobiography of Philip Snowden* (1934), i. 443–4, on Liberal leaders' leanings towards a negotiated peace from which they might derive political profit.

[2] CO-ORDINATION OF ALLIES' WAR AIMS. LETTER FROM LANSDOWNE. *Daily Telegraph*, 29 Nov. 1917; *Riddell War Diary*, 296 ('L. G. The point is that at the moment we could not secure favourable terms. That being so, the letter is harmful').

[3] Charteris, *At G.H.Q.*, 335–9; *Private Papers of Douglas Haig*, 294; Hankey, *Supreme Command*, ii. 756; Arno J. Mayer, *Political Origins of the New Diplomacy, 1917–1918* (New Haven, 1959), 313; Owen, *Tempestuous Journey*, 448; *Riddell War Diary*, 303, 306; Field-Marshal Sir William Robertson, *Soldiers and Statesmen, 1915–1918* (1926), ii. 276–84.

considered central or eastern Europe as an area of serious concern to Great Britain. And, in the 'New Imperialist' view, the war had by now brought substantial and important gains to the Empire. Germany's colonies, apart from East Africa, had long been conquered. The 'consolidation' of the 'Southern British World' had more recently been largely accomplished. From the Cape to Cairo, from Cairo to Calcutta, British hegemony was now unchallenged by any major power. The South African commander in German East Africa had at last been able to announce on 1 December that the territory 'had been completely cleared of the enemy'. Colonel von Lettow-Vorbeck's force had indeed withdrawn southwards, only to invade the adjoining Portuguese colony of Mozambique. 'BRITISH EAST AFRICA' was the title of the leader run in *The Times* of 5 December celebrating the conquest. The German enclave between the British possessions in Africa had been eliminated, and therewith the only base for German sea-power in the Indian Ocean.[1]

In the 'Middle East', from Egypt to India, the British position had been transformed during the past year. In November and early December 1917 General Allenby's troops had inflicted a severe defeat upon the opposing Turkish forces and their commander had entered in triumph into the city of Jerusalem on 11 December. The Balfour declaration of 2 November, viewing 'with favour the establishment in Palestine of a national home for the Jewish people', would serve to keep the French out of Palestine and the British in. The whole of 'Arabia', roused by the activities of Major T. E. Lawrence and other British irregulars, was now effectively in the British sphere of influence. The Turkish 'presence', maintained only by scattered garrisons along the Red Sea Coast and a railway line running north from Medina, was besieged rather than occupying. Most of 'Mesopotamia', including the vilayets of Baghdad and Basra, was controlled by British troops.[2] The Bolshevik Government had

[1] *Diary of Lord Bertie*, ii. 219; Hankey, *Supreme Command*, ii. 685; *House Papers*, iii. 241; War Office announcement, 3 Dec. 1917 ('Thus the whole of the German overseas possessions has passed into our hands and those of our Belgian allies'), as printed in *Daily Telegraph*, 4 Dec. 1917.
[2] 'The prime mission of your force is the establishment and maintenance of British influence in the Baghdad *vilayet*.' (Telegram, C.I.G.S. to Lt.-Gen. Sir W. R. Marshall, 22 Nov. 1917, Brig.-Gen. F. J. Moberly, *The Campaign in Mesopotamia*, iv (1927), 87–88.) Cf. earlier instructions, above, pp. 157 and 220.

ordered the withdrawal of the Russian garrisons from northern Persia, and the new British commander of the Mesopotamia force, General Marshall, was being pressed to begin occupation of this area. Indian Army authorities had established a post at Meshed, in north-east Persia. A small British party under General Dunsterville of the Indian Army was preparing to pass through Persia on the way to the Caucasus to organize resistance against the Turks. The 'Southern British World', patrolled by British sea-power, was now in being, its limits being formed by a semicircle including the entire Indian Ocean and passing through Africa from the Cape of Good Hope to Egypt, from Palestine through India to Australia.[1]

In the last month of 1917 there was therefore much 'peace talk'. The withdrawal of Russia from the war and the seizure of its government by the Bolsheviks, commonly regarded as enemies of civilized society, made possible the payment of territorial 'compensation' to the Central Powers in exchange for the evacuation of the occupied territories in the West. General Smuts conferred in Geneva with Count Mensdorff, former Austrian Ambassador to London, and held out hopes of Russian Poland, which had in fact already been promised to the Austrians by the German Government. 'I expect', the South African statesman said in his report, 'that she [Austria] will strain every nerve to induce Germany to accept moderate terms.'[2] Efforts were made in vain to induce the Turks to enter into peace negotiations at a prisoner-of-war exchange conference in Switzerland.[3]

On 5 January the Prime Minister, in a much publicized speech on war aims formulated in collaboration with the Liberal and Labour leaders, 'went', as he told Lords Reading and Riddell immediately afterwards, 'as near peace as I could'.[4] Any

[1] Isaac Deutscher, The Prophet Armed: Trotsky, 1879–1921 (Oxford, 1954), 360; L. C. Dunsterville, Adventures of Dunsterforce (1921), 11–21; W. Marshall, Memories of Four Fronts (1929), 282–3; Brig.-Gen. F. J. Moberly, Campaign in Mesopotamia, iv (1927), 89, 98–107; Leonard Stein, Balfour Declaration (1961), 548; The Times, 10 Nov. 1917, third leader, 7 (2) ('we may rejoice that by reaching Tikrit SIR STANLEY MAUDE has practically completed his conquest of the Baghdad vilayet'); Field-Marshal Earl Wavell, The Palestine Campaigns (3rd edn., 1931), 53–56, 115–68, 179, Allenby (1940), 236. [2] Lloyd George, War Memoirs, ii. 1489. [3] Ibid. 1478–90, 1504–9; Lord Beaverbrook, Men and Power, 1917–1918 (1956), 193 n.; Callwell, Henry Wilson, ii. 49; Private Papers of Douglas Haig, 286; Hammond, Scott, 214–15, 232. [4] Riddell War Diary, 304.

intent to change the German constitution was now disclaimed. 'After all, that is a question for the German people to decide.' 'The first requirement' for peace, now as always, was 'the complete restoration . . . of the independence of Belgium. . . .' 'Next comes the restoration of Serbia, Montenegro, and the occupied parts of France, Italy, and Rumania.' There must be a 'reconsideration' of the status of Alsace-Lorraine. But 'I will not attempt to deal with the question of the Russian territories now in German occupation'. As for Turkey,[1]

While we do not challenge the maintenance of the Turkish Empire in the homelands of the Turkish race with its capital at Constantinople—the passage between the Mediterranean and the Black Sea being internationalized and neutralized—Arabia, Armenia, Mesopotamia, Syria, and Palestine are in our judgment entitled to a recognition of their separate national conditions.

What the exact form of that recognition in each particular case should be need not here be discussed, beyond stating that it would be impossible to restore to their former sovereignty the territories to which I have already referred.

None of these overtures, however, met with any success. The German High Command was determined to take the offensive in the West. With Germany's star in the ascendant, neither Austria nor Turkey was now desirous, or indeed able, to desert their ally on the terms proffered by Great Britain. The war would go on. Ludendorff so willed it.

The British Government, however, was determined that at any rate the war would not be conducted in the old reckless untraditional way. The keynote of future policy was sounded in an address to the House by Sir Auckland Geddes, Minister of National Service, on 14 January. 'Since August, 1914 we

---

[1] Prime Minister's Speech on War Aims (5 Jan. 1918), Appendix III to *The War Cabinet Report for the Year 1917* (1918 [Cd. 9005]), 230–5. See also Louis Fischer, *Soviets in World Affairs, 1917–1918* (2nd edn., Princeton, 1951), i. 51; *House Papers*, iii. 270; Address by the British Prime Minister (Lloyd George) before the Trade Union Conference at London, 18 January 1918 ('The moment the Germans show a disposition to negotiate peace on equitable terms—the terms have been stated and they are terms which the Labour Party Staff itself in substance adopted—then there will be no reluctance to enter into negotiations'). Enclosure, Consul-General Landon to Sec. State, 19 Jan. 1918, U.S. Department of State. *Papers Relating to the Foreign Relations of the United States. Supplement. The World War, 1918*, i. 76 (Washington, 1933).

have trodden some strange paths, and they have brought us little profit for treading. Let us return to the faith of our fore-fathers, and recognize that on the sea and by the sea we live.' Henceforth the man-power needs of the Navy, however implausible; of the Air Services under the control of the newly constituted Air Ministry; of shipbuilding; of the construction of aeroplanes and tanks (and, to set shipping free of food production, of timber felling and the provision of fuel storage accommodations) were to receive absolute priority over the Army. Carelessness in regard to casualties would no longer be tolerated.[1]

The Government was finally also able to enforce a far-reaching purge of the military and naval staffs. Admirals Bacon and Jellicoe were dismissed summarily though with careful regard for timing. The consequent resignation of Sir Edward Carson, ostensibly on Irish affairs, caused no great stir. The new First Sea Lord, the genial Admiral Wester Wemyss, devoted himself to encouraging the 'younger seamen' and recreating the offensive spirit. The War Office staff had a reputation for routine competence, if not for impartiality, but Robertson its chief was for the moment saved from dismissal only by Lord Derby's threatened resignation. Derby himself, however, backed by Robertson, enforced upon Sir Douglas Haig the dismissal or transfer of the chief staff officers at G.H.Q., a generally mediocre and subservient group of men. General Kiggell, who had broken down in something like remorse on witnessing for the first time the battlefields at Passchendaele, was sent to the Channel island of Jersey. General Charteris, who had long pandered to Haig's desire to hear of the enemy's failing morale, was given a job in Transportation at G.H.Q. And so it went on. Haig as yet was spared, but Smuts and Hankey were sent to the front to recommend another suitable Commander-in-Chief. They failed to discover one.[2]

---

[1] 5 *Parliamentary Debates* (Commons), ci, cols. 59–65 (the quote from Geddes is in col. 60); *Mil. Opns. Fr. and Bel. 1918*, i. 51.
[2] Beaverbrook, *Men and Power*, 180, 364–73; Charteris, *At G.H.Q.*, 277, 286; R. Churchill, *Derby*, 300–2; Lloyd George, *War Memoirs*, ii. 1367, 1370; *Private Papers of Douglas Haig*, 272–3, 276–8; Hankey, *Supreme Command*, ii. 755 ff.; *Mil. Opns. Fr. and Bel. 1918*, i. 55–56; *The Times*, 27 Dec. 1917, first leader, 7 (1) ('A CHANCE FOR THE YOUNGER SEAMEN'); Letter, B. H. Liddell Hart to the Editor, *The Spectator*, 3 Jan. 1958; John Terraine, *Douglas Haig* (1963), 384–90.

On the general policy to be pursued in the West during the forthcoming year (both in France and in Italy)[1] the War Cabinet, the Chief of the Imperial Staff, and the Military Representatives on the Allied Supreme War Council were in agreement. It was to be purely defensive. The British role was to hold on until the Americans finally arrived in substantial numbers. General Foch might argue in favour of making plans for a 'disengaging' counter-offensive following or coincident with the German onslaught, but neither Haig nor Pétain took this 'theory' seriously. Bring back the men from Salonika, Haig remarked, then it would be time to talk of offensives![2]

Even so Haig told himself and others, including, it may be, the War Cabinet, that 'the best defence would be to continue our offensive in Flanders'. 'Though', he told Repington, in order that the latter might throw his weight into a press campaign to force the Government to provide the desired men, 'the continuation of the Flanders offensive is the best way he knows of attracting and using up the Boches, he cannot go on with it if he is not adequately supplied with drafts.'[3]

The War Cabinet were consequently all the more determined not to furnish the drafts.[4] Not that they lacked excuses, for the whole man-power problem was difficult and even dangerous. After several years of 'using up' the German reserves, 'Germany had the power, which the French and British lacked, of keeping her divisions up to establishment'.[5] Some two hundred thousand men might be secured through applying conscription to Ireland, and this measure the 'generals'—notably Sir Henry Wilson, a member of the Irish Protestant ascendancy like so many other career officers in the British Army—vehemently backed, for political rather than military reasons. The removal of the more

[1] The Italians at this stage were in no mood to launch further offensives on their front.

[2] *AF*, vi (1), 39–40, Annexes nos. 179, 242, 287; Winston S. Churchill, *The World Crisis, 1911–1918* (4-vol. Odhams Press edn.), iv. 1221; Lloyd George, *War Memoirs*, ii. 1806–11; *Mil. Opns. Fr. and Bel. 1918*, i. Appendixes (1935), no. 2, pp. 9–14; Robertson, *Soldiers and Statesmen*, ii. 282–4.

[3] *Private Papers of Douglas Haig*, 278; Repington, *First World War*, ii. 173. See also Hankey, *Supreme Command*, ii. 756; *Mil. Opns. Fr. and Bel. 1918*, i. 37, ii. 475; *AF*, vi (1), Annexe no. 156.

[4] L. S. Amery, *My Political Life*, ii (1953), 134–5; Churchill, *World Crisis*, iv. 1220–1, 1227–8; Hankey, *Supreme Command*, ii. 1801; Earl Lloyd George, *Lloyd George* (1960), 187–8.

[5] *Mil. Opns. Fr. and Bel. 1918*, i. 49.

restless spirits, it was urged, would tranquillize the country. Yet might not the effect be rather to stir it into open and this time widespread insurrection? The trade unions were another source of man-power, but these were becoming increasingly restive and many of their members were both frankly reluctant to serve and in a position to make that reluctance effective. Already the unions had helped to compel the Prime Minister to deliver his war aims speech of 5 January 1918, given neither to the Commons nor to a newspaperman, but to a trades union congress in hopes of inducing organized labour to release more men for the services.[1]

The War Office demanded another six hundred thousand 'A' men to fill up the ranks in France until July 1918. It was estimated that by the end of March the deficit of the British Armies there would amount to a quarter of a million. A Cabinet Committee on man-power policy recommended that of the one hundred and fifty thousand 'A' men the Ministry of National Service hoped to prize loose from industry one hundred thousand should go to the Army and the remainder to the Navy.[2] The divisions on the Western Front would be reduced from twelve to nine battalions. The Military Members of the Army Council solemnly protested that the acceptance of the committee's recommendations would be 'taking an unreasonably grave risk of losing the War and sacrificing to no purpose the British Army on the Western Front'. In the speech by Sir Auckland Geddes already cited, delivered a week after this protest, the Minister stated that 'if we are to expand the Navy and the Air Force as we propose, and to maintain the Armies in the field, it is necessary to proceed immediately to raise in this country 420,000 to 450,000 men from among those now in civil life. [This was the] absolute minimum.'[3]

---

[1] Callwell, Henry Wilson, ii. 5–6; Private Papers of Douglas Haig, 299; House Papers, iii. 349; Lloyd George, War Memoirs, ii. 1593–1601; Auckland Geddes, 14 Jan. 1918, 5 Parliamentary Debates (Commons), ci. 70 (Rank-and-file trade union resistance might 'force the Government to send out the wounded men again and again . . . to drag out their fathers . . . to stop leave'); The Times, 21 Dec. 1917, first leader, 7 (1/2) ('The defection of Russia and the demands of the Italian campaign impose a fresh and unforeseen drain upon our Armies. Are we going to meet it? The answer rests very largely with the trade unions').

[2] These were in addition to 'the 120,000 boys which the Army would get naturally in the first half-year'. (Lieut.-Col. C. à Court Repington, The First World War, 1914–1918 [Boston, 1921], ii. 180, Entry for 10 January 1918.)

[3] 5 Parliamentary Debates (Commons), ci. 66.

The impression was none the less created in *The Times* leaders that all four hundred and fifty thousand were scheduled for the Army. Colonel Repington resigned in protest from that journal in consequence and went to the extreme High Tory *Morning Post*, the only journal of consequence henceforth to support unreservedly the military demands.[1]

The 'Home Forces', numbering over a million, were another source of man-power for the armies in France.

The Cabinet committee had estimated the number of men in the Home Forces available for drafts at 449,000. But to keep Field-Marshal Haig firmly on the leash the Government decided, apparently on War Office advice, to keep a reserve of (perhaps) one hundred and twenty thousand men in England, ready in case of need, rather than to send it to France. The General Staff recommended this course in part to conserve public morale; for soldiers sent to the Front were by now regarded by their families as unlikely to return whole. Haig had expressed his belief that he would be able to hold his present front with the forces already at his disposal for eighteen days.[2]

By these astonishing expedients the Government was enabled (though on how unsound a basis!)[3] still to coexist with Haig and

---

[1] Charteris, *At G.H.Q.*, 273–4 ('D. H. does not agree about the German strategy for 1918. He says that the correct strategy for them is to play a waiting game and not commit themselves to a big attack. . . . It makes no difference to our immediate plans which are to get every man we can over here'); Beaverbrook, *Men and Power*, 376–7; Lloyd George, *War Memoirs*, ii. 1589; *Mil. Opns. Fr. and Bel. 1918*, i. Appendixes, pp. 30–34; Repington, *First World War*, ii. 187, 197; Robertson, *Soldiers and Statesmen*, i. 314–19; *The Times*, 16 Jan. 1918, ENGINEERS AND MAN-POWER, Parliamentary Correspondent ('The country has been virtually stripped of all young and fit men in non-essential industries, and the Government believes that they can secure 450,000 men for the Army, and at the same time maintain the maximum output of tonnage, aeroplanes, certain other engines of war, and food'), p. 7 (4); *Morning Post*, first leader, 5 Feb. 1918.

[2] *Mil. Opns. Fr. and Bel. 1918*, i. 52 n.; Capt. B. H. Liddell Hart, Talk with Colonel E. Allanson, 19 Aug. 1937, Liddell Hart files.

[3] Churchill from December 1917 onwards consistently urged that Haig be (1) adequately reinforced, (2) forbidden to mount an offensive prior to a German attack. Such a policy in itself, however, would not have caused G.H.Q. to prepare the Army in France any the less inefficiently for the German onslaught, and would have made repairing the initial disaster even more difficult. 'In the event 174,379 men (including 32,384 for Dominions forces and 7,359 labour and non-fighting troops) were sent to France before 21 March in addition to one division from Italy—190,000 men in all compared with the original demand for that period of 350,000 men.' (Lord Hankey, *The Supreme Command, 1914–1918* [1961], ii. 802.) A General Reserve under Foch, as proposed by the Prime Minister, was undoubtedly the best solution.

Robertson without either surrendering the fundamentals of its strategic policy or incurring any political risk. But in the Eastern theatres of war, or at any rate in Palestine, open conflict proved unavoidable.[1]

There were now over three-quarters of a million Empire troops, including twelve British infantry divisions, serving in Greece, Mesopotamia, and Palestine.[2] The new French Prime Minister, Georges Clemenceau, hitherto no friend of the Salonika expedition, had at Lloyd George's and Orlando's promptings consented to recall the unpopular Sarrail—an action he took without ceremony—and replaced him by the energetic yet friendly Guillaumat. In spite of the opportunities for offensive action offered by the steady withdrawal of German troops from Macedonia to the Western Front, the Military Representatives concurred in recommending not only a defensive policy in Greece but also preparations for the evacuation of Salonika or even an eventual general withdrawal.[3]

With these moves the British General Staff could be well content. But with the Turkish War it was a different story. On the one hand, the C.I.G.S. was now insistent that in view of the Russian collapse 'we must cut down in Mesopotamia and Palestine to a defensive minimum'; on the other, the Prime Minister exuberantly reminded the House that 'The British Empire owes a good deal to side shows'[4] and pressed for further gains. In Mesopotamia the reluctant General Marshall was urged to use his diminished forces to expand the area under his control still further into Persia.[5]

---

[1] Churchill, *World Crisis*, iv. 1220–8; Owen, *Tempestuous Journey*, 449–50.

[2] *Mil. Ops. Fr. and Bel. 1918*, i. 13–14, 52 n.

[3] Military Representatives. Joint Notes No. 1 and 4, *AF*, vi (1), Annexes nos. 179, 203; Cyril Falls, *Military Operations, Macedonia*, ii (1935), 46–54; Lloyd George, *War Memoirs*, ii. 1914–17; Mermeix, *Sarrail et les armées d'Orient* (Paris, 1920), 293–4.

[4] '[The capture of Baghdad and Jerusalem] . . . will have a permanent effect on the history of the world. . . . The British Empire owes a great deal to side-shows. During the Seven Years' War . . . the events which are best remembered by every Englishman are not the great battles on the Continent of Europe, but Plassey and the Heights of Abraham; and I have no doubt at all that, when the history of 1917 comes to be written, and comes to be read ages hence, these events in Mesopotamia and Palestine will hold a much more conspicuous place in the minds and in the memories of the people than many an event which looms much larger for the moment in our sight.' The Prime Minister, 20 Dec. 1917. (5 *Parliamentary Debates* (Commons), c. 2211.)

[5] *Campaign in Mesopotamia*, iv. 97, 103–4, 109–10; *Mil. Opns. Fr. and Bel. 1918*, i. Appendixes, no. 2, pp. 9–14; *The Times*, 14 Dec. 1917, THE MILITARY SITUATION—

The real clash came over the exploitation of Allenby's victories in Palestine. Comparison was naturally drawn between these brilliant operations, which made extensive use of surprise, deception, and an unorthodox disposition of force, and the disappointments of Passchendaele and Cambrai. Of even greater import to the War Cabinet was the manifest error in both Allenby's and the General Staff's estimates of the preceding October as to further needed reinforcements.[1] The E.E.F. had in fact occupied Jerusalem without any. The War Cabinet, or at any rate the Prime Minister, suspected Robertson of deliberate deception, and decided to dismiss him. In this intention they had provisionally been thwarted by Lord Derby. These past quarrels, however, presented the worst possible background for the discussions between the General Staff and the War Cabinet on the future conduct of the Turkish campaign.[2]

Even before the occupation of Jerusalem the Seventh Division had been ordered from Mesopotamia to Allenby's command. The War Cabinet now desired preferably an advance north to Aleppo, thus occupying the entire Mediterranean littoral and severing the Turkish railway to Mesopotamia, but at any rate the occupation of all Palestine between 'Dan and Beersheba'. Allenby was understandably puzzled by the Biblical reference (Judges xx. 1), for 'Dan' no longer existed, but cautiously indicated that by next summer he might with his present force be able to advance to the Sea of Galilee. He could not deploy further troops until his railway-line was doubled. Meanwhile the General Staff urged a defensive policy and the withdrawal of at least one division to the Western Front.[3]

On the last day of 1917 the War Cabinet asked the Military Representatives to the Allied Supreme War Council for their opinion on the prospects for the Turkish War. Henry Wilson and Leopold Amery (who had been appointed political secretary of the British section of the Allied Supreme War Council and

A BRIEF REVIEW (By our Military Correspondent), 7 (1); Arnold Wilson, *Mesopotamia, 1917–1920*, ii. 6.

[1] See above, pp. 260–1.

[2] Amery, *Political Life*, ii. 135–6; Beaverbrook, *Men and Power*, 187–8, 364–9; R. Churchill, *Derby*, 301–2; Lloyd George, *War Memoirs*, ii. 1092.

[3] Cyril Falls, *Military Operations Egypt and Palestine*, ii (1) (1930), 293–6; *Campaign in Mesopotamia*, iv. 97; Lloyd George, *War Memoirs*, ii. 1093; Robertson, *Soldiers and Statesmen*, ii. 187–9, 272–6; Wavell, *Palestine Campaigns*, 173.

personal representative of Milner and Lloyd George) set themselves and their substantial staff to work. Between them they produced a lengthy memorandum on general military policy forecasting a stalemate in the West during 1918 and urging 'a decisive offensive against Turkey with a view to the annihilation of the Turkish Armies and the collapse of Turkish resistance'.[1]

So far so good, but would the other Military Representatives agree? The United States was not at war with Turkey, so General Tasker Bliss could not very well offer any opinion. He of course did not append his signature. Italy, on the other hand, had been promised Smyrna and had ambitions in the Eastern Mediterranean. The French Military Representative, General Weygand, was not interested in the Turkish War but, as Foch's spokesman and representative, wished to see the French Chief of General Staff's policy on the necessity of a counter-offensive in France prevail over the passive stance of Pétain.[2] An 'annexure' was accordingly added recommending that Haig and Pétain be instructed to draw up plans for the Western Front in accordance with Foch's 'counter-offensive' strategy. The 'Military Representatives feel obliged to add that France will be safe during 1918 *only* under certain conditions', one of them being

That the French and British forces in France are continuously maintained at their present total aggregate strength.

After all these negotiations and adjustments took place ('Stitching is not strategy!') Generals Weygand, Wilson, and Cadorna presented the resultant document, Joint Note No. 12, dated 21 January 1918, to the Supreme War Council for its approval.[3] The Westerners were naturally disgruntled at this turn of events. Haig noted that in the course of the year he would have

---

[1] Joint Note No. 12, *Mil. Opns. Fr. and Bel. 1918*, i, Appendixes, no. 9, pp. 37–42; Amery, *Political Life*, ii. 129, 137; Callwell, *Henry Wilson*, ii. 51–52; Robertson, *Soldiers and Statesmen*, ii. 276.

[2] See above, p. 280.

[3] Joint Note No. 12 and Annexes, *Mil. Opns. Fr. and Bel. 1918*, i, Appendixes, nos. 9, 10, pp. 37–44; *AF*, vi (1), 48, 50–51; British Section, 'A' Branch, A.S.W.C. papers on 'Future Operations in Palestine' ('It is upon rapidity of railway construction that we must depend for our success in the advance to Aleppo') and on 'Strategical Objectives in Mesopotamia and Palestine', 20 Jan. 1918. Records of the Supreme War Council, National Archives, Washington, D.C.

to reduce 16 to 18 divisions, and the French '(if attacked) . . . some 50'. Yet with these facts before it,[1]

the Versailles War Council writes a volume advising an offensive to annihilate the Turks in Palestine, as well as a great combined Franco-British one on the Western Front.

Wilson, when asked by Robertson how he reconciled the trickle of man-power to the Western Front with his proposals and conditions, replied[2]

that it was quite simple, that if our effectives were kept up we were safe, and if not then we were unsafe, and that I wanted to fix the responsibility on the Prime Ministers—which is where it must rest.

The C.I.G.S. did not take this view. He advised the War Cabinet against the acceptance of Note 12 and wrote Haig he would resign if overruled. Meanwhile, Colonel Repington, who appears to have been kept well informed,[3]

saw a distinguished soldier this afternoon [18 Jan.] The Boches have now 165 divisions in the West—two more than the total of the Allies —and they are coming in at the average rate of nine a month. A nice moment to reduce our infantry by a quarter[4] and to go prancing off to the Holy Land to win the war there! This soldier thought that it was quite time for me to repeat my indiscretion about the shells. Everything else had been tried without avail. The War Office had failed to move the Government fool from its folly, and the only chance of averting defeat was for me and some honest editor to speak out.

On 30 January the third session of the Allied Supreme War Council convened at Versailles.

For the first and last time the 'Conseil Suprême de Volaille' (the phrase is Lord Esher's) now became the organization in which Allied grand strategy was formally determined. Hitherto the British had succeeded in dominating the new institution. The British section of the Council was the first of the four national sections to be created and by far the most fully staffed.

[1] *Private Papers of Douglas Haig*, 280.
[2] Callwell, *Henry Wilson*, ii. 54.
[3] Repington, *First World War*, 191. See also ibid. 178, 181; *AF*, vi (1), 187–8; Callwell, *Henry Wilson*, 50; *Mil. Opns. Fr. and Bel. 1918*, i. 67–68.
[4] Presumably a reference to the reduction of divisions from twelve to nine battalions. (Brig.-Gen. J. E. Edmonds, *Mil. Opns. Fr. and Bel. 1918*, i. 52 n.)

'Versailles, indeed,' Amery later recalled, 'went some way towards achieving what I had always aimed at, namely a measure of British control over the whole war policy of the Allies.'[1] But of course as yet the powers of the Military Representatives had been purely advisory, and the advice they had offered quite consistent with that of the British General Staff. The Council, constituted at Rapallo, had devoted its first working session, at the beginning of the previous December, to putting the Military Representatives to work. The new French Prime Minister, Georges Clemenceau, though initially sceptical of the innovation, had been so far won over by Lloyd George and Henry Wilson as to deliver a businesslike introductory speech drafted by Hankey requesting recommendations for 'the overthrow, first of all, of Germany's allies'. As yet no occasion within the Council for disagreement with either M. Clemenceau—so far more formidable a personality than his predecessors—or with the British General Staff, or with the three commanders-in-chief upon the Western Front, had arisen. This lack was soon to be remedied.[2]

The two resolutions discussed at length at the third session, Joint Notes No. 12 and No. 14—the latter urging as 'imperative' the formation of a General Reserve for the whole of the Allied forces both in France and Italy—were both of British origin. The concept of a general reserve, first designed 'for keeping a certain number of divisions away from Haig and Pétain, and which those men could only draw on with permission of Versailles, or of Robertson and Foch',[3] appears to have originated, at any rate within senior levels, with General Wilson, who had drafted the joint note. Faced with the growing menace on the Western Front, which was deathly quiet during most of this long interim, neither political nor military authorities in

---

[1] Amery, *Political Life*, ii. 123–31.
[2] Callwell, *Henry Wilson*, ii. 32, 38; *Journals and Letters of Reginald Viscount Esher* (1934–8), iv. 176; Hankey, *Supreme Command*, ii. 731–3; *Papers Relating to the Foreign Relations of the United States, The Lansing Papers, 1914–1920* (Washington, 1940), ii. 190–303, and esp. 240 ff. (Report of General Tasker H. Bliss, Military Representative of the United States on the Supreme War Council); Lloyd George, *War Memoirs*, ii. 1650–2; Minutes, second session, Allied Supreme War Council, 1 December 1917, Versailles. Records of the Supreme War Council, National Archives, Washington, D.C.
[3] Callwell, *Henry Wilson*, ii. 50. See also A. M. Gollin, *Proconsul in Politics* (1964), 467–70.

France and England could deny the desirability of the principle of such a reserve. Where the troops constituting the reserve were to come from and who was to command them—a 'Generalissimo', the Chiefs of Staff, or the Military Representatives— were more controversial questions. At a meeting of the Military Representatives, General Weygand stated that the existence of such a reserve could be justified only if provided with a commander-in-chief, to which Wilson replied: a unified command was impossible, a general reserve none the less in itself highly desirable, and some other arrangement to deal with it equally desirable![1]

The session, held in the Trianon Palace, proved lively. General Foch, now French Chief of General Staff, made his proposals for a counter-offensive in the West, but these were met by the gloomiest predictions from Haig and Pétain on the declining strength of their respective armies during the course of the year. Foch's attempts to persist in discussion of the paucity of men supplied from England were waved down by Lloyd George: the number of men sent to France, he warned, was solely the business of His Majesty's Government.[2]

On this occasion Lloyd George's objection was sustained in council by Clemenceau. But henceforth 'Tiger' made use of his famous claws. Since the man-power for the Western Front could not be furnished, he observed, the concluding recommendation of Joint Note No. 12 on a Turkish offensive was automatically cancelled. Besides, the Allies could really not afford to go looking for victory on the Euphrates. Great Britain's right to engage in these 'distant expeditions' could of course not be denied; but let her do so on her own responsibility, not on that of the Supreme Council!

This suggestion Lloyd George was unwilling to adopt; for he needed to be able to say that the Government had acted upon military advice. Nothing, he conceded, could compensate for defeat on the Western Front, but the Allies had always been

---

[1] Callwell, *Henry Wilson*, ii. 50–51, 53–55; *AF*, vi (1), Annexes nos. 267, 284; *U.S. Army, 1917–19, Policy-Forming Documents*, 1160–1 (M.R.S., 19 Jan. 1918).

[2] *AF*, vi (1), 62; Callwell, *Henry Wilson*, ii. 55; *Mil. Opns. Fr. and Bel. 1918*, i. 72–74; Repington, *First World War*, ii. 208–9; Robertson, *Soldiers and Statesmen*, ii. 289–90; *U.S. Army, 1917–1919, Policy-Forming Documents*, 185–7; Minutes, first meeting, 30 January 1918, third session, A.S.W.C., Versailles. Records of the Supreme War Council, National Archives, Washington, D.C.

'overinsured' in that theatre. Abandonment of the offensive in the East would procure no more than two divisions for the West. How could the Entente win the war without attaining, somehow, somewhere, a victory?[1]

The meeting adjourned without a decision, but immediately thereafter Amery drafted a compromise adopted by the Entente ministers with the proviso (apparently oral) that no action was to be taken in the Eastern theatre for another two months, by which time (as proved indeed to be the case) the situation in the West would be clarified. Joint Note No. 12 was to be accepted,[2]

the British Government having made it clear that, in utilizing in the most effective fashion the forces already at its disposal in the Eastern theatre, it has no intention of diverting forces from the Western Front or in any way relaxing its effort to maintain the safety of that front, which it regards as a vital interest of the whole Alliance.

Note 12, with its 'annexure' on a counter-offensive still further watered down,[3] was adopted the next day, upon which Robertson in council roundly condemned the Turkish offensive. It was not a practicable plan; to attempt it would be very dangerous and detrimental to the prospects of winning the war. Haig said nothing. As the C.I.G.S. reminded the Prime Minister immediately thereafter, Fisher's silence at the War Council meeting which three years earlier had decided upon the Dardanelles operations had been generally condemned—by Lloyd George among others—and it was essential that this ambiguity, from which disaster had sprung, should not be repeated. Lloyd George, angered, remained unmollified.[4]

[1] *AF*, vi (1), 63–64; *Private Papers of Douglas Haig*, 281; *Mil. Opns. Fr. and Bel. 1918*, i. 74–75; Robertson, *Soldiers and Statesmen*, ii. 286; *U.S. Army, 1917–1919, Policy-Forming Documents*, 188; Minutes, second meeting, 31 January 1918, third session, A.S.W.C., Versailles. Records, National Archives, Washington, D.C.

[2] *Mil. Opns. Fr. and Bel. 1918*, i. 75; Amery, *Political Life*, ii. 140.

[3] Primarily on Pétain's insistence. The original resolution opined that 'the armies of the Entente . . . should . . . in case the enemy does attack . . . be able ultimately to engage the whole of their forces in a combined offensive *as extensive and powerful as possible*'. The words here italicized were deleted and for them were substituted 'as far as our effectives permit'. (*Mil. Opns. Fr. and Bel. 1918*, i. *Appendixes*, Appendix 10, pp. 43–44.)

[4] Amery, *Political Life*, ii. 140; Callwell, *Henry Wilson*, ii. 56; *Private Papers of Douglas Haig*, 281; Hankey, *Supreme Command*, ii. 768–9; *Mil. Opns. Fr. and Bel. 1918*, i. 75–76; Repington, *First World War*, ii. 208; Robertson, *Soldiers and Statesmen*, ii.

There remained only the question of the General Reserve. 'The Supreme War Council decides on the creation of a General Reserve *for the whole of the Armies on the Western, Italian, and Balkan fronts.*'¹ The command would be entrusted to the Military Representatives (save for Weygand, to be replaced in this instance by Foch), sitting as an 'Executive Committee'.² Robertson was expressly excluded by the British Prime Minister, who, however, at the same session nominated the French Chief of Staff, General Foch, as 'President' of the Committee. The Military Representatives on the Committee would 'transmit its orders to the Armies of the several countries'. 'Whether Milner was to command the cavalry was not settled', Colonel Repington commented on a projected and yet more complicated version of this curious arrangement. The participants adjourned shortly afterwards leaving Robertson to sit long afterwards head in hand, furious and bewildered. 'This really was a triumph,' Wilson wrote in his diary, '. . . the long duel between me and Robertson has ended in his complete defeat. . . . I wonder will he resign?'³

Not without a fight, in which the Prime Minister on his return to London took the initiative. The Army Council, to be sure, immediately began to raise difficulties over the command of the General Reserve. But on 7 February the C.I.G.S. left London for the coast 'to shake off the effects of a bad cold', and Lloyd George, urged on by Milner, promptly took advantage of Robertson's absence to prepare his dismissal.⁴

286–8, *From Private to Field-Marshal* (1921), 317–18; *U.S. Army, 1917–1919, Policy-Forming Documents*, 191–2; Minutes, third meeting, 1 February 1918, third session, A.S.W.C. Records, National Archives.   ¹ Present writer's italics.

² General Wilson had observed just before the opening of the session that the statesmen of the Entente 'were inclined to a board of officers, and Lloyd George was ready to accept Versailles; but Clemenceau said he could not agree to Weygand'. (Maj.-Gen. Sir C. E. Callwell, *Field-Marshal Sir Henry Wilson* [1927], ii. 55.)

³ Callwell, *Henry Wilson*, ii. 56–57. See also Hankey, *Supreme Command*, ii. 769; Lloyd George, *War Memoir*, ii. 1637–42; *Mil. Opns. Fr. and Bel. 1918*, i. 77–78, 80; Repington, *First World War*, ii. 204–9; Robertson, *From Private to Field-Marshal*, 330–1; Peter E. Wright, *At the Supreme War Council* (1921), 61–62; *U.S. Army, 1917–1919, Policy-Forming Documents*, 189–90; Minutes, fourth and fifth meetings, 1–2 February 1918, third session, A.S.W.C. Records, National Archives (M. Clemenceau, 'As we could not have a single Commander-in-Chief, such as a Hannibal or a Charlemagne, we might at least have a Commander of Reserves').

⁴ R. Churchill, *Derby*, 306–9; Lloyd George, *War Memoirs*, ii. 1670–2; Robertson, *From Private to Field-Marshal*, 333–4, *Soldiers and Statesmen*, i. 231–320.

By this time, the major press lords, who, as Lloyd George told Haldane a few weeks later, had to be propitiated in the same fashion as their political forebears, the great territorial magnates of the eighteenth century, had been gradually secured. Lord Rothermere, proprietor of five important newspapers and brother of Lord Northcliffe, had been made the first Minister for Air the preceding November. Lord Beaverbrook was appointed Minister of Information on 10 February, and he immediately thereafter prevailed upon Northcliffe, greatest of the 'press lords', to accept the post of Director of Enemy Propaganda. The Northcliffe press, the Prime Minister might well feel, was in his pocket.[1]

At first the Prime Minister desired simply to dismiss the C.I.G.S., giving him the Northern Command with headquarters at York for consolation, replacing him by Plumer or Haig himself. The latter was asked through Derby to come to London for a 'talk . . . in the strictest confidence', meaning 'without feeling it your duty to report what took place to Robertson'. This, however, was too simple a move to satisfy Lloyd George, nor would the change have made it any easier for the War Cabinet to obtain more palatable military advice in London. So Lloyd George next proposed that Robertson and Henry Wilson exchange their present positions. Superficially this manœuvre was a stroke of genius in Lloyd George's best *combinazione* style. The advantages were apparent. Henry Wilson as C.I.G.S. was personally congenial to Lloyd George and Milner, highly ingenious, and willing to work with rather than against the War Cabinet. The new command function of the Military Representatives made it easier to represent the change as no slight to Robertson. Of course the latter's appointment would also mean that the advice emanating from Versailles would no longer be welcome, but after the recent confrontation with Clemenceau the British Prime Minister may well have determined that the usefulness of the Council as an organ of British influence had ended. If, on the other hand, Robertson refused, as probably he would, all the better. Lloyd George firmly decided upon this Machiavellian scheme and together

---

[1] Beaverbrook, *Men and Power*, 82–86, 217–18, 266–9, 277–8; Lloyd George, *War Memoirs*, ii. 1110–13; Dudley Sommer, *Haldane of Cloan: His Life and Times, 1856–1928* (1960), 352–3.

with Derby drew up a detailed draft defining the respective
functions and powers of the C.I.G.S. and the Military Representative. Much to the War Cabinet's relief, Field-Marshal
Haig, now in London, gave the Prime Minister to understand
he would accept Robertson's supersession. These preliminaries
once completed, Lloyd George wrote Milner on the 9th that
'Wully is to be told to-morrow by Macpherson [the Under-
Secretary for War], who is motoring over to Eastbourne to
communicate the news to him'.[1]

All was not however destined to go so smoothly. Clemenceau
had not yet finished making trouble for the Prime Minister; not
all the newspaper proprietors had been won over. Colonel
Repington, according to the testimony, which there is no reason
for doubting, of his own published diary, had been asked by the
French statesman to come to Paris during the Council Session.
Immediately this had ended 'Tiger' had given 'the Playboy of
the Western Front' detailed information on what had transpired
with a request (as translated by Repington) to 'stop the side-
shows and send us men'. Repington, nothing loath once again
to destroy a government and kill another side-show, penned
perhaps the most vitriolic composition of his journalistic career.[2]
Returned by the censor 'NOT to be published', the article none
the less appeared with minor emendations under the heading

THE WAR COUNCIL

PARIS DISCUSSIONS

REMARKABLE REPORT

in the *Morning Post* of 11 February.

The article was certainly remarkable; it is not easy to remember a parallel 'indiscretion' in the long and acrid history of
civil–military relations. 'Prime Ministers and others', Repington
began,

have recently resolved themselves into a Council of War, have revelled
in strategy, and have exclusively occupied themselves in teaching
soldiers how and where to make war.

[1] Lloyd George, *War Memoirs*, ii. 1673. See also ibid. 1671–2; Callwell, *Henry Wilson*, ii. 58; R. Churchill, *Derby*, 308–10, 315–16; *Private Papers of Douglas Haig*, 283–4; Hankey, *Supreme Command*, ii. 776.

[2] Repington, *First World War*, ii. 200, 207–10, 212, 228; Wright, *At the Supreme Council*, 70, 169–70.

The plan to 'knock out' Turkey, the refusal to provide reinforcements for the Western Front or to permit discussion thereof, the creation of a reserve for counter-attack under 'a committee of military busy-bodies'—these were all truthfully if intemperately summarized. References to the Prime Minister's 'poltroonery' were liberally interspersed and the Army Council and the House of Commons exhorted to action. 'I hope that Parliament will extract a definite promise from Mr. Lloyd George that neither this side-show nor any other will be permitted to take place.' 'My opinion', Repington concluded,

is that by starving our Armies in the field, by advocating adventures contrary to the advice of his legitimate military advisers, and by approving a decision which deprives our Commander in France of his full command, Mr. Lloyd George has clearly and finally proved his incapacity to govern England in a great war. This is the situation which Parliament must clear up in such manner as it thinks best.

The first leader on the same page shared its new Military Correspondent's indignation.[1]

We suggest also to Mr. Asquith that it is his clear duty as Leader of the Opposition to probe this matter and to find out if there is anything in the suspicions and reports of this manifold intrigue against the Military Chiefs. And we warn the country that there is a very serious danger at the present time of the skill and valour of our soldiers being brought to nought by political ideas which are founded upon no sound principle of strategy but are merely the reflection of the politician's instinct to find any way round rather than the straight way through.

The Repington disclosures, however, were too sensational for Asquith to use freely. On the man-power issue the Liberal party could give the generals no comfort. Though the Liberal leaders and the War Office were at one on the Turkish War, they could hardly afford to discuss the matter openly in the House. For reasons of security, therefore, both Asquith in the debate the following day and the Government in its subsequent prosecution

---

[1] *The Morning Post*, 11 Feb. 1918. See also ibid., 5 Feb. (article by Repington on p. 4) and first leader of 12 Feb. 1918 ('EXPERT OR AMATEUR? . . . There was the Antwerp disaster, the Dardanelles gamble, the Salonika entanglement, the Mesopotamia tragedy . . . some military Pliable . . . found to give a favourable opinion . . . [for each]. . . . There is a Judas in every twelve'); Ian Colvin, *Life of Lord Carson*, iii (1936), 319-20; Repington, *First World War*, ii. 228-9.

of Repington and the editor of the *Morning Post*, concentrated upon the General Reserve scheme, ignoring the other, more vital issues.[1]

The debate in the House of 12 February had therefore an air of unreality. Asquith could only express, unconvincingly, 'the confidence of the nation and of the Empire in the two great soldiers, Sir Douglas Haig, our Commander-in-Chief, and Sir William Robertson, the head of our General Staff at home. . . . Having seen a good deal myself of soldiers, there are no two men in the whole of Europe whose military judgement I would more unhesitatingly accept.' This pomposity was followed by a question whether any change affecting either had been made. Lloyd George in reply accused the Liberal leader of publicly demanding 'information which any intelligence officer on the other side would gladly pay large sums of money to get', refused to furnish it, and scored an effective point by informing the House that he had offered to give Asquith the requested information in private. 'The House of Commons, if it is not satisfied, has in my judgement but one way of dealing with the situation; it can change that Government.' It was not Asquith's day. Gossip had it that the fall of the Government would be followed by the formation of an Asquith–Lansdowne cabinet whose primary aim it would be to seek peace as soon as possible. 'This', F. S. Oliver wrote Carson, '*is the central dominating consideration.*' The 'Ulster pirate' was careful to stay away from London during the crisis.[2]

However ineffective Asquith's intervention, the debate none the less frightened Lloyd George into retreat. The whole scheme for quietly jettisoning Robertson and replacing him by Wilson had blown up in the Prime Minister's face. The Government, he decided, would have to bear with Robertson as C.I.G.S. a little longer. Robertson, who had earlier been (rather contemptuously?) offered the post at Versailles, which he had rejected, was now pressed to take whichever of the two he desired. It was assumed that he would prefer to remain where he was. The 'agreement' of 9 February on the powers of the C.I.G.S. and

[1] Lloyd George, *War Memoirs*, ii. 1678–9; Repington, *First World War*, ii. 248; Wright, *At the Supreme War Council*, 71.

[2] *Diary of Lord Bertie*, ii. 264–5, 282; Colvin, *Carson*, iii. 318–19, 322–4; Maj.-Gen. Sir Frederick Maurice, *Haldane*, ii (1939), 51–52; 5 *Parliamentary Debates* (Commons), ciii (12 Feb. 1918), 6–92.

the Military Representative, tailored for Sir Henry Wilson, would have to serve for Sir William Robertson. The command of the General Reserve would remain entrusted to the Versailles Committee, and therefore the Order in Council of January 1916 giving the C.I.G.S. sole powers to give orders to the armies in the field would have to be revoked; but otherwise the functions of the C.I.G.S. remained unaffected. He would 'continue to be the supreme military adviser of the Government', and would in that capacity advise the Cabinet on whatever recommendations the Military Representative at Versailles might submit.[1]

Lloyd George, however, had been rather too clever. Robertson, despite appeals from the King and from Derby to stay where he was, continued to take his stand on the point of principle. He would not consent to any arrangement but the one that seemed obvious to him and everyone else save the distracted War Cabinet: the direct subordination of the Military Representative to the Chief of Staff. But with Robertson as C.I.G.S. this would mean complete defeat for the War Cabinet, the nullification of all their efforts since Caporetto; and Milner and Barnes talked of resignation if Robertson's demands were met.[2]

Having manœuvred himself into a corner through his own excessive subtlety, the Prime Minister had no choice but to fight it out. At the War Office an 'Ulster crisis' atmosphere prevailed. The post of C.I.G.S. was now first offered, not to Henry Wilson, who was generally mistrusted in the Army, but to the 'sound' Plumer, who promptly refused it in a telegram indicating his support of Robertson on the General Reserve command question. The Government was now in a 'very critical' position.[3] Fortunately they too could now, more or less plausibly, proclaim their attachment to a principle with greater public appeal than that of efficient military administration: 'civilian control' as opposed to 'military supremacy'. Sir Douglas Haig,

[1] Callwell, *Henry Wilson*, ii. 59–60; R. Churchill, *Derby*, 315–16, 322; Hankey, *Supreme Command*, ii. 777; Lloyd George, *War Memoirs*, ii. 1684–6.
[2] Beaverbrook, *Men and Power*, 408–12; R. Churchill, *Derby*, 317–18; Hankey, *Supreme Command*, ii. 777; Lloyd George, *War Memoirs*, ii. 1685–6; Robertson, *Private to Field-Marshal*, 335; Gollin, *Proconsul*, 478–82.
[3] Hankey, *Supreme Command*, ii. 778. See also ibid. 777; Callwell, *Henry Wilson*, ii. 61; R. Churchill, *Derby*, 326–7; Brigadier the Viscount Dillon, *Memories of Three Wars* (1951), 108; Victor Bonham-Carter, *Soldier True* (1963), 345–8.

summoned to London once again through Derby, once again promised not to cause difficulties. The King, who urged Robertson's retention, was threatened in no uncertain terms by the Prime Minister.[1]

Mr. Lloyd George told me [wrote Lord Stamfordham, the King's private secretary] that the question of Sir William Robertson had now reached a point that if His Majesty insisted upon his (Sir W. R.) remaining in office on the terms he laid down the Government could not carry on, and the King would have to find other Ministers. The Government *must* govern, whereas this was practically military dictation.

All save Robertson now gave way. The latter having once again refused to continue in office or become Military Representative on the new terms, despite an appeal from the Prime Minister himself, the Government issued a note to the Press the night of the 16th that the C.I.G.S. had resigned and that Sir Henry Wilson would assume his post. Robertson the next day denied his resignation to the Press and, according to gossip retailed to Bertie, ordered Wilson out of his office.[2]

The former C.I.G.S., however, received little support. Derby, as frantically urged by the *Morning Post* and more temperately by the King, resigned more than once; but each time withdrew his resignation, reasoning that his 'loyalty' was due not to Robertson alone but to Haig as well. Curzon, whose sympathies on this particular issue were reputed to be with Robertson, had retired to the country. The Army Council did not resign. Discerning no support, Robertson accepted the offer of the Eastern Command on the 18th and withdrew from the centre of affairs.

Lloyd George's triumph was complete. In the debate of the following day the Prime Minister demanded that the House either support or dismiss him, and after an unpleasant passage at arms Asquith retreated. 'I do not ask the House . . . to pronounce its opinion one way or the other on this question.' Looking back, Lloyd George and his followers discerned the

---

[1] Beaverbrook, *Men and Power*, 410, 412; *Private Papers of Douglas Haig*, 285 ff.; Lloyd George, *War Memoirs*, ii. 1689.

[2] *Diary of Lord Bertie*, ii. 262; Hankey, *Supreme Command*, ii. 778–9; Robertson, *Private to Field-Marshal*, 336; *Morning Post*, 18 Feb. 1918, p. 7.

defeat of a decisive bid by the High Command for military supremacy over the civil authority.[1]

The 'victory', however, had been won with the co-operation, or at any rate the acquiescence, of the Field-Marshal Commander-in-Chief, who oddly enough condemned Robertson for having been insufficiently Western.[2] In exchange, the War Cabinet had to pay Haig's price, and that price was the abandonment of the ostensible cause of the entire controversy—the General Reserve. During his second visit to London, on 17 February, Haig made it quite clear to Bonar Law and to Lloyd George that he would be relieved of his command rather than part with any of his divisions to the General Reserve.

With Robertson as both C.I.G.S. and a member of the Versailles Executive Committee the Government could and would have insisted on Haig contributing to the General Reserve but could not have proceeded with a 'decisive offensive against Turkey'. After dismissing the C.I.G.S. and replacing him with the generally distrusted Sir Henry Wilson the Government could go on with the Turkish War but was no longer in a position to exert any pressure on Haig. By replacing Robertson with Haig's consent the War Cabinet sacrificed the prerequisite for a successful defence on the Western Front to the freedom to proceed with the offensive against Turkey. If they were not aware of this at the time they should have been.[3]

With Robertson out of the way, planning for the Turkish War could continue unhindered. On 28 January 1918, one day before the third session of the Supreme War Council, the War Cabinet had deputed General Smuts to proceed to Egypt to

---

[1] Christopher Addison, *Four and a Half Years* (1934), ii. 488, *Politics from Within, 1914–1918* (1924), ii. 239; Beaverbrook, *Men and Power*, 208–14, 414; Callwell, *Henry Wilson*, 62; R. Churchill, *Derby*, 332–4, 346; Hankey, *Supreme Command*, ii. 779; Lloyd George, *War Memoirs*, ii. 1668–9, 1687; 5 *Parliamentary Debates* (Commons), ciii (19 Feb. 1918), 633–54; Repington, *First World War*, ii. 233; Robertson, *Soldiers and Statesmen*, i. 236–7; *Morning Post*, first leaders, 12 and 14 ('If the race of STANLEY no longer throws up a great man it might at least yield a true man, a man who would stick to his word, to his faith, to his officers, and not merely to his office. And if Mr. Lloyd George is not a CHATHAM, he might at least have the imagination to recognise military greatness where it exists, as in Sir William Robertson') Feb. 1918; *The Times* first leaders of 18 and 20 Feb. 1918 (which support the War Cabinet decision).
[2] Cooper, *Haig*, ii. 233; *Private Papers of Douglas Haig*, 283.
[3] *Private Papers of Douglas Haig*, 287; Lloyd George, *War Memoirs*, ii. 1689.

consult with the chief British commanders in Palestine and Mesopotamia. The mission under Smuts and Amery left London a week later and, after several days' consultation with Allenby in Egypt and Palestine, Smuts wired home his recommenda-tions.[1] The 'gist' of these, commented the irrepressible Colonel Meinertzhagen, then in the War Office Military Operations directorate, 'is to strengthen Allenby and press on to Aleppo at the expense of France'. Two more divisions were to be transferred from Mesopotamia, where the British forces were to adopt a purely defensive role, and the Indian cavalry division from France. Allenby would first occupy the Valley of Jordan, then destroy the Turkish Hejaz railway just to the east, and by slow stages proceed north along the coast. The main body would advance only along with the railway in process of construction up the coast. 'Vast' quantities of rail and considerable labour would be required, Smuts reported. Even so, the railway, and therefore Allenby's army, would advance rather less than one mile a day.

Allenby's plans (as incorporated by Smuts) were generally accepted by the War Cabinet, and 'the Bull' was told to proceed. One division was ordered from Mesopotamia and all the Indian cavalry regiments from France. On 19 February Allenby's troops had already proceeded—with considerable difficulty—to accomplish the first step in the programme, the clearance of the Valley of Jordan. Jericho was captured on the 21st, three thousand three hundred and eighteen years after Joshua.[2]

In the Western theatre, by contrast, Haig's persistent refusal to allocate any of his divisions to the General Reserve prevented the formation of this body and precipitated the collapse of the Versailles Executive War Committee. On 6 February, while Henry Wilson was still the British member, the Committee, now renamed the Executive War Board (apparently to avoid the onus of waging 'war by committee'), formally requested the British, French, and Italian Commanders-in-Chief to contribute

---

[1] Lloyd George, *War Memoirs*, ii. 1922; Millin, *Smuts*, ii. 119; Robertson, *Soldiers and Statesmen*, ii. 189; Wavell, *Allenby*, 241.

[2] Callwell, *Henry Wilson*, ii. 65, 67, 69; Col. Richard Meinertzhagen, *Army Diary* (1960), 230, 233; *Mil. Opns. Egypt and Palestine*, ii (1), 298-9, 411-12; *Campaign in Mesopotamia*, iv. 114-15; Repington, *First World War*, ii. 236-7; Robertson, *Soldiers and Statesmen*, ii. 189; Wavell, *Allenby*, 242; *Palestine Campaigns*, 176-9.

a total of thirty divisions. Haig was asked to give six or seven. Affirmative replies were soon received from Pétain and Diaz, but none of any kind from the British Commander-in-Chief until 2 March.[1] This, when transmitted, was a blank refusal. By then Henry Wilson was no longer the British member on the Committee. In his place was General Rawlinson, Haig's nominee and one of his own army commanders.[2]

Haig would not be moved from his decision. Useless for the Executive Committee to point out that the divisions would be held directly behind his own front, to be not only employed when needed but also reinforced by the French and Italian components. Useless for the War Board to reduce Haig's quota to two divisions, the same number as had been ordered returned to him from Italy. Useless for Henry Wilson to impress 'on him the fact that by refusing to contribute to the General Reserve he was killing that body, and he would have to live on Pétain's charity, and he would find that very cold charity'.[3]

Sir Douglas Haig, who had been informed that in April he would receive barely eighteen thousand men, was determined to rely on his own force and not yield any of it to another commander, let alone the despised 'Versailles Committee'. G.H.Q., belatedly studying the problems of the defensive, misinterpreted an out-of-date German training manual and proceeded to lock up the best and most numerous of its troops for the defensive in the forward 'battle zone', where they were soon to be overrun.[4]

Pétain and Clemenceau's inaction completed the ruin of the General Reserve scheme. If Haig would not contribute, neither would Pétain. Clemenceau, who was already on bad terms with the Chief of Staff he had inherited, sided with Pétain. In case

[1] The delay may have been due to Sir Henry Wilson's having kept the original letter to Haig in his own pocket during the Robertson crisis, while forwarding only a draft copy.

[2] AF, vi (1), Annexe no. 332; Callwell, Henry Wilson, ii. 67; Lloyd George, War Memoirs, ii. 1713; Private Papers of Douglas Haig, 287-8; Mil. Opns. Fr. and Bel. 1918, i. 81-83; 5 Parliamentary Debates (Commons), ciii (19 Feb. 1918), 658.

[3] Callwell, Henry Wilson, ii. 69.

[4] Ibid. 65; Tasker H. Bliss, 'The Evolution of the Unified Command', Foreign Affairs, i. 2 (15 Dec. 1922), pp. 1-30; Cooper, Haig, ii. 238; Hankey, Supreme Command, ii. 781-2; Private Papers of Douglas Haig, 290; Mil. Opns. Fr. and Bel. 1918, i. 39, 41-42; Repington, First World War, ii. 159; Cyril Falls, The Great War (N.Y. Capricorn Books, 1961), 332 ('The misinterpretation of the German scheme lay in the fact that the Germans placed only one-third of the defending battalions in keeps, whereas the British locked up about two-thirds in them').

of trouble he himself, the aged statesman told Poincaré, would co-ordinate the action of the two armies![1]

It only remained to give the General Reserve a decent burial. This was done at the fourth session of the Supreme War Council held in London on 14 and 15 March. Further efforts to persuade Haig proved unavailing. The mortified Milner proposed, and Hankey drafted, a scheme to 'save our faces', whereby the name 'General Reserve' would be given to the French and British troops still in Italy, plus a quota of Italian divisions to be determined later. This was adopted. Foch then protested against the abandonment of the General Reserve, whereupon Clemenceau shouted him down. Foch's experiences at Supreme Council sessions had been discouraging, but his time would come.[2]

So matters rested. Seen from London, the prospects for the war against Turkey, now that consistent support from home was guaranteed, were surely good. As for the West, Haig, having sabotaged the organization designed to ensure his own and France's defence, would have to make do. Perhaps the Germans might not attack there after all?

On 21 March Allenby's forces began an (unsuccessful) operation—the raid to Amman—designed to destroy the El Hejaz railway. But in the West, on that same day, Ludendorff's armies struck.[3]

---

[1] Callwell, *Henry Wilson*, ii. 66, 68; *Private Papers of Douglas Haig*, 289; Lloyd George, *War Memoirs*, ii. 1715–20; Raymond Poincaré, *Au Service de la France*, x (Paris, 1933), 58.

[2] Callwell, *Henry Wilson*, ii. 69–70; *Private Papers of Douglas Haig*, 292–3; Hankey, *Supreme Command*, ii. 782; Owen, *Tempestuous Journey*, 469–70; Minutes, fourth session, 14–15 March 1918, A.S.W.C. Records, National Archives; *U.S. Army, 1917–1919, Policy-Forming Documents*, 240–1.

[3] Callwell, *Henry Wilson*, ii. 70; *Private Papers of Douglas Haig*, 292; 5 *Parliamentary Debates* (Commons), ciii (7 Mar. 1918), 2161; Wavell, *Palestine Campaigns*, 180.

EPILOGUE

'The most urgent task . . . is the establishment of British control of the Caspian and of a secure line of communication to it from Baghdad.'
GENERAL SIR HENRY WILSON,
British Military Policy, 1918–1919, 25 July 1918.

THE series of German offensives on the Western Front during the spring and early summer of 1918 brought to a head—but also to an end—the internal conflicts which constitute the theme of the present study. The massive attacks of 21 March and 9 April against Haig's armies riveted the attention of England and the Empire upon the Western Front, imposed for the first time in the history of the war an harmonious command and staff system, and led to an overt parliamentary challenge the failure of which made manifest to everyone the real strength of the Lloyd George Coalition and helped to ensure its continuance for another four and a half years.

As soon as the gravity of Ludendorff's first offensive was manifest the chief care of the War Cabinet was to find the man-power for Haig earlier denied him. Among the steps taken were the recall of troops from Italy, from Greece, and from Palestine. No further reinforcements would be sent to any theatre save the Western Front. The instructions for Allenby's offensive (the opening phase of which had failed) were hurriedly cancelled; and Allenby was enjoined to adopt a policy of 'active defence'.[1]

Neither these measures, however, nor the extension of the age for military service, nor the proclaimed application of conscription to Ireland, could in themselves save the British Army in France from defeat or destruction. The reserves which General Pétain had promised Haig in case of need were slow in arriving, and the French Army itself prepared to fall back toward Paris while the British retreated to the Channel ports. German troops were pouring into the gap thus created between the two armies.

---

[1] Brig.-Gen. J. E. Edmonds, *Military Operations, France and Belgium, 1918* (1935–47), ii. 9–11, 190; *Military Operations, Italy, 1915–1919* (1949), 156; Cyril Falls, *Military Operations, Egypt and Palestine* (1928), ii (2), 413, 421; *War Memoirs of David Lloyd George* (2-vol. Odhams Press edn.), ii. 1727–8.

There was of course no General Reserve. Lord Milner was
sent out to France to find out the truth of the situation; 'the
real question now,' as he reported to his colleagues, 'was how
much in the way of reserves could be got out of the French, and
how quickly it could be got'. The only way to obtain continued
and rapid French assistance and an end to the southerly retreat
of Pétain's northern flank proved to be the acceptance of
General Foch as supreme commander. Haig, Henry Wilson, and
Lord Milner all agreed on the necessity of this course. Lord
Milner's, however, was the responsibility; and so unpopular
with the War Cabinet was his decision[1] to encharge Foch 'to
co-ordinate the action of the Allied Armies on the Western
Front' that a new emissary—Churchill—was immediately
designated to return to France to see Clemenceau. On 3 April
Lloyd George himself at Beauvais told Clemenceau that a
French 'Commander-in-Chief' was impossible.[2]

The compulsion of events was, however, unavoidable. After
Ludendorff's second attack beginning 9 April, this time on the
British front, Haig was desperate for assistance;[3] and on the 14th
the Prime Minister informed Clemenceau that there was no
longer any objection to Foch's designation as Commander-in-
Chief of the Allied Armies operating in France. Four days later
Derby was removed to the Paris Embassy and replaced as
Secretary of State for War by Lord Milner. General Rawlinson
and his troupe of forty staff officers left Versailles to return to
Sir Douglas Haig's command. Rawlinson was replaced as Mili-
tary Representative by a comparatively junior officer, Major-
General Charles J. Sackville-West, to whom Sir Henry Wilson
communicated his instructions on a direct telephone line.[4]

[1] Reached on 26 March at the emergency Anglo-French governmental–military
conference at Doullens.
[2] Maj.-Gen. Sir C. E. Callwell, *Field-Marshal Sir Henry Wilson* (1927), ii. 81;
Lloyd George, *War Memoirs*, ii. 1740; General Mordacq, *Le commandement unique—
Comment il fut réalisé* (Paris, 1929), 114; Memorandum by Lord Milner, 27 March
1918, *The National Review*, vol. 115, No. 690 (August, 1940), p. 170; Historical
Division, Department of the Army, *United States Army in the World War, 1917–1919,
Policy-Forming Documents, American Expeditionary Forces* (Washington, 1942), 253–4,
264, 274–7.
[3] It was on 11 April that the Field-Marshal issued his 'backs to the wall' order.
'Every position must be held to the last man: there must be no retirement. With
our backs to the wall, and believing in the justice of our cause, each one of us must
fight on to the end.' (As cited in Duff Cooper, *Haig* [1936], ii. 273.)
[4] Duff Cooper, *Haig*, ii (1936), 275 ff.; *Private Papers of Douglas Haig, 1914–1919*

The consequence of these changes were entirely beneficial for the smooth working of the now most efficient British military supreme command system. In the War Cabinet the vacancy created by Lord Milner's departure was filled by Austen Chamberlain. Lloyd George's political strength was thereby increased; but the War Cabinet itself, divested of its 'mainstay', faded into the background, as was to be the case again a quarter of a century later. So did the Allied Supreme War Council. During the remainder of the war the most important function of that organization was to serve as a means of combined Allied pressure on President Wilson to sanction and support the Japanese invasion of Russia. British war direction was henceforth conducted daily by what Amery called the 'X' Committee: the Prime Minister, the Secretary of State for War, and the C.I.G.S. as responsible officers; the indispensable Hankey as recorder and suggester; Amery, now Milner's personal assistant secretary, as an insistent reminder of the requirements and privileges of the New Imperialism.[1]

The appointment of Foch as supreme commander proved altogether beneficial to both G.H.Q. and the British Government. Haig soon discovered that London now generally left him alone; he had never, as he told Henry Wilson more than once, felt so free and so little vexed by interference and questioning. For Milner, who appears henceforth to have acted with the greatest tact, the Field-Marshal expressed the highest esteem, in striking contrast to his opinion of the 'loyal' Derby. The 'X' committee found Haig's subordination equally useful. On the one hand they doubtless estimated Foch's advice above that of Haig; on the other the demands of a foreigner were politically easier to refuse.[2]

Not that the Government's political difficulties, after a long-delayed eruption in early May, were very real. On 7 May the

(1952), Robert Blake (ed.), 301 ff.; Lord Hankey, *The Supreme Command, 1914–1918* (1961), ii. 794; *Mil. Opns. Fr. and Bel. 1918*, i. 88, n. 2; Mordacq, *Le commandement unique*, 132 ff.; Lieut.-Col. C. à Court Repington, *The First World War, 1914–1918* (Boston 1921), 260; *U.S. Army, 1917–1919, Policy-Forming Documents*, 323–4.
[1] L. S. Amery, *My Political Life*, ii (1953), 155, 157; Hankey, *Supreme Command*, ii. 816; Sir Charles Petrie, *Life and Letters of the Right Hon. Sir Austen Chamberlain* (1939–40), ii. 113–17.
[2] Callwell, *Henry Wilson*, ii. 116–17, 125; Brig.-Gen. John Charteris, *At G.H.Q.* (1931), 315; *Private Papers of Douglas Haig*, 304–6; *Mil. Opns. Fr. and Bel. 1918*, ii. 542.

Morning Post appeared with a startling letter from Major-General Sir Frederick Maurice. Maurice had been Director of Military Operations under the Robertson régime, but had been discharged by Sir Henry Wilson and was currently unemployed. General Maurice's letter accused the Government of a series of 'mis-statements . . . in the House of Commons' during the past month: 'Versailles', despite Bonar Law's statement to the contrary, had forced Haig to extend his front prior to the German offensive; Haig's fighting strength, despite Lloyd George's sophistries, had been diminished before the great battle. The Prime Minister, Maurice added, had made an incorrect statement on the numbers of 'white divisions' on duty in the Turkish theatres.[1]

The foolishness of General Maurice's action takes one's breath away. His motives were unselfish enough, if short-sighted; the command in France had greatly resented the Government's statements, which they rightly interpreted as an attempt to fasten on G.H.Q. the responsibility for the March defeats. Lloyd George's claim in his speech of 9 April that the Army in France 'was considerably stronger on' 1 January 1918 than on 1 January 1917 had aroused widespread ire. But, though the Maurice letter ended,[2]

I have . . . decided . . . that my duty as a citizen must override my duty as a soldier, and I ask you to publish this letter in the hope that Parliament may see fit to order an investigation into the statements I have made

—he himself took no further action to ensure that friendly M.P.s would be further informed of the facts in the case. Whether through—in the circumstances—a rather misplaced sense of propriety or simply lack of forcefulness, General Maurice failed to see the matter through. He left London directly and held no communications with 'politicians'. Brigadier-General Sir Bonham-Carter—formerly Director of Training at G.H.Q., and brother of Asquith's private secretary—was deputed by a number of senior officers at G.H.Q. to go to London to lay the facts before Asquith, but appears to have arrived too late to be of service.[3]

---

[1] The 'Maurice letter' is reprinted in Robert Blake, *The Unknown Prime Minister: The Life and Times of Andrew Bonar Law, 1858–1923* (1955), 369–70.   [2] Ibid.
[3] *Autobiography of Margot Asquith* (Penguin, 1936), ii. 217–18; Victor Bonham-Carter, *In a Liberal Tradition* (1960), 174–5; Charteris, *At G.H.Q.*, 308; Cooper, *Haig*, ii. 278; Maj.-Gen. Sir Frederick Maurice, *Haldane*, ii (1939), 153, *Intrigues*

PLATE 14

His Majesty the King with British Army Commanders at Buckingham Palace, 19 December 1918
Left to right: Sir William Birdwood, Sir Henry Rawlinson, Sir Hubert Plumer, H.M. The King, Sir Douglas Haig, Sir Henry Horne, Sir Julian Byng

The crucial issue presented by the Maurice letter was of course not the technical accuracy of Bonar Law's and Lloyd George's statements, on which much could and has been said on both sides; but whether Haig had been adequately reinforced prior to the March offensive. But on this controversy Asquith was at a disadvantage; for during the preceding winter he had given no support to the Army demands for man-power. The Prime Minister's speech of 9 April, which had so aroused the soldiers' resentment, had concluded with the proposals that the age liability for conscription be raised from forty to fifty; and Asquith had then expressed his opinion that this action, as well as conscription in Ireland, would be unwise.[1]

Whether for these or other reasons the debate of 9 May was badly fumbled by the 'Squiffites', and superbly conducted by Lloyd George. On the 7th Bonar Law announced that the truth or falsity of his and the Prime Minister's statements was to be determined by a two-man judicial 'court of honour', the members of which Asquith himself would be welcome to choose. Asquith refused to accept this, demanded a select Committee of the House, and pressed for a preliminary debate, the better to discredit the Government as the standing of his own had been depreciated.[2]

The debate took place on the 9th, and permanently destroyed Asquith's personal political power. Amery had persuaded the Unionist 'War Committee' to view the motion as a device to return a thoroughly discredited war leader back into power, and Lloyd George in a speech of great skill hammered on the same theme. Asquith had[3]

been responsible for the conduct of this War for two years. If this Motion be carried, he will again be responsible for the conduct of

---

of the War (1922), 34–35; Repington, *First World War*, ii. 275 ('Charlie Burn, just back from France, says . . . that if our Army be rounded up, the soldiers mean to make themselves very unpleasant here'); U.S. Department of State. *Papers Relating to the Foreign Relations of the United States.* Supplements. *The World War, 1918,* i. 205 (Telegram, Page to Sec. State, 10 Apr. 1918).

[1] Letter, Lloyd George to Bonar Law, 10 Apr. 1918 ('It looks as if the Asquithians meant to challenge an issue on Irish conscription. . . . They are relying on the 40–50 call-up'), Lord Beaverbrook, *Men and Power, 1917–1918* (1956), 248; Great Britain. *5 Parliamentary Debates* (Commons), civ (9, 12 Apr. 1918), 1337–70, 1908–12.

[2] *5 Parliamentary Debates* (Commons), cv (7, 8 May 1918), 1981–4, 2181.

[3] Ibid. cv (9 May 1918), 2371.

the War. Make no mistake! This is a Vote of Censure upon the Government. If this Motion were carried we could not possibly continue in office, and the right hon. Gentleman, as the one who is responsible for the Motion, would have to be responsible for the Government.

The Prime Minister was further able to show that the statements on man-power and divisional strength attacked by Maurice had come from that general's own office. There was much to be said in reply to this, but apparently no one had the knowledge for effective rebuttal. Carson, deserted by his followers the day before, now pleaded with Asquith to withdraw his motion. No further speeches came from the 'Squiffite' leaders, and a Liberal backbencher pleaded in vain for 'some little light or leading' as the bells rang as the signal to divide. Not one Unionist voted for Asquith's motion, which was defeated by 293 votes to 106. Once again Lloyd George had won a battle with the 'soldiers',[1] and this time in the arena that he really feared and with results that were indisputable.

After this debate Lloyd George ceased to look over his shoulder at the House of Commons, and energetically began preparations for dissolution and new elections. The 'issue', he told Lord Riddell, 'will really be who is to run the war'. In the current temper of the British people, if the Pemberton Billing case were any indication,[2] there was no doubt that they would not choose Asquith.[3]

Thus the Government had recovered its freedom of action to wage the war as it chose. For the first time since Haldane twelve years before had conceived the idea of an Expeditionary Force, policy and strategy became genuinely harmonized and complementary. Yet, as is so often the case with internal conflicts involving great issues, the 'triumph' of the Government

---

[1] Sir Douglas Haig disapproved of Maurice's action.

[2] Pemberton Billing, elected an independent M.P. in 1916, claimed in his journal, the Vigilante, that the Germans had subverted 47,000 prominent Englishmen and women through homosexual vice. He was accused of criminal libel; the court proceedings—in which Haldane and both Mr. and Mrs. Asquith were said to be listed in the German 'Black Book'—were a disgrace to wartime justice. The jury found Billing not guilty.

[3] Parl., 2347–406; Amery, Political Life, ii. 154; Blake, Unknown Prime Minister, 378–9; Repington, First World War, ii. 298; Lord Riddell's War Diary, 1914–1918 (c. 1933), 349; The Round Table, No. 31 (June 1918), p. 603.

was attained only after the original struggle had lost its meaning. That indeed was why final 'victory' was possible. The March offensive made the Maurice letter irrelevant. There was no basis for an 'Easterners–Westerners' controversy after March 1918, just as there had been none before December 1914. On vital strategic issues and on major operations there were henceforth no direct clashes between the Government, the General Staff, or the chief commands; though the cleavage between policy and operations due to the distance from what was desirable to what was operationally possible remained as deep and unbridgeable as ever. Henceforth the differences between 'soldiers' and 'statesmen' were of emphasis and nuance.

Until mid-July the Government and General Staff exerted their best efforts to reinforce the Western Front. Between the 21st of March and the end of August some six hundred and fifty thousand Empire troops were sent to Sir Douglas Haig's command. Both moving appeals and offers of shipping space were addressed to President Wilson; American soldiers began arriving in France first at the rate of one hundred and twenty thousand a month, later much more rapidly. Twelve battalions were withdrawn from Salonika, and all white infantry units save the 54th Division from Palestine. The proposal of the C.I.G.S. to transfer this division also to France was overruled in a meeting of the Committee of Prime Ministers of the Imperial War Cabinet in June.[1]

At this time the general military situation continued to appear desperate. The March and April attacks had, it is true, been beaten off; and fortunately Foch had refused to act on Wilson's proposal to evacuate Dunkirk and flood the surrounding areas. The psychological effect of these blows had been so great, however, that on 16 May Balfour and Robert Cecil for the Government, supported by Asquith and Herbert Samuel for the Opposition, made what sounded uncommonly like a plea for peace negotiations. No reasonable and responsible offer, they stressed, no matter where its origin, would be refused careful consideration. In June the German Foreign Minister, von Kühlmann, publicly stated that the war could hardly come

[1] Hankey, *Supreme Command*, ii. 817–18; Lloyd George, *War Memoirs*, ii. 1811 ff.; *Mil. Opns. Fr. and Bel. 1918*, i. 52 n. 1, ii. 10–11; General Sir Archibald Wavell, *Allenby* (1940), 263.

to an end by military means alone. Preliminary soundings between British and German negotiators appear to have taken place at a prisoner-of-war conference in The Hague, but on Ludendorff's insistence Kühlmann was promptly dismissed for his temerity. The British Government once again had no choice but to continue the struggle.[1]

But on what basis? On 27 May the German forces attacked the French front in Champagne, which promptly buckled. British leaders immediately began to speculate on the possible consequences of a French capitulation followed by that of Italy. Evacuation of the British armies from the Continent would then be necessary, and preparations for such a débâcle were made.[2]

It is only against this background of both real and apparently impending disaster that the Allied intervention in Russia can be understood. The Entente Governments had consistently refused to admit to themselves the depth of Russian war-weariness. The Bolshevik seizure of power appeared to them both shocking and unnatural, and therefore transitory. The Treaty of Brest-Litovsk made possible, they believed, German exploitation of Russian resources and even Russian man-power. 'Unless we are prepared to sit down', wrote Milner, '—watch Germany like a *boa constrictor*, gradually swallowing Russia, the only thing to do is to resort to Allied Military Intervention to stop her.'[3] The German blows upon the Western Front between March and June caused both British and French authorities to

[1] Callwell, *Henry Wilson*, ii. 90, 92; Lord Newton, *Retrospection* (1941), 261–2; 5 *Parliamentary Debates* (Commons), cvi (16 May 1918), 577 (MR. BALFOUR. '. . . now the condition of international affairs has got to its present condition in Europe, it is not a good thing necessarily to discourage informal attempts at conversations. . . . If any representative of any belligerent country desires seriously to lay before us any proposals, we are prepared to listen to them. . . . Certainly the last thing I should lay down would be that the door must be shut to any kind of informal approach which had any element of authenticity, and which had adequate credentials'), 586 (MR. ASQUITH. '. . . The Secretary of State for Foreign Affairs said . . . that the British Government has closed no door to overtures in the direction of an honourable peace. . . . From whatever quarter, be it with adequate authority and with real good faith, if an appeal be made which is not merely rhetorical, but which is based upon substantial considerations—from whatever quarter such an appeal be directed to them, they would not, I am certain, turn to it a deaf ear. Let that be clear'), 622, 625–6, cvii (20 June 1918), 569–71; Pierre Renouvin, *La Crise européenne et la première guerre mondiale* (3rd edn., Paris, 1948), 556–9; *U.S. For. Rels. 1918, Supplement I*, vol. i. 251–2 (Letter, Reading to Sec. State, 7 Jan. 1918).
[2] Callwell, *Henry Wilson*, ii. 103, 119; Hankey, *Supreme Command*, ii. 809, 813.
[3] *The History of The Times*, iv. *1912–1948* (1952) (2), 1071–2.

cast about almost blindly for a means of alleviating the punishment their troops—and nations—were receiving. Even the mere
creation of further disorder requiring the use of German troops
might fulfil this intention.[1]

To these compelling—if not very rational[2]—motives for the
intervention in Russia must be added, for the British, two others:
the desire to make Japan a more influential factor in the war
against Germany and fear for the security of the Empire south
and east of the Caspian Sea.

If France and Italy were to be defeated, then the war would
change its character. Henceforth it would be a war between
Eurasia—the 'heartland', and the great 'rim' powers—the
British Empire, the United States of America and, it was hoped,
Japan. The danger, however, was that Japan, whose military
operations had hitherto been of a distressingly selfish nature,
might withdraw from the war altogether and make terms with
Germany. The way of avoiding this calamity, it was argued,
was to let Japan take Siberia and urge the Japanese to send
troops along the Trans-Siberian railway until they eventually
came into hostile contact with German troops.[3]

What a mirage! The fear of German and Turkish penetration
of the Empire and incitement to disaffection, though greatly

---

[1] France. Les Armées françaises dans la Grande Guerre [AF], vii (2), Annexe no.
2448; U.S. For. Rels. 1918 Russia, ii. 135-7, 148-9, 315-17, 482.

[2] General Bliss, the American Military Representative to the Supreme War
Council, noted as early as February that 'The fact is, in regard to this whole
Russian matter, that the feeling over here has become somewhat "panicky" '.
(Letter, Bliss to Secretary of War Baker, 25 February 1918. Box 74, Tasker H. Bliss
Papers, Library of Congress, Washington, D.C.)

[3] Winston S. Churchill, The World Crisis, 1911–1918 (4-vol. Odhams Press edn.),
iv. 1236; George F. Kennan, Russia Leaves the War (Princeton, 1956), 474-5;
Pierre Renouvin, La question d'Extrême Orient, 1840–1940 (Paris, 1946), 303 n. 1;
Transcript of 11 June 1918, meeting of the Imperial War Cabinet. . . . Borden
Papers ('Lloyd George survey[ed] the war situation in terms of black despair. The
possibility of complete defeat in France had to be considered . . . with the British
Empire and the United States left standing alone, as England had been left in the
days of Napoleon. Full attention, therefore, must be turned to beginning interven-
tion in Russia as the one means, should disaster strike, of carrying on the war'),
Gaddis Smith, 'Canada and the Siberian Intervention, 1918–1919', American
Historical Review, lxiv, No. 4 (July 1959), 867; Betty M. Unterberger, America's
Siberian Expedition, 1918–1920 (Durham, N.C., 1956), 25, 27–29; U.S. For. Rels.
Russia 1918, ii. 49, 315–17; W. K. Hancock, Smuts: The Sanguine Years, 1870–1919
(Cambridge, 1962), 477–80. Japanese policy is discussed in James William Morley,
The Japanese Thrust into Siberia, 1918 (N.Y., 1957). See also A. M. Gollin, Proconsul
in Politics (1964), 557, 562–3, 565–6.

exaggerated, had a more solid basis, and would be assuaged by the employment of British and Indian troops. With the defeat of Russia the 'Mesopotamia' force was no longer well placed to act as a 'barrier' to German and Turkish operations eastward. The troops of Germany and Turkey could now pass virtually unopposed (save by each other) through Trans-Caucasia. Batum was in fact occupied by the Turks on 15 April and Tabriz on 14 June. Sevastopol was taken by the Germans on 1 May. Should these forces then gain command of the Caspian Sea, there was nothing to prevent them from advancing through Trans-Caspia to Afghanistan and beyond, exhorting the hitherto obedient 'native' subjects of the British Empire to revolt and slaughter on their way. The task of British strategy during the next twelve months, Sir Henry Wilson wrote in his survey on 'British Military Policy, 1918–1919', dated 25 July, was to ensure command of the Caspian Sea. 'Your main attention', the C.I.G.S. had warned the Commander-in-Chief of the Mesopotamian force, 'must be directed towards Persia and the Caspian.'[1]

Whether spontaneous or inspired, the revolt of the Czech troops[2] at the end of May—while conveniently located along the Trans-Siberian railway from Samara to Irkutsk, a distance of some 2,500 miles—presented an occasion too good to be missed. At the end of June Czech forces seized Vladivostock, which was placed under the 'protection' of the Allies a week later. The Japanese still refused to invade Siberia without President Wilson's permission. The Supreme War Council session of 2–4 July addressed a solemn appeal to the American President, and this proved effective.[3]

[1] Brig.-Gen. F. J. Moberly, *Campaign in Mesopotamia*, iv (1927), 187. See also ibid. 143–5, 183, 187–8; *Mil. Opns. Fr. and Bel. 1918*, iv. App. V, pp. 527–49 (paragraph 61*v* reads 'The most urgent task . . . is the establishment of British control of the Caspian and of a secure line of communication to it from Baghdad'). See also *AF*, viii (3), Annexe no. 22; Lord Ronaldshay, *Life of Curzon* (1928), iii. 209–12; Kennan, *Russia Leaves the War*, 187

[2] These former prisoners-of-war for the Austro-Hungarian Army had been fighting on the Eastern Front under Russian military direction, but under the political control of the newly formed Czechoslovak national committee, precursors to the Czechoslovak Government. After the treaty of Brest-Litovsk they were to be transferred to the Western Front.

[3] Churchill, *World Crisis*, iv. 1301; George F. Kennan, *The Decision to Intervene* (Princeton, 1958), 151–64, 277, 393; Lloyd George, *War Memoirs*, ii. 1900–8; *U.S. For. Rels. 1918, Russia*, ii. 271; Minutes, seventh session, 2–11 July 1918, A.S.W.C.,

On 3 August the Allied intervention in Russia began.[1] The substantial Japanese and American forces at Vladivostock were preceded by an English garrison battalion (the 'Die-Hards') of eight hundred men from Hong Kong. At the same time a British-officered force of some 1,500 troops occupied Archangel in north Russia. Detachments of Dunsterforce arrived at Baku after having sailed on the Caspian from Enzeli, in Persia, followed by General Dunsterville himself with some 560 men on the 17th. A small group of Indian troops under General Malleson of the Indian Army—the 'Malleson Mission'— crossed the Russian border from Persia east of the Caspian to gain control of, and if need be to destroy, the railway from the port of Krasnovodsk eastwards. The hope, if not the belief, behind these separate ventures was that the various Allied forces would capture the railways from Archangel to Perm, from Perm to Vladivostock, followed by a move north of the 'patriotic' Russian troops in the Caucasus.[2]

The story of the British adventure in Russia is told elsewhere.[3] Both Japanese and Americans proved unwilling to move beyond Siberia, but the 'Die-Hard' battalion proceeded along the Trans-Siberian railway in hopes of lifting Czech morale. Despite recurrent Japanese obstruction the battalion reached Omsk by 18 October. The Czechs were unable to capture Perm, and none of them ever arrived at Archangel, where the Entente Ambassadors had gathered to welcome the regeneration of a 'new' Russia. The British command in north Russia had to content itself with occupying the surrounding countryside; and both in Archangel and Vladivostock great, though largely unsuccessful, efforts were made to recruit and train Russian soldiers

Versailles. Records of the Supreme War Council, National Archives, Washington, D.C.

[1] Some two hundred British marines had been landed at Murmansk on 6 March, with the tacit consent of the Bolshevik Government.

[2] *Campaign in Mesopotamia*, iv. 202–5, 209–10, 212–13, 216–18; Dunsterville, *Adventures of Dunsterforce*, 207–9, 226; Kennan, *Decision to Intervene*, 408, 417–18; W. Malleson, 'The British Military Mission to Turkistan, 1918–20', *Journal of the Royal Central Asian Society*, ix, pt. 2 (1922), pp. 98–99, and Col. J. K. Tod, 'The Malleson Mission to Transcaspia in 1918', in the same journal for January 1940, pp. 45–67; Charles Maynard, *The Murmansk Venture* (1928), 55; Leonid Strakhovsky, *Intervention at Archangel* (Princeton, 1944), 14–28, 261–4; Col. J. Ward, *With the 'Die-Hards' in Siberia* (1920), 2–3; John Albert White, *Siberian Intervention* (1950), 258.

[3] See in particular Richard H. Ullman, *Anglo-Soviet Relations, 1917–1921*, vol. i, *Intervention and the War* (Princeton University Press, 1961).

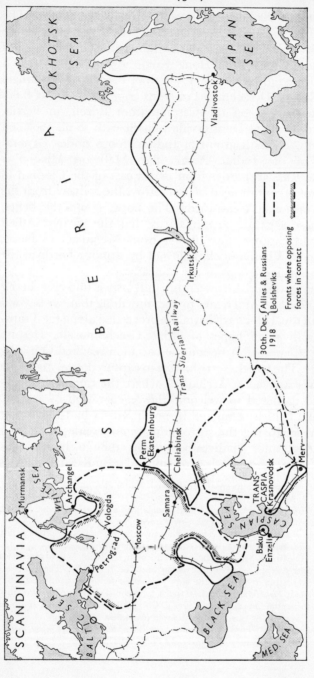

Map 8: Intervention in Russia, 1918.

Adapted from map in *The War Cabinet—Report for the Year 1918*

Legend:
30th. Dec. 1918 — Allies & Russians / Bolsheviks
Fronts where opposing forces in contact

under British officers to fight against either Germans or Bolsheviks. The latter were by now commonly regarded as 'tools'
of the Central Powers.[1]

In southern Russia Baku was attacked by Turkish forces on
26 August, and on 14 September 'Dunsterforce' departed from
the city. 'This is a bother,' the C.I.G.S. noted in his diary, 'it
breaks the chain from Baghdad to Archangel.'[2] No such chain,
however, really existed; and General Dunsterville's activities
had been astonishingly effective. Naval guns and ammunition
had been transported overland from Basra to Baghdad to
Enzeli, and long before the armistice British 'command' of the
Caspian, through the employment of captured Russian vessels,
had been secured. Trans-Caspia was now in British hands; the
occupation of Krasnovodsk was looked on as permanent.[3]

On the need of the Russian intervention in the summer of
1918 both General Staff and Government were agreed, though
the former were perhaps more insistent.

The immediate military result of the attacks of early August
was the conclusion of a Bolshevik–German alliance on 27
August which enabled the German command to transport five
hundred thousand troops to the Western Front. The attacks
also revived and extended the civil war in Russia, which lasted
for two more years. In the light of these facts no comment on
the wisdom and justice of the Allied intervention in Russia
appears necessary, or indeed desirable.[4]

The success of the counter-attack ordered by Foch for 18 July
after the failure of Ludendorff's fourth and final blow against
the French at Rheims afforded some leisure for reflection upon
future strategy. The second Imperial War Cabinet, meeting in
London, was a suitable occasion.

For the immediate future it was clear that no British or
Empire troops should or could be withdrawn from the Western

---

[1] Sir Edmund Ironside, *Archangel, 1918–1919* (1953), 35, 37; Strakhovsky, *Intervention at Archangel*, 92–93, 97; *U.S. For. Rels. 1918, Russia*, i. 632–6, ii. 368, 386, 540; Ward, *With the 'Die-Hards' in Siberia*, 9–10, 63 ff., 103–8.

[2] Callwell, *Henry Wilson*, ii. 125.

[3] *Campaign in Mesopotamia*, iv. 213, 227, 247. See also Dunsterville, *Adventures of Dunsterforce*, 270 ff., and C. H. Ellis, *The Transcaspian Episode, 1918–1919* (1963), *passim*.

[4] Callwell, *Henry Wilson*, ii. 109; William Chamberlain, *The Russian Revolution, 1917–1921* (N.Y., 1935), ii. 37; Pierre Renouvin, *Les crises du XXᵉ siècle*, i (Paris, 1957), 107.

Front. The line of battle was still too uncomfortably close to the Allies' vital political and communication centres. The Western Front was not yet entirely secure. The 'X' Committee had hopes, comparable to those of the year before, of transferring several divisions to Allenby just for the winter; but an exchange of cablegrams between London and Jerusalem once more made clear the impracticability of such a scheme.[1]

Nothing of any real importance, it was agreed, could be accomplished in any theatre save the Russian and 'Caspian' in 1918. What of 1919? The C.I.G.S., in the very able paper of 25 July already cited, was clear that to postpone beyond the summer of 1919 the final attack on the Western Front would be impossible. It must either be delivered or else the war must come to a stop. The British share in this offensive, of which General Foch would assume the command, would be essentially a tank assault. Over the forthcoming months the divisional and man-power strength of the British army in France ought to be drastically reduced, and machine-guns, tanks, and aircraft increased. The urgings and achievements of Churchill from the Ministry of Munitions had already accomplished much in this last direction. Meanwhile the Prime Minister manœuvred to bring pressure on the French to agree to a contraction of the British line. In Greece it was hoped that all British divisions could be withdrawn. In Palestine the 'active defence' could continue.[2]

Wilson's paper was greeted by considerable grumbling on the part of the 'frocks'. 'Wully redivivus', complained Lloyd George. The Committee of Prime Ministers had no wish to commit themselves to 1919 or to any other date.[3]

Even so, no other practicable general plan of action was suggested and the C.I.G.S. paper in its emphasis on mechanical warfare undoubtedly indicated the right road. Pétain's head-quarters came to a similar conclusion: 'La bataille de 1919 sera

---

[1] Callwell, *Henry Wilson*, ii. 113; Hankey, *Supreme Command*, ii. 821; *Mil. Opns. Egypt and Palestine*, ii (2), pp. 447–8.

[2] British Military Policy, 1918–1919. Henry Wilson, C.I.G.S. General Staff, War Office. 25 July 1918. *Mil. Opns. Fr. and Bel. 1918*, iv. App. V, pp. 527–49; Churchill, *World Crisis*, iv. 1315–22, 1345–52; Lloyd George, *War Memoirs*, ii. 1877; Frank Owen, *Tempestuous Journey: Lloyd George His Life and Times* (N.Y., 1955), 491.

[3] Hankey, *Supreme Command*, ii. 830. See also ibid. 831–2; Callwell, *Henry Wilson*, ii. 118–19; G. Smith, 'Canada and the Siberian Intervention', *AHR* (July 1959), 867–8.

la bataille de l'aviation et des chars d'assaut.' By then the
British Armies in France had already demonstrated before
Amiens the character of the next stage of land warfare.[1]

Of the victories in France in August and September which
gradually beat the German forces back to and beyond the line
of March 1918 the British Government and General Staff had
no advance knowledge. The British Armies in France played a
pre-eminent part in these combined assaults. It was Sir Douglas
Haig who proposed to General Foch the plan for a tank attack
before Amiens, and the extraordinary psychological effect of
that blow, concerning which Ludendorff has given such
striking testimony, was due to both British arms and British
brains. The War Cabinet was informed by the British representative at Foch's headquarters on 8 August, the day of the attack.
The Foch Government awarded Haig the 'médaille militaire'.
No word of congratulation to the armies in France, however,
came from London. Instead Haig was warned by the C.I.G.S.
not to incur heavy casualties if he went on to attack the Hindenburg line. Haig's customary optimism now revived, however,
and on 15 September he expressed his intention to hold a
cavalry pursuit exercise. In the general offensive of 25 September, in which the Belgian, British, French, and American
armies participated ('tout le monde à la bataille'), Marshal Foch
acted as cheer-leader, a necessary function. Once again the
British armies proved the most successful. The German armies,
though retaining their cohesion and fighting power, now fell
slowly backwards. Lloyd George relented and on the 9th,
having 'just heard from Marshal Foch of the brilliant victory',
sent Haig a telegram congratulating him on the achievements
of 'the past two days!'[2]

No one in a position of authority had as yet any conception
that the Germans or their allies were due to crack, or rather to
fall apart. The general débâcle of all four of the Central Powers,
when it came, was precipitated and largely caused by an

[1] *AF*, vii (1), Annexe no. 1036 (G.Q.G. Armies of the North and North East,
29 Aug. 1918).
[2] Callwell, *Henry Wilson*, ii. 125, 127; Hankey, *Supreme Command*, ii. 829–30;
Erich Ludendorff, *My War Memories* (1919), ii. 674; General Mordacq, *Le ministère
Clemenceau: journal d'un témoin* (1930 ff.), ii. 185; *Mil. Opns. Fr. and Bel. 1918* (1935–
47), iv. 383; Maxime Weygand, *Mémoires*, i (1953), 589.

offensive from Greece, a theatre, as the reader is well aware, which had been a source of irritation, not of hope, to British authorities for the past three years. In June, Clemenceau had appointed General Franchet d'Espèrey to the command in Greece in place of Guillaumat, who was recalled to France. This move had been taken without consulting the British, for which omission Lloyd George launched a violent tirade against Clemenceau at the Supreme War Council session of early July. D'Espèrey, with Clemenceau's support, worked tirelessly to launch an offensive against Bulgaria. That nation was known to be indignant at Germany's failure to award it the Dobrudja in the Rumanian peace treaty of May 1918; and in June a new ministry under Malinov came into power.[1]

The British forces in Greece had now been reduced to less than one hundred and forty thousand, and were still unequipped for mountain warfare. British authorities were as always in favour of bribing Bulgaria to leave the war at the expense of Greece and Serbia. But on 4 September General Guillaumat came over to London to obtain British consent to participation of British forces in the offensive. All parties and authorities had long agreed the new Venizelist Greek Army, which had obtained a small success at Skra di Legen on 30 May, would melt away if it were not kept active. This argument proved sufficient. After all, the C.I.G.S. remarked, 'we should not go in until after the Serbian success'.[2]

On 15 September the offensive against Bulgaria began. Two good French divisions were used to 'break the crust'; and they

---

[1] *AF*, viii (3), Annexe no. 259; Callwell, *Henry Wilson*, ii. 113; Cyril Falls, *Military Operations, Macedonia* (1935), 11, 102, 321–2; Renouvin, *La crise européenne*, 520–1, 591–2.

[2] Lloyd George, *War Memoirs*, ii. 1919. See also ibid. 1917–18; *AF*, viii (3), p. 90; Hankey, *Supreme Command*, ii. 837; Shane Leslie, *Mark Sykes* (1923), 240; *Mil. Opns. Macedonia*, ii. 105, 109–11, 113 ('What happened was that the British authorities at home gave their approval to the attack but did not supply the means which General Milne declared to be necessary'), 115–17; Letter, General Bliss to Secretary of War Baker, 22 and 31 July 1918, Versailles ('One serious thing was admitted by all . . . that the Greek Army would melt away before the coming winter, just as the Serbian Army had to a considerable extent done, if no hope were given to them of an offensive movement by which they might win back lost territory. The Allied forces in Macedonia cannot afford to lose the Greek contingent because, on the strength of it they have withdrawn a very considerable British and French force for use on the Western Front'), Tasker H. Bliss Papers, Library of Congress, Washington, D.C.

were followed by the forces of the Serbian Army who overcame the greatest handicaps in terrain and transport to reconquer their motherland. The British infantry attack on the right of the line was a failure, but British aircraft helped to turn the retreat elsewhere into a rout. The Serbians proceeded to overrun Serbia and approach the Austrian border; the retreating Bulgarian Army revolted against their own Government, which on the 29th, less than two weeks after the beginning of the offensive, was forced to conclude an armistice with the victorious Franchet d'Espèrey.[1]

Meanwhile, on 18 September, General Allenby, without instructions from London, launched another masterly surprise cavalry offensive at Megiddo. The failures in the spring had led him once again to exploit the virtues of surprise and deception. What was now called the Arab Northern Army under the leadership of Major Lawrence cut the Turkish railway lines from Deraa. Having thus riveted the Turkish Command's attention inland, Allenby dispatched his cavalry along the coast. The two Turkish armies in Palestine and Syria, numbering some one hundred thousand, were rounded up, dispersed, or destroyed. Only some seventeen thousand escaped north.[2]

It was the Bulgarian surrender, however, exposing Constantinople to capture, which led the Turkish Government to sue for peace. The approach of the Serbians to Bosnia and Herzegovina determined the Austro-Hungarian command to withdraw troops to the east from the Italian front, thus convincing General Diaz that the time had come to allow himself to be persuaded by Marshal Foch's repeated urgings and return to the attack. It was the approach of Franchet d'Espèrey's forces that determined the subject nationalities within the Austrian Empire to open revolt. In the course of the next four weeks the Empire had split into four independent units and the Royal and Imperial Army of the Habsburgs no longer existed. And it was the Bulgarian surrender that caused Ludendorff, hard pressed as his armies were upon the Western Front, to inform the Kaiser and the 'frocks' that the war must be brought to an end without

[1] Général Paul Azan, *Franchet d'Espèrey* (Paris, 1949), 209–10; Liddell Hart, *A History of the World War, 1914–1918* (1934), 481.
[2] Liddell Hart, *History of the World War*, 553–62; Field-Marshal Earl Wavell, *Palestine Campaigns* (3rd edn., 1931), 203–16.

delay. On 4 October the German Government addressed a request for a peace based on the fourteen points and an immediate armistice to President Wilson. Clemenceau informed Lloyd George and his party of the German plea the next day. The conclave found the information difficult to believe, but went into a little dance before returning to work.[1]

Henceforth, as this Paris colloquy indicated, it was the Turkish War that the British Government and staff were determined to prosecute to a victorious conclusion. Germany was to be granted armistice terms as lenient—save for the naval provisions —as the French and Americans could be made to accept. Turkey, however, was to lose by conquest all her territories south and east of Anatolia and must conclude her armistice with a British and not a French commander. British prestige demanded no less.

Franchet d'Espèrey had ordered all but one of the British divisions under his command to participate in his projected drive north and west to the Danube and beyond, with Dresden as the last stop. Such employment Lloyd George flatly refused to consider—the proper course was for Milne's troops to be put under Allenby and march directly upon Constantinople. The Prime Minister therefore threatened to withdraw Milne from d'Espèrey's command. Clemenceau thereupon gave way and instructed d'Espèrey to allow the British to go off to the Turkish War, though still nominally under the French commander-in-chief. One British division was to be sent toward the Danube to show the flag![2]

With the Turkish collapse visibly impending, Milne's forces would act as occupiers rather than conquerors. Allenby however urged on his own forces and the Arab Northern Army the occupation of all of the area ascribed by the Franco-British agreement of May 1916 ('Sykes–Picot') on the division of the Ottoman Empire to the French sector of the still-to-be-created Arab State. Damascus was captured at the end of September, evoking dithyrambic enthusiasm from Amery. Henry Wilson had suggested as early as 23 September on behalf of the War

[1] *AF*, viii (3), Annexe no. 1735; Hankey, *Supreme Command*, ii. 841, 853; Renouvin, *La crise européenne*, 587, 594–9, 615, 617.
[2] *AF*, viii (3), Annexe no. 1381; Callwell, *Henry Wilson*, ii. 131–4; Hankey, *Supreme Command*, ii. 840–3; Lloyd George, *War Memoirs*, ii. 1947–51; *Mil. Opns. Macedonia*, ii. 277.

Cabinet 'a cavalry ride up to Aleppo', the northernmost city of the Arab 'state'. Homs was captured on the 15th, and Aleppo itself, by an Arab detachment, on the 26th. General Marshall's forces meanwhile were instructed to gain all the ground possible toward Mosul.¹

Before they could take Mosul the Turkish armistice had been negotiated. On 11 October Admiral Calthorpe, British Commander-in-Chief, Mediterranean, arrived at the island of Lemnos from Malta. General Townshend came from Constantinople shortly thereafter, to act as 'intermediary' from the new Turkish Government, and on the 25th a British vessel conveyed the Turkish plenipotentiaries from Mytilene to Lemnos. The French naval commander on the island was excluded from the discussions, and the armistice signed with the British alone on 30 October. The provisions did not include the cession of the city of Mosul, but General Marshall proceeded to occupy it and the entire Mosul vilayet none the less.²

Meanwhile the British Government prepared and hoped for peace with Germany. Sir Douglas Haig, summoned from France, gave his opinion on 19 October to the Prime Minister, Milner, and Bonar Law that the German armies were still a most effective force. There was no reason why, as they shortened their lines from 250 to 155 miles by withdrawing to the German frontiers, the German armies should not continue fighting into the spring or indeed indefinitely. To this conclusion there was general agreement. A 'soft' peace must therefore be accepted. Only the C.I.G.S. disagreed, and for curious reasons. If the war continued, Lloyd George might finally agree to the actual imposition of conscription in Ireland!³

¹ Amery, *Political Life*, ii. 169 ('It is just the same now as in the past: Plassey and the Heights of Abraham have mattered far more in history than Leuthen or Rossbach, though the last two were the events that figured biggest in the minds of the devotees of the "main theatre" of those days'); Callwell, *Henry Wilson*, ii. 126; *Campaign in Mesopotamia*, iv. 259; Brig.-Gen. Sir James E. Edmonds, *A Short History of World War I* (1951), 312; Lieut.-Gen. Sir William Marshall, *Memories of Four Fronts* (1929), 318; *Mil. Opns. Egypt and Palestine*, ii (2), 605, 609–10, 616; Wavell, *Palestine Campaigns*, 222–3.

² Commandant Laurens, *Le commandement naval en Méditerranée* (Paris, 1931), 321–30; Lloyd George, *War Memoirs*, ii. 1974–7; Marshall, *Memories of Four Fronts*, 324–5; *Mil. Opns. Macedonia*, ii. 265–6; Sir Henry Newbolt, *Naval Operations*, iv (1931), 351–6; Renouvin, *La crise européenne*, 615–16, 624–5; Maj.-Gen. Charles Townshend, *My Campaign in Mesopotamia* (1920), 381.

³ Callwell, *Henry Wilson*, ii. 138, 140–1; *Private Papers of Douglas Haig*, 332–9;

President Wilson's hints, in his messages to the German Government of 8 and 14 October, that the Germans should rapidly rid themselves of the Kaiser, therefore met with no enthusiasm in London. In an interview appearing in the *Evening Standard* of 17 October Lord Milner cautioned that it must not be unthinkingly assumed that the Germans 'were in love with militarism'. Unsuccessful efforts were made by the British delegation at Versailles, led by the Prime Minister, to soften the severe armistice terms formulated by Marshal Foch on the grounds that there were really no prospects for believing that the Germans would accept them.[1]

But of course they did. The Italian victory of Vittorio Veneto, in which once again British troops played a notable part, left Germany vulnerable from the south and south-west. The Allied Supreme War Council and its Military Representatives, together with Foch and Haig, mutually agreed—wilfully ignoring the achievements of Franchet d'Espèrey's armies— that the efforts on the Western Front would henceforth be complemented by an offensive from Italy across the Alps into Bavaria. As for the Allied Armies of the East, let them be transported to Trieste![2]

Such a clumsy cavalcade proved unnecessary. On 9 November the Kaiser fled to Holland and a German republic was proclaimed. Throughout central and eastern Europe appeared the spectre of communism. British leaders—both 'frocks' and 'brasshats'—now saw in 'Bolshevism' as well as in defeated 'Prussian militarism' a deadly enemy. But if eastern Europe was once again menaced, the security, prestige, and power of the British Empire was now greater than ever before in its history. On 12 November the Allied fleets, with the British in the lead,

Hankey, *Supreme Command*, ii. 849–50; Lloyd George, *War Memoirs*, ii. 1882–4, 1968–74; *Mil. Opns. Fr. and Bel. 1918*, v. 394–9.
[1] Callwell, *Henry Wilson*, ii. 133–49; Hankey, *Supreme Command*, ii. 854–63; *History of The Times*, iv (2), pp. 376–7, 1091–3; Lloyd George, *War Memoirs*, ii. 1954–64, 1968–74, 1979–80; *Naval Opns.*, v. 368; Petrie, *Austen Chamberlain*, ii. 123–5; *U.S. For. Rels. 1918*, Suppl. I, vol. i, p. 422; Hancock, *Smuts*, i. 493–5.
[2] *AF*, viii (3), Annexe no. 1751; Callwell, *Henry Wilson*, ii. 147; *Mil. Opns. Macedonia*, ii. 277–8; Renouvin, *La crise européenne*, 611; Resolutions in Regard to Operations against Germany through Austria. 4 November 1918. Eighth session, A.S.W.C. Records of the Supreme War Council, National Archives, Washington, D.C.

EPILOGUE 321

steamed through the Straits into the Black Sea, now like the
Caspian a British lake. In the last days of the conflict the War
Cabinet, over the objections of the Government of India, had
ordered the occupation by Malleson's troops of Merv, north of
the Afghanistan and Persian frontiers. Sir Percy Cox reigned as
British Minister in Teheran. British troops were now stationed,
emblems of British rule, from Merv to Baku, from India to
Egypt, from Cairo to Pretoria. Europe should be left to 'stew in
its own juice', but 'from the left bank of the Don to India is our
interest and preserve', the C.I.G.S. wrote in his diary. 'All the
Cabinet agreed. Our real danger now is not the Boches but
Bolshevism.'[1]

The victory over Germany was undone in a decade, the
Empire in a generation. 'Bolshevism' is with us yet, while the
relationship of the United Kingdom to the Continental Powers
is as ambiguous and uncertain as ever.

Such an outcome, after so titanic a struggle, may be disappointing to some. Others, however, will be less impressed by
the discrepancy between aims and achievements than by the
sheer vitality and resource shown throughout the crisis. 'Between 1914 and 1918 Britain displayed a creative vigour, driving energy and relentless purpose such as had not been seen
there since the 1850's.'[2] Similar attributes were manifested in
1940–5. The philosopher/psychologist William James once
called attention to the need of a 'moral equivalent for war' as
focus of a society's creative energy. Never has this observation
seemed more pertinent. Would the problems—less stark, but
still crucial—of stalemate peace evoke in Great Britain the same
determination and resourcefulness as she has displayed in time
of war? If so, all her friends could be increasingly confident
about the prospects, not only for Britain, but for the West.

[1] Callwell, *Henry Wilson*, ii. 147–8. See also *Campaign in Mesopotamia*, iv. 329–31;
Hankey, *Supreme Command*, ii. 864 ('British prestige is higher than it has ever been
before. So is Lloyd George's'); Marshall, *Memories of Four Fronts*, 328; Malleson,
'British . . . Mission to Turkistan', *Journal of the Royal Central Asian Society* (1922),
99–100; Letter, General Bliss to Secretary of War Baker, 10 November 1918,
Versailles (' . . . there was running through the minds of all the high political men
the fear of revolution and Bolshevism in Germany and their belief that the only
barrier against the spread of it would be to leave the German army sufficiently
armed to put down such revolution'). Tasker H. Bliss Papers, The Library of Congress, Washington, D.C.
[2] Correlli Barnett, *The Swordbearers* (1963), 358.

BIBLIOGRAPHY[1]

I. UNPUBLISHED SOURCES

George Arthur Papers. National Register of Archives, Historical Manuscripts Commission, Public Record Office.
Asquith Papers. The Bodleian Library, Oxford.
Campbell-Bannerman Papers. The British Museum.
Committee of Imperial Defence, Records, 1902-1909. Public Record Office.
Capt. B. H. Liddell Hart. Personal files.
Arthur Henderson Papers. Library, Trades Union Congress.
Kitchener Papers. National Register of Archives.
Directorate of Military Operations and Intelligence, War Office, Records, 1902-1908. Public Record Office.
Records of the Supreme War Council. Record Group 120. American Expeditionary Forces. National Archives, Washington, D.C.
Tasker H. Bliss Papers. Division of Manuscripts, The Library of Congress, Washington, D.C.
The writer also obtained much of value from correspondence and personal interviews with, among others, the late Lord Hankey, Capt. B. H. Liddell Hart, and Maj.-Gen. E. L. Spears.

II. PUBLISHED SOURCES

A. RECORDS OF PERSONAL EXPERIENCE—MEMOIRS, BIOGRAPHIES, LETTERS, AND DIARIES.
B. OFFICIAL DOCUMENTS, OFFICIAL MILITARY HISTORIES, AND SPEECHES.
C. DAILY AND WEEKLY PRESS.
D. SECONDARY STUDIES.[2]

A. RECORDS OF PERSONAL EXPERIENCE—MEMOIRS, BIOGRAPHIES, LETTERS, AND DIARIES

ADDISON, CHRISTOPHER, *Four and a Half Years: A Personal Diary from June 1914 to January 1919*, 2 vols., 1934.
—— *Politics from Within, 1911-1918*, 2 vols., 1924.
Les carnets de guerre d'Albert Ier Roi des Belges, Brussels, 1953.
ALDROVANDI, MARESCOTTI, L., *Guerra Diplomatica: Ricordi e Frammenti di Diario (1914-1919)*, Milan, 1936.

---

[1] The place of location or publication is London unless otherwise indicated.
[2] These frequently contain important documentary evidence; the volumes by Beaverbrook and Winston Churchill (particularly the latter) are both personal testimonies and major historical works.

AMERY, LEOPOLD, *My Political Life*, vol. ii: *War and Peace, 1914–1929*, 1953.

AMIGUET, PHILIPPE, *La vie du prince Sixte de Bourbon*, Paris, 1934.

ARTHUR, SIR GEORGE, *General Sir John Maxwell*, 1932.

—— *Life of Lord Kitchener*, 3 vols., 1920.

—— *Not Worth Reading*, 1938.

ASHMEAD-BARTLETT, E., *The Uncensored Dardanelles*, 1928.

ASQUITH, EARL OF OXFORD AND, *Memories and Reflections, 1852–1927*, 2 vols., Boston, 1928.

AZAN, GÉNÉRAL PAUL, *Franchet d'Espèrey*, Paris, 1949.

BACON, ADMIRAL SIR REGINALD, *The Dover Patrol, 1915–1917*, n.d.

—— *The Life of John Rushworth, Earl Jellicoe*, 1936.

BARNES, GEORGE, *From Workshop to War Cabinet*, 1924.

BARROW, GENERAL SIR EDMUND GEORGE, *Life of General Sir Charles Carmichael Monro*, 1931.

Diary of Lord Bertie of Thame, 1914–1918, Lady Algernon Gordon Lennox (ed.), 1924.

BIRKENHEAD, LORD, *F. E.: The Life of F. E. Smith, First Earl of Birkenhead*, 1959.

BLAKE, ROBERT, *The Unknown Prime Minister: The Life and Times of Andrew Bonar Law, 1858–1923*, 1955.

BONHAM-CARTER, VICTOR, *In a Liberal Tradition* (includes personal memoirs of General Charles Bonham-Carter), 1960.

Robert Laird Borden: His Memoirs, Toronto, 1938.

BOWLE, JOHN, *Viscount Samuel: A Biography*, 1957.

BRADFORD, ADMIRAL SIR EDWARD E., *Life of Admiral of the Fleet Sir Arthur Knyvet Wilson*, 1923.

BRIDGES, LIEUTENANT-GENERAL SIR TOM, *Alarms and Excursions*, 1938.

BUCHANAN, SIR GEORGE, *My Mission to Russia and Other Diplomatic Memories*, 1923.

CALLWELL, MAJOR-GENERAL SIR C. E., *Experiences of a Dug-Out, 1914–1918*, 1920.

—— *Field-Marshal Sir Henry Wilson: His Life and Diaries*, 2 vols., 1927.

—— *Life of Sir Stanley Maude*, 1920.

CAMBON, PAUL, *Correspondance, 1870–1924*, vol. iii, Paris, 1946.

CHALMERS, REAR-ADMIRAL W. S., *Life and Letters of David, Earl Beatty*, 1951.

CHAPMAN-HUSTON, MAJOR DESMOND, *The Lost Historian: A Memoir of Sir Sidney Low*, 1936.

CHARTERIS, BRIGADIER-GENERAL JOHN, *At G.H.Q.*, 1931.

—— *Field-Marshal Earl Haig*, 1929.

CHURCHILL, RANDOLPH, *Lord Derby, 'King' of Lancashire: the official life of Edward Earl Derby, 1865–1948* (1959).

CHURCHILL, WINSTON S., *Great Contemporaries*, 1937.

COLLIER, BASIL, *Brasshat: A Biography of Field-Marshal Sir Henry Wilson*, 1961.

COLVIN, IAN, *The Life of Lord Carson*, vol. iii, 1936.

DAVIES, JOSEPH, *The Prime Minister's Secretariat, 1916–1920*, Newport, 1952.

DILLON, BRIGADIER THE VISCOUNT, *Memories of Three Wars*, 1951.

Old Men Forget: The Autobiography of Duff Cooper, 1953.
DUFF COOPER, *Haig*, 2 vols., 1935–6.
DUGDALE, BLANCHE E. C., *Arthur James Balfour*, 2 vols., 1936.
DUNSTERVILLE, L. C., *Adventures of Dunsterforce*, 1921.
ESHER, REGINALD VISCOUNT, *Journals and Letters*, Maurice V. Brett (ed.), 4 vols., 1934–8.
FAY, SIR SAM, *War Office at War*, 1937.
Fear God and Dread Nought: The Correspondence of Admiral of the Fleet Lord Fisher of Kilverstone, Arthur J. Marder (ed.), vol. iii, *Restoration, Abdication, and Last Years, 1914–1920*, 1959.
FISHER, ADMIRAL OF THE FLEET LORD, *Memories*, 1919.
—— *Records*, 1919.
FITZROY, SIR ALMERIC, *Memoirs*, 2 vols., n.d.
FOCH, MARÉCHAL, *Mémoires pour servir à l'histoire de la guerre de 1914–1918*, 2 vols., Paris, 1931.
FRENCH OF YPRES, FIELD-MARSHAL VISCOUNT, *1914*, 1919.
Some War Diaries, Addresses, and Correspondence of Field-Marshal the Right Honourable the Earl of Ypres, Gerald French (ed.), 1937.
FRENCH, MAJOR THE HON. GERALD, *Life of Field-Marshal Sir John French*, 1931.
GEORGE, WILLIAM, *My Brother and I*, 1958.
GOUGH, GENERAL SIR HUBERT, *The Fifth Army*, 1931.
GRAVES, PHILIP, *Life of Sir Percy Cox*, 1941.
GREY OF FALLODON, VISCOUNT, *Twenty-Five Years, 1892–1916*, N.Y., 1925.
GWYNN, DENIS, *The Life of John Redmond*, 1932.
The Private Papers of Douglas Haig, 1914–1919: Being selections from the private diary and correspondence of Field-Marshal the Earl Haig of Bemersyde, K.T., G.C.B., O.M., &c., Robert Blake (ed.), 1952.
THE COUNTESS HAIG, *The Man I Knew*, 1936.
HALDANE, VISCOUNT, *Before the War*, 1920.
Richard Burdon Haldane: An Autobiography, 1929.
HAMILTON, GENERAL SIR IAN, *Gallipoli Diary*, 2 vols., 1920.
HAMILTON, MARY AGNES, *Arthur Henderson*, 1938.
HAMMOND, J. L., *C. P. Scott of the Manchester Guardian*, 1934.
HANBURY-WILLIAMS, MAJOR-GENERAL SIR JOHN, *The Emperor Nicholas II as I Knew Him*, 1922.
HANCOCK, W. K., *Smuts: The Sanguine Years, 1870–1919*, 1962.
HANKEY, LORD, *The Supreme Command, 1914–1918*, 2 vols., 1961.
HENDRICK, BURTON J., *The Life and Letters of Walter H. Page*, 2 vols. in one, 1924.
HEWINS, W. A. S., *The Apologia of an Imperialist. Forty Years of Empire Policy*, 2 vols., 1929.
HOARE, SIR SAMUEL, *The Fourth Seal*, 1930.
The Intimate Papers of Colonel House, Arranged as a Narrative by Charles Seymour, 4 vols., 1926–8.
HYDE, H. MONTGOMERY, *Carson: The Life of Sir Edward Carson, Lord Carson of Duncairn*, 1953.
IRONSIDE, SIR EDMUND, *Archangel, 1918–1919*, 1953.

JAMES, ADMIRAL SIR WILLIAM, *A Great Seaman: The Life of Admiral of the Fleet Sir Henry F. Oliver*, 1956.

JELLICOE OF SCAPA, ADMIRAL OF THE FLEET VISCOUNT, *Crisis of the Naval War*, 1920.

—— *The Submarine Peril: The Admiralty Policy in 1917*, 1934.

JOFFRE, MARÉCHAL, *Mémoires, 1910–1917*, 2 vols., Paris, 1932.

KEYES, ADMIRAL OF THE FLEET SIR ROGER, *Naval Memoirs, 1910–1918*, 2 vols., 1934–5.

KNOX, MAJOR-GENERAL SIR ALFRED, *With the Russian Army, 1914–1917*, 2 vols., 1921.

LESLIE, SHANE, *Mark Sykes*, 1923.

LLOYD GEORGE, EARL, *Lloyd George*, 1960.

LLOYD GEORGE, DAVID, *The Great Crusade*, 1918.

—— *War Memoirs*, 2 vols., Odhams Press edn., 1938.

LYTTON, NEVILLE, *The Press and the General Staff*, 1920.

MACDONAGH, MICHAEL, *In London During the Great War: The Diary of a Journalist*, 1935.

MCKENNA, STEPHEN, *Reginald McKenna, 1863–1943*, 1948.

MACREADY, GENERAL, *Annals of an Active Life*, 2 vols., n.d.

MAGNUS, PHILIP, *Kitchener: Portrait of an Imperialist*, 1958.

MALLESON, W., 'The British Military Mission to Turkistan, 1918–1920', *Journal of the Royal Central Asian Society*, ix, pt. 2, 1922, pp. 98 ff.

MARSHALL, GENERAL WILLIAM, *Memories of Four Fronts*, 1929.

MASTERMAN, LUCY, *C. F. G. Masterman: A Biography*, 1939.

MAURICE, MAJOR-GENERAL SIR FREDERICK, *Intrigues of the War*, 1922.

—— *The Life of General Lord Rawlinson of Trent*, 1928.

—— *Haldane: The Life of Viscount Haldane of Cloan*, 2 vols., 1937–9.

MAYNARD, CHARLES, *The Murmansk Venture*, 1928.

MEINERTZHAGEN, COLONEL RICHARD, *Army Diary, 1899–1926*, 1960.

MILLIN, SARAH GERTRUDE, *General Smuts*, 2 vols., 1936.

MORDACQ, GÉNÉRAL, *Le ministère Clemenceau: journal d'un témoin*, 4 vols., 1930–1.

NABOKOFF, CONSTANTIN, *Ordeal of a Diplomat*, 1921.

NAPIER, LIEUTENANT-COLONEL H. D., *The Experiences of a Military Attaché in the Balkans*, n.d.

NEWTON, P. C., *Lord Lansdowne: A Biography*, 1929.

—— *Retrospection*, 1941.

NICOLSON, HAROLD, *King George the Fifth: His Life and Reign*, 1952.

OWEN, FRANK, *Tempestuous Journey: Lloyd George His Life and Times*, N.Y., 1955.

PAINLEVÉ, PAUL, *Comment j'ai nommé Foch et Pétain*, Paris, 1923.

PALÉOLOGUE, MAURICE, *La Russie des Tsars pendant la grande guerre*, 3 vols., Paris, 1921–2.

PALMER, FREDERICK, *Bliss, Peacemaker: The Life and Letters of General Tasker Howard Bliss*, N.Y., 1934.

PETRIE, SIR CHARLES, *Life and Letters of the Right Hon. Sir Austen Chamberlain*, 2 vols., 1939–40.

—— *Walter Long and His Times*, 1936.

POINCARÉ, RAYMOND, *Au Service de la France: Neuf années des souvenirs*, Paris, 10 vols., 1926–33.

POUND, REGINALD, and GEOFFREY HARMSWORTH, *Northcliffe*, 1959.

REPINGTON, LIEUTENANT-COLONEL C. À COURT, *The First World War, 1914–18. Personal Experiences*, 2 vols., Boston, 1921.

Journal d'Alexandre Ribot et Correspondances Inédites 1914–1922, Paris, 1936.

RIBOT, ALEXANDRE, *Lettres à un ami*, Paris, 1921.

Portrait of an Admiral: The Life and Papers of Sir Herbert Richmond, Arthur J. Marder (ed.), 1952.

Lord Riddell's War Diary, 1914–1918, 1933.

ROBERTSON, FIELD-MARSHAL SIR WILLIAM, *From Private to Field-Marshal*, 1921.

—— 'Relations with the Government, 1916–1918', *British Legion Journal*, Earl Haig Memorial Number, vol. vii, no. 9 (March 1928), 236.

—— *Soldiers and Statesmen, 1914–1918*, 2 vols., 1926.

RODD, SIR JAMES RENNELL, *Social and Diplomatic Memories (Third Series), 1902–1919*, 1925.

RONALDSHAY, LORD, *Life of Curzon*, 3 vols., 1928.

SALVIDGE, STANLEY, *Salvidge of Liverpool*, 1934.

SAMUEL, VISCOUNT, *Grooves of Change*, N.Y., 1946.

SIMS, REAR-ADMIRAL WILLIAM SOWDEN, *Victory at Sea*, 1920.

SIXTE DE BOURBON, PRINCE, *L'offre de paix séparée de l'Autriche (5 Décembre 1916– 12 Octobre 1917)*, Paris, 1920.

SNOWDEN, PHILIP, *Autobiography*, 2 vols., 1934.

SOMMER, DUDLEY, *Haldane of Cloan: His Life and Times, 1856–1928*, 1960.

SPENDER, J. A., and CYRIL ASQUITH, *Life of Herbert Henry Asquith, Lord Oxford and Asquith*, 2 vols., 1932.

SUAREZ, GEORGES, *Briand: Sa Vie—Son Œuvre*, vols. 3–4, Paris, 1939–40.

TAYLOR, H. A., *Robert Donald*, 1934.

TOWNSHEND, MAJOR-GENERAL CHARLES, *My Campaign in Mesopotamia*, 1920.

TREVELYAN, G. M., *Grey of Fallodon*, Longmans Library edn., 1940.

WARD, COLONEL J., *With the 'Die-Hards' in Siberia*, 1920.

WAVELL, GENERAL SIR ARCHIBALD, *Allenby*, 1940.

WESTER-WEMYSS, ADMIRAL OF THE FLEET LORD, *The Navy in the Dardanelles Campaign*, 1924.

WEYGAND, MAXIME, *Mémoires*, vol. i, *Idéal Vécu*, Paris, 1953.

WICKHAM STEED, HENRY, *Through Thirty Years*, 2 vols., 1924.

WRENCH, JOHN EVELYN, *Alfred Lord Milner: The Man with No Illusions*, 1958.

—— *Geoffrey Dawson and Our Times*, 1955.

WRIGHT, CAPTAIN PETER E., *At the Supreme War Council*, 1921.

B. OFFICIAL DOCUMENTS, OFFICIAL HISTORIES, AND SPEECHES

BEAN, C. E. W. (gen. ed. and principal author), *The Official History of Australia in the War of 1914–1918*, 12 vols., Sydney, 1921–43 (numerous edns.)

British Documents on the Origins of the War, 1898–1914, G. P. Gooch and Harold Temperly (eds.), 1926–38.

DICKINSON, G. LOWES, *Documents and Statements Relating to Peace Proposals and War Aims (December 1916–November 1918)*, 1919.

DUGUID, COLONEL A. FORTESCUE, *Official History of the Canadian Forces in the Great War, 1914–1919*, vol. i, Ottawa, 1938.

France. Ministère de la Guerre. État-Major de l'Armée. Service Historique, *Les armées françaises dans la Grande Guerre*, 11 'tomes' (23 vols. of text, 56 vols. of appendixes), unfinished, Paris, 1922–37.

Great Britain. 'Correspondence relative to the Peace Proposals made by His Holiness the Pope to the Belligerent Powers on August 1, 1917. August–October 1917', *British and Foreign State Papers, 1917–1918*, cvi, 1921, pp. 575–89.

Great Britain. *Dardanelles Commission. First Report*, Cd. 8490, 1917; *The Final Report of the Dardanelles Commission* (Part II—Conduct of Operations, &c.), Cmd. 371.

Great Britain. *History of the Great War*: Based on official documents by direction of the Historical Section of the Committee of Imperial Defence, 1920–49.

The Merchant Navy, Sir Archibald Hurd, 3 vols., 1921–9.

Military Operations, Brigadier-General J. E. Edmonds (general editor and chief compiler): *East Africa*, unfinished, Lieutenant-Colonel Charles Hordern, 1 vol., 1941; *Egypt and Palestine*, Captain Cyril Falls and Lieutenant-General Sir G. MacMunn, 2 vols., 1928–30; *France and Belgium*, J. E. Edmonds, Cyril Falls, Wilfred Miles. 13 vols. of text, plus maps and appendixes, 1922–48; *Gallipoli*, Brigadier-General C. F. Aspinall-Oglander, 2 vols., 1929–32; *Italy, 1915–1919*, J. E. Edmonds, 1949; *Macedonia*, Cyril Falls, 2 vols., 1933–5; *Campaign in Mesopotamia*, Brigadier-General F. J. Moberly, 4 vols., 1923–7; *Togoland and the Cameroons, 1914–1916*, Moberly, 1 vol., 1931. This series does not contain any account of British military operations in Russia in 1918.

Naval Operations, Sir Julian Corbett and Sir Henry Newbolt, 5 vols., 1920–31. Volumes 1 and 3 have also been printed in later edns. The second edn. of vol. 3 contains important additional material on Jutland.

Seaborne Trade, C. Ernest Fayle, 3 vols., 1920–4.

The War in the Air, Walter Raleigh and H. A. Jones, 6 vols., plus 1 vol. of appendixes, 1922–37.

Great Britain. History of the Ministry of Munitions, 12 vols., 1921–2.

Great Britain. *Mesopotamia Commission. Report of the Commission Appointed by Act of Parliament to Enquire into the Operations of War in Mesopotamia*, Cd. 8610, 1917.

Great Britain. Parliament. *Parliamentary Debates*: House of Commons and House of Lords, 1914–18.

Great Britain. The War Cabinet, Reports for the Years 1917 and 1918, Cd. 9005, 1918. Cmd. 325, 1919.

Great Britain. War Office. *Statistics of the Military Effort of the British Empire during the Great War, 1914–1920*, 1922.

JONES, R. B., 'Anglo-French negotiations, 1907: a memorandum by Sir Alfred Milner', *Bulletin of the Institute of Historical Research*, xxi, 1958, pp. 224–7.

LALOY, ÉMILE, *Les documents secrets des archives du ministère des affaires étrangères de Russie*, Paris, 1919.

MILNER, LORD, *Fighting for Our Lives.* Speech . . . Plymouth, 21 February 1918, Constable, 1918.

—— Memoranda on the Petrograd Conference of 1917 and the Doullens Conference of 1918, *National Review*, cxv, Aug. 1940, Nov. 1940, cxvii, Nov. 1941.

Official Statements of War Aims and Peace Proposals, James Brown Scott (ed.), Washington, 1921.

U.S.S.R. *Constantinople et les détroits*: documents secrets de l'ancien ministère des affaires étrangères de Russie; trad. intégrale de l'édition soviétique du Commissariat du peuple des affaires étrangères par S. Volski, G. Gaussel et V. Paris; revue et annotée par Georges Chklaver, Paris, Les éditions internationales, 2 vols., 1930–2.

U.S.S.R. Historical Commission, Central Executive Committee, *Mejdounarodnia Otnochenia v epokhou imperialisma*, third series, 1914–17, 10 vols. to March 1916, Moscow, 1930 *et seq.*

United States. Historical Division, Department of the Army, *United States Army in the World War, 1917–1919*, vol. 2, *Policy-Forming Documents, American Expeditionary Forces* (Washington, 1948).

United States. Department of State, *Papers Relating to the Foreign Relations of the United States* (Washington):
Supplement: The World War, 9 vols., 1928–33.
The Lansing Papers, 1914–1920, 2 vols., 1939–40.
Russia, 1918–1919, 4 vols., 1931–7.

War Speeches by British Ministers, 1917.

C. DAILY AND WEEKLY PRESS

Daily Chronicle
Daily Telegraph
Evening Standard
Manchester Guardian
Morning Post
The Nation
Sunday Times
The Times
Westminster Gazette

D. SECONDARY STUDIES

ALLEN, W. E. D., and PAUL MURATOV, *Caucasian Battlefields: A History of the Wars on the Turco-Caucasian Border, 1828–1921*, Cambridge, 1953.

ASTON, GEORGE, 'The Entente Cordiale and the Military Conversations', *Quarterly Review*, April 1932.

BEAVERBROOK, LORD, *Men and Power, 1917–1918*, 1956.

—— *Politicians and the War, 1914–1916*, 2 vols., N.Y., 1928, London, n.d., but *c.* 1932.

BLISS, TASKER H., 'The Evolution of the Unified Command', *Foreign Affairs*, i, no. 2, N.Y., December 1922.

BRAND, CARL F., *British Labour's Rise to Power*, Stanford, 1941.

CHURCHILL, WINSTON S., *The World Crisis, 1911–1918*, 4 vols. Odhams Press edn., n.d., but *c.* 1949.

CIVRIEUX, COMMANDANT DE, *L'offensive de 1917 et le commandement du général Nivelle*, Paris, 1919.

CONTAMINE, HENRY, *La Revanche, 1871–1914*, Paris, 1957.

CRUTTWELL, C. R. M. F., *A History of the Great War, 1914–1918*, Oxford, 2nd edn., 1936.

—— *The Role of British Strategy in the Great War*, 1936.

DEWAR, GEORGE A. B., Assisted by LIEUTENANT-COLONEL J. H. BORASTON, *Sir Douglas Haig's Command, December 19, 1915, to November 11, 1918*, 1923.

DUNLOP, COLONEL JOHN K., *Development of the British Army, 1899–1914*, 1938.

EHRMAN, JOHN, *Cabinet Government and War, 1890–1940*, Cambridge, 1958.

ELLIS, C. H., 'Operations in Transcaspia, 1918–1919, and the 26 Commissars Case', St. Antony's Papers. Number 6, *Soviet Affairs* (ed.) David Footman (N.Y., 1959), pp. 131–53.

FAINSOD, MERLE, *International Socialism and the World War*, Cambridge, Mass., 1935.

FALLS, CYRIL, *The Great War*, N.Y., 1961, Capricorn Books edn.

FOOTMAN, DAVID, *Civil War in Russia*, 1961.

GORDON, DONALD C., 'The Colonial Defence Committee and Imperial Collaboration: 1885–1904'. *Political Science Quarterly* (Columbia University, N.Y.), vol. lxxvii, no. 4 (December 1962), pp. 526–45.

GOTTLIEB, W. W., *Studies in Secret Diplomacy during the First World War*, 1957.

GRAUBARD, STEPHEN R., *British Labour and the Russian Revolution*, Cambridge, Mass., 1956.

HALÉVY, ELIE, *Imperialism and the Rise of Labour*, Paperback edn., 1961.

—— *The Rule of Democracy*, Paperback edn., 1961.

—— *The World Crisis of 1914–1918*, 1930.

The History of The Times, vol. iv, *1912–1948*, 2 parts, 1952.

KENNAN, GEORGE F., *The Decision to Intervene*, Princeton, 1958.

—— *Russia Leaves the War*, Princeton, 1956.

KING, JERE CLEMENS, *Generals and Politicians: Conflict Between France's High Command, Parliament and Government, 1914–1918*, Berkeley, 1951.

LARCHER, MAURICE, *La guerre turque dans la guerre mondiale*, 1926.

LAURENS, COMMANDANT, *Le commandement naval en Méditerranée*, Paris, 1931.

LIDDELL HART, CAPTAIN B. H., *A History of the World War, 1914–1918*, 1934.

—— 'The Basic Truths of Passchendaele', *Journal of the Royal United Service Institution*, civ, no. 616, November 1959, 433–9.

—— *The Tanks: The History of the Royal Tank Regiment and its predecessors: Heavy Branch Machine-Gun Corps, Tank Corps, and Royal Tank Corps, 1914–1945*, 2 vols., 1959.

—— *Through the Fog of War*, 1938.

LINK, ARTHUR S., *Woodrow Wilson and the Progressive Era, 1910–1917*, 1954.

LOW, SIDNEY, 'The Cabinet Revolution', *The Fortnightly Review*, ci, February 1917, pp. 205–17.

MARDER, ARTHUR J., *From the Dreadnought to Scapa Flow: The Royal Navy in the Fisher Era, 1904–1919*, vol. i, *The Road to War, 1904–1914*, 1961.

MAY, ERNEST R., *The World War and American Isolation, 1914–1917*, Cambridge, Mass., 1959.

MAYER, ARNO J., *Political Origins of the New Diplomacy, 1917–1918*, New Haven, 1959.

MEYNELL, HILDAMARIE, 'The Stockholm Conference of 1917', *International Review of Social History*, v, pts. 1 and 2, Amsterdam, 1960, pp. 1–25.

MOOREHEAD, ALAN, *Gallipoli*, 1959, Arrow edn.

MORDACQ, GÉNÉRAL, *Le commandement unique: comment il fut réalisé*, Paris, 1929.

MORISON, STANLEY, 'Personality and Diplomacy in Anglo-American Relations, 1917', *Essays Presented to Sir Lewis Namier*, 1956.

MORLEY, JAMES WILLIAM, *The Japanese Thrust into Siberia, 1918*, N.Y., 1957.

OLIVER, FREDERICK SCOTT, *Ordeal by Battle*, 1915.

PIERREFEU, JEAN DE, *G.H.Q. Secteur I: trois ans au grand quartier général par le rédacteur du 'communiqué'*, 2 vols., Paris, 1920.

PINGAUD, ALBERT, *Histoire diplomatique de la France pendant la Grande Guerre*, 3 vols., Paris, 1938–40.

PITT, BARRIE, *1918: The Last Act*, 1962.

RENOUVIN, PIERRE, *La crise européenne et la première guerre mondiale*, 3rd edn., Paris, 1948.

ROCH, WALTER, *Mr. Lloyd George and the War*, 1920.

ROSKILL, CAPTAIN S. W., 'The U-Boat Campaign of 1917 and Third Ypres', *Journal of the Royal United Service Institution*, civ, no. 616, November 1959, 440–2.

SALTER, J. A., *Allied Shipping Control*, Oxford, 1921.

SMITH, C. JAY, *The Russian Struggle for Power: A Study of Russian Foreign Policy during the First World War*, 1956.

SMITH, GADDIS, 'Canada and the Siberian Intervention, 1918–1919', *American Historical Review*, lxiv, no. 4, July 1959, pp. 866–77.

SPEARS, BRIGADIER-GENERAL E. L., *Prelude to Victory*, 1939.

STEIN, LEONARD, *The Balfour Declaration*, 1961.

STRAKHOVSKY, LEONID, *Intervention at Archangel*, Princeton, 1944.

TAYLOR, A. J. P., *Politics in the First World War*, The Raleigh Lecture on History, British Academy, 1959.

TOD, COLONEL J. K., 'The Malleson Mission to Transcaspia in 1918', *Journal of the Royal Central Asian Society*, January 1940, pp. 45–67.

TRASK, DAVID F., *The United States in the Supreme War Council: American War Aims and Inter-Allied Strategy, 1917–1918*, Wesleyan University Press, 1961.

TYLER, J. E., *The British Army and the Continent, 1904–1914*, London, 1938.

ULLMAN, RICHARD H., *Intervention and the War: Anglo-Soviet Relations, 1917–1921*, vol. i, Princeton, 1961.

WAVELL, FIELD-MARSHAL EARL, *The Palestine Campaigns*, 1931, numerous reimpressions.

WILSON, ARNOLD, *Loyalties: Mesopotamia: a personal and historical record*, 2 vols., Oxford, 1936.
WULLUS-RUDIGER, J., *La Belgique et l'équilibre européen*, Paris, 1935.
WYNNE, CAPTAIN G. C., 'Pattern for Limited (Nuclear) War: The Riddle of the Schlieffen Plan', *Journal of the Royal United Service Institution*, November 1957–February 1958.

III. SUPPLEMENT

BARNETT, CORRELLI, *The Swordbearers: Studies in Supreme Command in the First World War*, 1963.
BONHAM-CARTER, VICTOR, *Soldier True: The Life and Times of Field-Marshal Sir William Robertson, Bart., G.C.B., G.C.M.G., K.C.V.O., D.S.O., 1860–1933*, 1963.
ELLIS, C. H., *The Transcaspian Episode, 1918–1919*, 1963.
FLEMING, PETER, *The Fate of Admiral Kolchak*, 1963.
GARDNER, BRIAN, *The Big Push: A Portrait of the Battle of the Somme*, 1961.
—— *German East: The Story of The First World War in East Africa*, 1963.
GOLLIN, A. M., *Proconsul in Politics: A Study of Lord Milner in Opposition and in Power*, 1964.
HEUSTON, R. F. V., *Lives of the Lord Chancellors, 1885–1940*, 1964.
HIGGINS, TRUMBULL, *Winston Churchill and the Dardanelles: A Dialogue in Ends and Means*, 1964.
JENKINS, ROY, *Asquith*, 1964.
LOCKWOOD, P. A., 'Milner's Entry into the War Cabinet, December 1916', *The Historical Journal*, Cambridge, vii, 1 (1964), pp. 120–34.
MACKINTOSH, JOHN P., 'The Role of the Committee of Imperial Defence before 1914', *English Historical Review*, lxxvii, no. 304 (July 1962), pp. 490–503.
McCORMICK, DONALD, *The Mask of Merlin: A Critical Biography of David Lloyd George*, 1964.
MIDDLEMAS, ROBERT KEITH, *The Master Builders* (includes section on Sir John Norton-Griffiths), 1963.
MONGER, G. W., *The End of Isolation: British Foreign Policy, 1900–1907*, 1963.
NELSON, HAROLD I., *Land and Power: British and Allied Policy on Germany's Frontiers, 1916–19*, 1963.
OLSON, MANCUR, JR., *The Economics of the Wartime Shortage: A History of British Food Supplies in the Napoleonic War and in World Wars I and II*, Durham, North Carolina, 1963.
PUBLIC RECORD OFFICE, *List of Papers of the Committee of Imperial Defence to 1914*, 1964.
—— *List of Cabinet Papers 1880–1914*, 1964.
SALTER, LORD, *Memoirs of a Public Servant*, 1961.
TAYLOR, A. J. P., *The First World War: An Illustrated History*, 1963.
TERRAINE, JOHN, *Douglas Haig: The Educated Soldier*, 1963.
—— *The Western Front, 1914–1918*, 1964.
The American Heritage History of World War I, N.Y., 1964.

THOMAS, D. H., 'The Use of the Scheldt in British Plans for the Defence of Belgian Neutrality, 1831–1914', *Revue belge de philologie et d'histoire*, xli, no. 2, Brussels, 1963, pp. 449–70.

WILLIAMS, M. J., 'Thirty Per Cent: A Study in Casualty Statistics', *Journal of the Royal United Service Institution*, cix, No. 633, February 1964, pp. 51–55.

INDEX

Abadan Island, 43.

Addison, Dr. Christopher, 153, 242.

Admiralty, 16, 21, 32, 33, 51, 68, 75, 79, 118, 175, 227; insists on keeping North Sea clear, 13; prewar concept of war with Germany, 17–21; Transport Department, 21; in 1914, 32; commissions 'lighters', 51; and Dardanelles expedition, 59, 68–71, 75, 93, 110–11; new direction of (June 1915), 82–83; Sea Lords favour acceptance of Fisher's resignation, 82; decides against general fleet action, 141; helplessness against submarine menace, 176–7; misleading statistics on shipping entering British ports, 226, 228; and convoys, 227, 229; obtains use of American warships, 236; mid-1917 reorganization of, 240; advocacy of campaign in Flanders, 243; fears loss of English Channel, 243, 245; and Flanders campaign, 244, 246, 250, 252 n., 256; purge of naval staff, 279. *See also* Board of Admiralty, *individual first sea lords*.

Adriatic, fear of loss of control of, 264.

Afghanistan, 13; fear of German-Turkish advance on, 310.

Agadir. *See* Moroccan Crises.

Air Ministry, 279.

Air Services, manpower needs of, 279.

Air warfare, 249, 251.

Aircraft, 314; squadrons transferred from Western Front to rear, 249; in Palestine, 250; in Bulgaria, 317.

Aisne, River, 37, 40.

Albania, Serbian Army in, 112.

Albert, King of the Belgians, 39; opposed to offensive on Belgian soil, 135; convinced of failure of Flanders campaign, 251.

Albert-Bapaume, 148 n.

Aleppo, 285 n.; eventual advance to pressed by Government, 298; capture of, 318–19.

Alexandretta, 52.

Alexandria, 75.

Alexieff, Gen., 133 n., 155, 158.

Algeciras. *See* Moroccan Crises.

Allenby, Gen., 314, 318; appointed to Palestine command, 231, 258; revitalizes force, 258; estimate on forces needed to occupy Palestine, 260, 280; enters Jerusalem, 276; clash over exploitation of victories, 284; reinforced by Seventh Division, 284; War Cabinet approves plans for eventual advance to Aleppo, 298; clearance of Valley of Jordan and capture of Jericho, 298; raid to Amman, 300; enjoined to adopt policy of 'active defence', 301; destroys Turkish armies in Palestine and Syria, 317; urges occupation of Syria, 318.

Allied Armies in the East, 257 n.; to be transported to Trieste, 320.

Allied conferences. *See* Allied Supreme War Council, Calais, Chantilly, Entente, London, Paris, Petrograd.

Allied Supreme War Council, 280, 302, 316; prehistory, 259–60, 262–3; as vehicle of British influence, 259; launching of, 264–6; brainchild of Henry Wilson, 266; Versailles chosen as location for, 266–7; constitution of, 267; House of Commons debate on, 269; press opinions on, 269 n.; Military Representatives recommend defensive in Greece, 283; British section urges decisive offensive against Turkey, 284–5; Military Representatives concur in Joint Note No. 12, 285; early British domination of, 286; first sessions, 287; third session (Jan.–Feb. 1918), 286–90; constitutes General Reserve, 287–8, 290; adopts Joint Note No. 12, 289; new command function of Military Representatives, 290, 291; collapse of General Reserve and of Executive War Committee, 298; burial of General Reserve at fourth session (Mar. 1918), 300; new British Military Representative subordinate to C.I.G.S., 302; loses importance, 303; accused of forcing Haig to extend front, 304; appeal to President Wilson for invasion of Siberia, 310; and armistic terms, 320; agrees on final offensive from Italy across the Alps, 320.

Allies. *See* Entente.

334 INDEX

Alsace-Lorraine, 27, 95 n., 123, 124, 185, 234, 278.
'Alternate advisers' scheme, 259, 260–1.
Altham, Lieut.-Col. E. A., 5.
Amara, 157.
American Expeditionary Force: initially limited to one division in French sector, 236; expansion during German spring offensives, 307.
Amery, Leopold, 128, 318; appointed to War Cabinet secretariat, 192; expounds imperialist strategy, 194–6; views Allied Supreme War Council as vehicle of British influence, 259, 287; on British section of A.S.W.C., 284–5; drafts compromise for adoption of Joint Note No. 12, 289; mission to Middle East, 298; on 'X' Committee, 303; and conduct of Maurice debate, 305.
Amiens, 25; tank attack before, 315.
Amman, raid to, 300.
Ancre, battle of the, 162–4.
Anglo-Japanese Alliance (1902), 3.
Anthoine, Gen., 247, 254, 255.
Antwerp, 55, 81; in prewar planning, 13–14; Royal Naval Division sent to, 38; fall of, 39–40.
Anzac, 93, 111.
Arab Northern Army, 317, 318.
Arab revolt, 156.
Arabia, in British sphere of influence, 276, 278.
Arabic, 225.
Archangel, 141; British occupation of, 311.
Armenia, 194, 219, 220, 278.
Armies (British): First, 63, 113; Second, 249; Third, 258, 273; Fourth, 143, 148; Fifth, 162–4.
Armies (French): First, 254; Sixth, 146.
Army Corps: IV, 112.
Army Council, 11, 32, 109, 142; creation of, 7; diminution in powers of (1915), 114; reports manpower needs for 1917, 177; protests War Cabinet committee recommendations on manpower, 281; raises difficulties on command of General Reserve, 290; exhorted to action by Col. Repington, 293; does not resign at dismissal of Robertson, 296.
Army of the Caucasus (Russian), 217, 221; to accord operations with British, 219; advances through Persia, 220; lapses into inactivity, 223.
Arras, 63, 215.
Artillery, 134–5.
Artois, 72, 74, 88, 94.
Ashmead-Bartlett, Ellis, 87, 104.

Asquith, Herbert H., 37, 49, 51, 54, 57, 61, 62, 70, 73, 76, 77, 79, 82, 87, 89, 94, 98, 100, 108, 115, 116, 122 n., 128, 139, 141, 142, 149, 161, 165 n., 169, 170, 180, 216 n., 240 n., 256, 258, 262, 304, 306 n.; as war leader, 181–2; fails to dislodge Campbell-Bannerman, 10; becomes prime minister, 15; refers (1911) to 'treaty obligations to France', 16; convenes Committee of Imperial Defence, 19; appoints Churchill to Admiralty, 21; permits Cabinet ignorance of French staff talks, 23; unable to stop staff talks, 24; appoints Gen. Douglas as C.I.G.S., 25; on War Council, 34; reluctant to resolve disagreements, 34; determines continuance of party government, 35; enrages opponents, 36; dissatisfied at stalemate in West (Dec. 1914), 48; publicizes Dardanelles in Commons, 64; reports Greek offer of military support at Gallipoli, 66; refrains from convening War Council, 69, 71; offers Sir John French condolences on May attack, 74; announces formation of new government, 77; agrees to formation of Munitions of War Committee, 78; agrees to coalition government, 80; accepts Fisher's resignation, 81–82; angry at Kitchener on 'shells' crisis, 83; on Dardanelles Committee, 84; attempts to exclude Kitchener from Calais conference, 90 n.; reconstitutes General Staff, 84, 98–99; insists on preparation of plan for evacuation of Gallipoli, 103; and compulsion issue, 107; persuades Kitchener to visit Gallipoli, 108; reorganizes supreme command, 109–15; on new War Committee, 109, 125; recalls Sir John French, 110; announces casualty figures to 1916, 121; definition of war aims, 122–3; and Grey–House memorandum, 124; opposition to, 127–9; decrees continuance of British forces in Greece, 132; acquiesces in Chantilly resolutions, 169; invites military-naval opinions on winning the war, 175; relations with Grey, 182 n.; fall of, 187, 199; refrains from immediate parliamentary challenge, 201; more congenial to military than Lloyd George, 204; opposed to Commons secret session, 230; rejects overture to enter government, 240; assures Haig of support, 241, 254; on importance of clearance of Ostend and

G.H.Q. (France), 32, 67 n., 78, 113, 143, 146, 148, 149, 158, 161, 215, 255; disapproval of Dardanelles, 77; wants re-creation of General Staff, 84; becomes independent power, 129; demands of, 129–30; unfavourable position prior to Chantilly conference, 162; welcomes fall of Asquith Coalition, 203; Gen. Nivelle's lack of prestige with, 211; visit of Carson to, 241; advocacy of campaign in Flanders, 243; confronted with Government opposition to Flanders campaign, 245; forced to accept French participation in Flanders campaign, 247; boomerang effect of Cambrai on, 271–4; whitewash inquiry into Cambrai, 273; not opposed to negotiated peace, 275; dismissal or transfer of chief staff officers, 279; desires unlimited manpower, 282 n.; defective plannings for defensive, 299; sends emissary to Asquith, 304. See also Haig, Western Front.

Galicia, 1915 offensive in, 74, 95 n.
Galilee, Sea of, 284.
Gallipoli Peninsula, 52 n., 67, 68 n., 69, 74, 76, 104, 110, 112 n., 116; naval strike decided on, 54; military occupation urged, 60; bombardment of outer forts, 61; landing on, 71, 73; Navy leaves, 87–88; Gen. Monro's visit to, 106; evacuation of, 111, 115, 131; and Lloyd George, 180. See also Dardanelles expedition.

'Garden Suburb', 192.
Garvin, J. L., 200.
Gaza, assaults on, 221–2, 257.
Geddes, Sir Auckland: sounds seapower as keynote of future strategic policy, 278–9; states need to raise 450,000 men from civil life, 281.
Geddes, Sir Eric, appointed First Lord of the Admiralty, 240.
General election: question of, 201–2; Lloyd George prepares for after Maurice debate, 306.
General Reserve, 282 n., 302; origins of concept of, 287; command question, 288, 290, 290 n., 295; Allied Supreme War Council decides on creation of under Executive Committee headed by Foch, 290; abandoned as quid pro quo for Haig's acquiescence in dismissal of Robertson, 297; ruin of, 298–300; name to be given to French and British troops in Italy, 300.
General Staff, 21, 130, 154, 251, 270–1, 283, 287, 313; creation of, 7, 16;

on Belgian neutrality, 9, 12–15, 20; on war with Germany, 14–17, 24, 26, 27; is absorbed into G.H.Q., B.E.F., 32, 49; price of its decision to support France over Belgium, 38; prewar opinions on attack on Dardanelles, 61; re-creation of (1915), 84; on capture of Baghdad, 105; advises evacuation of Gallipoli, 110; insists on withdrawal from Greece, 112; in 1916, 125; on Verdun and the Somme, 146; on need for continued offensive on the Somme, 153; on German manpower in 1916, 155; asked for opinion on winning the war, 175; demands destruction of military domination of Prussia, 175; prepares weekly intelligence summaries, 192; distrust of Lloyd George, 204; and Rome conference of Jan. 1917, 208; orders exploitation of victory at Gaza, 221; agrees to reinforcement of E.E.F., 257; estimate on further reinforcements for Allenby, 260, 284; advises keeping reserve in England, 282; urges defensive policy in Palestine, 284; reinforcement of Western Front, 307; no advance knowledge of Allied 1918 counteroffensives, 315.

Generals: free hand in 1916, 130–1; political support for, 179–80; victory in battle only war aim, 183; welcome fall of Asquith Coalition, 203; personalities of leaders, 204–5; aristocratic background, 205–6; look on Lloyd George War Cabinet as personal enemies, 217; temporary realignment of Lloyd George with, 231; loss of public's faith in, 270–1, 273.

George V, 66, 76, 113, 169, 216, 221, 295; desires recall of Sir John French, 107; supports Robertson's refusal to visit Russia, 158; fears general election, 201; long support of Haig, 207–8; sees Prince Sixte of Bourbon on peace with Austria, 247–8; threatened by Prime Minister, 296.

German Army, 27, 39, 187; prewar, 9, 12–14, 19–20, 22 n.; in 1914, 27, 36–40, 45; successes dictate British strategy for remainder of 1915, 97; British aim the destruction of, 134, 184; 1916 increase in manpower, 155; tactical withdrawal on Western Front, 215; supposed deterioration of, 250, 255, 273; command determined on offensive in the West, 274, 278; offensives of 1918, 301; estimated as still most effective force, 319.

paign, 249; convinced of failure of,
251, 252 n.; careful not to hamper
Haig's operations, 254; in state of
nervous depression, 255; abdication
no less complete than Asquith's, 256;
groping toward new military system,
256; reinforces army in Palestine,
257; offers its command to Gen.
Smuts, 258; demands capture of
Jerusalem, 258; seeks arrangements
to neutralize or outflank Robertson,
259–63; avoids commitment on
Supreme Council, 260; proposes
offensive against Turkey, 260, 261;
reviews strategic situation at 'Council
of War', 261; and French–Wilson
memoranda, 262; launches Allied
Supreme War Council, 264–5; orders
divisions sent to Italy, 265; at
Rapallo, 267; publicly arraigns
Allied strategy in Paris speech, 267–8;
defends Allied Supreme War Council
in House of Commons, 269; believed
to 'inspire' press attacks on military,
271; speech on war aims (Jan. 1918),
277; why given to trades union congress, 281; presses for further gains
in Mesopotamia and Palestine, 203;
suspects Robertson of deception over
estimate of reinforcements for Palestine, 284; prepares dismissal of Gen.
Robertson, 290; proposes that
Robertson and Wilson exchange
positions, 291; attacked by Col. Repington in *Morning Post*, 293; frightened into retreat by consequent
Commons debate, 294; forced to
fight it out by Robertson's intran-
sigence, 295; triumph over fall of
Robertson, 296–7; and acceptance of
Foch as Allied Commander-in-Chief,
302; on 'X' Committee, 303; claims
the Army in France stronger than in
1917, 304, 305; superb conduct of
Maurice debate, 305; on need for
intervention in Russia, 309 n.; tirade
against Clemenceau on appointment
of d'Espèrey, 316; threatens withdrawal of British troops from
d'Espèrey's command, 318; attempts
to soften armistice terms, 320.
Lloyd George Coalition: significance of
advent to power, 196; owes formulation to House of Commons, 197;
political background, 198; formation
of, 199; Conservatives hold key posts
in, 199; uneasy relations with House
of Commons, 197–8, 200–2, 239;
initial principal strategic themes,
209; envisages negotiated peace, 233;

ministerial changes of July 1917,
240; narrow victory in House of
Commons, 242; sanctions Flanders
campaign, 251–2, 256; desires to
reconstruct new strategy, 256; favourable to negotiated peace?, 275; real
strength made manifest by Maurice
debate, 301, 306; recovers freedom
of action, 306; hint at peace negotiations, supported by Asquithian
Opposition, 307; no advance knowledge of Allied 1918 counter-offensives,
315.
Lodz, 45.
London: first German air raid on (June
1917), 249; second, 251.
London, Anglo-French Conference of
Mar. 1917, 216.
London, Treaty of (on Italian entry),
74 n., 248.
Long, Walter, 242; demands industrial
compulsion, 85; supports Lloyd
George Coalition, 199.
Loos, 147.
Lords, House of, 104, 128 n.; 179; Grey
transferred to, 182. *See also* Parlia-
ment.
Ludendorff, Gen. Erich von, 62, 186,
247 n., 301, 302, 308, 315; deter-
mined on offensive in West, 278; de-
mands German Government request
armistice, 317–18.
Lusitania, 75, 225.
Lytton, Maj. Neville, 213.

Macedonia, 72, 132; Serbia agrees to
concede, 98; withdrawal of German
troops from, 283.
Machine-gun, 63, 134, 143, 272, 314.
McKenna, Reginald, 23, 127 n.; re-
placed as First Lord of the Admiralty,
21, 24; on War Council, 34 n.; and
Dardanelles Committee, 194; on new
War Committee, 109, 125; proffers
resignation on conscription, 126.
Mackensen, Gen., 153, 154.
Macready, Gen. Sir Nevil, 186 n.
Mahon, Lieut.-Gen. Bryan T., 101,
112.
Malleson Mission, 311; control of rail-
way in Trans-Caspia, 311; occupa-
tion of Merv, 321.
Malmaison, French victory at, 256;
Cambrai as British counterpart to,
272.
Malta, 319.
Manchester Guardian, 207; on Allied
Supreme War Council, 269 n.; at-
tacks military conduct of the war,
270–1.

INDEX

150; wrecked by German offensives of 1917, 234. *See also* Army of the Caucasus.

Russian Navy, destroyed in 1905, 4, 73.

Russian Revolution: first military effects, 222–3; challenges European order, 235; Bolshevik seizure, 308.

Sackville-West, Maj.-Gen. Charles J., appointed British Military Representative to Allied Supreme War Council, 302.

Saint-Nazaire, 36.

Saint-Omer, 129.

Salisbury, 3rd Marquess of (Cecil Robert A. T.), 3; reproves speculation on British reaction to Belgian invasion, 5 n.

Salisbury Plain, 60.

Salonika, 52, 57–58, 106, 111, 156, 168, 228, 280; landings at, 101, 112; question of withdrawal from, 112, 114–15; British 1915 policy on reviewed, 117; troop strength and policy in, 131–2; 1916 offensive from, 150–2, 169; reinforcements for urged (Oct. 1916), 154; 60th Division sent, 155; rejection of proposal to reinforce, 197, 208; connexion with Turkish War, 222; operations of spring 1917, 222; British to withdraw from, 231; Allied Supreme War Council military staff recommends preparations for evacuation of, 283; withdrawal of twelve battalions from, 307. *See also* Allied Armies in the East; Salonika Army, British; Greece; Mahon; Milne; Sarrail; Guillaumet; Espèrey, d'.

Salonika Army, British, 132, 152, 156; 'last chance' for, 222.

Samara, 310.

Sambre, River, 20, 21.

Samuel, Sir Herbert, 200; supports government-hinted plea for peace negotiations, 307.

San, River, 74.

Sanderson, Sir Thomas, 8.

Sari Bair Range, 93.

Sarrail, Gen. Maurice, 97, 106, 132, 169; popularity with parliamentary left, 96; initial operations in Serbia, 112; 1916 'offensive', 150, 152; attack in support of Nivelle offensive, 221–2; British request dismissal of, 231; to command Western Front?, 260; recall of, 283. *See also* Salonika.

Sassoon, Sir Philip, on victory at Cambrai, 272.

Sauvigny, Commandant Bertier de, 214.

Sazonov, replaced as Russian foreign minister, 174.

Scapa Flow, 27.

Scheldt Estuary, 13, 39.

Schelighorn, 20.

Schleswig-Holstein, 8, 123.

Schlieffen–Moltke plan, 22 n.

Second Coalition. *See* Lloyd George Coalition.

Second International, 235.

Secretary of State for War, 109; diminution in powers of (1915), 114–15 n.; after death of Kitchener, 142. *See also* Kitchener, Lloyd George, Derby, Milner.

Selborne, 2nd Earl of (William W. Palmer): on Dardanelles Committee, 84; sensitive to prestige factor, 87; unable to obtain information from Hamilton, 92.

Serbia, 54, 57, 101, 108, 122, 124, 132, 152; in Bosnian Crisis, 14 n.; repulses (1914) attempts at conquest, 45; crushed (1915), 97; Entente pressure on, 97, 98; Bulgarian attack on, 98; Greek help for?, 100; 1915 invasion of, 101, 104, 112, 121; decision to abandon, 103–4; Serb despair at partial British withdrawal from Greece, 256; Allied reconquest of, 317.

Serbian Army, 106, 316 n.; flees to Albania, 112; reconstitution of, 132; capture of Monastir, 169; reconquest of Serbia, 317.

Sereth, River, 169.

Sevastopol, taken by Germans, 310.

'Shells' question, 35, 76–80, 83, 88.

Sherif Hussein, 156.

Shipping: prohibitive losses of 1917, 226–8, 236, 245. *See also* Submarine war.

Shipping Controller, 236.

Siberia: Japanese occupation of, 309; Japanese and Americans unwilling to move beyond, 311.

Silesia, 45, 52.

Simon, Sir John A., resigns over conscription, 126.

Sims, Adm. William S., 228 n.; stresses success of convoys, 238.

Sinai Peninsula, 156; cleared of Turkish troops, 220–1.

Sixte of Bourbon, Prince, role in Austrian peace feelers, 247–8.

Skra di Legen, 316.

Smallwood, Mr., M.P., 274.

Smith, Frederick E., 161; arrest of, 129; circulates analysis of Somme battle to Cabinet, 147.

PRINTED IN GREAT BRITAIN
AT THE UNIVERSITY PRESS, OXFORD
BY VIVIAN RIDLER
PRINTER TO THE UNIVERSITY